The Complementarity Regime of the International Criminal Court

Ovo Catherine Imoedemhe

# The Complementarity Regime of the International Criminal Court

## National Implementation in Africa

Springer

Ovo Catherine Imoedemhe
Leicester, United Kingdom



The author.

ISBN 978-3-319-46779-5 ISBN 978-3-319-46780-1 (eBook)
DOI 10.1007/978-3-319-46780-1

Library of Congress Control Number: 2016960328



Printed on acid-free paper

This Springer imprint is published by Springer Nature
The registered company is Springer International Publishing AG
The registered company address is: Gewerbestrasse 11, 6330 Cham, Switzerland

*I would like to dedicate this book to the memories of my father David Obowhodo Ojarikre who passed away on 20 July 2012 and my brother Emmanuel Ariomaghwa Ojarikre whose untimely death in an auto crash on 16 June 2016 robbed the world of a humane, kind and compassionate vibrant man who would have contributed immensely to the promotion of a world full of laughter, kindness and peace. The demise of my brother is a huge lesson to me and to all who knew him of the futility and vanity of all the struggles of life. Whilst I still have breath, all that counts is ensuring togetherness, peace, love and joy to every soul, and I am highly motivated in the pursuit of friendship and togetherness as epitomised in the complementarity regime of the International Criminal Court to stamp out atrocities and ensure peace in our world.*

# Acknowledgements

I appreciate the help and divine guidance of my indwelling partner, the Holy Spirit. I am thankful to the Lord God Almighty and my Saviour Jesus Christ who preserved and sustained me and provided the resources that were necessary to complete this book.

This book is an offshoot from my PhD thesis, and I am immensely grateful to my supervisors, Drs Troy Lavers and Eki Omorogbe, for their tireless efforts, encouragements and support. I am also grateful to Drs Loveday Hodson, Paolo Vargiu and Yassin Brunger and Professors Katja Ziegler and Elizabeth Wicks of the School of Law, University of Leicester, for their huge support. The completion of this book would not have been possible without the support of my spiritual father Rev Dr Efe Obuke and his family in Louisiana, United States of America. Thank you for your immense support in every way.

I would like to thank Dr Solomon Ukhuegbe, Professors Atsegbua, Chianu, Inegbedion, Omoruyi, Idubor, Odiase-Alegimenlen, Aniekwu, Kalu and Aigbokhaevbo all of the Faculty of Law, University of Benin, Benin City, Nigeria, for their mentorship and guidance in completing this book. I also appreciate the mentorship of Professor Chris Ohurogu whose insights into ICL and IHL were a great impetus for me to pursue this ambition; thanks also to Dr Ngozi Stewart for being a vital part of the process.

I would also like to thank my mother Agnes Ojarikre and my siblings, Aaron, Benedict, Ese, Obruche, TG and Gift, for their prayers and encouragements. I am indebted to my family, especially to my husband Walter, who was never too busy to read and discuss pertinent issues relating to this book, thereby coaxing the work to completion; thank you 'my love and my lord' for your unflinching support. Big hugs to my princess Oyarelemi, who took charge of the home when I became extremely busy and immersed in writing, becoming 'mom' to everyone, including me, whilst also excelling in her academics. I am so proud of you Lemmy! Thank you. Special hugs and thanks to my 'Anointed Generals' Oghenakogie and Aghunopua, to whom I owe everything.

# Contents

# Table of Abbreviations

| | |
|---|---|
| ACHPR | African Charter on Human and Peoples' Rights |
| Af.HRJ | African Human Rights Journals |
| Afr J. Int'l & Comp L | African Journal of International and Comparative Law |
| A-G | Attorney General |
| AI | Amnesty International |
| AJIL | American Journal of International Law |
| ALR | Albany Law Review |
| Am.J.Int'l.L | Amsterdam Journal of International Law |
| AMF/CFT | Anti-Money Laundering/Counter Financing of Terrorism |
| API | Additional Protocol I |
| APII | Additional Protocol II |
| App | Appendix |
| APRM | African Peer Review Mechanism |
| Art/arts | Article/articles |
| ASF | African Standby Force |
| ASF | Avocats sans Frontières (Lawyers without Borders) |
| ASIL | American Society of International Law |
| ASP | Assembly of States Party |
| ASR | African Security Review |
| AU | African Union |
| BBC | British Broadcasting Corporation |
| BIA | Bilateral Immunity Agreement |
| Brklyn J. Int'l L | Brooklyn Journal of International Law |
| Cal. L. Rev | California Law Review |
| CJL&J | Canadian Journal of Law and Jurisprudence |
| CAR | Central African Republic |
| CCAIL | Code of Crimes Against International Law |
| Ch | Chapter |
| ChiJ Int'lL | Chinese Journal of International Law |
| CICC | Coalition for the International Criminal Court |

| | |
|---|---|
| CID | Criminal Investigation Department |
| CIPD | Centre for International Peace and Development |
| CJL&J | Canadian Journal of Law & Jurisprudence |
| CJN | Chief Justice of Nigeria |
| CLF | Criminal Law Forum |
| CLJ | Cambridge Law Journal |
| CLP | Current Legal Problems |
| CLR | Columbia Law Review |
| CLR | Criminal Law Forum |
| Cor Int'l LJ | Cornell International Law Journal |
| CPI | Corruption Perceptions Index |
| Crim LR | Criminal Law Review |
| CSPRI | Civil Society Prison Reform Initiative |
| CUP | Cambridge University Press |
| DENJILP | Denver Journal of International Law and Politics |
| Dept | Department |
| DPP | Director of Public Prosecutions |
| DRC | Democratic Republic of the Congo |
| DRT | Demobilisation and Resettlement Team |
| ECOWAS | Economic Community of West African States |
| ed/eds | Editor/Editors |
| Edn | Edition |
| EFCC | Economic and Financial Crimes Commission |
| EJIL | European Journal of International Law |
| EL Rev | European Law Review |
| FARDC | Armed Forces of the Democratic Republic of the Congo |
| FCT | Federal Capital Territory, Abuja |
| FICJC | Forum for International Criminal Justice and Conflict |
| FJSC | Federal Judicial Service Commission |
| Fla. J. Int'l. L | Florida Journal of International Law |
| FRPI | Front for Patriotic Resistance in Ituri |
| FWLR | Fawehinmi Law Report |
| Ga. J. Int'l & Comp. L | Georgia Journal of International & Comparative Law |
| GIABA | Inter-Governmental Action Group Against Money Laundering in West Africa |
| Goe.J.Int'l L | Goettingen Journal of International Law |
| Harv. Int'l LJ | Harvard International Law Journal |
| Harv.HRJ | Harvard Human Rights Journal |
| Hast Int'l & Comp. L. Rev | Hastings International & Comparative Law Review |
| HRLC | Human Rights Law Centre |
| HRLR | Human Rights Law Review |
| HRQ | Human Rights Quarterly |

| | |
|---|---|
| HRW | Human Rights Watch |
| IBA | International Bar Association |
| ICC | International Criminal Court |
| ICCLR | International Centre for Criminal Law Reform |
| ICCM | International Criminal Court Manual |
| ICD | International Crimes Division |
| ICJ | International Court of Justice |
| ICL | International Criminal Law |
| ICLQ | International & Comparative Law Quarterly |
| ICLR | International Criminal Law Review |
| ICPC | Independent Corrupt Practices and Other Related Offences |
| ICRC | International Committee of the Red Cross |
| ICTJ | International Centre for Transitional Justice |
| ICTR | International Criminal Tribunal for Rwanda |
| ICTY | International Criminal Tribunal for the Former Yugoslavia |
| IGP | Inspector-General of Police |
| IHL | International Humanitarian Law |
| ILC | International Law Commission |
| ILE | International Law Essays |
| ILSAJ. Int'l & Comp. L | International Law Students Association Journal of International and Comparative Law |
| Int'l Org | International Organisation |
| IRC | Independent Review Committee |
| IRRC | International Review of the Red Cross |
| J.L&Soc. Cha. | Journal of Law and Social Challenge |
| JAL | Journal of African Law |
| JEM | Justice and Equality Movement |
| JICJ | Journal of International Criminal Justice |
| JSC | Justice of the Supreme Court |
| LCP | Law and Contemporary Problems |
| LEN | Law Enforcement Network |
| LFN | Laws of the Federation of Nigeria |
| LJIL | Leiden Journal of International Law |
| LQR | Law Quarterly Review |
| LRA | Lord's Resistance Army |
| LS | Legal Studies |
| MAF | Mustapha Akanbi Foundation |
| Mich J. Intl.L | Michigan Journal of International Law |
| n/notes | Footnote/footnotes |
| NATO | North Atlantic Treaty Organization |
| NBA | Nigerian Bar Association |
| NDPP | National Director of Public Prosecution |
| NELR | New England Law Report |
| NGO | Non-Governmental Organisation |

| | |
|---|---|
| NILD | National Implementing Legislation Database |
| NJC | National Judicial Council |
| NOPRIN | Network on Police Reform in Nigeria |
| Nor.J.Int'l.L | Nordic Journal of International Law |
| NPF | Nigerian Police Force |
| NPS | Nigerian Prison Service |
| NWLR | Nigeria Weekly Law Report |
| NWULRev. | Northwestern University Law Review |
| NYUJIL&P | New York University Journal of International Law and Politics |
| OAU | Organisation of African Unity |
| OHCHR | Office of the United Nations High Commission on Human Rights |
| OSJI | Open Society Justice Initiative |
| OSV | Other Situations of Violence |
| OTP | Office of the Prosecutor |
| OUP | Oxford University Press |
| Para/paras | Paragraph/paragraphs |
| PCIJ | Permanent Court of International Justice |
| PrepCom | Preparatory Committee |
| PRIO | Peace Research Institute Oslo |
| PSC | Peace and Security Council |
| PSC | Police Service Commission |
| Pt/pts | Part/parts |
| PTCI | Pre-Trial Chamber I |
| PTCII | Pre-Trial Chamber II |
| QLR | Queen's Lancashire Regiment |
| Que. Rev. Int'l L | Quebecois Review of International Law |
| R | Rules |
| Res | Resolution |
| Rev.IL&P | Review of International Law and Politics |
| RPE | Rules of Procedure and Evidence |
| RULAC | Rule of Law in Armed Conflicts |
| s/ss | Section/sections |
| SA ICC Act | South African International Criminal Court Act |
| SA | South Africa |
| SAN | Senior Advocate of Nigeria |
| SC | Supreme Court |
| SCCED | Special Criminal Court on the Events in Darfur |
| SCSL | Special Court for Sierra-Leone |
| Sing.JInt'l&Comp L. | Singapore Journal of International Comparative Law |
| SIPRI | Stockholm International Peace Research Institute |
| SJSC | State Judicial Service Commission |

| | |
|---|---|
| SL J. Int'l L. | Sri Lanka Journal of International Law |
| SPLM | Sudanese People's Liberation Movement |
| TMG | Tribunal Militaire de Garnison (Military Tribunals) |
| UTFL-Rev | University of Toronto Faculty of Law Review |
| UC Davis J. Int'l L& P | University of California Davis Journal of International Law & Policy |
| UCDP | Uppsala Conflict Data Program |
| UICC | Understanding the International Criminal Court |
| UK ICC Act | United Kingdom International Criminal Court Act |
| UK | United Kingdom |
| UN Doc | United Nations Documents |
| UNHCHR | United Nations High Commission on Human Rights |
| UNODC | United Nations Office on Drugs and Crimes |
| UNSC | United Nations Security Council |
| UNSMIL | United Nations Support Mission in Libya |
| UNSW | University of New South Wales |
| UNTS | United Nations Treaty Series |
| UP | University Press |
| UPR | Universal Periodic Review |
| US | United States |
| US Dept. of State | United States Department of State |
| USA | United States of America |
| UTFL-Rev | University of Toronto Faculty of Law Review |
| VJIL | Virginia Journal of International Law |
| VJIL | Virginia Journal of International Law |
| Vol/Vols | Volume/volumes |
| Yale J.Int'l.L | Yale Journal of International Law |
| Yale L.J | Yale Law Journal |
| YB | Yearbook |

# Chapter 1
# The International Criminal Court as the New Paradigm to Close Impunity Gaps

**Abstract** This chapter discusses the different ways through which the international community continues to combat international crimes. Hitherto, international crimes included piracy *jure gentium*, slavery and slave trade. However, the international crimes discussed in this book are those recognised as constituting serious concern to the international community as a whole and these are the crimes listed in the Rome Statute; genocide, war crimes, crimes against humanity and aggression. Originally, international criminals were prosecuted by the Nuremberg and Tokyo International Military Tribunals, which were perceived as lopsided, as the prosecution focused only on the victims. Thereafter, the ad hoc tribunals of the former Yugoslavia and Rwanda established in the 1990s, achieved a lot in the field of international prosecution of international crimes. Despite the success of the ad hoc tribunals, their ad hoc nature and certain questions, such as the huge burden of costs, as well as the need for a permanent institution, were left unanswered. Consequently, the creation of the International Criminal Court (ICC) by the Rome Statute appeared to have solved the problem and yet even after the first ten years of the functioning of the ICC, there are new challenges regarding the implementation of the complementarity regime which is the pillar upon which the Court stands.

International criminal law encompasses the law that proscribes international crimes, such as genocide, war crimes, crimes against humanity and potentially, aggression,[1] and the principles and procedures governing the investigation and prosecution of these crimes.[2] In an attempt to ensure accountability for such serious crimes, the international community established the International Criminal Court (the ICC or the Court).[3] The Rome Statute of the International Criminal Court (the 'Rome Statute') adopted at the diplomatic conference in Rome, Italy in 1998,[4]

---

[1]Though included in the Rome Statute in article 5(1)(d), the crime of Aggression has only been defined at the first Review Conference of the Rome Statute held in Kampala Uganda May-June 2010. The jurisdiction of the ICC over the crime would be activated in January 2017.

[2]Cryer (2011), p. 4. (Cryer *et al.*).

[3]Scheffer and Cox (2008), p. 3.

[4]The Rome Statute of the International Criminal Court, July 17, 1998, 2187 UNTS 90 (entered into force on 1 July 2002) http://legal.un.org/icc/statute/romefra.htm (Accessed 16 November 2013). (Rome Statute).



O.C. Imoedemhe, *The Complementarity Regime of the International Criminal Court*, DOI 10.1007/978-3-319-46780-1_1

created the ICC in accordance with the proposition, arguably, that international prosecution is most appropriate for international crimes.[5]

The desire of the international community to establish a permanent international court dates back to the Second World War. In the aftermath of the Second World War (World War 11), the international community employed the use of the Tokyo and Nuremberg Military Tribunals for the prosecution of those who were suspected to have committed international crimes. As is common knowledge, the trials were widely perceived as lopsided, as they were held by the Allied Forces against the leaders of Nazi Germany and therefore classified as 'victor's justice'. In the 1990s new ad hoc tribunals were set up; the International Criminal Tribunals for the former Yugoslavia (ICTY) and the International Criminal Tribunals for Rwanda (ICTR). The contributions made by these tribunals to the international community as a whole has been analysed by Guénaël Mettraux.[6] Despite the success of the ad hoc tribunals, the ICC was established in 1998.

The dominant theme of the Rome Statute which established the ICC is complementarity, which gives states the primary responsibility to investigate and prosecute international crimes and the ICC to intervene only where certain conditions exist. This chapter will trace the trajectory of the effort of the international community in combating international crimes that culminated in the complementarity regime of the ICC. This is important because although the international criminal justice system established under the Rome Statute set up a permanent international institution—the ICC—it nevertheless puts the primary responsibility of prosecuting international crimes on states.[7] This is a reversal of functions, as previous tribunals had primacy of jurisdiction over national courts.

The first president of the International Criminal Tribunal for the former Yugoslavia (ICTY), Antonio Cassese, once noted that the 'the tribunal can be likened to a giant without arms and legs yet it needs artificial limbs to walk and work and these artificial limbs are state authorities'.[8] As it were, the ad hoc tribunals had concurrent jurisdictions with domestic courts but had primacy over them.[9] Under the Rome Statute, however, the reverse is the case, as states have primacy of jurisdiction while the ICC is complementary to national jurisdictions. This means that despite creating an international court, the expectation of the international community is that states should bear the primary responsibility of investigating and prosecuting international crimes.

[5]Jessberger (2010), pp. 209, 214; Cassese (2010), pp. 123, 127.

[6]Mettraux (2010).

[7]Burke-White (2002–2003), pp. 1–24; Werle (2009), p. 117; Stahn (2008), pp. 87–113.

[8]See Cassese (1998), pp. 2, 13.

[9]See Article 9(2) ICTY Statute UN Doc S/RES/827 1993 and Article 8(2) ICTR Statute UN Doc. S/RES/955 1994.

## 1.1 The Different Phases: From Nuremberg/Tokyo IMTs, Yugoslavia and Rwanda Ad Hoc Tribunals to the Complementarity of the ICC

In the course of World War II the Allied Powers, the United States, the United Kingdom, France and the Soviet Union,[10] issued several declarations concerning the punishment of war criminals.[11] It was announced that a United Nations War Crimes Commission would be set up for the investigations of war crimes and on 20 October 1943 the Commission was established.[12] The three main Allied Powers namely, the United States, the United Kingdom and the Soviet Union issued joint statement that the German war criminals should be judged and punished in the countries in which their crimes were committed. However, the major criminals whose offences had no particular geographical location should be punished by the joint decision of the governments of the Allies. This agreement was drafted in proceedings and deliberations leading to the conference held in London from 26 June to 8 August 1945.[13]

The Allied Powers signed the London Agreement and Charter, which became the basis for the trials at the International Military Tribunals (IMT) established at Nuremberg and for the Far East Tokyo.[14] The Tribunals were established for the just and prompt trial and punishment of the major war criminals of the European Axis.[15] The jurisdiction of the Tribunals was outlined in Article 6 of the Nuremberg Charter, which defined the crimes the defendants were charged with, namely, crimes against peace, war crimes and crimes against humanity.[16]

Details of the trials and convictions by the Nuremberg and Tokyo Tribunals have been recorded and any further analysis of whether they were right or wrong is

[10]In 1991 the Soviet Union witnessed disintegration into 15 separate states and the Russian Federation continued in its stead.

[11]Although other countries later signed and ratified the London Agreement, only these four countries participated in the London Conference in 1945 (In accordance with Article 5, the following governments expressed their adherence to the Agreement: Greece, Denmark, Yugoslavia, The Netherlands, Czechoslovakia, Poland, Belgium, Ethiopia, Australia, Honduras, Norway, Panama, Luxemburg, Haiti, New Zealand, India, Venezuela, Uruguay and Paraguay).

[12]'Declaration on German Atrocities' 20 October 1943. The determination of the Allies to punish the major war criminals of the European Axis first found expression in the Moscow Conference in 1943 cited in: Document: A/CN.4/5 The Charter and Judgment of the Nuremberg Tribunal—History and Analysis: Memorandum Submitted by the Secretary-General 1–100, 3.

[13]Agreement for the Prosecution and Punishment of the Major War Criminals of the European Axis, and Charter of the International Military Tribunal London 8 August 1945.

[14]The Nuremberg and Tokyo Military Tribunals (IMT) were the first international criminal tribunals. For detailed record of the judgments of the Nuremberg Tribunal see 'International Military Tribunal (Nuremberg) Judgment of 1 October 1946'. Available at http://crimeofaggression.info/documents/6/1946_Nuremberg_Judgement.pdf (Accessed 30 June 2016).

[15]Nuremberg Charter, Article 18 (c) provided for expedited trials.

[16]Nuremberg Charter, Article 6.

beyond the scope of this book. However, the trial at the Nuremberg Tribunal is worthy of mention because of the fundamental principles of international law, albeit, international criminal law that were laid down in the judgments. In the case between the Four Allied Powers against the 22 German war criminals,[17] the defendants were tried and convicted of war crimes, crimes against humanity and aggression in violation of international treaties. The Nuremberg Tribunal found that certain of the German war criminals planned and waged aggressive wars against 12 nations and were therefore guilty of this series of crimes.[18] In The Hague Convention 1899, the signatory powers agreed that no high contracting party would have recourse to arms except there was first recourse to the good offices or mediation of one or more friendly powers.[19] A similar clause was inserted in the Convention for Pacific Settlement of International Disputes of 1907.[20] Furthermore, certain provisions of the Treaty of Versailles of 1919 were also breached by the defendants.[21] It was argued that since Germany was party to these international treaties, their violations by its nationals meant that they had to be prosecuted.

There are diverse views about the genuineness or otherwise of these trials and as is commonly known, the summary nature of the trials appeared to confirm the fact of a 'victor's justice' for which these trials and convictions are reputed. Detailed analyses of these issues are beyond the scope of this book. However, certain important principles were laid down by the Nuremberg Tribunal which became cornerstone principles on which subsequent jurisprudence of ad hoc tribunals and international criminal courts were founded. Some of these principles will be mentioned briefly below.

---

[17]The United States of America, The French Republic, the United Kingdom of Great Britain and Northern Ireland and the Union of Soviet Socialist Republics v Hermann Wilhelm Göring, Rudolf Hess, Joachim von Ribbentrop, Robert Ley, Wilhelm Keitel, Ernst Kaltenbrunner et al (22 defendants in all). Robert Ley was reported to have committed suicide on 25 October 1945.

[18]These nations were Austria, Belgium, Czechoslovakia, Greece, Denmark, Luxemburg, Norway, Poland, The Netherlands, then Union of Soviet Socialist Republics, the United States and former Yugoslavia.

[19]Convention (II) with Respect to the Laws and Customs of War on Land and its Annex: Regulations Concerning the Laws and Customs of War on Land. The Hague 29 July 1899. Available at http://www.opbw.org/int_inst/sec_docs/1899HC-TEXT.pdf (Accessed 20 May 2016).

[20]Convention (IV) Respecting the Laws and Customs of War on Land and its Anne: Regulations Concerning the Laws and Customs of War on Land. The Hague 18 October 1907. Available at http://www.opbw.org/int_inst/sec_docs/1907HC-TEXT.pdf (Accessed 20 May 2016). Other treaties of mutual guarantee, arbitration and non-aggression were entered into between Germany and Belgium, France, Great Britain and Italy, at Locarno in 1925. Other treaties were between Germany, The Netherlands and Denmark and between Germany and Luxemburg and between Germany, Denmark and Russia in 1926, 1929 and 1939 respectively were referred to.

[21]The Treaty of Versailles 28 June 1919. Specifically, Arts 242-44, 80, 99, 100 were breached in relation to the demilitarised zone of the Rhineland, the annexation of Austria, the incorporation of the district of Memel and the Free City of Danzig.

### 1.1.1 *Nullum crimen sine lege, nulla poena sine lege*

The first is the principle of Nullum *crimen sine lege, nulla poena sine lege* (there can be no punishment of crime without a pre-existing law), argued on behalf of the defendant as a fundamental principle of law both domestic and international. It was submitted that *ex post facto* punishment is abhorrent to the law of all civilized nations, that no sovereign power had made aggressive war a crime at the time the alleged criminal acts were committed.[22] No statute had defined aggressive war, no penalty had been fixed for its commission, and also no court had been created to try and punish offenders.[23] However, the Tribunal noted that;

> [I]t is to be observed that the maxim "*nullum crimen sine lege*" is not a limitation of sovereignty, but is in general a principle of justice. To assert that it is unjust to punish those who in defiance of treaties and assurances have attacked neighbouring States without warning is obviously untrue, for in such circumstances the attacker must know that he is doing wrong, and so far from it being unjust to punish him, it would be unjust if his wrong were allowed to go unpunished.[24]

Making reference to several international treaties to which Germany was a party,[25] the Tribunal noted that 'occupying the positions they did in the Government of Germany, the defendants, or at least some of them, must have known of the treaties signed by Germany, outlawing recourse to war for the settlement of international disputes; they must have known that they were acting in defiance of all International Law when in complete deliberation they carried out their designs of invasion and aggression.'[26] On this point the Tribunal noted that the maxim has no application to the case.

It was further argued that The Hague Convention 1907 and other international treaties mentioned did list a number of conducts as crimes, but nowhere in these laws was any sentence prescribed, nor any mention made of a court to try and punish offenders. In response to this the Tribunal noted that for many years, military tribunals have tried and punished individuals guilty of violating the rules of land warfare laid down by the Convention.[27]

---

[22]IMT Judgment of 1 October 1946 in *The Trial of German Major War Criminals. Proceedings of the International Military Tribunal Sitting at Nuremberg, Germany* Part 22 (22nd August 1946 to 1st October 1946) available at http://crimeofaggression.info/documents/6/1946_Nuremberg_Judgement.pdf (Accessed 30 January 2016) (hereinafter 'IMT Judgment 1946').

[23]Ibid, 52.

[24]Ibid.

[25]For example, The Hague Convention 1907; the Treaty of Versailles 28 June 1919; the League of Nations 1924 Protocol for the Pacific Settlement of International Disputes and the General Treaty for the Renunciation of War generally known as the Pact of Paris or the Kellogg-Briand Pact 27 August 1928 were binding on 63 nations including Germany, Italy and Japan at the outbreak of the war in 1939.

[26]IMT Judgment 1946, 52.

[27]Ibid.

> In the opinion of the Tribunal, those who wage aggressive war are doing that which is equally illegal, and of much greater moment than a breach of one of the rules of the Hague Convention.[28]

Interpreting the Kellogg-Briand Pact,[29] the Tribunal noted that it must be remembered that 'International Law is not the product of an international legislature, and that such international agreements as the Pact of Paris have to deal with general principles of law, and not with administrative matters of procedure. The law of war is to be found not only in treaties, but in the customs and practices of States, which gradually obtained universal recognition, and from the general principles of justice applied by jurists and practised by military courts. This law is not static, but by continual adaptation follows the needs of a changing world.'[30]

The Tribunal further noted that Article 227 of the Treaty of Versailles provided for the constitution of a special Tribunal, composed of representatives of five of the Allied and Associated Powers which had been belligerents in the First World War.[31] Thus, by Article 228 of the Treaty, the German Government expressly recognised the right of the Allied Powers 'to bring before military tribunals persons accused of having committed acts in violation of the laws and customs of war.'[32] Consequently the *nullum crimen sine lege* argument was defeated and the Tribunal demonstrated that the body of treaty laws that existed prior to the commencement of the war were sufficient to ground prosecution and conviction.

### *1.1.2 Individual Criminal Responsibility*

The second principle was that of individual criminal responsibility. Previously, international law concerned the actions of sovereign states and provides no punishment for individuals. Consequently, where the act in question is an act of state, those who carry it out were not personally responsible, but were protected by the doctrine of the sovereignty of the state for which they acted. The Nuremberg Tribunal rejected these submissions and noted that international law imposes duties and liabilities upon individuals, as well as upon states.

---

[28]Ibid.

[29]The Kellogg-Briand Pact 27 August 1928.

[30]IMT Judgment 1946, 53.

[31]Article 227 of the Treaty of Versailles 1919.

[32]Article 228 of the Treaty of Versailles provides: 'The German Government recognises the right of the Allied and Associated Powers to bring before military tribunals persons accused of having committed acts in violation of the laws and customs of war. Such persons shall, if found guilty, be sentenced to punishments laid down by law. This provision will apply notwithstanding any proceedings or prosecution before a tribunal in Germany or in the territory of her allies'. See also, Arts 229 & 230.

> Crimes against International Law are committed by men, not by abstract entities, and only by punishing individuals who commit such crimes can the provisions of International Law be enforced.[33]

In placing the protection of individuals at the heart of the international legal regime, the old 'state-centric' model of international law was changed forever.[34] Thus, the Tribunal noted that the principle of international law, which under certain circumstances protects the representatives of a state, cannot be applied to acts which are condemned as criminal by international law.[35] The authors of these acts cannot shelter themselves behind their official position in order to be freed from punishment in appropriate proceedings. Article 7 of the Charter expressly declares:

> The official position of defendants, whether as heads of State, or responsible officials in government departments, shall not be considered as freeing them from responsibility, or mitigating punishment.[36]

Consequently, the very essence of the Charter is that individuals have international duties which transcend the national obligations of obedience imposed by the individual state. He who violates the laws of war cannot obtain immunity while acting in pursuance of the authority of the state if the state in authorising action moves outside its competence under international law.[37]

Furthermore, in response to the submission on behalf of the defendants that in doing what they did they were acting under superior orders, and therefore cannot be held responsible for the acts committed by them, the Tribunal noted that Article 8 of the Charter provides: 'the fact that the defendant acted pursuant to orders of his Government or of a superior shall not free him from responsibility, but may be considered in mitigation of punishment.'[38] This also put paid to the defence of superior orders, although such defence may be argued in mitigation of the punishment, but does not exclude liability. According to the Tribunal, 'the true test..., is not the existence of the order, but whether moral choice was in fact possible'.[39]

### 1.1.3 *The Establishment of the ICTY and the ICTR*

As noted earlier, the point of the above analysis is to state the origin and the principles upon which international prosecution of international crimes is founded.

---

[33]IMT Judgment 1946, 55.

[34]Mansell and Openshaw (2013), p. 126.

[35]IMT Judgment 1946, 55.

[36]Nuremberg Charter, Article 7. This Article has been reproduced verbatim in all Statutes of the ICTY, ICTR and the ICC.

[37]IMT Judgment of 1946, p. 56.

[38]Nuremberg Charter, Article 8. This Article has also been reproduced verbatim in all Statutes of the ICTY, ICTR and the ICC.

[39]IMT Judgment of 1946, 56–57.

The principles analysed are, amongst others, cornerstone principles of international criminal law and they are enshrined in subsequent statutes that established ad hoc tribunals. At the Nuremberg Tribunal, Prosecutors were drawn from the four Allied Powers and in the end, Justice Robert Jackson the Chief Prosecutor for United States said;

> Of course, it would be extravagant to claim that agreements or trials of this character can make aggressive war or persecution of minorities impossible, just as it would be extravagant to claim that our federal laws make federal crime impossible. But we cannot doubt that they strengthen the bulwarks of peace and tolerance...[40]

True to the words of Justice Jackson, the prosecution of the war criminals by the Nuremberg and Tokyo Tribunals did not stop aggressive war or the persecution of minorities, as there were reported widespread atrocities all over the world subsequently and specifically in the former Yugoslavia in 1991. This prompted the United Nations Security Council in accordance with Chapter VII of the Charter of the United Nations to set up the International Criminal Tribunal for the former Yugoslavia (ICTY).[41] The aim was to put an end to such crimes, to restore peace and security and to bring stability back to the region, as well as with a view of punishing those responsible for the atrocities.

For this purpose, the Statute of the 'International Criminal Tribunal for the Prosecution of Persons Responsible for Serious Violations of International Humanitarian Law Committed in the Territory of the former Yugoslavia since 1991' was adopted.[42] The Statute gave the ICTY jurisdiction to prosecute those who were suspected to have violated international humanitarian law committed on the territory of the former Yugoslavia since 1991, to prosecute violations of Grave breaches of the Geneva Conventions of 1949 and other serious violations of the laws or customs of war, genocide, and crimes against humanity.[43] Although the jurisdiction of the ICTY and that of domestic courts were concurrent, the former was given primacy over the latter.[44] Furthermore, Article 29 placed a binding obligation on states to cooperate with the ICTY in its investigation and prosecution.

The ICTY was situation specific,[45] as it was a reaction of the international community to quell the atrocities and the gross violations of international

---

[40] Robert H Jackson, *The Reminiscences of Robert H. Jackson* (1947) available at The Robert H. Jackson Centre at https://www.roberthjackson.org/article/london-agreement-charter-August-8-1945/ (Accessed 26 July 2016).

[41] In accordance with its Chapter VII power under the United Nations Charter, on 22 February 1993 the United Nations Security Council put in motion the establishment of the International Criminal Tribunal for the former Yugoslavia (ICTY) in response to the widespread violations of international humanitarian law in the region of the former Yugoslavia.

[42] Security Council Resolution 827 (1993) UN Doc. S/RES/827 25 May 1993 adopted the Statute of the International Criminal Tribunal for the former Yugoslavia which established the ICTY.

[43] ICTY Statute, Articles 6 & 8.

[44] ICTY Statute, Article 9.

[45] Other Tribunals such as the Special Court for Sierra Leone (SCSL), the Extraordinary Chambers in the Courts of Cambodia (ECCC) and the Special Tribunal for Lebanon (STL) were also

humanitarian law in the particular situation. Therefore, although it was a good and arguably a quick response, aimed at restoring peace and stability, the ICTY could not stop other atrocities that took place in other places. Thus, in 1994, Rwanda witnessed severe catastrophic violations of a scale that alarmed the entire world.[46] In reaction to this new violence the Security Council established the International Criminal Tribunal for Rwanda (ICTR) in 1994.[47] Apart from slight nuances, the Statute of the ICTR was similar to that of the ICTY. The jurisdiction *ratione temporis* and *ratione loci* of the ICTR relate to the crimes committed in Rwanda or neighbouring states between 1 January 1994 and 31 December 1994.[48] As was the case with the ICTY, the ICTR had concurrent jurisdiction with national courts but had primacy over domestic courts in relation to the crimes within its jurisdiction.[49]

Both the ICTY and ICTR have made huge contributions to the jurisprudence of international prosecutions of international crimes, however, as their names indicate, they were temporary measures to make up for the lack of will or ability of national courts.[50] Therefore, as the works of the ad hoc tribunals have gradually come to an end, a Residual Mechanism, which comprised of two branches, both in Arusha Tanzania and in The Hague Netherlands, was put in place to cover any future functions of both the ICTR and the ICTY respectively. The mandate of the Residual Mechanism includes the continuation of ad hoc activities, such as trials and appeals, protection of witnesses and sentencing.[51]

---

established only for specific situations. See The Agreement between the United Nations Security Council and the government of Sierra Leone was for the SCSL 'to prosecute persons who bear the greatest responsibility for serious violations of international humanitarian law and Sierra Leonean law committed in the territory of Sierra Leone since 30 November 1996'; signed on 16 January 2002. The ECCC was established by an agreement between the United Nations and the Government of Cambodia for the prosecution of 'senior leaders of Democratic Kampuchea and those who were most responsible for the crimes and serious violations of Cambodian penal law, international humanitarian law and custom, and international conventions recognised by Cambodia, that were committed during the period from 17 April 1975 to 6 January 1979'. The Special Tribunal for Lebanon (STL) was established to hear one or more specific cases, namely 'persons responsible for the attack of 14 February 2005 resulting in the death of former Lebanese Prime Minister Rafiq Hariri and in the death or injury of other persons' and other connected cases; Article 1, Statute of the Special Tribunal for Lebanon, S/RES/1757.

[46] Prunier (1995).

[47] Security Council Resolution 955 (1994) UN Doc. S/RES/955. The Security Council expressed 'grave concern at the reports indicating that genocide and other systematic, widespread and flagrant violations of international humanitarian law have been committed in Rwanda'.

[48] ICTR Statute, Article 7.

[49] Ibid.

[50] Theodor Meron, 'From Ad Hoc Tribunals to the Residual Mechanism: A New Model of International Criminal Tribunals' being paper delivered at Fordham University School of Law New York 27 October 2012.

[51] Ibid.

## 1.2 The Rome Statute of the International Criminal Court

In addition to the ad hoc nature of the ICTY and ICTR and the costs of their maintenance, there had been discussions for over 50 years to establish a permanent international court.[52] This culminated in the adoption of the Rome Statute of the International Criminal Court by the plenipotentiaries of states in Rome Italy on 17 July 1998. The Rome Statute is based on the non-retroactivity principle, presumably, to avoid the *Nullum crimen sine lege* (no crime without law) maxim, for which the ad hoc tribunals were criticised, because arguably, the conducts for which the suspects of those situations were prosecuted and convicted were not criminalised at the time of their commission. Therefore Article 11 of the Rome Statute stipulates that the Court has jurisdiction only with respect to crimes committed after the entry into force of the Statute, which is 1 July 2002.[53] The dominant theme of the Rome Statue is complementarity, which makes the ICC to exercise secondary jurisdiction where there is a lack of will or ability on the part of states to act.

However, complementarity presents several challenges. First, inactivity in conducting genuine domestic investigation and prosecutions is diverse and it is now linked to inability. There are capacity issues in connection with an absent or ineffective legislative framework for implementation, limited expertise on the part of investigators, prosecutors and judges, and the national judicial system's lack of resources. Therefore, states may have the will and intent to investigate and prosecute perpetrators of international crimes but may lack the resources, expertise and capacity, as well as functioning independent judiciaries. Second, there may be unwillingness on the part of states to conduct genuine domestic prosecutions where there is governmental complicity in the commission of the crimes. This will result in political interference in the judicial system and unwillingness to secure the arrest and surrender of the suspects.

In order to overcome some of the practical challenges, this book suggests that complementarity should be interpreted and applied as a mutually inclusive concept in which both the ICC and states share the responsibility of investigating and prosecuting international crimes. Mutual inclusivity of complementarity further implies that there must be an appropriate legal framework and the institutional capacity to investigate and prosecute international crimes domestically. This is critical to the international criminal justice system because, by their nature, international crimes often require the direct or indirect participation of a number of individuals in positions of governmental authority.[54] For example, the definition of torture in the Convention against Torture requires the involvement of a public

[52]Hunt (2004), pp. 56–70, 57.

[53]See also Articles 22–24 Rome Statute.

[54]Report of the International Law Commission, 'Overview of the Rome Statute' 1996 http://untreaty.un.org/cod/icc/general/overview.htm. Accessed 4 January 2010; Kleffner (2009), p. 2.

(government) official as perpetrator or co-perpetrator.[55] In the Rome Statute, torture comes under crimes against humanity[56] and together with other acts that constitute that crime, there is a further requirement that such acts should have been committed 'in furtherance of a state or organisational policy'.[57] The question then is whether a state or government which is an alleged perpetrator or co-perpetrator can actually prosecute itself. Examples of this scenario are the cases of Sudan[58] and Kenya,[59] which are examined in Chap. 4.

Therefore, there is unwillingness on the part of national authorities where they are implicated as suspects, as well as inability to act in times of conflict. Inability may be attributed to either a lack of political will on the part of a government to prosecute its own citizens or to the inadequacy of institutions.[60] Added to the primary responsibility to investigate and prosecute international crimes, states are further required to cooperate fully with the ICC.[61] However, the lack of domestic implementing legislation consistent with the Rome Statute, as well as the fact of non-party states can undermine cooperation and render arresting and prosecuting suspects problematic.[62] Changeable obligations for states parties and non-party states may hinder cooperation by some states. For example, the United Nations Security Council Resolution 1593 of 31 March 2005[63] by which the Security Council referred the situation in Darfur Sudan to the ICC specifically urged the government of Sudan to cooperate fully with the Court.[64] Also, Security Council

[55]Convention Against Torture and Other Cruel, Inhuman or Degrading Treatment or Punishment 1465 UNTS 85 10 December 1984, Art 1.

[56]See Rome Statute, Art 7(1)(f).

[57]See Rome Statute, Art 7(2)(a).

[58]See *The Prosecutor v. Omar Hassan Ahmad Al-Bashir* ICC-02/05-01/09. See also Amnesty International, 'UN: Demand Al-Bashir's Surrender to the International Criminal Court' 20 September 2013. Available at http://www.amnesty.org/en/news/un-demand-al-bashir-s-surrender-international-criminal-court-2013-09-20 (Accessed 30 January 2014). The ICC issued two arrest warrants against President Omar Al-Bashir of Sudan in 2009 and 2010, yet Sudan claims to carry out carry out prosecution domestically for which reason it asserts that the ICC has no jurisdiction.

[59]See *The Prosecutor v. Uhuru Muigai Kenyatta* ICC-01/09-02/11 and *The Prosecutor v. William Samoei Ruto and Joshua Arap Sang* ICC-01/09-01/11 President Uhuru Muigai Kenyatta and Vice President William Ruto of the Republic of Kenya are currently standing trial before the ICC for their alleged role in the 2007 post-election violence that resulted in the death of over 1000 people in Kenya.

[60]See Kleffner (2009) Complementarity in the Rome Statute and National Criminal Jurisdictions (oxford Online Scholarship) 209–310.

[61]See part 9 of the Rome Statute on International Cooperation and Judicial Assistance particularly Arts 86–89 on General Obligation to Cooperate.

[62]Oosterveld et al. (2002), p. 25 in Roper and Barria (2008), pp. 457–476.

[63]United Nations Security Council Resolution 1593 S/RES/1593 (2005) Adopted by the Security Council at its 5158th Meeting on 31 March 2005 http://www.icc-cpi.int/NR/rdonlyres/85FEBD1A-29 F8-4EC4-9566-48EDF55CC587/283244/N0529273.pdf (Accessed 30 January 2014).

[64]Ibid, para 2.

Resolution 1970 of 26 February 2011, which referred the situation in Libya to the ICC, put the same obligation to cooperate on Libya.[65] However, other non-party states are not put under similar obligation.[66]

Nevertheless, the sustainability of the ICC rests greatly on the success of the complementarity regime; states parties, having been saddled with the primary responsibility to investigate and prosecute international crimes, must therefore be well-equipped to do so. Otherwise, the effectiveness of the ICC will be undermined and the credibility of the international criminal justice system as a whole may be called into question.

## 1.3 The Journey So Far: The ICC and African States

The ICC came into force on 1 July 2002, and in its first 10 years of operational phase (2002–2012), the Court only secured one conviction. On 14 March 2012, the ICC had its first verdict against an African, Thomas Lubanga Dyilo,[67] the leader of a militia in the Democratic Republic of Congo. Thomas Lubanga was convicted of war crimes of conscripting and enlisting children under the age of 15 years into the Patriotic Force for the Liberation of Congo (FPLC) and using them to participate actively in hostilities within the meaning of Articles 8(2)(b)(xxvi) and 25(3)(a) of the Rome Statute.[68] He was sentenced on 10 July 2012 to 14 years' imprisonment.[69] In addition, the ICC recorded a second verdict in 2014 in the *Katanga*[70] case. The Trial Chamber II found Germain Katanga guilty of one count of crimes against humanity of murder and four counts of war crimes (murder, attacking a civilian population, destruction of property and pillaging) on 7 March 2014 and he was sentenced to 12 years' imprisonment on 23 May 2014.

There are several questions on why the ICC appears to be fixated on the African region, that question is dealt with in Chap. 5. However, here, we are concerned with the activities of the ICC generally and the member states of its founding Statute—the Rome Statute. The rationale is that implementation of the complementarity regime has to be state-specific; all states parties to the Rome Statute are expected to ensure they take the vanguard role to investigate and prosecute international crimes.

---

[65]United Nations Security Council Resolution 1970 S/RES/1970 (2011) Adopted by the Security Council at its 6491st Meeting on 26 February 2011 http://www.icc-cpi.int/NR/rdonlyres/081A9013-B03D-4859-9D61-5D0B0F2F5EFA/0/1970Eng.pdf (Accessed 30 January 2014).

[66]Ibid, para 5.

[67]*The Prosecutor v Thomas Lubanga Dyilo* ICC-01/04-01/06.

[68]Articles 8 and 25 of the Rome Statute provides for war crimes and individual criminal responsibility respectively.

[69]Details can be found on the ICC website, Situation in the Democratic Republic of the Congo *The Prosecutor v Thomas Lubanga Dyilo* ICC-01/04-01/06 updated 10 February 2016. Available at https://www.icc-cpi.int/iccdocs/PIDS/publications/LubangaENG.pdf (Accessed 20 May 2016).

[70]*The Prosecutor v Germain Katanga* ICC-01/04-01/07.

The problem is that the where, when and how to implement complementarity are left entirely to individual state.

Presently, there are ten situations resulting in 21 cases before the ICC,[71] all from the African continent with the exception of Georgia.[72] Of the ten situations, four were referred by the respective state government themselves otherwise known as 'self-referrals'. This is discussed in detail in subsequent chapters, but the question may be asked here of why these African states chose to refer to the ICC situations within their jurisdictions with alleged perpetrators that arguably are their nationals and for which by the complementarity regime they are meant to be primarily responsible to investigate and prosecute? Situations in Uganda,[73] Central African Republic (CAR),[74] the Democratic Republic of the Congo (DRC)[75] and Mali[76] were referred to the ICC by the states' respective governments. Two countries, Sudan and Libya, were referred by the Security Council,[77] the Chief Prosecutor's *proprio motu* actions were in Kenya and Georgia.[78] Although not a party at the time, Cote d'Ivoire made a declaration pursuant to Article 12(3) of the Rome Statute accepting the juris-

[71]See situation and cases before the ICC available at http://www.icc-cpi.int/en_menus/icc/situations%20and%20cases/Pages/situations%20and%20cases.aspx (Accessed 5 June 2013).

[72]On 27 January 2016 the Prosecutor was authorised to open *proprio motu* investigation in and around South Ossetia Georgia for the alleged crimes against humanity and war crimes committed in the context of an international conflict between 1 July to 10 October 2008.

[73]Press Release, 'ICC – President of Uganda refers situation concerning the Lord's Resistance Army (LRA) to the ICC' ICC-20040129-44 29 January 2004. Available at http://www.icc-cpi.int/en_menus/icc/press%20and%20media/press%20releases/2004/Pages/president%20of%20uganda%20refers%20situation%20concerning%20the%20lord_s%20resistance%20army%20_lra_%20to%20the%20icc.aspx.

[74]Press Release, 'ICC – Prosecutor Receives Referral Concerning Central African Republic' ICC-OTP-20050107-86, 7 January 2005. Available at http://www.icc-cpi.int/en_menus/icc/press%20and%20media/press%20releases/2005/Pages/otp%20prosecutor%20receives%20referral%20concerning%20central%20african%20republic.aspx.

[75]Press Release, 'ICC – Prosecutor Receives Referral of the Situation in the Democratic Republic of Congo' ICC-OTP-20040419-50 19 April 2004. Available at http://www.icc-cpi.int/en_menus/icc/press%20and%20media/press%20releases/2004/Pages/prosecutor%20receives%20referral%20of%20the%20situation%20in%20the%20democratic%20republic%20of%20congo.aspx.

[76]'Referral Letter by the Government of Mali' ICC-01/12 13 July 2012. Available at http://www.icc-cpi.int/NR/rdonlyres/A245A47F-BFD1-45B6-891C-3BCB5B173F57/0/ReferralLetterMali130712.pdf.

[77]See the United Nations Security Council Resolutions 1593 (2005) and 1970 (2011) which referred the situations in Darfur Sudan and Libya respectively to the ICC (notes 22 & 24).

[78]With respect to Georgia, the Prosecutor was authorised to open investigation in January 2016. The Kenya situation commenced since 2010, 'Situation in the Republic of Kenya and Authorisation to Open an Investigation' ICC-01/09 31 March 2010. Available at http://www.icc-cpi.int/en_menus/icc/situations%20and%20cases/situations/situation%20icc%200109/Pages/situation%20index.aspx.

diction of the ICC in October 2003.[79] This was confirmed in May 2011. Technically, such declarations constitute self-referral.

Taking into consideration the limited mandate of the ICC, which is to prosecute those who bear the greatest responsibility, and the complementarity regime, collaboration with national jurisdictions is imperative for its effective functioning. According to William Schabas, 'there seems to be a paradox: the ICC is independent and interdependent at the same time. It cannot act alone. It will achieve efficiency only if it works closely with other members of the international community.'[80] Therefore, there is the need for states to adopt implementing legislation in conformity with the Rome Statute and develop institutional capacity to carry out their primary responsibility of investigating and prosecuting international crimes, as well as cooperate with the ICC where the need arises.

In addition to all self-referrals to the ICC so far coming from the African region, Africa constitutes the largest regional bloc support for the ICC in terms of ratification of the Rome Statute. Presently there are 124 state parties to the Rome Statute, 34 from Africa, 19 from Asia-Pacific States, Eastern European States constitute 18, Latin American and Caribbean States 28 and Western European and other states make up 25. Paradoxically, the implication of these ratifications does not translate to implementing complementarity at the national levels. Therefore, it is either that there is a lack of understanding of what the complementarity regime means or there is a lack of will or ability to implement it in reality.

Nigeria is a federation comprising 36 states and a Federal Capital Territory (FCT), Abuja.[81] Since gaining independence in 1960, Nigeria has had 12 presidents or heads of government, eight of whom presided over a total of 29 years of military rule.[82] During this period, Nigeria had six constitutions (including one that never entered into force),[83] four constitution drafting processes and four programs of transition from military to civilian rule.[84] In addition, Nigeria has had three civilian

[79]Cote d'Ivoire is the 34th African State party to the Rome Statute, having deposited its instrument of ratification on 15 February 2013.

[80]William Schabas in Ray Murphy, 'Gravity Issues and the International Criminal Court' (2006) 17(3/4) CLR 281–315.

[81]The Constitution of the Federal Republic of Nigeria 1999. (The 1999 Constitution). Available at http://www.nigeria-law.org/ConstitutionOfTheFederalRepublicOfNigeria.htm ss 2 & 3.

[82]There have been several military regimes in Nigeria: Aguiyi Ironsi (1966); Yakubu Gowon (1966–1975); Murtala Mohammed (1975–1976); Olusegun Obansanjo (1976–1979); Mohammadu Buhari (1983–1985); Ibrahim Babaginda (1985–1993); Sani Abacha (1993–1998); Abdusallami Abubakar (1998–1999).

[83]The 1989 Constitution drafted under the Ibrahim Babangida regime was abrogated following the annulment of the Presidential elections of June 1993. See *Attorney General of Anambra State & Others v Attorney General of the Federation* [1993] NWLR (Pt 302) 692.

[84]With the exception of the regime of Mohammadu Buhari (December 1983-August 1985), every military regime in Nigeria showed an intention to design and implement a transition to a civilian government. See Awa Kalu, 'the Democratisation of Nigeria: More Bullets or Ballot?' in *Lawyers Biannual* (1994) 40.

regimes, two constituent assemblies and one civil war.[85] With a population estimated at 168 million, Nigeria is Africa's most populous nation.[86]

Although under preliminary examination, Nigeria is not currently a situation country before the ICC.[87] However, regardless of whether indictments will result from these inquiries or not, complementarity puts the primary responsibility to investigate and prosecute international crimes on states. A corollary of this duty is for individual states to undertake a study of how they may review their laws to incorporate the crimes in the Rome Statute. Thus, ratification of the Rome Statute alone is not sufficient; thereafter, states need to take further steps to enact implementing legislation in conformity with the Rome Statute and ensure they have credible institutions to investigate and prosecute international crimes, should the need arise.

From this stand point, virtually any state party to the Statute could be selected as a case study to illustrate the capacity to investigate and prosecute international crimes domestically. However, since all situations, but one, currently before the ICC are from Africa and because there seems to be a lack of understanding on the part of a number of African states as to what their obligations are under the complementarity regime, it is logical to investigate how African states can take proactive steps to ensure the institutional capacity and a legal framework in line with the Rome Statute. Moreover, failure to do this will not only invoke the complementary jurisdiction or interference of the ICC, which can result in tension and antagonism, but it will also lead to case overload for the ICC.

Nigeria ratified the Rome Statute in 2001,[88] which means that by implication, the ICC has jurisdiction over Rome Statute crimes committed in the territory of Nigeria or by its nationals, from 1 July 2002, the date of coming into force of the ICC.[89] From November 2005 to September 2012, the ICC received 59 communications in relation to the situation in Nigeria inviting the OTP to activate its Article 15 *proprio-motu* powers to investigate atrocities that were committed in Nigeria.[90] Of these, 26 were outside the jurisdiction of the ICC, 5 were found to warrant further analysis and 28 communications were made part of a preliminary

[85]The Nigerian Civil war began in 1967 and formally ended on 15 January 1970.

[86]In October 2006, a national population census put Nigeria's population at 140,003,542. With an annual growth rate of 3.2 per cent since 1991, Nigeria's population is estimated at 168 million belonging to about 250 ethnic groups. See Legal Notice on the Publication of the 2006 Census Vol 94(4) Federal Republic of Nigeria Official Gazette 19 January 2007 B50. Available at www.population.gov.ng/pop_figure.pdf.

[87]Nigeria is presently under preliminary examination by the office of the Prosecutor and may potentially come before the ICC before the end of this research. (See *infra* notes 43–50).

[88]Nigeria deposited its instrument of ratification on 27 September 2001.

[89]Report on Preliminary Examination Activities 2012 (OTP Report November 2012) para 76. Available at http://www.icc-cpi.int/NR/rdonlyres/C433C462-7C4E-4358-8A72-8D99FD00E8CD/285209/OTP2012ReportonPreliminaryExaminations22Nov2012.pdf (Accessed 20 November 2013).

[90]Ibid, para 75.

examination, which was made public in 2010.[91] The alleged crimes which the OTP is currently analysing include killings, rape and sexual violence, abductions and torture, all attributed to members of the Boko Haram sect.[92]

'Boko Haram', which means 'western education is sinful', is a Salafi-jihadi Muslim group that operates mainly in North-Eastern Nigeria but has launched attacks in other parts of the country including Abuja, Kaduna and Plateau States.[93] To date, no arrest warrant has been issued for any of the crimes. However, the OTP has determined that there is a reasonable basis to believe that crimes against humanity, namely, acts of murder and persecution, have been committed by members of Boko Haram in Nigeria.[94] Since July 2009, members of Boko Haram have launched widespread and systematic attacks that have resulted in the killing of over 1200 civilians in different parts of Nigeria, with the scale and intensity of the attacks increasing over time.[95] Consequently, the Prosecutor decided that the preliminary examination in Nigeria should progress to phase 3 (admissibility),[96] with a view to assessing the gravity of the crimes and whether Nigeria is conducting genuine proceedings in relation to those who bear the greatest responsibility.[97]

Similarly, the governments of the DRC, Uganda and Kenya have ratified the Rome Statute since 2002 and 2005 respectively. Although both the DRC and Uganda became state parties since the beginning of the operational phase of the ICC, they were quick to refer situations in their territories to the ICC instead of taking responsibility to act. The probable reason for these will be discussed in detail in the book, but suffice it to mention here that these are some of the reasons that prompted the writing of this book. Do African states parties to the Rome Statute have the legal framework and institutional capacity to investigate and prosecute crimes under the Statute? What legislation and institutional expansion are necessary and can be made available for African states, and Nigeria in particular, to carry out

---

[91]Ibid.

[92]Ibid, paras 81, 84, 85 & 86.

[93]The group is known officially as *Jama'atu Ahlis Sunna Lidda'awati wal-jihad*, Arabic for 'group of Islamic fundamentalist committed to propagating the Prophet's teachings and jihad'. See OTP, 'Situation in Nigeria Article 5 Report' 5 August 2013; paras 8 & 30. (OTP Article 5 Report on Nigeria 2013) Available at http://www.icc-cpi.int/iccdocs/PIDS/docs/SAS%20-%20NGA%20-%20Public%20version%20Article%205%20Report%20-%2005%20August%202013.PDF (Accessed 29 November 2013).

[94]OTP Article 5 Report on Nigeria 2013, para 128.

[95]Ibid, para 15.

[96]Ibid, paras 2 & 17; OTP Report November 2012, para 96 (The OTP retains four main phases in its preliminary examination process. Phase 1 includes an initial assessment of all information on alleged crimes; Phase 2 involves a determination whether the preconditions to the exercise of jurisdiction under Article 12 of the Rome Statute are satisfied and whether the alleged crimes fall under the subject matter jurisdiction of the ICC. Phase 3 involves analysis of admissibility in terms of complementarity and gravity. Having concluded its preliminary examination, the office takes into account the gravity of the crimes, the interests of victims and examines whether there is a reasonable basis to proceed in phase 4).

[97]Ibid, para 131.

the investigation and prosecution of international crimes? How does the relationship between the ICC and the African Union affect the implementation of the complementarity regime? What are the challenges that states parties face in implementing the Rome Statute?

## 1.4 Conclusion

The birth of international criminal law and the international prosecution of international crimes can be traced to the creation of the IMTs in Nuremberg and Tokyo after World War II. These were reinforced by the setting up of the ad hoc Tribunals in the 1990s to deal with specific situations. However, as their nomenclature depicts, they were 'ad hoc' reactions to atrocities that were already committed and disasters that already occurred and to that extent, even though they arguably served the aim of international criminal justice, they were far from being the once-for-all solution that was needed. Debatably, that solution came in the adoption of the Rome Statute in 1998, which created the ICC as a permanent institution and the new paradigm to deal with perpetrators of international crimes and to close impunity gap.

Paradoxically, the Rome Statute created the ICC and yet put the primary responsibility to investigate and prosecute international crimes on states. The ICC can only exercise jurisdiction when states have failed to act or where the situation is of exceptional gravity. As discussed in this chapter, this is a reverse position with previous tribunals, because hitherto, although the ad hoc tribunals had concurrent jurisdictions with states, they nevertheless had primacy over states where there were conflicts. As would be revealed later in this book, most of the situations and cases before the ICC have state officials as perpetrators or co-perpetrators, this leads to the question of how a state who is implicated in a crime prosecute itself or how would a state whose situation is referred to the ICC by the Security Council or by the *proprio motu* action of the Chief Prosecutor be willing to cooperate with the ICC in investigation and prosecution?

Whilst it is axiomatic that so far the ICC seems fixated on Africa and has secured two convictions of Africans since its inception, most of the cases were referred to the ICC by the respective African states themselves. This makes it imperative for African states to look inwards and find how they can take charge of their affairs including taking primary responsibility to investigate and prosecute international crimes and implementing complementarity which they have gladly undertaken to do by generously signing and ratifying the Rome Statute. It may be argued that the self-referrals reflect African states' support for the ICC to stamp out impunity or it may have been due to lack of will, inability, lack of resources, lack of a legal framework and institutional capacity, or could it be a result of a lack of understanding of how complementarity is meant to work in reality? The next chapter presents a critical analysis of the complementarity regime both in Article 17 and as envisioned in other provisions of the Rome Statute.

## References

Burke-White W (2002–2003) A community of courts: towards a system of international criminal law enforcement. Mich J Int'l L 24:1–24

Cassese A (1998) On the current trends towards criminal prosecution and punishment of breaches of international humanitarian law. EJIL 9:2, 13

Cassese A (2010) The rationale for international criminal justice. In: Cassese A (ed) The Oxford companion to international criminal justice. OUP, p 123

Cryer R (2011) Darfur: complementarity as the drafters intended? In: Stahn C, ElZeidy M (eds) Complementarity from theory to practice. CUP, pp 1097–1119

Hunt D (2004) The international criminal court: high hopes, creative ambiguity and an unfortunate mistrust in international judges. JICJ 2:56–70, 57

Jessberger F (2010) International v. National Prosecution of International Crimes. In: Cassese A (ed) The Oxford companion to international criminal justice. OUP, pp 209–214

Kleffner JK (2009) Complementarity of the Rome Statute and National Criminal Jurisdictions. Oxford Scholarship Online, p 2. www.oxfordscholarshiponline.com. Accessed 15 Mar 2012

Mansell W, Openshaw K (2013) International law: a critical introduction. Hart Publishing, p 126

Mettraux G (2010) International crimes and the ad hoc tribunals. Oxford Scholarship Online

Oosterveld V, Perry M, McManu J (2002) How the world will relate to the court: the co-operation of states with the international criminal court. FILJ 25

Prunier G (1995) The Rwanda crisis: history of a genocide. Columbia University Press, New York

Report on Preliminary Examination Activities 2012 para 76. Available at http://www.icc-cpi.int/NR/rdonlyres/C433C462-7C4E-4358-8A72-8D99FD00E8CD/285209/OTP2012ReportonPreliminaryExaminations22Nov2012.pdf. Accessed 20 Nov 2013

Roper S, Barria L (2008) State co-operation and international criminal court bargaining influence in the arrest and surrender of suspects. LJIL 21(2):457–476

Scheffer D, Cox A (2008) The constitutionality of the Rome Statute of the international criminal court. JCLC 98:3

Stahn C (2008) Complementarity: a tale of two notions. CLF 19:87–113

Werle G (2009) Principles of international criminal law, 2nd edn. TMC Asser, The Hague

# Chapter 2
# The Complementarity Regime of the Rome Statute: An Analysis of Its Components

**Abstract** This chapter presents a critical analysis of complementarity both in Article 17 and as envisioned in other provisions of the Rome Statute and proposes a mutually inclusive interpretation of complementarity. The complementarity components of 'unwillingness', 'inability', 'genuinely' and 'gravity' are scrutinised. Subsequently, the decisions of the Pre-Trial Chambers of the ICC on admissibility challenges under Article 19, all of which favour mutual inclusivity, are also examined. Such an analysis, and the insight it reveals, are imperative for identifying the way forward for both the Court and state parties to the Rome Statute, and is particularly relevant in light of ongoing controversy and misunderstandings regarding the role of the ICC in serving the interests of justice for victims of international crimes. It is argued that the relationship between the Court and states which have had cases before it has often been antagonistic, whereas a mutually inclusive interpretation of complementarity best suits the aims of the Statute. Three models of complementarity are examined-passive, positive and proactive-, two of which have already been implemented to some degree but which have proven unsatisfactory. The last, the proactive complementarity model, is advocated as the most suitable model, as it mirrors the proposal for mutual inclusivity, and thereby would ensure that the ICC and national jurisdictions work in cooperation and collaboration rather than in either competition or isolation.

Complementarity forms the cornerstone of the Rome Statute of the International Criminal Court.[1] As a mechanism that puts the primary responsibility to investigate and prosecute international crimes on states, complementarity envisages clear interactions between domestic criminal justice systems and the ICC.[2] Nevertheless, while literature is replete with scholarly debates on how collaboration between the

---

[1]See Pre-Trial Chamber II decision in *Prosecutor v Joseph Kony, Vincent Otti, Okot Odhiambo and Dominic Ongwen* ICC-02/04-01/05-377 10 March 2009 para 34. (Decision on the Admissibility of the case under Article 19(1) of the Statute). See also Trial Chamber I, *Prosecutor v Lubanga*, Decision on the Practice of Witness Familiarisation and Witness Proofing icc-01/04-01/06 8 November 2006 para 34 & 38 (describing complementarity as 'one of the cornerstones of the Rome Statute').

[2]Kleffner (2009); 99–162, 309–310; Burke-White (2008b), pp. 53–108. (Burke-White 'Proactive Complementarity').

 
O.C. Imoedemhe, *The Complementarity Regime of the International Criminal Court*, DOI 10.1007/978-3-319-46780-1_2

two justice systems could be achieved,[3] the practical applications pose a serious challenge to the functioning of the ICC.

In light of the practical difficulties associated with the implementation of the principle, this chapter includes a discussion of the component elements of complementarity and the proposal that complementarity should be perceived as a mutually inclusive concept. This means that both the ICC and national systems share the responsibility of ensuring that perpetrators of international crimes are prosecuted. This further implies that certain legal frameworks and institutional capacities are necessary for states to implement the Rome Statute domestically. Therefore the analysis of the component elements of complementarity will help shape the understanding of both the ICC and states in its implementation.

This chapter is divided into three sections. The first section discusses complementarity as a principle under the Rome Statute. The twin concepts of 'jurisdiction' and 'admissibility' and their relationship with 'complementarity' are also examined in this section. This is important because although 'complementarity' is the basis of the compromise which created the ICC, the word does not appear anywhere in the Rome Statute.[4] It is a derivative of the word 'complementary', which itself appears only twice in the Statute.[5] Therefore it is important to note that complementarity is realised through admissibility provisions.

In the second section, the fundamental components of complementarity are evaluated. These elements, which are also referred to as 'complementarity thresholds' or simply as 'elements', include 'unwilling', 'unable', 'genuinely' and 'gravity'. Clarifying these elements is important because they constitute the bedrock on which the principle of complementarity is founded. They determine which forum is best suited for the prosecution of a particular case: the ICC or a national court. Analysis within this section reveals some deficiencies in the definition of the elements, which necessitates clarification from the ICC. The second section further incorporates an evaluation of other provisions of the Rome Statute in which complementarity has been envisioned. For instance, articles 18, 19 and 20, which regulate admissibility challenges, clearly articulate interactions between the ICC and states. This analysis strengthens a mutually inclusive interpretation of complementarity.

Section three examines emerging models of complementarity. These models include passive, positive and proactive complementarity.[6] Passive complementarity was reflected in the initial application of the concept, whereby the ICC was

---

[3]See for example Robinson (2012b), p. 165; Sriram and Brown (2012), pp. 219–244; Stahn and El-Zeidy (2011) (Stahn & ElZeidy *Complementarity Theory to Practice*); Ebobrah (2011), pp. 663–688; Robinson (2010), pp. 67–102 (Robinson, Mysterious Complementarity); Schabas (2008b), p. 5 (Schabas, Uncomplementary Thoughts).

[4]Perrin (2006), pp. 301–326. (Perrin, 'Making Sense of Complementarity'); Doherty and McCormack (1999), pp. 147–180. (Doherty & McCormack, 'Complementarity as a Catalyst').

[5]Rome Statute, para 10 of the Preamble & art 1.

[6]Burke-White (2008a), pp. 59–85 (Burke-White 'Positive Complementarity').

perceived as a court of last resort.[7] Subsequently however, positive complementarity, which promotes cooperation and interaction between the ICC and states, was considered as the appropriate characterisation of the relationship between states and the ICC. Finally, it is argued that Article 93(10) of the Rome Statute could be used to promote the proactive complementarity model which would ensure that the ICC and national jurisdictions work in collaboration rather than in either isolation or even in contention.

## 2.1 The Principle of Complementarity

### *2.1.1 What Is Complementarity*

'Complementarity' denotes a situation in which two or more different things improve or emphasize each other's qualities or complete one another.[8] While the term was first coined to describe a phenomenon in physics,[9] it can generally apply to a situation in which the description of the whole of a system in one picture is impossible as there are complementary images which do not apply simultaneously but nevertheless exhaust the whole only together.[10] The American English Dictionary defines complementarity as 'a principle of law which stipulates that jurisdictions will not overlap in legislation, administration, or prosecution of crime'.[11] The latter definition accords with the meaning attributed by the state plenipotentiaries at the Rome Conference to the concept as used in the context of the relationship between the ICC and national jurisdictions.[12] In effect, complementarity is meant to close gaps in the task of prosecuting perpetrators of international crimes.

However, more than just eliminating jurisdictional gaps, complementarity under the Rome Statute awards national courts with precedence to exercise jurisdiction over international crimes. The priority given to domestic authorities is driven by the fact that under contemporary international criminal law, states are obligated to investigate and prosecute international crimes.[13] It is only when they fail to do so

---

[7]Hall (2011), p. 1017.

[8]Collins English Dictionary 21st Century Edition (5th edn London Harper Collins Publishers 2001) 327; See also Ebobrah (2011), p. 666.

[9]Bohr (1950), pp. 51, 54; Bohr (1958), p. 74; Englard (1995), pp. 191–192.

[10]Levin (2001), pp. 249–260, 255.

[11]Available at http://oxforddictionaries.com/definition/american_english/complementarity (Accessed 2 February 2013). In Physics, complementarity is defined as the concept that two contrasted theories, such as the wave and particle theories of light, may be able to explain a set of phenomena, although each separately only accounts for some aspects.

[12]Rome Statute, Article 17.

[13]ElZeidy (2011), pp. 71–141 (ElZeidy, Genesis of complementarity). See also Holmes (1999), pp. 41–78, 41–42 (noting that many states argued that they are under an obligation to prosecute international crimes and thus an international court cannot enjoy a primary role in this regard).

that the ICC steps in to remedy their deficiencies. Consequently, to ensure an appropriate legal framework and institutional capacity domestically, national and international jurisdictions cannot be deemed mutually exclusive,[14] but rather that the two systems exist simultaneously to complete the functions of each other.

However, contrary to the perception of mutual inclusivity, William Schabas describes the term 'complementarity' as a 'misnomer' because it establishes a relationship between international and national justice systems that is far from complementary.[15] According to him, the two systems function in opposition and to some extent with hostility *vis-a-vis* each other.[16] Therefore, despite being conceived as a jurisdictional mechanism for the allocation of cases to the most effective forum, complementarity is inherently antagonistic.[17] Similarly, Robert Cryer noted that the understanding of complementarity at its inception was that the ICC was to exist in a slightly antagonistic relationship with domestic jurisdictions.[18] Accordingly, the ICC is meant to prod states to prosecute and step in when they fail to do so.

In line with the antagonistic perspective, Immi Tallgren describes complementarity as 'an open container of contradictory or at least inconsistent arguments' which reflects the deeply rooted postures on international criminal law and international jurisdiction in criminal matters.[19] He discussed complementarity not as a principle or a legal concept but as conceptualised in two trends of argument. First is the 'Butler ICC interpretation'[20] (the Butler) which sees complementarity as a means of restricting the role of the ICC and its scope of jurisdiction.[21] The Butler interpretation rests upon the unconditional presumption of national omnipotence in the field of international criminal law.[22] Accordingly this trend of thought aims to reduce the jurisdiction of the ICC to be exceptional.

The second explanation according to Tallgren, is the 'Master ICC interpretation'[23] (the Master) in which complementarity represents the process of unification

---

[14]ElZeidy (2011), pp. 72–73; See also ElZeidy (2008), pp. 1–5.

[15]Schabas (2007), p. 175. (Schabas *Intro to the ICC*).

[16]Ibid.

[17]Schabas (2008b), p. 6.

[18]Robert Cryer (2011), pp. 1097–1119.

[19]Tallgren (1998), pp. 107–137, 123.

[20]Ishiguro (1990) Cited in Tallgren Ibid, 124. (The story of the Butler was made famous by Ishiguro in his book).Why 'Butler'? A butler is supposed to stay in the background and coordinate a scene just by his mere existence, to enter when it is necessary, to be around but not use any visible gestures of power. Never is a butler supposed to be too loud or draw extraordinary attention to himself. The allegiance of a butler to his master is unquestionable.

[21]Ibid.

[22]Ibid.

[23]Tallgren, '. . .And why "Master"? A master regards "others" as able servants and wishes to make them hardworking and loyal companions in achieving a greater goal. A master aims at sovereignty of decisions and control of the situation. A tolerant master may, however, let the little mice dance on the table in his absence, but only when it is he who chooses the music . . .' cited in Tallgren.

of criminal law. Since the responsibility for punishing international crimes lies with the international community as a whole, the Master is concerned that giving states the primary responsibility to prosecute international crimes would undermine its power.[24] Presumably, the Master wants to achieve status, independence and authority, and therefore seeks to ensure that complementarity is constructed in such a way as to make the application coherent. Accordingly, Tallgren notes that espousing to monistic attempts to refer to the international criminal law system as a single coherent framework of values makes complementarity a fallacy.[25]

Similarly, Frédéric Mégret argues that there are differences in the exercise of criminal justice.[26] First, a line of inefficiency appears in all 'human and therefore fallible' justice systems. Second, the amount of resources that states are able to invest in maintaining proper justice systems varies widely.[27] Therefore, criminal proceedings are necessarily dependent on the means at the disposal of the state and on the degree of authority which it is able to exert.[28] As a consequence, Mégret argues that it is not possible to demand a uniform application in all systems which satisfies the minimum legal standards of international law.[29]

Notwithstanding the foregoing arguments, complementarity appears to be the best attempt thus far by the international community to ensure accountability for international crimes. Therefore it is argued that national and international jurisdictions should not be deemed to be mutually exclusive. Rather, the complementarity regime should be perceived as offering an opportunity to achieve an inclusive fight against impunity. Its implementation at the national level would culminate in the success and sustainability of the ICC. Without it, the ICC may soon become overburdened with referrals. The next subsection discusses the concept as stipulated in the Statute.

### 2.1.2 Complementarity in the Rome Statute

The word 'complementarity' does not appear anywhere in the Rome Statute, which consequently does not allow for a precise definition. However, Mohammed ElZeidy notes that as a legal concept it has existed since the Treaty of Versailles in 1919 in which the Allies authorised the Germans to try some of the war criminals themselves in Leipzig, Germany.[30] In contemporary times, the term 'complementary jurisdiction' appeared in the 1994 ILC Draft Statute which proposed that the ICC be

---

[24]Ibid.

[25]Tallgren (2002), pp. 561–595, 568–569.

[26]Mégret (2005).

[27]Ibid.

[28]Ibid.

[29]Ibid.

[30]ElZeidy (2011), pp. 71–78 (noting that complementarity is not a novel concept. Rather it dates back to the twentieth century, covering over a period of 79 years and ending with the Rome Statute); Bergsmo and Webb (2012), pp. 688, 691.

'complementary to national criminal justice systems...'[31] Subsequently, the French word '*complèmentaritè*' which corresponds with 'complementarity' and is a derivative of 'complementary' entered into the parlance of the Rome Statute negotiations as it aptly captured the relationship between the ICC and national courts.[32]

Yet, the term 'complementary' was used only twice in the Rome Statute. Paragraph 10 of the Preamble and Article 1 provide that the 'Court shall be *complementary* to national criminal jurisdiction'.[33] Nonetheless, complementarity is implied in all articles, including the preamble, making it an overriding theme of the Statute. For example, the preamble declares that it is 'the duty of every state to exercise its criminal jurisdiction over those responsible for international crimes',[34] and further states that the prosecution of international crimes '...must be ensured by taking measures at the national level...'[35] Thus the preamble affirms that the ICC does not have sole or even primary jurisdiction.

The choice of 'complementarity' as a means of jurisdictional allocation was not however without obstacles. The concerns that states expressed during the negotiations that led to the adoption of the Rome Statute culminated in the preference for complementary jurisdiction.[36] At the top on the list was the issue of state sovereignty, which remains the fulcrum of the law of nations.[37] In fact, the establishment of the ad hoc tribunals in the 1990s[38] and later the ICC were seen as encroachments on sovereignty.[39] Nevertheless state sovereignty remains strong as obligations of international law are in turn formed by the consent of sovereign states themselves.[40]

Since the potential loss of sovereignty was a major concern for states, they were reluctant to create the ICC without ensuring that their interests would be preserved.[41] For example, following the final meeting of the Preparatory Committee

[31]See 1994 ILC Draft Statute Report of the International Law Commission on the Work of its Forty-Sixth Session 2 May to 22 July 1994 UN Doc A/49/10 43–44.

[32]Doherty and McCormack (1999).

[33]Rome Statute, para 10 of the Preamble and Article 1 (*emphasis added*).

[34]Rome statute, para 6 of the Preamble.

[35]Rome statute, para 4 of the Preamble.

[36]Issues of concern include sovereignty, the scope of jurisdiction of the ICC and the *proprio motu* powers of the Prosecutor. See Gaeta (2004), pp. 949–952, 950. (Noting that 'it is well known that the Court was begotten by many but born against the will of some powerful countries...').

[37]Brownlie (2008), p. 289, Shaw (2008), pp. 487–490; Harris (2010), pp. 161–170.

[38]Statute of the International Criminal Tribunal for the Prosecution of Persons Responsible for serious Violations of International Humanitarian Law Committed in the Territory of the Former Yugoslavia since 1991 SC Res 827 UN Doc S/Res/827 (25 May 1993) ('ICTY Statute'); Statute of the International Criminal Tribunal for the Prosecution of Persons Responsible for Genocide and Other Serious Violations of Humanitarian Law Committed in the Territory of Rwanda and Rwandan Citizens Responsible for genocide and Other Such Violations Committed in the Territory of Neighbouring States Between 1 January and 31 December 1994 SC Res 1315 UN Doc 5/RES/955 (6 November 1994) ('ICTR Statute').

[39]Jessberger and Geneuss (2012), pp. 1081–1094, 1085.

[40]See Kittichaisaree (2001), p. 247.

[41]Bekou (2011), pp. 830–852, 836.

in anticipation of the Rome Conference,[42] the United States Senator Jesse Helms, Chairman of the Senate Committee on Foreign Relations, sent a letter to then Secretary of State Madeleine Albright objecting to the court. He stated that he was 'unalterably opposed to the creation of the permanent UN criminal court because any permanent judiciary within the UN system would…grant the UN a principal trapping of sovereignty'.[43] He added that a 'treaty establishing such a court without the clear US veto will be dead on arrival at the Senate Foreign Relations Committee'.[44]

States' concerns were allayed in part by restrictions on the points at which the ICC could assert its jurisdiction.[45]

> The drafters of the Rome statute having determined that as a matter of principles, national jurisdiction should have primacy were faced with the question of when the ICC could assume jurisdiction. The solutions developed were both complex and politically sensitive, reflecting the concerns of states over national sovereignty and the potentially intrusive powers of an international institution.[46]

Consequently, as long as a state can effectively investigate and prosecute international crimes, the sovereignty of the state will remain unaffected and the state will be free from ICC intervention.[47]

Sovereignty and other concerns necessitated the ultimate choice of 'complementary jurisdiction' for the ICC. Having come into force, however, the complementarity regime of the Rome Statute is phenomenal, as states are required to play a vanguard role in ensuring international criminal justice within their domestic spheres. While some have hailed it as the bedrock of the ICC,[48] others have raised objections to it.[49] Some reasons for the objections are that states where international crimes have occurred and are likely to occur, particularly in conflict and post conflict areas, lack the competence, ability and political will to prosecute their nationals who may be responsible for such crimes.

As will be shown in subsequent chapters, national courts face some challenges because legislation, institutional capacity and due process may be lacking and trials may be fraught with irregularities and biases. For example, the Specialised Courts

---

[42]Upon the submission of the final Draft Statute for the ICC by the ILC to the United Nations General Assembly (UNGA) in 1994 and recommendations of the *ad hoc* Committee 1995, the UNGA created the Preparatory Committee (PrepCom) on the Establishment of the ICC. In its primary responsibility to prepare a consolidated draft text for the establishment of the ICC the PrepCom held six sessions between 1996 and 1998.

[43]Letter from Jesse Helms, Senator for North Carolina to Madeleine Albright Secretary of State dated 26th March 1998 cited in van der Vyver (2010), p. 163.

[44]Ibid.

[45]Williams and Schabas (2008), pp. 605–625, 606.

[46]Holmes (2004), p. 260.

[47]Yang (2005), pp. 121–132; Kim (2003), pp. 258–259.

[48]See Broomhall (2003), p. 84; Ryngaert (2011), pp. 855–885. See also Pre-Trial Chamber II decision in *Joseph Kony et al* and Trial Chamber I decision in *Lubanga* (above note 1).

[49]Lattanzi (2001), pp. 181–182; Easterday (2009).

in which Sudan purports to prosecute those responsible for the atrocities in Darfur,[50] routinely sentenced unrepresented suspects to death after secret trials involving confessions obtained through torture.[51] Complementarity is thus described as a 'double-edged' sword.[52] On the one hand, it may reflect the willingness of states to take the lead in bringing the perpetrators of international crimes to justice. On the other hand, it may expose perpetrators to national judicial systems that are far less likely than the ICC to provide them with due process, increasing the probability of malicious prosecutions and wrongful convictions.[53]

Implementation of complementarity remains a challenge. The ICC has begun formal investigations and prosecutions in 10 situations resulting in 21 cases. Of the ten situation countries before the ICC, four were self-referrals.[54] Although not a party to the Rome Statute at the time, Cote d'Ivoire accepted the jurisdiction of the ICC in 2003 by Art 12(3) declaration.[55] Arguably, this is tantamount to a self-referral, particularly with the confirmation of acceptance of jurisdiction by the president in December 2010 and May 2011. This underscores the importance of national implementation of complementarity.

Self-referral was not contemplated in the Rome Statute, as it was perceived that states would be concerned if they have to defer to the ICC in respect of their own nationals. A demonstration of this underlying concern is rooted in the American opposition to the Rome Statute and the ICC.[56] This was reflected in the fear that accepting the Statute will eventually mean that the ICC would exercise jurisdiction over United States Servicemen, possibly at the malicious behest of one of United States many enemies in the community of nations,[57] which made the United States to withdraw from the Rome Statute.[58]

---

[50]Although not a state party to the Rome Statute, the situation in Darfur Sudan was referred to the ICC by the United Nations Security Council Resolution 1593 of 31 March 2005. Subsequently, Sudan purports to be able and willing to investigate and prosecute the perpetrators domestically.

[51]See U.S. Dept of State, 'Country Reports on Human Rights Practices, Sudan' (2005), http://www.state.gov/g/drl/rls/hrrpt/2005/61594.htm. See also Human Rights Watch, 'Lack of Conviction: The Special Criminal Court on the Events in Darfur' 1 (2006).

[52]Jon Heller (2006), pp. 255–280 (Heller, Shadow Side of Complementarity).

[53]Ibid, 256. See also Williams and Schabas (2008), p. 628. (Noting that complementarity may require an assessment of the quality of justice from the stand point of procedural and substantive fairness).

[54]The governments of Uganda, the DRC, CAR and Mali referred situations in their states to the ICC in 2003, 2004, 2005 and 2012 respectively. Available at the ICC website http://www.icc-cpi.int/en_menus/icc/situations%20and%20cases/Pages/situations%20and%20cases.aspx (Assessed 8 March 2013). See also Akhavan (2011), pp. 283–303, 287.

[55]Cote d'Ivoire became a party to the Rome Statute on 15 February 2013.

[56]Turns (2004), pp. 337, 338.

[57]Scheffer (1999), p. 12; Newton (2002), p. 35.

[58]The Rome Statute was signed by the US President Bill Clinton on 31 December 2000 with the proviso that it will not be transmitted to Congress for ratification; the administration of President George W Bush subsequently withdrew the US signature and indicated the US intention not to become a party to the Statute: US Department of State Press Statement, 6 May 2001. Available at http://www.state.gov/r/pa/prs/ps/2002/9968.htm.

Louise Arbour former Chief Prosecutor of the ICTY also noted; 'I can't think of a single state that will voluntarily defer to the jurisdiction of the ICC if one of their nationals is implicated'.[59] The debate had focused on how states could aggressively and fairly pursue domestic prosecution so as to prevent the ICC's intervention.[60] According to Antonio Cassese, self-referrals are an opportunity to use the ICC as some sort of 'bad bank', 'as a means of exposing dangerous rebels internationally so as to dispose of them through the judicial process of the ICC'.[61] Similarly, Florian Jessberger and Julia Geneuss noted that self-referring is a mechanism by which states outsource their obligation to investigate and prosecute international crimes, 'hijack' the court and tie up financial resources that could otherwise have been used for investigations *proprio-motu*.[62] Certainly, the practice of self-referrals ultimately turns the very idea of complementarity inside out.

Critical to the success of the ICC is not how situations are referred to it by states which, according to complementarity, should be engaged in carrying out investigation and prosecution themselves. Rather it is how these states demonstrate the willingness and ability to prosecute international crimes domestically. This will be discussed in subsequent chapters, but first, it is necessary to outline the provisions in the Rome Statute on complementarity and how the ICC has assessed complementarity in the cases before it. As noted, the debate on the principle of complementarity revolves around 'jurisdiction' and 'admissibility' provisions. The next section analyses the relationship between these two concepts and how they are entwined with the principle of complementarity.

## 2.2 Evaluating the Twin Concepts of Jurisdiction and Admissibility

The Rome Statute distinguishes between two related concepts; jurisdiction and admissibility. Jurisdiction refers to the legal parameters of the ICC's operations in terms of subject matter (jurisdiction *ratione materiae*),[63] time (*ratione temporis*),[64] space (*ratione loci*) as well as individuals (*ratione personae*).[65] The preconditions

[59] 'The Protection of Human Rights through International Criminal Law: A Conversation with Madame Justice Louise Arbour, Chief Prosecutor for the International Criminal Tribunals for the Former Yugoslavia and Rwanda' (1999) 57 *U Toronto Faculty of Law Rev* 83 97.

[60] Ellis (2003), pp. 215, 224–225.

[61] Cassese (2006), pp. 434–441, 436; Cassese (2009), pp. 21–30, 25 (noting that by self-referrals states use the Court as a means of de-legitimizing and cornering their political and military opponents).

[62] Jessberger and Geneuss (2012), pp. 1081–1094.

[63] Rome Statute, Articles 5–8 stipulate the Crimes within the Jurisdiction of the Court.

[64] Rome Statute, Article 11 refers to crimes committed after the entry into force of the Statute; which suggests that the Rome Statute cannot be applied retroactively.

[65] Schabas (2007), p. 172.

to the exercise of jurisdiction by the ICC are prescribed in Article 12. This article stipulates that the court may exercise jurisdiction over crimes committed on the territory of a state party or by nationals of states parties to the Rome Statute. The Court may also exercise jurisdiction over non-party states who have made an Article 12(3) declaration accepting the jurisdiction of the ICC over crimes committed in their territories.[66] Situations in the territories of states non-party to the Rome Statute may also come under the jurisdiction of the ICC where such situations are referred to it by the United Nations Security Council acting under its Chapter VII powers of the United Nations Charter.[67] Consequently, jurisdiction only identifies the scope of the Court's legal authority over a situation.

Admissibility on the other hand relates to when the court can effectively try a matter over which it has jurisdiction. Considerations of admissibility arise after the ICC has upheld jurisdiction. For this reason, jurisdictional provisions (articles 5–16) logically precede those on admissibility (articles 17–19),[68] since if the Court does not have jurisdiction over a situation, there is no need to conduct an admissibility analysis.[69] On the other hand, the ICC may have jurisdiction over a situation, yet the matter will be inadmissible if certain conditions are not met.[70] The admissibility criteria are contained in Article 17, which states:

> Having regard to paragraph 10 of the Preamble and article 1, the Court shall determine that a case is inadmissible where:
>
> (a) The case is being investigated or prosecuted by a State which has jurisdiction over it, unless the State is unwilling or unable genuinely to carry out the investigation or prosecution;
>
> (b) The case has been investigated by a State which has jurisdiction over it and the State has decided not to prosecute the person concerned, unless the decision resulted from the unwillingness or inability of the State genuinely to prosecute;
>
> (c) The person concerned has already been tried for conduct which is the subject of the complaint, and a trial by the Court is not permitted under article 20, paragraph 3;
>
> (d) The case is not of sufficient gravity to justify further action by the Court.[71]

The foregoing reveals four conditions in which a case will be inadmissible and the ICC is expected to defer to a national proceeding.[72] The conditions are: (a) a domestic investigation or prosecution is in progress; (b) a domestic investigation has been completed with a decision not to prosecute; (c) a trial has been completed or (d) the case is deemed not to be sufficiently serious.[73] Admissibility criteria

[66]Cote d'Ivoire and the Palestinian National Authority made such declarations in 2003 and 2009 respectively.

[67]See Rome Statute, Article 13(b). The referrals of the situations in Darfur Sudan and Libya to the ICC in 2005 and 2011 respectively are examples.

[68]Ryngaert (2011), p. 874.

[69]Ibid.

[70]Schabas (2007), p. 172.

[71]Rome Statute Art 17 (1).

[72]Robinson (2010).

[73]Rome Statute, Article 17(1)(d).

could thus be broadly categorised into two. First, the ICC must carry out an assessment of the national justice system to see whether a state could reasonably be expected to investigate or prosecute genuinely.[74] Second, the ICC must determine that the matter indeed warrants its intervention.[75] This implies that the ICC may decide not try a case which comes under its jurisdiction due to other considerations. Therefore there is a need to consider the trigger mechanisms for investigation by the ICC.

### 2.2.1 *Admissibility and Trigger Mechanisms for ICC Investigation*

Under the Rome Statute, three trigger mechanisms based on which the ICC may commence investigation into a situation are identified. The prosecutor may act upon referrals by state parties[76] or by the United Nations Security Council[77] or on his own motion (*proprio motu*) on the basis of information received from any reliable source.[78] Pursuant to these trigger mechanisms, the governments of Uganda, the DRC, CAR, Mali and technically Cote d'Ivoire have referred situations in their states to the ICC.[79] The cases on Darfur, Sudan and Libya were triggered by Security Council referrals, while Kenya and Georgia were the Prosecutor's *proprio motu* action.

None of these mechanisms, however, automatically triggers investigation because the Prosecutor is further required to consider whether there is a 'reasonable basis' to proceed.[80] The determination of a 'reasonable basis' to proceed relates to jurisdiction and admissibility, and also to prosecutorial discretion,[81] which is a consideration of whether the ICC investigation would serve the interests of justice.[82] Furthermore, Rule 104(1) of the Rule of Procedure and Evidence enjoins that, for the purpose of determining whether there is a reasonable basis to proceed

[74] *The Prosecutor v Thomas Lubanga Dyilo*, Decision on the Prosecutor's Application for a Warrant of Arrest, ICC-01/04-01/06 10 February 2006, para 29.

[75] Rome Statute, Article 17(1)(d).

[76] Rome Statute, Articles 13(a) & 14. See Akhavan (2011).

[77] Article 13(b).

[78] Articles 13(c) & 15.

[79] Notably, the Central African Republic (CAR) has referred situations to the ICC twice, first in December 2004 and second in May 2014. This has resulted in the situations being separated at the ICC by 'Central Africa Republic' representing the first referral and the 'Central African Republic II' as the second referral. This is inevitably so, as the situations related to different times, locations, as well as different crimes and alleged perpetrators.

[80] See Article 53(1) for state and Security Council referrals and Article 53(3) for *Proprio motu* investigations.

[81] Stigen (2011), pp. 503, 504.

[82] Rome Statute, Article 53(1)(c).

under Article 53(1), the Prosecutor is to analyse the seriousness of the case based on the information available to him.[83] The Prosecutor may seek additional information from states, organs of the United Nations, intergovernmental and non-governmental organisations or other reliable sources as appropriate.[84]

Through the admissibility provisions and the trigger mechanisms, the Rome Statute reinforces the well-established right of sovereign states to enforce international criminal law.[85] In the *Muthaura et al*[86] case the Appeals Chamber noted that by stipulating the substantive conditions under which a case is inadmissible before the ICC, Article 17 sets out how to resolve a conflict of jurisdiction between the ICC and a national court.[87] This implies that complementarity confers a right on states to investigate and prosecute international crimes which, unless waived or rescinded, a case is inadmissible before the ICC.

As regards waiver of this right, several questions arise as to how to establish 'unwillingness', 'inability', and 'genuineness' and what may constitute 'sufficient gravity'. These elements represent complementarity thresholds, yet they are not clearly defined by the Rome Statute. Therefore, the next subsection analyses these thresholds within the context of the jurisprudence of the ICC.

### 2.2.2 *Clarifying the Elements of Complementarity*

Presently, there are no parameters by which complementarity can be evaluated. This is because the jurisprudence of the ICC to date does not encompass an inclusive analysis or interpretation of all the components of complementarity. For example, in the *Lubanga*[88] case, the ICC interpreted the phrase 'case is being investigated' in Article 17(1)(a). Consequently, the Pre-Trial Chamber I (PTCI) formulated and applied the 'same person same conduct' test to decide that for a case to be inadmissible before the ICC, investigations at the national level must encompass the

---

[83]Rule 104(1) RPE.

[84]Rule 104(2).

[85]Newton (2001), p. 67. See also Robinson Mysterious Complementarity (2010).

[86]Situation in the Republic of Kenya, *The Prosecutor v. Francis Kirimi Muthaura, Uhuru Muigai Kenyatta and Mohammed Hussein Ali* ICC-01/09-02/11-274 30-08-2011 1/43 NM PT OA Available at http://icc-cpi.int/iccdocs/doc/doc1223134.pdf (Judgment on the Appeal of the Republic of Kenya against the decision of Pre-Trial Chamber II of 30 May 2011 entitled 'Decision on the Application by the Government of Kenya Challenging the Admissibility of the Case Pursuant to Article 19(2)(b) of the Statute). ('*Muthaura et al* case').

[87]Ibid, para 36.

[88]*The Prosecutor v. Thomas Lubanga Dyilo*, Decision concerning Pre-Trial Chamber I Decision of 10 February 2006 and the Incorporation of Documents into the Record of the Case against Mr Thomas Lubanga Dyilo, 24 February 2006, ICC-01/04-01/06-8-Corr.

same person and the same conduct for which the suspect is being tried before the ICC.[89]

The 'same person same conduct' test has been applied by the ICC in other cases[90] to reject the admissibility challenge by states. In the *Muthaura et al* case, the Appeals Chamber noted that the 'same person same conduct' test does not compel a prosecution or conviction of a particular person by national authorities. Rather it compels only a genuine investigation or prosecution of that person.[91] Thus under Article 17(1)(a), the first question is whether the same case is being investigated by both the ICC and a national jurisdiction.[92] Consequently, Kenya's argument that it was investigating suspects in the 'same hierarchical level' with those indicted by the ICC failed to establish that it was investigating the same suspects as the ICC.[93]

In the decision of the PTCI of 31 May 2013 in the *Saif Al-Islam Gaddafi*[94] case, the phrase 'case being investigated' was again considered and the 'same person, same conduct' test was applied but adjusted to 'substantially' the same conduct.[95] The PTCI did not consider the element of unwillingness. According to the Chamber, consideration of 'unwillingness' was not necessary at the admissibility

[89]Ibid, para 31.

[90]See for example *The Prosecutor v Mr Germain Katanga* ICC-01/04-01/07-1497 OA 8 (Oral Decision of the Trial Chamber II of 12 June 2009 on the Admissibility of the Case) para 81-82; *The Prosecutor v. Ahmad Muhammad Harun and Ali Muhammad Ali Abd-Al-Rahman* Decision on the Prosecution Application under Article 58(7) of the Statute, 27 April 2007, ICC-02/05-01/07-1-Corr, para. 24; *The Prosecutor v. Mathieu Ngudjolo Chui*, Decision on the evidence and information provided by the Prosecution for the issuance of a warrant of arrest for Mathieu Ngudjolo Chui, 6 July 2007, ICC-01/04-01/07-262, para. 21; *The Prosecutor v. Omar Hassan Ahmad Al Bashir*, Decision on the Prosecution's Application for a Warrant of Arrest against Omar Hassan Ahmad Al Bashir, 4 March 2009, ICC-02/05-01/09-2-Conf, para. 50 (public redacted version in ICC-02/05-01/09-3); and *The Prosecutor v. Bahr Idriss Abu Garda*, Decision on the Prosecutor's Application under Article 58, 7 May 2009, ICC-02/05-02/09-1-Conf, para. 4 (public redacted version in ICC-02/05-02/09-12-Anxl), The same approach was taken by Pre-Trial Chamber II in *The Prosecutor v. Kony et al.*, Decision on the Admissibility of the Case under Article 19(1) of the Statute, 10 March 2009, ICC-02/04-01/05-377, paras 17–18; *The Prosecutor v. William Samoei Ruto, Henry Kiprono Kosgey and Joshua Arap Sang*, Decision on the Application by the Government of Kenya Challenging the Admissibility of the Case Pursuant to Article 19(2)(b) of the Statute, 30 May 2011, ICC-01/09-01/11-101, para. 54; *The Prosecutor v. Francis Kirimi Muthaura, Uhuru Muigai Kenyatta and Mohammed Hussein Ali,* Decision on the Application by the Government of Kenya Challenging the Admissibility of the Case Pursuant to Article 19(2)(b) of the Statute, 30 May 2011, ICC-01/09-02/11-96, para. 48; Pre-Trial Chamber III in *The Prosecutor v. Jean-Pierre Bemba Gombo*, Decision on the Prosecutor's Application for a Warrant of Arrest against Jean-Pierre Bemba Gombo, 10 June 2008, ICC-01/05-01/08-14-tENG (Translation notified 17 July 2006), para. 16.

[91]*Muthaura et al* case, para 31.

[92]Ibid, paras 36, 40 & 41.

[93]Ibid, para 41.

[94]*The Prosecutor v. Saif Al-Islam Gaddafi and Abdullah Al-Hussein* ICC-01/11-01/11-344-Red Decision of the Pre-Trial Chamber I on the Admissibility of the case against Saif Al-Islam Gaddafi 31 May 2013. http://www.icc-cpi.int/iccdocs/doc/doc1599307.pdf (*Saif Al-Islam* case).

[95]Ibid, paras 73, 77.

challenge stage since the Chamber found that Libya was unable genuinely to investigate and prosecute the suspect not least because of its inability to apprehend him.[96]

From the jurisprudence of the ICC it appears that the problem of overlap between national and international jurisdictions has been given an abstract solution through the complementarity regime without an interpretive guide.[97] This is because as noted by the Appeals Chamber in the *Katanga*[98] case, in considering whether a case is inadmissible under Article 17(1)(a) and (b), two questions must be asked. The first is empirical; whether there are on-going investigations or prosecutions at the domestic level. The second is whether there have been investigations in the past and the state having jurisdiction has decided not to prosecute the person concerned.[99] It is only when these questions are answered in the affirmative that an examination of unwillingness and inability becomes necessary.[100] As both elements, along with genuineness and sufficient gravity, are separate from the consideration of whether or not an investigation is being carried out, it is important to see how the ICC would evaluate these elements, in the event that an admissibility challenge is brought on the basis of one of them.

#### 2.2.2.1 Unwilling

Three types of unwillingness are mentioned in Article 17(2). First, a state is deemed unwilling when the proceedings were or are being undertaken or the national decision was made for the purpose of 'shielding' the person concerned from criminal responsibility.[101] Moreover, in the *Katanga* case, the Pre-Trial Chamber II (PTCII) held that a state that does not intend to shield a person but rather wants the person to be prosecuted by the ICC is not an unwilling state under the terms of Article 17.[102] The rationale behind this decision is hardly comprehensible because it poses the question as to why a state would prefer to have its nationals prosecuted by the ICC when complementarity gives it the primary duty to prosecute.[103]

[96]Ibid paras 204, 205, 206, 215 & 216.

[97]Easterday (2009).

[98]*The Prosecutor v. Germain Katanga*, Decision on the evidence and information provided by the Prosecution for the issuance of a warrant of arrest for Germain Katanga, 6 July 2007, ICC-01/04-01/07-4.

[99]*Katanga* case, para 20.

[100]Ibid, para 78.

[101]See article 17(2)(a).

[102]*Prosecutor v Germain Katanga and Mathieu Ngudjolo Chui* Case No ICC-01/04-01/07-123tENG (Reasons for the Oral Decision on the Motion Challenging the Admissibility of the Case under Art 19) 16 June 2009.

[103]Politi (2011), pp. 142–149.

A better argument may be that self-referral constitutes a demonstration of a state's willingness but also its inability to prosecute.[104]

Unwillingness could stem from the lack of an appropriate legal framework, lack of institutional capacity or of political will, as demonstrated in the Kenya *Muthaura et al.* case. In this case, the Appeals Chamber observed that Kenya submitted 29 annexes in support of its admissibility challenge, yet none of the annexes related to the suspects before the ICC.[105] The Appeals Chamber further noted that Kenya's claim that the Commissioner of Police had confirmed that the suspects were being exhaustively investigated by the CID/DPP team lacked specificity.[106] Arguably, these could be interpreted as revealing a goal of shielding the suspects. The Appeals Chamber further noted dissonance not only between the suspects being investigated by the Kenyan authorities and by the ICC but also in the crimes for which the suspects were being investigated, as the crimes against humanity for which the suspects were brought before the ICC were not at that time known to Kenyan domestic law.

The second type of possible unwillingness is where there has been an 'unjustified delay' in the proceedings which is deemed inconsistent with an intent to bring the person concerned to justice.[107] However, the Statute does not give a definition of what could constitute an unjustified delay; rather, the decision is left to the ICC. Arguably, unjustifiable delay may be occasioned by the lack of requisite implementing legislation and inadequate institutions to carry out proceedings. Again, in the *Muthaura et al* case, Kenya's delay in taking investigative steps could arguably be linked to the lack of implementing legislation at the time.[108]

Third, unwillingness is further implied in situations where the proceedings were not or are not being conducted 'independently or impartially',[109] or in a manner which, in the circumstances, is inconsistent with an intent to bring the person concerned to justice.[110] Unwillingness could further be determined with 'regard to the principles of due process recognized by international law'.[111] These include the presumption of innocence, non-retroactivity of criminal law, the right to a public hearing, the

---

[104] Ibid.

[105] *Muthaura et al* case, para 67.

[106] Ibid, para 68.

[107] Article 17(2)(b).

[108] *Infra* (Text to notes 83–85 in Ch 4).

[109] Cherif M Bassiouni, *Introduction to International Criminal Law* (2003) 518; see also Ellis (2003), p. 236 ('A case will fall under the jurisdiction of the ICC because of the unwillingness of a State to prosecute or investigate when it is found that... the proceedings are not independent and impartial'.); Solera (2002), pp. 145, 166 (noting '...a State is unwilling to prosecute when the competent domestic court is not independent or impartial').

[110] Article 17(2)(c).

[111] See the Chapeau of Article 17(2). 'In order to determine unwillingness...the court shall consider, having regard to the principle of due process recognised by international law...'.

right to obtain free legal assistance, the right to be informed, the right to examine the witnesses and the right to remain silent.[112]

In line with the due process requirement, Carsten Stahn argued that alternative justice mechanisms at the domestic level must meet basic fair trial standards.[113] Again the implication of a mutually inclusive construction of complementarity is that states would reflect and uphold the general principles of criminal law and strive to maintain international standards as explicated in the Rome Statute.

Furthermore there is the possibility of varying degrees of willingness being exhibited by rival branches of a particular state's authorities.[114] This may arise due to internal differences within a state which are not envisaged in the Rome Statute. For example, the judiciary may be willing whereas the executive is not. Investigators may be willing but an unwilling military may frustrate and hinder investigative efforts.[115] Therefore unwillingness in one branch of government may create inability in another branch that is sincerely attempting to investigate or prosecute. There is also a possibility of selective willingness where state authorities may be eager to investigate crimes by rebel groups but may be reticent with respect to the investigation of government forces.[116]

#### 2.2.2.2 Unable: Inability and Inactivity

Inability is the second element of complementarity identified under Article 17. In reaching the determination of inability, there are two cumulative sets of considerations.[117] The first is inability as a consequence of the 'collapse' or 'unavailability' of the national judicial system. The use of the terms 'inability', 'collapse' and 'unavailability' thus imply certain political circumstances that could render holding trials impossible. The words further suggest a lack of expertise in the field of international criminal law including judges, prosecutors, and other court personnel.[118] Clearly, analysis of a state's judicial system and political climate is necessary in determining ability or the lack thereof to prosecute.

---

[112]See Part 3 on General Principles of Criminal Law and Art 55 Rome Statute.

[113]Carsten (2005), pp. 695, 713.

[114]Informal Expert Paper: 'The Principle of Complementarity in Practice' ICC-01/04-01/07-1008-AnxA 30 March 2009 ('Informal Expert Paper') http://www.icc-cpi.int/iccdocs/doc/doc654724.pdf (Accessed 2 March 2013). (Members of the Expert Group include Xabier Agirre, Antonio Cassese, Rolf Einar Fife, Hakan Friman, Christopher Hall, John Holmes, Jann Kleffner, Hector Olasolo, Norul Rashid, Darryl Robinson, Elizabeth Wilmshurst and Andreas Zimmermann).

[115]Ibid, para 45.

[116]Ibid. See also the self-referral by the Government of Uganda of the Lords Resistance Army (LRA) in Northern Uganda to the ICC. Available at http://www.icc-cpi.int/en_menus/icc/situations/nothern%20uganda.aspx (Assessed 26 February 2013).

[117]Yang (2005).

[118]Informal Expert Paper, (note 114) paras 49 & 50.

In the admissibility challenge by Libya in the *Saif Al-Islam*[119] case, the PTCI noted the efforts deployed by Libya under extremely difficult circumstances to improve security conditions, rebuild institutions and to restore the rule of law.[120] In particular, the Chamber observed the specific measures taken by the Libyan government to enhance capacity.[121] These were in relation to the proposed strategy to improve the effectiveness of accountability of the police service, the security of the courts and of participants in the proceedings.[122] It also noted the proposed strategy to reform the detention centres and to bring practices of torture to an end.[123] In spite of these measures, the Chamber found that Libya continues to face multiple challenges as it cannot exercise its judicial powers fully across the entire territory. Consequently, Libya's national system was found unavailable according to the terms of Article 17(3) of the Statute.[124]

The second aspect of the inability consideration is inability with respect to apprehending the accused, or obtaining evidence or testimony such that proceedings cannot be carried out.[125] In the admissibility challenge by Libya, the PTCI observed that the Libyan Code of Criminal Procedure contained provisions that could sustain the prosecution of Saif Al-Islam. These include Article 59 of the Libyan Code, which provides for confidentiality of investigations, and Article 106, which guarantees a defendant's right to a lawyer during investigation.[126] The PTCI observed that additional rights of accused persons are guaranteed under other provisions of the Libyan Code.[127]

Nevertheless, the Chamber found that there had been no concrete progress towards transferring Saif Al-Islam from his detention centre in Zintan.[128] The Chamber further expressed concerns over the issues raised by the United Nations Support Mission in Libya (UNSMIL) about instances of torture and death arising from torture in detention centres and concluded that Libya was not able to assume full control of the detention facilities.[129] Also Libya's capacity to obtain the necessary testimony was in doubt, as the Chamber observed 'clear inability of

---

[119]*Saif al-Islam* case (note 94).

[120]Ibid, para 200.

[121]Ibid, para 204.

[122]Ibid.

[123]Ibid.

[124]Ibid, para 205.

[125]Rome Statute, Art 17 (3).

[126]Ibid.

[127]For example, Art 435 of the Libyan Code safeguards the accused right to review evidence presented against him and forced confessions are inadmissible in criminal proceedings. Also, under Article 9 of the Code the accused has the right to be informed of his fights and duties and Article 4 of the Libyan Prisons Act requires the defendant to be held in prison prepared for that purpose.

[128]*Saif Al-Islam* case paras 206, 207.

[129]Ibid, para 209.

judicial and governmental authorities to ascertain control and provide adequate protection for witnesses'.[130]

Based on the decision of the PTCI in the Libya admissibility challenge in the *Saif Al-Islam* case, it can be deduced that 'inability' may not only refer to situations of armed conflict resulting in the total or substantial collapse of a national judicial system. Rather, inability may include the lack of institutions or lack of judges and prosecutors who are trained in international criminal law. This point is underscored by Libya's submission that it was in the process of 'approaching the Bar Associations of Tunisia and Egypt in order to obtain suitably qualified and experienced counsel...'[131] The PTCI rejected this point on the grounds that Libya did not demonstrate that it was taking any concrete steps to overcome the deficiencies.[132]

Closely linked to inability is 'inactivity'.[133] Inactivity was developed by the office of the Prosecutor based on the theory of 'uncontested admissibility'.[134] In the *Katanga*[135] case, the PTCII held that inaction on the part of a state having jurisdiction renders a case admissible before the Court regardless of any question of unwillingness or inability.[136] Following this position by the PTCII in the *Katanga* case, it would appear that referral was deemed appropriate on account of inaction by the Ugandan government. The ICC and Uganda, which claimed to be incapacitated by its inability to apprehend members of the LRA agreed that a consensual division of labour is the most logical and effective approach.[137]

In authorising the issuance of arrest warrants in the case, the PTCII invoked a letter of 28 May 2004 from the government of Uganda stating that it had been 'unable to arrest...persons who may bear the greatest responsibility for the relevant crimes' and that 'the ICC is the most appropriate and effective forum for the investigation and prosecution...'[138]The letter further noted that the Ugandan government 'has not conducted and does not intend to conduct national proceedings in relation to the persons...'[139]

The rationale is that armed groups divided by conflict may oppose prosecutions at each other's hand and yet agree to a prosecution by the ICC for reasons of

[130]Ibid, paras 209, 211.

[131]Ibid, para 213.

[132]Ibid, para 214.

[133]Robinson, Mysterious Complementarity (above note 3) 76 (noting that the word 'inactivity' is not used in Article 17 but the Pre-Trial Chamber in the *Lubanga* case erroneously used it in interpreting when a case becomes admissible before the ICC. He agrees however, that a case is admissible where there is inaction on the part of a state in a particular case). See also El-zeidy The Genesis of Complementarity (above note 13) 137.

[134]Williams and Schabas (2008), pp. 615–616.

[135]*Prosecutor v. Germain Katanga et al* (note 102).

[136]Ibid, para 37.

[137]Williams and Schabas (2008).

[138]Ibid, 616. See also Schabas (2008b), p. 6.

[139]Ibid; Schabas (2008a), p. 29; Stahn and Sluiter (2009), p. 239.

neutrality and impartiality.[140] The state, in such a case, waives its right of primacy of jurisdiction to trigger the jurisdiction of the ICC and the case is admissible before the ICC as long as the state with jurisdiction remains inactive.

#### 2.2.2.3 Genuinely

As with complementarity thresholds of unwillingness and inability, there are no parameters in the Rome Statute for determining the third element of 'genuinely'. In arriving at the term, other words like 'ineffective', 'good faith', 'diligently' and 'sufficient grounds' were considered and rejected for being too subjective.[141] The term 'genuinely' that was finally adopted, bears close semblance to 'good faith'; however, the later was deemed to be too constricted.[142]

'Genuinely', open to interpretation by the court, is an adverb that explains what kind of investigation or prosecution a state must be willing and able to conduct in order to make a case inadmissible before the ICC—namely, a genuine one.[143] It could further be argued that requiring states to conduct genuine investigations and prosecutions, as opposed to investigations and prosecutions of any kind indicates that the drafters intended to make due process a criterion of major importance.[144]

The phrase 'unless the state is unwilling or unable genuinely to carry out the investigation or prosecution' presupposes something real and sincere, having the value claimed without a form of pretence. In the *Muthaura et al*[145] case, the Appeals Chamber observed that the report on the investigations into the post-election violence did not include any reference to the suspects.[146] The report also did not reveal any investigative steps taken by the Kenyan investigation team.[147] A genuine investigation would thus encompass detailed report of investigative steps taken in a particular case. Therefore in determining whether the actions of a state are genuine, the ICC looks beyond the domestic laws or implementing legislation and objectively examines whether the motives and broad context of the state's actions are real and sincere.

---

[140]Kress (2004), pp. 944–948. See also 'Paper on Some Policy Issues before the Office of the Prosecutor' ICC-OTP September 2003 1-9, 5. http://www.icc-cpi.int/NR/rdonlyres/1FA7C4C6-DE5F-42B7-8B25-60AA962ED8B6/143594/030905_Policy_Paper.pdf (Assessed 26 February 2013).

[141]Holmes (1999), p. 49.

[142]Ibid. See also Holmes Complementarity *vs.* National Courts (2004), p. 266.

[143]Jon Heller (2006).

[144]Jon Heller Ibid.

[145]*Muthaura et al* case (note 86).

[146]Ibid, para 53.

[147]Ibid, para 68.

#### 2.2.2.4 Sufficient Gravity

Another complementarity element is 'sufficient gravity'. Two prong components to the determination of admissibility are complementarity and gravity.[148] Crimes falling within the jurisdiction of the ICC have been designated 'serious crimes',[149] yet the Rome Statute provides for the additional admissibility consideration of 'sufficient gravity'.[150] Thus, even where subject-matter jurisdiction is satisfied, the ICC must determine whether the case is severe enough to justify further action. Factors relevant in assessing gravity include the scale, the nature, the manner of commission and the impact of the crimes.[151] Therefore, isolated instances of criminal activity do not meet the gravity threshold.

One way of assessing gravity for the purpose of determining prosecutorial priorities is to look at absolute numbers. This is exemplified in the actions taken by the first Chief Prosecutor of the ICC Luis Moreno-Ocampo with respect to situations in Uganda in one case and the United Kingdom in another.[152] Upon receipt of information regarding the activities of British troops in Iraq, the Prosecutor noted that there were only 4–12 victims, which does not meet the requirement of sufficient gravity.[153] On the other hand, regarding the situation in Uganda, the Prosecutor noted;

> . . .we examined information concerning all groups that had committed crimes in the region. We selected our first case based on gravity. Between July 2002 and June 2004, the [Lord's Resistance Army] was allegedly responsible for at least 2200 killings and 3200 abductions in over 850 attacks. It was clear that we start with the Lord's Resistance Army.[154]

The analysis of the complementarity thresholds reveals that so far, the case law of the ICC relates to waivers or inaction and the Court has not had the opportunity to interpret the other constituent elements of unwillingness and genuineness. Although some of these complementarity thresholds may be inferred in the cases as they do overlap, the decisions of the ICC have focused on the 'same person same conduct' test as a result of admissibility challenges by states which claimed to be carrying out investigations domestically. The Pre-Trial Chamber has further interpreted 'inability' in light of the deficiencies of Libya's judicial system, including its inability to procure the suspect, witnesses and evidence.

---

[148] Schabas (2007), pp. 171–175; Williams and Schabas (2008), p. 613.

[149] Rome Statute, para 4 of the Preamble.

[150] Rome Statute, Articles 17 (1) (d), 53 (1) (b) and 53 (2) (b).

[151] Luis Moreno-Ocampo OTP, Draft Policy Paper on Selection Criteria.

[152] See Williams and Schabas (2008), pp. 621–622.

[153] See 'Letter of Prosecutor dated 9 February 2006' (Iraq) http://www.icc-cpi.int/library/organs/otp_letter_to_senders_re_Iraq_9_Febraury_2006.pdf (assessed 10 February 2009), 7–8. See also Gaja (2008), p. 45.

[154] See 'Statement by Luis Moreno-Ocampo, Prosecutor of the International Criminal Court, Fourth Session of the Assembly of States Parties' at The Hague 28 November to 3 December 2005. 2.

It is submitted that the cumulative effect of Article 17 makes it imperative for states to start investigation and prosecution and it would be for the ICC, if it wishes, to assert and prove that the state is unwilling or unable genuinely to carry out the proceedings. Thus far, the reverse has been the case. This underlines that for states to assume their primary role to investigate and prosecute international crimes, appropriate legal framework and institutional capacity in conformity with the Rome Statute is imperative.

The complementarity thresholds analysed above are entwined in the admissibility provisions in Article 17. The Article is certainly the focus of complementarity and it is usually the central point of complementarity discussions.[155] However, the broader interplay and division of labour between national jurisdictions and the ICC envisaged in the Rome Statute makes complementarity a dominant theme that is woven through many other Articles of the Rome Statute.[156] The next section evaluates complementarity framework under Articles 18-20 of the Rome Statute and the relevant Rules of Procedure and Evidence (RPE).

### 2.2.3 *Evaluating Complementarity Under Articles 18, 19 and 20*

The Rome Statute, supplemented by its Rules of Procedure and Evidence (RPE),[157] establishes a comprehensive though complex procedure for complementarity. The procedure reinforces the approach of allowing national proceedings to take primacy of jurisdiction unless there are compelling reasons to intervene. The argument here is that, though not specifically stated, complementarity appears to be central to the procedures articulated in Articles 18, 19 and 20 and the relevant RPE. This section analyses these provisions to support the view of a mutually inclusive interpretation of complementarity. The underlying objective is to give states the first opportunity to prosecute.

Article 18 stipulates deferral procedures by which the OTP could suspend its action to allow for a state's investigation. Article 19 specifies the determination of jurisdiction and admissibility by the ICC and the need to balance the interests of states and the requirements of effective investigation.[158] Article 20 establishes the *ne bis in idem* rule,[159] which forbids trying a person before the ICC with respect to criminal conduct for which the person has been convicted or acquitted by another court.[160]

---

[155]Robinson (2012a), pp. 177–178.

[156]Articles 1, 18, 19, 20, 89(4), 90, 93(10), 94.

[157]International Criminal Court, Rules of Procedure and Evidence, U.N. Doc. PCNICC/2000/1/Add.1 (2000).

[158]Broomhall (2003), p. 88.

[159]Rome Statute, Article 20(1) & (2). The rule against double jeopardy.

[160]Ibid.

Where there is a state referral or the prosecutor initiates *proprio-motu* investigation and believes that there is a reasonable basis to proceed, Article 18 will apply.[161] The Article requires the prosecutor to inform all states parties, as well as other states which would normally exercise jurisdiction, of his intention to conduct an investigation. Regardless of whether the Prosecutor conducts its preliminary examination upon the receipt of a referral by a state or upon the receipt of communication,[162] there are procedural mechanisms by which admissibility is determined. First, Article 53(1)(b) and Rule 48 of the RPE require an admissibility assessment to be conducted during the preliminary examination of a situation prior to the initiation of an investigation. Second within 30 days after the Prosecutor's notification of the initiation of an investigation into a situation, Article 18 allows a state to assert that the relevant situation is inadmissible and obtain a deferral as a result of its national proceedings.

Furthermore, Article 18 provides for confidential and limited information with a view to protecting witnesses and evidence and prevents alleged perpetrators from absconding. However, Rule 52 RPE obliges the Prosecutor to provide ample information so that a state may determine if it is examining the same situation. If the information is insufficient then the state may request additional information under the Rule.

As illustrated in the *Muthaura et al* case, with respect to proceedings relating to preliminary admissibility challenges under Article 18, the likely cases are often imprecise because the investigations of the Prosecutor are in their initial stages.[163] In the case, even though the Prosecutor had received information and a list of alleged perpetrators, his preliminary examination into the situation was necessary to confirm the suspects. Thus, no individual suspects had been identified by the Prosecutor at that stage, and there was no clear determination or legal classification of the exact conduct.[164] The relative vagueness of the cases in Article 18 proceedings is further reflected in Rule 52(1) of the RPE which speaks of information about the acts that may constitute crimes referred to in Article 5, relevant to the purposes of Article 18(2).[165]

Article 18(2) and Rule 53 provide that the information must be sufficiently detailed to demonstrate that the state is indeed conducting investigation or has investigated the criminal acts contained in the information provided by the Prosecutor in the original notification.[166] Article 18(7) and Rule 55 authorise a state to

[161]Ibid, article 18(1).

[162]Pursuant to its literal wording, Art 18 does not appear to apply when the Prosecutor opens an investigation as a result of a referral by the Security Council.

[163]*Muthaura et al* case, (note 86) para 38.

[164]Ibid.

[165]*Muthaura et al* case, (note 86) para 38.

[166]Rome Statute, Art 18 (2) & Rule 53 RPE. See also *Muthaura et al* case para 41 (Kenya failed to provide detailed information about the investigative steps it purported to have taken with respect to the suspects before the ICC).

challenge the ruling of the Pre- Trial Chamber. Thereafter, pursuant to Article 82(1) (a) the Pre-Trial Chamber and eventually the Appeals Chamber decide on the admissibility of the situation.[167]

As it relates to the original notification, both the Statute and the Rules encourage a dialogue between the state and the Prosecutor to ensure that there is no overlap in their respective areas of interest. This implies that where the Prosecutor is uncertain about the nature of national proceedings, he should request additional information from the state.[168] This is further reinforced by Article 18(5) which allows the Prosecutor to request periodic updates from the state on the progress of the investigations. Where the Prosecutor is not convinced of the genuineness of national proceedings or the proceedings cover a different situation, he may seek authorisation for an investigation from the Pre-Trial Chamber.[169] Admittedly, these provisions may slow down the process of initiating an investigation and may make obtaining of evidence, accused persons and witnesses more difficult.[170] However, the underlying objective is to allow states to have primary jurisdiction.

Article 19 together with Rules 58-62 RPE relate to situations in which there are challenges to the exercise of jurisdiction by the ICC and the admissibility of cases before it. Under this Article, questions of jurisdiction and admissibility may be raised either by the ICC, the Prosecutor, the accused person, a state with jurisdiction or a state from which acceptance of jurisdiction is required under Article 12.[171] These questions can be raised regardless of the triggering mechanism. However, in *proprio-motu* investigations by the Prosecutor under Article 15, a determination by the Prosecutor of a reasonable basis to proceed and an authorisation from the Pre-Trial Chamber must be completed. This is followed by compliance with Article 18 (notification to states by the Prosecutor and authorisation by the Pre-Trial Chamber where a state requests a deferral). Once these criteria are met and the Prosecutor decides to proceed, jurisdiction and admissibility issues become relevant.

Article 19 permits states or accused persons to make challenges only once and at the earliest possible time.[172] This is to ensure speed in the process. To facilitate the process, the Rules entrust the relevant Chamber with the authority to set its own procedures without any obligation for a hearing.[173] Notwithstanding, possible delays exists, as states that potentially have jurisdiction may bring challenges at different times. In addition, the Statute and the Rules allow victims to make representation.[174]

---

[167]Olasolo (2007), p. 157.

[168]Ibid.

[169]See *Lubanga* case.

[170]See generally Article 18 Rome Statute and Rules 53–57 RPE.

[171]Rome Statute, article 19 (2) (a), (b) & (c).

[172]Rome Statute, article 19(5).

[173]See Stigen (2011).

[174]Rule 59 limits the opportunity of making representation to those victims or their legal representatives who have previously communicated to the Court in relation to the case before it.

The interactions envisaged between the ICC and national jurisdictions in these procedures are further depicted in Article 19(11). The provision anticipates that the Prosecutor must at all times be abreast with proceedings at the national level by requesting periodic update on the status of such proceedings. These interactions have the advantage of demonstrating to the state that though the Prosecutor may have deferred to its national investigation, he remains interested in the situation and may reactivate his investigation should doubts emerge as to the genuineness of the state's actions.[175] Nevertheless, the overall objective of these procedures is to allow states the first opportunity to prosecute.

Furthermore, embedded in the *ne bis in idem* rule is the principle of complementarity. The rule forbids the ICC from reopening a case that has been prosecuted by a state with jurisdiction, whether resulting in either acquittal or conviction.[176] In effect, the rule maintains jurisdictional interactions between the ICC and domestic courts as well as protects an accused person from being punished twice for the same crime.[177]

However, the rule admits of exceptions expressed in Article 20(3) by which the ICC could reopen a case where proceedings in the domestic court were undertaken for the purpose of shielding the person concerned from criminal responsibility for crimes within the jurisdiction of the ICC. The Court is also permitted to reopen the case when the proceedings were not conducted independently or impartially in accordance with the norms of due process recognized by international law and were conducted in a manner which, in the circumstances, was inconsistent with an intent to bring the person concerned to justice.[178] The question remains as to what may constitute a proceeding that shows a 'purpose of shielding'. As the Kenya Appeals Decision reveals, Kenya's failure to indicate that it was investigating the same suspects that were before the ICC showed a purpose of shielding.

Furthermore, while the Rome Statute encourages national authorities to comply with 'principles' or 'norms' of due process recognised by international law[179]; the question of how this could be implemented is not addressed. A case simply becomes admissible before the ICC where particular national proceedings fall short of international standards and show a 'purpose of shielding' or an 'inconsistency' of intent.[180] Thus, the Prosecutor must show additional bad faith on the part of the state or, in the case of inconsistency, a lack of good faith. The risk of improper standards and proceedings that do not meet the threshold of independence and impartiality would be particularly high where the police and security forces are subject to their own courts.

---

[175] Holmes (2004), p. 275.

[176] Rome Statute, Art 20(1) & (2).

[177] Bernard (2011), pp. 863–880.

[178] Rome Statute, Article 20(3).

[179] Rome Statute, Articles 17(2) and 20(3).

[180] Broomhall (2003), p. 89.

The complementarity procedures analysed in this section envision some interactions and interdependence between the ICC and national jurisdictions. Whilst the Rome Statute entitled these provisions 'admissibility challenges' which attribute antagonism to the relationship, it is proposed that allowing such admissibility challenges actually reinforces the belief that domestic efforts are preferred. Furthermore, the monitoring of national prosecutions by the Prosecutor and the division of labour makes the relationship between the ICC and states a mutually inclusive rather than an exclusive one. The principle of complementarity was reaffirmed at the first review conference held in Kampala Uganda in 2010, during which different models of complementarity, particularly positive complementarity, were discussed. This indicates that complementarity is the future of the ICC. Therefore, the next section discusses emerging models of complementarity.

## 2.3 Emerging Models of Complementarity

Models of Complementarity have been analysed by ElZeidy.[181] He conceptualized complementarity from the peace treaties of World War I according to which he argues that the concept of complementarity is not novel but that it has existed as early as 1919.[182] Consequently, he noted that complementarity models include amicable, mandatory and optional complementarity.[183] He posits that dating back to Nuremberg and Tokyo Tribunals, the nature of the crimes under consideration made amicable complementarity the best option since the crime of aggression, for example, could not be left to the jurisdiction of national courts. Accordingly the philosophy was that the tasks would be divided and performed in two jurisdictions in a friendly manner.[184]

ElZeidy further maintains that mandatory complementarity model could be seen from the plain reading of the chapeau of Article 17.[185] He postulates that the provision 'The Court shall determine that a case is inadmissible...' suggests a mandatory requirement on the part of states to investigate and prosecute cases arising within their jurisdictions.[186] However, optional complementarity has emerged in the procedure of self-referral by which a state waives its right to prosecute, preferring rather to refer a situation within its jurisdiction to the ICC. This is

---

[181]ElZeidy (2011), pp. 77–78.

[182]Ibid 80–83. (noting that under Articles 228–230 of the Treaty of Versailles 1919, Germany initially agreed to hand over suspected criminals to the Allies for trials, but subsequently asked permission to try alleged war criminals in its domestic court. The allies granted the request on condition of setting aside German courts' judgement in case of unsatisfactory result).

[183]ElZeidy (2011), p. 126.

[184]Ibid.

[185]Ibid, 136.

[186]Ibid, 137.

the reverse scheme of the ‘mandatory model’ as it was not due to the ICC’s determination, but rather it was because the state itself voluntarily decided to renounce the exercise of its jurisdiction.[187]

The mutually inclusive interpretation of complementarity proposed in this book, was also articulated by ElZeidy, in which he noted that a mutually inclusive interpretation mirrors the amicable model of complementarity.[188] This is exemplified in the jurisprudence of the ICC to prosecute only those who bear the greatest responsibility as it is impossible for the ICC to investigate and prosecute all perpetrators of international crimes.

The mutually inclusive interpretation of complementarity is adopted and expanded here to propose a model that envisages clear interactions and division of labour between the ICC and domestic jurisdictions. Therefore, a mutually inclusive complementarity will ensure that states incorporate Rome Statutes crimes into their domestic law and ensure institutional preparedness to prosecute those crimes. This is important because the optional model discussed by Elzeidy, which is reflected in states’ referral of situations to the ICC instead of taking action domestically will not occur. Consequently, this section analyses emerging models of complementarity—passive, positive and proactive—from the point of view of the Rome Statute and other scholarly debates since the inception of the ICC.

This book supports the proactive complementarity model because its importance to the overall success of the ICC is in demonstrating that understanding complementarity from a mutually inclusive perspective would mean that both national jurisdictions and the ICC are proactive in implementing complementarity. This means that states and the ICC would not wait until there are situations before they act. Rather states would take advantage of Article 93(10) to request assistance from the ICC in ensuring legal framework and institutional capacity that are in conformity with the Rome Statute.

### *2.3.1 Passive Complementarity*

One view of complementarity which was prevalent during the drafting of the Rome Statute was mainly passive, where the ICC would simply be a court of last resort.[189] As succinctly argued by Ann-Marie Slaughter;

> One of the most powerful argument for the International Criminal Court is not that it will be a global instrument of justice itself-arresting and trying tyrants and torturers worldwide-but that it will be a backstop and trigger for domestic forces for justice and democracy...[190]

[187]ElZeidy (2008), pp. 212–214, 229.

[188]Ibid.

[189]Hall (2011), p. 1017.

[190]Slaughter (2003), p. 34.

In other words, the ICC would make few or no contributions to international justice if states fulfilled their obligation to investigate and prosecute international crimes.[191] This also conferred an obligation on states not only to ensure that international crimes were defined in their national criminal laws but that there were institutions and expertise to carry out justice.

Passive complementarity meant that the ICC would be dormant until its jurisdiction was triggered either by state parties or the Security Council referrals. Consequently, this model of complementarity undermined the *proprio-motu* powers of the Prosecutor whereby the Prosecutor is empowered to initiate investigations and prosecutions on his own following information received from states.[192] Arguably, it was thought that the Prosecutor would rarely use the *proprio-motu* powers, as that would run counter to states' sovereignty and the principle of non-intervention. While the ICC was passive or dormant waiting for states to take on their primary responsibility, states on the other hand, were passive because they perceived the ICC as an institution endowed with the expertise and resources to investigate and prosecute international crimes—the mindset of the era of ad hoc tribunals.

As an initial model, passive complementarity could not last for a long time because the lack of understanding of complementarity on the part of states soon resulted in referrals of situations from some African states to the ICC.[193] In addition, the Prosecutor has exercised its powers under Article 15 with respect to Kenya and subsequently Georgia. As a result, passive complementarity gave way to positive complementarity.

### 2.3.2 *Positive Complementarity*

Articulating positive complementarity, the first Prosecutor of the ICC, Luis Moreno-Ocampo said that the ICC should be viewed as a success when it has no cases, due to the availability and ability of national courts to try persons responsible for the crimes described in the Rome Statute.[194]

> As a consequence of complementarity, the number of cases that reach the court should not be a measure of its efficiency. On the contrary, the absence of trials before the court, as a consequence of the regular functioning of national institutions would be a major success.[195]

[191]Hall, ibid.

[192]Rome Statute, art 15.

[193]See Self-Referrals (note 54).

[194]International Criminal Court, Office of the Prosecutor, 'Paper on Some Policy Issues Before the Office of the Prosecutor (2003) (OTP Policy Paper) available at http://www.amicc.org/docs/ocampoPolicy/Paper9=03.pdf.

[195]Moreno-Ocampo (2003).

The strategic priority would be that, rather than compete with national jurisdictions, the OTP would 'encourage national proceedings wherever possible'.[196] In its 2006 Policy Paper,[197] the OTP further expounded the model by introducing what has since become known as 'a positive approach to complementarity'.[198]

Nevertheless, there seems to have been a shift in the above connotation of positive complementarity because at the Review Conference held in Kampala Uganda,[199] positive complementarity was defined as 'all activities whereby national jurisdictions are strengthened . . .to conduct genuine national investigations and trials. . .without involving the Court in capacity building, financial support and technical assistance, but instead leaving these actions and activities for States, to assist each other on a voluntary basis'.[200]

The three categories of support for national jurisdictions identified were legislative assistance, technical assistance, capacity building and physical infrastructure.[201] Different scenarios in which assistance could be provided were discussed, including assistance before, during and after situations arise, and assistance in situations where the Court is investigating and prosecuting and where it is not.[202] Most significantly, actors involved in positive complementarity were discussed, and the limited role that the ICC should play in positive complementarity was highlighted.[203] As a result of its judicial mandate and limited budget, the ICC was not to be actively involved in capacity building but to focus its resources on investigating and prosecuting the crimes under its jurisdiction.[204] Of crucial importance was the point that the 'Court is not a development agency'.[205]

The position taken at the Review Conference reveals that there has been a shift in the meaning of positive complementarity as formulated by the OTP. Whilst the

---

[196]Luis Moreno-Ocampo, Prosecutor of the ICC, Statement of the Prosecutor to the Diplomatic Corps (12 February 2004) available at http://www.icc--cpi-.int/library/organs/otp/LOM_20040212_en.pdf.

[197]ICC-Office of the Prosecutor, *Report on Prosecutorial Strategy* (2006). Available at http://www.icc-cpi.int/NR/rdonlyres/D673DD8C-D427-4547-BC69-2D363E07274B/143708/ProsecutorialStrategy20060914_English.pdf (Accessed 11 January 2013).

[198]Burke-White (2008a).

[199]In accordance with article 123 of the Rome Statute the first review conference was held in Kampala Uganda 31 May to 11 June 2010. The conference had about 4600 representatives of States parties, observers, intergovernmental and nongovernmental organisations participating. Available at http://www.icc-cpi.int/menus/icc/press%20release/review%20conference.org (Assessed 12 October 2010).

[200]Report of the Bureau on Stocktaking: Complementarity Annex IV ICC-ASP/8/Res.9 adopted at the 10th plenary meeting, on 25 March 2010 para 4. (hereinafter 'Stocktaking on Complementarity') Available at http://www.icc-cpi.int/iccdocs/asp_docs/RC2010/ICC-ASP-8-Res.9-Annex.IV-ENG.pdf (Accessed 16 May 2012) (Stocktaking on Complementarity), para 16.

[201]Ibid, para. 17.

[202]Ibid, paras 19–26.

[203]Ibid, paras 27–45.

[204]Ibid, para. 4.

[205]Ibid.

OTP intended some collaboration between the ICC and states in its formulation of positive complementarity, the Review Conference emphasised collaboration, but only amongst states, civil society and non-governmental organisations.[206] It is submitted that the interdependent relationship between the ICC and national jurisdictions with respect to complementarity needs further clarification. It is recognised that states need some assistance to be able to investigate and prosecute international crimes; the question of how and who to ensure these have been left unanswered.

Admittedly, for positive complementarity to work, it is not enough to rely on the OTP to inspire national jurisdictions to undertake investigations and prosecutions. Although such encouragement is significant, it runs the risk of becoming a paper exercise if there is no strong national framework in place enabling states to exercise criminal jurisdiction.[207] Consequently, a more systematic approach towards empowering national legal orders is imperative. It is argued that proactive complementarity by which both the ICC and states are actively engaged in on-going processes at the domestic level is necessary for the implementation of complementarity.[208]

### 2.3.3 *Proactive Complementarity*

Proactive complementarity involves requests for assistance from states to the ICC and pragmatic cooperation from the ICC to build national justice systems to enable them carry out investigation and prosecution of international crimes domestically.[209] This could be achieved by the consensual sharing of burden between the ICC and national jurisdictions, a point on which scholars agree.[210] However, the point is highlighted by the use of the word 'catalyst' stating that the ICC could act as a catalyst to national jurisdictions.[211] The view point on the catalytic effect of the ICC often stems from the notice that the Prosecutor is required to give to states which usually have jurisdiction over a case that there are sufficient grounds for investigation.[212] According to Kleffner, the notice is meant to catalyse states into

---

[206]Stocktaking on Complementarity, para 4.

[207]Burke-White (2008a), p. 71.

[208]Burke-White (2008b), p. 57.

[209]The OTP has defined positive complementarity as 'a proactive policy of cooperation aimed at promoting national proceedings.' OTP, 'Prosecutorial Strategy 2009-2012' (1 February 2010) 5. Available at www.icc-cpi.int/NR/rdonlyres/66A8DCDC-3650-4514-AA62-D229D1128F65/281506/OTPProsecutorialStrategy20092013.pdf (Accessed 11 January 2013) (2009–2012 Prosecutorial Strategy).

[210]See Broomhall (2003), pp. 84, 86 (noting that the ICC might act as 'spur' to national proceedings); Kleffner (2009), p. 309; Perrin (2006); Burke-White (2008b).

[211]Kleffner, 309 (noting that the catalytic effect of the ICC would yield good result in which the ICC motivates national justice systems through the threat of international intervention).

[212]Rome Statute, Art 18(1).

prosecution and where that happens the states concerned can stop intervention by the ICC.[213] On the other hand where the state in question fails to act, the Prosecutor finds the failure or inaction as a reasonable basis to commence an investigation.[214]

However, this view of the ICC as having a catalytic role is coercive and has the effect of creating hostility between the ICC and states. It appears complex and may possibly be frustrated by lack of cooperation by states.[215] Therefore the state concerned may ignore the Prosecutor's notification and allow the one month time frame to elapse without carrying out any investigation. The consequence of this is that the case returns to the Prosecutor. Conversely, the state may react positively to the notification and commence an investigation, but could such action then be classified as genuine? These scenarios have been reflected to a large degree in the Kenya and Libya admissibility decisions. As analysed above, the admissibility challenges were rejected because the states failed to produce investigative steps and evidence of sufficient degree of specificity and probative value.[216]

The foregoing scenario is aptly captured by the term 'complementarity paradox' by Paolo Benvenuti,[217] who stated that:

> The ICC starts with a terrible disadvantage. It acquires complementary jurisdiction when states having primary jurisdictions are unwilling or unable genuinely to carry out investigation or prosecution. These states are usually those most connected with the crime... and consequently they are precisely those whose cooperation is essential [for effective ICC prosecution]. Why would those states genuinely unwilling to carry out investigation and prosecution be subsequently cooperative with the ICC?[218]

In view of the foregoing, it is argued in this book that the catalytic effect of the ICC should be conceptualised from the perspective of proactive complementarity. The argument is that both the ICC and states could rely on Article 93(10) to ensure a mutually inclusive and an interdependent relationship. Article 93(10) requires the ICC to 'cooperate with and provide assistance to a state conducting an investigation into a trial...' The assistance provided by the ICC to states, oriented as it were, in the opposite direction *vis-à-vis* the perspective in which cooperation was usually addressed, namely, from states to the ICC has been referred to as 'reverse cooperation' by Federica Gioia.[219] This book adopts Article 93(10) 'reverse cooperation' provision as a mechanism by which proactive complementarity could be achieved.

Complementarity and cooperation are two pillars on which the effective functioning of the ICC is founded. Cooperation would be discussed in detail in the subsequent chapter; it suffices to mention here that hitherto, references to

---

213 Kleffner, 314–315.

214 Ibid. See also the Decision of the PTCII in the admissibility Challenge in *Katanga et al,* (note 102).

215 Perrin (2006).

216 See *Saif Al-Islam* case (note 94) para 54; *Muthaura et al* case (n 86) para 61.

217 Benvenuti (1999), p. 21.

218 Benvenuti, 50.

219 Gioia (2011), pp. 807–828.

cooperation almost invariably focuses on cooperation that states are statutorily obliged to provide to the ICC. However, the Rome Statute does address cooperation as a two-way process i.e. as occurring not only from states to the ICC but also from the ICC to states.[220]

Under Article 93(10), the ICC is expected to cooperate with and provide assistance to a state upon a request from that state. The state's request may cover areas of investigations into trials with respect to conduct which constitutes international crimes and may also include conduct which constitutes serious crimes under national law.[221] The assistance the ICC could provide may include transmission of documents, statements or other types of evidence obtained in the course of an investigation or a trial conducted by the Court.[222] It is submitted that, notwithstanding the restrictive or limited assistance that the ICC may provide, states could take advantage of the provision to request the ICC for assistance and cooperation in their genuine attempt at investigating and prosecuting international crimes domestically. When engaged in these collaborations, the ICC and states would function proactively and as mutually inclusive institutions to carry out the task of prosecuting international crimes.

In the Kenya Appeals Decision, Kenya noted that it had filed a Request for Assistance pursuant to Article 93(10) and Rule 194 before the PTCI but it was denied.[223] Kenya claimed that it was unfair to have been denied the opportunity of relying on the evidence and assistance in its national investigation.[224] It is submitted that the use of Article 93(10) Request for Assistance in the Kenya admissibility challenge appeared late. It is proposed that states could use the Request for Assistance in advance, not waiting until cases are before the ICC and then using the Request for Assistance as a means for requesting an inadmissibility consideration.

It is important to note that under Article 93(10) cooperation and assistance from the ICC can only occur on 'request'.[225] This again is to safeguard the sovereignty of states, as the ICC may not want to intervene unless formally and expressly requested to. It is therefore incumbent on states to take advantage of this option. This is even more imperative as the OTP has established a Jurisdiction, Complementarity and Cooperation Division (JCCD), which has the remit to assist national proceeding where possible and to verify that those proceedings are genuine.[226]

The theoretical assumptions of complementarity both as initially conceived and as it has materialised since the beginning of the operational phase of the ICC require assessment against the background of a relationship between the ICC and states.

---

[220] Gioia, 808.

[221] Rome Statute, Art 93(10)(a).

[222] Rome Statute, Art 93(10)(b); Rule 194 RPE.

[223] *Muthaura et al* case, para 114.

[224] Ibid, paras 115–116.

[225] Gioia, Reverse Cooperation 815.

[226] Stigen (2011), p. 507; Kress (2004), p. 948. See also FIDH (2011), pp. 1–32, 8.

Thus according to Gioia, a friendly vision of complementarity relies on the assumption that the ICC is not meant to act as a censor of national jurisdictions but rather to allow for the most efficient sharing of competences between the ICC and states.[227] This chapter agrees with this proposition and notes that adopting proactive complementarity would facilitate constructive interplay between states and the ICC. It may further detract resources from the direct investigation and prosecutions that the ICC may want to undertake.[228]

While proactive complementarity offers a potentially effective and efficient means of allowing the ICC to fulfil its mandate, its implementation could raise new challenges. These include the practical difficulty of coordinating with national governments and the legal risks that could compromise the subsequent admissibility of a case before the ICC.[229] It is therefore suggested that a cautious strategy of proactive complementarity be adopted, with appropriate limits in order to achieve its full benefits and minimise its potential challenges.

## 2.4 Conclusion

Complementarity is the future of the ICC. However, the concept is yet to be fully interpreted and applied. Analysis of the components of complementarity revealed that they are still ill-defined. This is linked to the fact that most of the cases in which the ICC has had to give an interpretation have been cases in which states claimed to be carrying out investigations domestically. As in previous cases, in the admissibility challenges by the Kenyan and Libyan governments, the ICC only had the opportunity to determine whether the investigations encompassed the same person and substantially the same conduct. Although this is permissible under the Statute, it appears that complementarity is working in reverse.

This is because the clear wording of Article 17 means that it is for states to be actively engaged in investigation and prosecution and it would be for the ICC to allege and prove that the complementarity thresholds of 'unwillingness', 'inability', 'genuinely' or 'sufficient gravity' exist on the part of the state or situation for which reason it would assume jurisdiction over the case. In view of this dilemma, the ICC has constructed another threshold of 'inactivity'. Arguably, this is the result of lack of understanding that states bear the primary responsibility to prosecute international crimes. It is maintained that a proper understanding would make states incorporate international crimes into their domestic criminal law.

The lack of understanding is exemplified in the fact that of the ten situations before the ICC, four (or five since CAR referred two situations in 2004 and 2014) were referred by the states themselves. This raises the fundamental question

[227]Gioia, 817.

[228]Burke-White 'Proactive Complementarity', 83; Bergsmo et al. (2011), pp. 1052–1070, 1063.

[229]Stigen (2011), p. 507; Stahn (2008), pp. 87–113, 103.

whether the complementarity regime was intended to encourage self-referrals. It is acknowledged that two of the three trigger mechanisms are by referrals; either by states or the Security Council, however it is submitted that self-referrals seem to undermine the very purpose of complementarity. Be that as it may, the first 10 years of the functioning of the ICC has been described as the 'teething' period and therefore neither the ICC nor the states that referred situations in their territories are to blame.[230]

While it may be difficult to determine the precise application of complementarity even in the next decade, it is suggested that a mutually inclusive interpretation may be beneficial. This would make states to see the need to incorporate the crimes in the Rome Statute into their domestic criminal law, ensure institutional capacity and confidently investigate and prosecute the crimes domestically rather than refer to the ICC situations for which they are meant to be primarily responsible.

The emerging complementarity models point to the fact that proactive complementarity would be of value to states, the ICC and the international community as whole. The distinctive provision of Article 93(10) providing for a reverse cooperation from the ICC to states is the architecture of the model. An understanding of complementarity from this perspective would make both national jurisdictions and the ICC to collaborate for the purpose of closing impunity gaps as envisioned in the Rome Statute.

This implies that the duty of states under the complementarity regime goes beyond mere ratification of the Rome Statute. For effective burden-sharing between states and the ICC, there are certain requirements for the implementation of complementarity. The next chapter would discuss these requirements with a view to ensuring that states do not stop at ratification but to take a further step to integrate the Rome Statute crimes into their domestic criminal law and ensure institutional capacity to act.

## References

Akhavan P (2011) International criminal justice in the era of failed states: the ICC and the self-referral debate. In: Stahn C, Elzeidy M (eds) The international criminal court and complementarity: from theory to practice, vol 1. CUP, pp 283–303

Bekou O (2011) In the hands of the state: implementing legislation and complementarity. In: Stahn C, ElZeidy M (eds) The international criminal court and complementarity: from theory to practice, vol 1. CUP, pp 830–852

Benvenuti P (1999) Complementarity of the international criminal court to national criminal jurisdictions. In Lattanzi F, Schabas WA (eds) Essays on the Rome Statute of the international criminal court. p 21

Bergsmo M, Webb P (2012) International criminal courts and tribunals: complementarity and jurisdiction. In: Wolfrum R (ed) The Max Planck encyclopaedia of public international law, vol VIII. Max-Planck-Gesellschaft OUP, pp 688, 691

[230]Schabas (2011), pp. 493–509; Cassese (2006), pp. 434–441.

Bergsmo M, Bekou O, Jones A (2011) Complementarity and the construction of national ability. In: Stahn C, ElZeidy M (eds) The international criminal court and complementarity: from theory to practice, vol 2. CUP, pp 1052–1070
Bernard D (2011) *Ne Bis In Idem-* protector of defendants' rights or jurisdictional Pointsman? JICJ 9:863–880
Bohr N (1950) On the notion of causality and complementarity. Science 111:51
Bohr N (1958) Atomic physics and human knowledge. Inter Science Publishers
Broomhall B (2003) International justice and the international criminal court: between sovereignty and the rule of law. OUP, Oxford, p 84
Brownlie I (2008) Principles of international law. OUP, p 289
Burke-White W (2008a) Implementing a system of positive complementarity in the Rome system of justice. CLF 19:59–85
Burke-White W (2008b) Proactive complementarity: the international criminal court and national courts in the Rome system of international justice. Harv Int'l L J 49:53–108
Carsten S (2005) Complementarity, amnesties, and alternative forms of justice: some interpretative guidelines for the international criminal court. JICJ 3:695
Cassese A (2006) Is the ICC still having teething problems? JICJ 4(3):434–441
Cryer R (2011) Darfur: complementarity as the drafters intended? In: Stahn C, ElZeidy M (eds) Complementarity from theory to practice. CUP, pp 1097–1119
Doherty K, McCormack T (1999) Complementarity as a catalyst for comprehensive domestic penal legislation. UC Davis J. Int'l L & Policy 5:147–180
Easterday JS (2009) Deciding the fate of complementarity: a Colombian case study. Arizona J Int Comp Law 49
Ebobrah S (2011) Towards a positive application of complementarity in the African human rights system: issues of functions and relations. EJIL 22(3):663–688
Ellis MS (2003) The international criminal court and its implication for domestic law and national capacity building. Fla. J Int'l L 15:215
ElZeidy M (2008) The principle of complementarity in international criminal law: origin, development and practice. Martins Nijhoff Publishers, The Netherlands
ElZeidy M (2011) The genesis of complementarity. In: Stahn C, ElZeidy M (eds) Complementarity from theory to practice. CUP, pp 71–141
Englard I (1995) The idea of complementarity as a physical basis for pluralism in tort law. In: Owen DG (ed) Philosophical foundation of tort law, p 191
FIDH (2011) The office of the prosecutor of the international criminal court: 9 years on. No 579 1-32, 8. Available at http://fidh.org/IMG//pdf/cpiproc579ang.pdf
Gaeta P (2004) Is the practice of self-referrals a sound start for the ICC? JICJ 2:949–952
Gaja G (2008) Issues of admissibility in case of self-referrals. In: Politi M, Gioia F (eds) International Criminal Court and National Jurisdictions. Ashgate, p 45
Gioia F (2011) Complementarity and reverse cooperation. In: Stahn C, ElZeidy M (eds) The international criminal court and complementarity: from theory to practice, vol 1. CUP, pp 807–828
Hall C (2011) Positive complementarity in action. In: Stahn C, ElZeidy M (eds) Complementarity theory to practice. CUP, p 1017
Harris D (2010) Cases and materials on international law, 7th edn. Sweet and Maxwell, London
Holmes J (1999) The principle of complementarity. In Lee RS (ed) The international criminal court: the making of the Rome Statute, issues, negotiations and results. Kluwer, The Netherlands, pp 41–78, 41–42
Holmes JT (2004) Complementarity: national courts *versus* the ICC. In: Bekou O, Cryer R (eds) The international criminal court. Ashgate Dartmouth, p 260
Ishiguro K (1990) The remains of the day. Faber and Faber, London
Jessberger F, Geneuss J (2012) The many faces of the international criminal court. JICJ 10: 1081–1094

Jon Heller K (2006) The shadow side of complementarity: the effect of article 17 of the Rome Statute on national due process. CLF 17:255–280

Kim SY (2003) The international criminal court: a commentary of the Rome Statute. Wisdom House

Kittichaisaree K (2001) International criminal law. OUP

Kleffner JK (2009) Complementarity of the Rome Statute and National Criminal Jurisdictions. Oxford Scholarship Online, p 2. www.oxfordscholarshiponline.com. Accessed 15 Mar 2012

Kress C (2004) Self-referrals and waivers of complementarity: some considerations in law and policy. JICJ 2:944–948

Lattanzi F (2001) The international criminal court and national jurisdictions. In: Mauro Politi M, Nesi G (eds) The Rome Statute of the international criminal court: a challenge to impunity. Ashgate, pp 181–182

Letter of Prosecutor dated 9 February 2006 (Iraq). http://www.icc-cpi.int/library/organs/otp_letter_to_senders_re_Iraq_9_Febraury_2006.pdf. Assessed 10 Feb 2009, pp 7–8

Levin A (2001) Quantum physics in private law. Can. J L J 14:249

Mégret F (2005) What is 'Unwilling' or 'Unable' Jurisdiction Under Article 17 of the Rome Statute? Lessons from international law's theories of denial of justice. Que. Rev. Int'l L. Available at http://papers.ssrn.com/sol3/papers.cfm?abstract_id=1277523. Accessed 15 May 2012

Moreno-Ocampo L (2003) Prosecutor, international criminal court, statement made at the ceremony for the Solemn undertaking of the chief prosecutor of the international criminal court (16 June 2003). Available at http://www.icc-cpi.int/library/organs/otp/030616_moreno_ocampo_english_final.pdf. Assessed 10 Dec 2008

Newton M (2001) Comparative complementarity: domestic jurisdiction consistent with the Rome Statute of the international criminal court. MLR 20:167

Newton M (2002) Should the United States join the international criminal court? UC Davis J. Int'l L & P 9:35

Olasolo H (2007) The lack of attention to the distinction between situation and cases in national laws on cooperation with the ICC: special attention to the Spanish case. LJIL 20:157

Perrin B (2006) Making sense of complementarity: the relationship between the international criminal court and national jurisdictions. SL J. Int'l L. 18:301–326

Politi M (2011) Reflections on complementarity at the Rome conference and beyond. In Stahn C, ElZeidy M (eds) The international criminal court and complementarity: from theory to practice, vol 1. CUP, p 142

Robinson D (2010) The mysterious mysteriousness of complementarity. CLF 21:67–102

Robinson D (2012a) Three theories of complementarity: charge, sentence or process? HILJ 53: 165–182

Robinson D (2012b) Three theories of complementarity: charge, sentence or process? Harv. Int'l L. J 53:165. http://www.harvardilj.org/2012/04/online_53_robinson/. Accessed 28 June 2012

Ryngaert C (2011) Horizontal complementarity. In: Stahn C, Elzeidy M (eds) The international criminal court and complementarity: from theory to practice, vol 1. CUP, pp 855–885

Schabas WA (2007) An introduction to the international criminal court, 3rd edn. CUP

Schabas WA (2008a) Complementarity in practice: creative solutions or a trap for the court? In: Politi M, Gioia F (eds) International criminal court and national jurisdictions. Ashgate, p 29

Schabas WA (2008b) Complementarity in practice some uncomplementary thoughts. CLF 19:5

Schabas WA (2011) The international criminal court at ten. CLF 493–509

Scheffer D (1999) The United States and the international criminal court. AJIL 93:12–20

Shaw M (2008) International law, 6th edn. CUP, pp 487–490

Slaughter AM (2003) Not the court of first resort. The Washington Post, 21 December 2003 cited in Branden B, du Plessis M (eds) The prosecution of international crimes: a practical guide to prosecuting ICC crimes in commonwealth states. Commonwealth Secretariat 2005, p 34

Solera O (2002) Complementary jurisdiction and international criminal justice. Int Rev Red Cross 84:145

Sriram CL, Brown S (2012) Kenya in the shadow of the ICC: complementarity, gravity and impact. Int'l CLR 12(2):219–244
Stahn C (2008) Complementarity: a tale of two notions. CLF 19:87–113
Stahn C, El-Zeidy M (eds) (2011) Complementarity of the international criminal court: from theory to practice, vols I & II. CUP
Stahn C, Sluiter G (eds) (2009) The emerging practice of the international criminal court. Martinus Nijhoff Publishers, The Netherlands, p 239
Stigen J (2011) The admissibility procedures. In: Stahn C, ElZeidy M (eds) The international criminal court and complementarity: from theory to practice, vol 1. CUP, p 503
Tallgren I (1998) Completing the international criminal order. Nor. J. Int'l. L 67(2):107
Tallgren I (2002) The sensibility and sense of international criminal law. EJIL 13(3):561
Turns D (2004) Aspects of national implementation of the Rome Statute: the United Kingdom and selected other states. In: McGoldrick D, Rowe P, Donnelly E (eds) The permanent international criminal court: legal and policy issues. Hart Publishing, Oxford, p 337
Vyver JD (2010) Implementation of international law in the United States. Internationaler Verlag der Wissenschaften Frankfurt am Main, p 163
Williams S, Schabas W (2008) Article 17: issues of admissibility. In: Triffterer O (ed) Commentary on the Rome Statute of the international criminal court: observers' notes article by article, 2nd edn. Nomos Oxford Hart, Baden-Baden, pp 605–625
Yang L (2005) On the principle of complementarity in the Rome Statute of the international criminal court. Chi J Int'l L 4:121–132

# Chapter 3
# National Implementation of the Rome Statute of the International Criminal Court: Obligations and Challenges for States Parties

**Abstract** Certainly, beyond ratification, there are other requirements and obligations for state parties under the complementarity regime. Therefore, contrary to other international law instruments and by virtue of the complementarity regime, the Rome Statute implies that states should take certain steps after ratification. These steps include incorporating the Rome Statute crimes into their domestic criminal law, because national criminal laws do not usually encompass international crimes. In addition to incorporating international crimes into domestic law, it is also an obligation for states to put in place mechanisms that could allow them to cooperate fully with the ICC. In this chapter, these mechanisms known as complementarity and cooperation legislation (implementing legislation) are discussed in detail. Furthermore, analysis of how South Africa adopted its implementing legislation is carried out in order for other African states to follow the example.

With the exception of issues relating to the administration of justice and cooperation,[1] the Rome Statute does not expressly stipulate any requirement on how states should implement its provisions. Therefore, states are not specifically obliged to incorporate international crimes into their domestic criminal law. For this reason some scholars have argued that states do not have to integrate the Rome Statute crimes into their domestic criminal law.[2]

However, the central argument of this book is that the distinctive regime of the Rome Statute rests on two pillars, namely; cooperation and complementarity. Consequently it could be inferred that cooperation and complementarity legislation (implementing legislation) are necessary for states to implement the Rome Statute regime. Following the explication in the previous chapter, that complementarity should be perceived and applied as a mutually inclusive concept, in this chapter it is argued that implementing legislation is required for states to realise complementarity. The premise of this argument is that states' ratification of the Rome Statute constitutes consent to complementarity as a concept designed by states, to be

[1] See Articles 70(4)(a) and 86–92 relating to the adoption of legislation penalizing offences against the administration of justice and the obligation to cooperate fully with the ICC respectively.

[2] See *Infra* Sarah Nouwen and Frédéric Mégret (notes 45 & 48 respectively).

 

O.C. Imoedemhe, *The Complementarity Regime of the International Criminal Court*, DOI 10.1007/978-3-319-46780-1_3

operated by states and for the benefit of states,[3] and that it is for individual states to devise its implementation mechanism.

The importance of this argument is that in order to realise the benefit of complementarity, states would need to engage actively in the investigation and prosecution of international crimes domestically. To demonstrate their willingness and genuine ability to carry out this duty, it is argued that it is expedient for states to incorporate the crimes in the Rome Statute into their domestic criminal law. This is because international crimes and ordinary domestic crimes are not the same. This point is further strengthened by the jurisprudence of the Pre-Trial and Appeals Chambers of the ICC in which they have repeatedly rejected admissibility challenges brought by states with jurisdiction to try the same cases.[4] The basis for rejection has been that the states' assertions that they were investigating the suspects for the crimes they allegedly committed did not establish that the states' investigations actually covered the same persons and substantially the same conduct for which they were on trial before the ICC.[5]

How a treaty is implemented (that is, how it is given force under domestic law, or what legal changes are made to allow the state to act in accordance with its international obligations) often varies from state to state, legal system to legal system and from treaty to treaty.[6] In the case of the Rome Statute, issues of domestic implementation arise for both complementarity and cooperation.[7] The former relates to the integration of Rome Statute crimes into domestic criminal law to enable domestic prosecution of the crimes. The latter is necessary to support and facilitate the ICC and national jurisdictions in the investigation and prosecution of alleged perpetrators.

This chapter is divided into four sections. The first section discusses the rationale for implementing legislation. This is significant because admittedly, the Rome Statute does not expressly oblige states to enact implementing legislation. However, since states determine how to observe their obligations under international law and particularly in view of the distinctive complementarity regime, it is necessary for states to reflect on how to ensure its domestic implementation of complementarity.

Besides, for a state to successfully challenge the admissibility of a case before the ICC, the state has to prove that its domestic investigation encompasses both the same person and substantially the same conduct for which the suspect is standing

[3]Bekou (2011) (Stahn and ElZeidy *Complementarity Theory to Practice*), 830–852, 851–852.

[4]See Pre-Trial Chamber I in the *Saif Al-Islam* case (Text to note 94 in Ch 2); Pre-Trial Chamber II in the *Joseph Kony et al* case, Trial Chamber II in the *Germain Katanga* case (Text to note 102 in Ch 2) and the Appeals Chamber in the *Muthaura et al* (Kenya Appeals Decision) case (Text to note 86 in Ch 2).

[5]See the 'same person same conduct' test formulated in the *Lubanga* case and applied in the cases analysed in the preceding Chapter (Text to notes 88–90 Ch 2).

[6]International Centre for Criminal Law Reform and Criminal Justice Policy (ICCLR) (2012).

[7]Ibid.

trial before the ICC.[8] It is argued that to pass the 'same person same conduct' test, states would need to incorporate Rome Statute crimes into their domestic criminal law.

The second section discusses cooperation legislation. Although the Rome Statute expressly requests states to cooperate fully with the ICC, there is no precise provision requiring them to adopt cooperation legislation. This means that states may use pre-existing cooperation mechanisms. In this section, it is argued that existing cooperation mechanisms like extradition rules cannot be relied on by states because the cooperation regime under the Rome Statute is different from extradition procedures that exist between states. Therefore cooperation legislation is important, not least for the sole purpose of cooperating fully with the ICC, but also for states to benefit from the 'reverse' cooperation regime introduced in Article 93(10).

The third section examines complementarity legislation. The different methods by which states have integrated international crimes into their domestic criminal law are analysed and two main approaches are identified, namely; the minimalist and express criminalisation methods. Although the minimalist approach seems to be the easiest, the use of the express criminalisation method, by which the exact wordings of the definitions of crimes in the Rome Statute are adopted by states in their implementing legislation, is nonetheless advocated.

An analysis of how South Africa adopted its implementing legislation forms the basis of the discussion in the fourth section. There, it is admitted that several countries both from the common law and civil law traditions have enacted implementing legislation; however, the section's focus on South Africa is due to two reasons. First, as all cases, but one, currently before the ICC are from the African continent, it is deemed more relevant to examine an African state which has implementing legislation, with a view to other states in the region following the example. Second, South Africa offers a ready case study because it is the only African state that has adopted implementing legislation in conformity with the Rome Statute in advance.[9]

Three other African states that have passed implementing legislation are Kenya, Senegal and Uganda, but their legislation were adopted late. Kenya's implementing legislation, for example, was passed 2 years after its 2007/2008 post-election violence.[10] Kenya's inability to prosecute those involved in the post-election violence, is arguably linked to the lack of implementing legislation at the time. Similarly, Senegal was found guilty of delaying the adoption of local legislation in

[8] *Saif Al-Islam* case (Text to note 94 in Ch 2) para 74.

[9] Implementation of the Rome Statute of the International Criminal Court Act No 27 of 2002 Government Gazette No 23642 of 18 July 2002 (South African ICC Act). Available at http://www.info.gov.za/gazette/acts/2002/a27-02.pdf Also available http://www.iccnow.org/documents/SouthAfricaLegEng2002.pdf (Assessed 11 April 2013).

[10] The International Crimes Act 2008 (Kenya International Crimes Act), gazetted and entered into force January 2009. Available at http://www.kenyalaw.org/Downloads/Acts/The_International_Crimes_Act_2008.pdf (Accessed 30 June 2013).

the judgement of the International Court of Justice (ICJ) in the case between *Belgium v Senegal*.[11] Arguably, Uganda hastily passed its implementing legislation in March 2010 in order to secure its hosting of the first Review Conference held in May and June 2010.

This chapter proposes that to ensure proactive complementarity, ratification of the Rome Statute by states is only a starting point. Thereafter, it is imperative for states to adopt both cooperation and complementarity legislation to ensure domestic implementation of the Rome Statute. However, since this is not strictly required under the Statute, and the debate over whether implementing legislation is necessary for states is on-going, the basis for implementing legislation is discussed in the following section.

## 3.1 The Rationale for Implementing Legislation

It might seem out of place to consider the implementation of the Rome Statute in the national legal systems of states. This is because the Statute places no specific obligation upon states to implement the Statute's provisions *per se*.[12] While it does contain various requirements for states' cooperation with the ICC,[13] these relate exclusively to matters of investigatory, executory and trial procedures.[14] Consequently, these have been the subject of little or no controversy,[15] although the practical application of cooperation between the ICC and states remains a challenge.

With respect to complementarity legislation, it may further be argued that some of the crimes defined by the Rome Statute, as well as the general principles and the jurisdictional regimes applicable to them, had been recognised by international law prior to the adoption of the Statute.[16] As a consequence, the obligation on states to adopt the crimes into their domestic laws is derived from treaties.[17] Thus, a strong

[11]Questions Relating to the Obligation to Prosecute or Extradite (*Belgium v. Senegal*) ICJ decision of 20 July 2012 para 72–76. Available at http://www.icj-cij.org/docket/files/144/17064.pdf (Accessed 3 October 2012).

[12]Turns (2004), pp. 337–338.

[13]See Part 9 of the Rome Statute which imposes a general obligation on states parties to cooperate with the ICC in investigating and prosecuting the crimes within the Court's jurisdiction.

[14]See Forms of Cooperation (*infra* n 66).

[15]Turns (2004), p. 338.

[16]The Convention for the Prevention and Punishment of Genocide (1948) proscribed the crime of genocide, the Four Geneva Conventions of (1949) and the Additional Protocols I and II of 1977 (AP I & II) proscribed war crimes and crimes against humanity.

[17]See for example Article V of the Genocide Convention, Articles 49, 50, 129 and 146 of the First, Second, Third and Fourth Geneva Conventions respectively; Articles 85–87 AP I; Article 6 of the Torture Convention (1984) where states undertook to enact necessary legislation to give effect to the provisions of the Conventions.

point may be made that since the crimes have been recognised by international law, it is superfluous to require states to incorporate them into their domestic criminal law. Nevertheless, it is maintained that for the distinctive regime of the Rome Statute, complementarity legislation is necessary for states.

Admittedly, Article 1 of the Rome Statute does not require national implementation in express terms.[18] However, its formulation of complementarity, reiterates that primary jurisdiction over the crimes delineated in the Rome Statute is given to individual states. Obliquely, this implies a need for implementation. States must ensure that they are able to prosecute the crimes enumerated in Articles 6–8 of the Statute, not only theoretically, for example, by having the legal capability to assert jurisdiction to prosecute, but also in reality, by having the crimes listed in the Statute in their national criminal law.[19]

Logically, implementing legislation safeguards states' primary right to investigate and prosecute crimes which could potentially come under the jurisdiction of the ICC and more specifically to avoid being declared 'unable'.[20] This is because inability does not only apply to situations of failed states in which armed conflict has resulted in the substantial or total collapse of the national judicial system, but it equally applies to states' inability to carry out proceedings due to the substantial or total unavailability of its judicial system.[21] This form of inability may result from the absence or inadequacy of substantive legislation at the domestic level.[22] Thus, defects in domestic law, which might render the national judicial system substantially or totally unavailable, can make a case admissible before the ICC.[23]

Contrary to the assertion that implementing legislation is necessary for national implementation of the Rome Statute, the Statute does not expressly say that it is. In fact, the Statute's silence on the point has been read to mean that states may depend on ordinary domestic criminal law to prosecute international crimes. Surprisingly, this position was adopted by the Pre-Trial Chamber I (PTCI) in its decision of 31 May 2013 regarding the admissibility challenge by Libya in the *Saif Al-Islam Gaddafi*[24] case. The PTCI noted that 'a domestic investigation or prosecution for 'ordinary crimes' *to the extent that the case covers the same conduct* shall be considered sufficient'.[25] It is the Chamber's view that Líbya's current lack of

[18]Article 1 of the Rome Statute provides that the ICC shall be complementary to national criminal jurisdictions; other formulations of complementarity are to be found in paras 6 & 10 of the Preamble to the Statute.

[19]Turns (2004), p. 338.

[20]Kleffner (2003), pp. 86–113, 88.

[21]Ibid.

[22]Doherty and McCormack (1999), p. 152; Lattanzi (2001), p. 181; Gaeta (2002), pp. 975–1002, 998 (Cassese *et al*); Yang (2005), p. 124.

[23]Kleffner.

[24]*Saif Al-Islam* case (Text to note 94 in Ch 2).

[25]Ibid, paras 88, 108, 133, 200, 201 (emphasis added).

legislation criminalising crimes against humanity does not *per se* render the case admissible before the Court.[26]

Nevertheless, the Chamber assessed Libya's ability in relation to the Libyan Code of Criminal Procedure, amongst others, and found that Libya was unable to investigate Mr Gaddafi. The PTCI decision was founded on Libya's failure to provide the Chamber with 'enough evidence with a sufficient degree of specificity and probative value to demonstrate that Libya's investigations *covered the same conduct* as those with the ICC'.[27]

In rejecting the admissibility challenge, the PTCI made reference to the Appeals Chamber's previous decisions in the two Kenyan cases,[28] in which the Chamber upheld the validity of the 'same person same conduct' test thus:

> The defining elements of a concrete case before the Court are the individual and the alleged conduct. It follows that for such a case to be inadmissible under Article 17(1)(a) of the Statute, the national investigation must cover the same individual and substantially the same conduct as alleged in the proceedings before the Court.[29]

The 'case' as referred to in Article 17 of the Statute is characterised by two components: the person and the conduct. The PTCI further observed that while it is uncontested that national investigations must cover the 'same person',[30] the 'conduct' part of the test raises issues of interpretation and needs further clarification.[31]

Admittedly, the determination of what constitutes 'substantially the same conduct' as alleged in the proceedings before the Court will vary according to the concrete facts and circumstances of the case and therefore requires a case-by-case analysis.[32] However, it is argued that 'substantially the same conduct' cannot be interpreted in a manner that would allow variation in the underlying facts and incidents, as such a flexible interpretation would undermine the very purpose of complementarity.[33]

---

[26] Ibid, para 88.

[27] *Saif Al-Islam* case, paras 134, 135, 219 (emphasis added).

[28] Appeals Chamber, *The Prosecutor v William Samoei Ruto, Henry Kiprono Kosgey and Joshua Arap Sang* Judgement on the Appeal of the Republic of Kenya against the decision of Pre-Trial Chamber II of 30 May 2011 entitled 'Decision on the Application by the Government of Kenya Challenging the Admissibility of the case Pursuant to Article 19(2)(b) of the Statute' 20 August 2011 ICC-01/09-01/11-307 para 40; Appeals Chamber, *The Prosecutor v Francis Kirimi Muthaura, Uhuru Muigai Kenyatta and Mohammed Hussein Ali* Judgment on the Appeal of the Republic of Kenya against the decision of Pre-Trial Chamber II of 30 May 2011 entitled 'Decision on the Application by the Government of Kenya challenging the Admissibility of the case Pursuant to Article 19(2)(b) of the Statute' 30 August 2011 ICC-01/09-02/11-274, (hereinafter '*Muthaura et al* case') para 39.

[29] *Muthaura et al case* paras 39, 40, 41, 42 & 61.

[30] Ibid, paras 1, 40–43.

[31] *Saif Al-Islam* case, para 61.

[32] *Saif Al-Islam* case, para 77.

[33] Ibid, para 68.

The ordinary crimes for which Saif Al-Islam Gaddafi was being investigated were intentional murder, torture, incitement to civil war, indiscriminate killings, misuse of authority against individuals, arresting people without just cause and unjustified deprivation of personal liberty pursuant to articles 368, 435, 293, 296, 431, 433 and 434 of the Libyan Criminal Code.[34] On the other hand, the ICC arrest warrant for Saif Al-Islam was for the commission of murder and persecution as crimes against humanity under Article 7(1)(a) and (h) of the Statute.

It is maintained that the ordinary crimes for which Libya proposed to prosecute Saif Al-Islam are not the same as the crimes against humanity of murder and persecution, for which he is indicted before the ICC. Although not expressly stated by the PTCI, it is submitted that it is for this reason that the PTCI found Libya unable to investigate and prosecute and rejected the admissibility challenge. This argument finds support in the PTCI assertion that 'a domestic investigation or prosecution for ordinary crimes is sufficient *provided that it covers the same conduct'*.[35] In other words, to pass the 'same conduct' limb of the test, the domestic investigation of an ordinary crime must cover the same acts as stipulated in the Rome Statute and the ICC arrest warrant. It is argued that this is possible only when the domestic law incorporates the Rome Statute crimes because international crimes are not usually known to domestic criminal law.

In addition, the PTCI raised specific concerns regarding the ordinary crimes for which Saif Al-Islam was being investigated.[36] Two concerns noted by the Chamber were; first, that the crimes potentially applicable to Saif Al-Islam apply only to 'public officers' under Libyan legislation, which could raise problems, as Saif Al-Islam did not occupy a formal official position in Libya.[37] Second, since the crime of persecution was not known in Libyan law, the Chamber was not satisfied with Libya's claim that though discriminatory intent was absent, it was an aggravating factor which would be taken into account in sentencing under Articles 27 and 28 of the Libyan Criminal Code.[38]

Furthermore, the PTCI determined that the crimes which Libya proposed charging Saif Al-Islam with under Libyan legislation do not cover all aspects of the offences under the Rome Statute.[39] Consequently, the Chamber established that Libya failed to 'provide evidence with a sufficient degree of specificity and probative value to demonstrate that Libya's investigations covered the same conduct as those with the ICC'.[40]

The PTCI argument inevitably leads to the inference that if Libya had adopted implementing legislation and begun its investigation based on the same conduct as

[34]Ibid, paras 28 & 112.

[35]Ibid, paras 85, 86, 108, 133, 200, 201 (emphasis added).

[36]*Saif Al-Islam* case, para 108, 109.

[37]Ibid, para 109.

[38]ibid, para 111.

[39]Ibid, para 113.

[40]Ibid, paras 134, 135.

contained in the Rome Statute and the ICC arrest warrant, Libya would have been able to show the 'sufficient degree of specificity and probative value' required by the PTCI. Ultimately a state that challenges the admissibility of a case bears the burden of proof to show that the case is inadmissible.[41] Arguably, the central argument reflected in the PTCI decision in the *Saif Al-Islam* case, is that the lack of substantive and procedural penal legislation in conformity with the Rome Statute rendered Libya's judicial system unavailable.

It is submitted that the PTCI's assertion that states do not have to integrate the Rome Statute crimes into their domestic criminal law is supported by the Statute only to the extent that the Rome Statute is silent on it. In the *Lotus*[42] case however, the Permanent Court of International Justice (PCIJ) noted that as long as international law does not expressly prohibit something, it may be applied.[43] It is argued further that although not explicitly stated, such an obligation is implied and could be read into the Rome Statute, as it is not possible to 'put something on nothing and expect it to [stand], it will collapse'.[44] Complementarity can only stand on the effective criminal justice systems of states and the starting point for that effectiveness is criminalising the Rome Statute crimes domestically.

Nevertheless, the argument that states can prosecute the crimes in the Rome Statute on the basis of ordinary domestic crimes has been advanced by some scholars. Sarah Nouwen, for example, maintains that the Statute's only provision referring to a duty to prosecute is the sixth preambular paragraph, which states that it is the duty of every state to exercise criminal jurisdiction over those responsible for international crimes.[45] Accordingly, she argues that there is no obligation on states to proscribe the Rome Statute crimes in their domestic criminal law.[46] Moreover, the Statute does not oblige states to make use of their primary right to investigate and prosecute war crimes, crimes against humanity or genocide.[47] Similarly, Frédéric Mégret argues that rigorous legal reform in national criminal law is not strictly required under the Rome Statute.[48]

Notwithstanding the lack of an explicit obligation on states to enact implementing legislation, adopting such legislation is nonetheless necessary for the application of complementarity. In addition to the inferences derived from the PTCI's decision in the *Saif Al-Islam* case described above, such a position finds

[41] Ibid, para 52; *Muthaura et al* case, para 62; Pre-Trial Chamber I Decision in *Saif Al-Islam* case 7 December 2012 para 9; Pre-Trial Chamber I, Transcript of Hearing, 10 October 2012 ICC-01/11-01/11-T-3-Red-ENG, 64–65.

[42] *SS Lotus*, PCIJ Series A No 10 (1927) (*Lotus* case).

[43] ibid, 19.

[44] *Per* Lord Denning in *Macfoy v UAC Ltd* (1961) 3 WLR (PC) 1405, 1409.

[45] Nouwen (2011), p. 1127.

[46] Ibid.

[47] Ibid.

[48] Mégret (2011), pp. 361–390, 367–374 (noting that requiring states to adopt comprehensive implementing legislations goes beyond what is required under the Rome Statute).

support in a number of arguments. First, paragraph six of the preamble recalls states' duty to 'exercise [their] criminal jurisdiction…'[49] such a duty presupposes an obligation to ensure that the crimes in the Rome Statute are incorporated into national criminal law.

Second, the Statute affirms that 'the most serious crimes of concern to the international community as a whole must not go unpunished' and expresses that 'their effective prosecution must be ensured by taking measures at the national level…'[50] This provision, underpins the realistic assertion that not all international crimes committed in a particular situation can be prosecuted before the ICC.[51] In line with this position, it has been noted that the ICC only prosecutes those who bear the greatest responsibility for the gravest crimes.[52] By implication, an appropriate starting point for effective prosecution by states would be to either adjust domestic laws or make new laws to incorporate the international crimes. Without the crimes being reflected in national criminal laws, implementation of complementarity as envisaged in the Rome Statute lacks its principal pillar, namely, 'measures at the national level'.[53]

Third, effective prosecution at the national level is to fulfil the goal of putting 'an end to impunity for the perpetrators… and thus contributing to the prevention of such crimes'.[54] This implies that the complementary jurisdiction of the ICC denotes a system of international law enforcement that allocates primary responsibility to national criminal jurisdictions.[55] In such a system, the object of prosecuting with the effect of deterrence for the ultimate purpose of putting an end to impunity is undermined if states fail to adopt implementing legislation.

In agreement with this argument, the Informal Expert Group noted with regard to the principle of complementarity that, consistent with its mandate to help ensure that serious international crimes do not go unpunished, it should be a high priority for the Office of the Prosecutor to actively remind states of their responsibility to adopt and implement effective legislation.[56] This implies that proof of a state's

---

[49]Rome Statute, para 6 of the Preamble.

[50]Rome Statute, para 4 of the Preamble.

[51]Triffterer (2008), pp. 1–16, 11–12.

[52]See the PTCI decision of 10 February 2006 in the *Lubanga* and *Ntaganda* cases ICC-01/04-01/07; The ICC, 'Understanding the International Criminal Court' Available at http://www.icc-cpi.int/iccdocs/PIDS/publications/UICCEng.pdf paras 37 & 38; Aranburu (2013).

[53]Kleffner (2003), p. 93.

[54]Rome Statute, para 5 of the Preamble.

[55]Kleffner.

[56]Informal Expert Paper, 'The Principle of Complementarity in Practice (2009) (Text to n 114 in Ch 2), para 7. See also 'The Commonwealth Expert Group on Review of the Implementing Legislation for the Rome Statute' 23–25 February 2011 (Proposing a model law on the implementation of the Rome Statute by Commonwealth member states). Available at http://www.thecommonwealth.org/files/238381/FileName/LMM(11)17PICCStatuteandImplementationoftheGenevaConventions.pdf (Assessed 8 April 2013).

ability or willingness to investigate and prosecute international crimes and to cooperate with the ICC could be ascertained by its implementing legislation.[57]

According to the former Registrar of the ICC, implementing legislation underpins the Rome Statute structure, such that the whole system becomes ineffective without it.[58] She affirms that effective cooperation with the ICC is dependent upon the existence of implementing legislation at national levels.[59] Accordingly, to guarantee cooperation, legislative and sometimes constitutional amendments are needed, although their exact scope and legal form may vary from one state to another.

> . . .as an international institution without direct enforcement mechanisms, the Court heavily relies on cooperation from states. . .the Rome Statute is a two pillar system: a judicial pillar represented by the Court, and an enforcement pillar represented by the states, which undertook a legal obligation to cooperate with the Court through the Rome Statute. Cooperation is the inter-play between these two pillars, shown clearly by the fact that the Court requires the states to play their part in order for the system created by the Statute to work.[60]

The foregoing argument reveals that the ICC can only be an effective complement if states adopt the Statute's substantive law for the purpose of domestic prosecution. Where states fail to enact implementing legislation, gaps are left that would ultimately prevent perpetrators from being brought to justice at the domestic level. It may also culminate in a large number of situations and cases being referred to or being admissible before the ICC. Thus, in order for the ICC to effectively perform its complementary function, comprehensive implementing legislation is indispensable.[61]

The view expressed by the German government in the course of implementing the Rome Statute by adopting the Code of Crimes against International Law (CCAIL) in 2002 further exemplifies this understanding.[62] The government noted that adoption of the law was necessary in order to ensure, in light of the complementary prosecutorial competence of the ICC, that Germany is always able to prosecute crimes within the jurisdiction of the ICC.[63] Furthermore, the Dutch Minister for Foreign Affairs J.D. de Hoop Scheffer in his statement to the First

---

[57]Triponel and Pearson (2010), pp. 65–106.

[58]Remarks by Arbia (2009); Arbia and Bassy (2011), p. 65. (Effective 16 April 2013, Herman von Hebel became the Registrar of the ICC as Arbia's five year mandate ended on that date).

[59]Speech by Ms Silvana Arbia at the conference 'Justice for all? The International Criminal Court - 10 Year Review of the ICC' at the University of New South Wales (UNSW) Sydney Australia 14 February 2012. Available at http://www.icc-cpi.int/NR/rdonlyres/8C6B4B5B-D854-4F18-BA76-E0F687F2D60C/284274/Speech_10anniversary_Australia.pdf (Accessed 2 March 2013).

[60]Arbia, 'Justice for all'.

[61]Kleffner (2003), p. 94; See also Robinson (2002), pp. 1849, 1864; Greppi (2008), p. 69.

[62]Turns (2004), p. 379. (The final version of the Code of Crimes against International Law (CCAIL) entered into force on 30 June 2002: *Bundesgestzblatt* (*BGBI*) 2002, 1, 2254).

[63]Turns (2004), p. 379.

Assembly of States Parties, explained that complementarity requires states 'to ensure ratification is followed by swift action to bring national legislation into line, because the Rome Statute will be incomplete without implementation and enforcement...'[64] Similarly, as noted by Garapon:

> Complementarity is not just a mechanism for the ICC Prosecutor to bypass cases: it carries with it the hope for a more harmonious world in which we are all engaged, starting with the Third states. If this institution is not supported by respected states prepared to lend their weight in the service of justice in a coordinated development policy, complementarity will become purely cosmetic.[65]

The debate in this section has thus far focused on the justification for the adoption of implementing legislation by states. It is believed that it is first and foremost to the benefit of states to take on the investigation and prosecution of crimes in the Rome statute and second for the sustainability of the ICC. Once domestic criminal laws reflect the international crimes that come under the jurisdiction of the ICC, then it would be easy for them to investigate and prosecute with the international legal characterisation of the crimes. It is argued that it is only on this basis that primary jurisdiction has been given to states, as it is only then that states would be able to pass the 'same conduct' limb of the 'same person same conduct' test. Issues of implementing legislation relate principally to both complementarity and cooperation. Therefore, the next section discusses cooperation legislation.

## 3.2 Cooperation Legislation

There appears to be no debate on the need for cooperation legislation, as it is expressly declared in the Rome Statute that states are expected to cooperate fully with the ICC. However, it may be argued that states' duty to cooperate with the ICC does not necessarily demand an extensive cooperation regime as individual states may rely on pre-existing cooperation mechanisms available to them. The purpose of the analysis in this section is to argue that under the complementarity regime, distinct cooperation legislation is required for a number of reasons.

First, the general cooperation that the ICC may request from states parties are set out in Parts 9 and 10 of the Rome Statute. As described there, the cooperation envisaged could be broadly categorised into three areas: (1) the arrest and surrender of persons at the request of the Court; (2) other practical assistance with the Court's

[64]See Statement by the Dutch Minister for Foreign Affairs J.D. de Hoop Scheffer to the First Assembly of States Parties 9 September 2002 New York. Available at http://www.iccnow.org/html/NetherlandsASP9Sept02.doc (Assessed 30 March 2013).

[65]Garapon (2012), p. 21.

investigations and prosecutions and (3) general enforcement.[66] Of these, the arrest and surrender of persons at the request of the Court is arguably the most important because under the Rome Statute, trials *in absentia* are not permitted.[67] Thus, the effective functioning of the ICC is wholly dependent upon national procedures which can comply with a request for arrest, and facilitate the surrender of suspects in order to ensure the appearance in court of accused persons.[68]

Article 89(1) of the Rome Statute imposes a general duty on states to comply with a request for the arrest and surrender of an individual to the ICC.[69] However, the manner in which the arrest is to be executed and that of the surrender of the suspect to the ICC is left entirely to states to determine. This is understandably so since it would have been impossible for the drafters of the Rome Statute to provide a generic approach which could be followed by all states parties.[70] It would also have amounted to infringing too much on the sovereignty of states, as the perceived intrusiveness of the ICC was already a major concern.

In order to secure the presence of accused persons at proceedings before the ICC, the question of whether the cooperation regime under the Rome Statute could depend on existing extradition laws between states needs to be answered. Extradition is the traditional method of securing the presence of alleged perpetrators of crimes to stand trial or serve a sentence, and it is usually a consequence of a bilateral agreement between states.[71] The national legislation of some states contains provisions on extradition but the content varies from one state to another.[72]

A cornerstone of extradition law is the requirement of double criminality.[73] The rule of double criminality requires that the conduct with regard to which extradition is requested constitutes a crime according to the law of both the requesting and the requested state at the time of its commission.[74] This requirement is a means of ensuring reciprocity as well as protecting the individual requested against punishment for conduct that has not been criminalised by the requested stated.[75] Another

---

[66]See Parts 9 & 10 (Arts 86-111) of the Rome Statute. The forms of cooperation include general compliance with the ICC requests for cooperation (Art 87); Surrender of persons to the Court (Art 89); Provisional arrests pursuant to ICC requests (Art 92); identification or location of persons or items, taking and production of evidence, service of documents, facilitating witnesses' and experts' attendance before the ICC, temporary transfer of persons, examination of sites (e.g. mass graves), execution of search and seizure Orders, protection of witnesses, freezing of sequestration of property and assets (Art 93); and enforcement of sentences (Arts 103–107), fines and forfeiture orders (Art 109). See also Rastan (2008), pp. 431–456.

[67]See Rome Statute, art 63.

[68]Bekou and Shah (2006), pp. 499–544, 523; Katz (2003), pp. 25–30.

[69]Rome Statute, Article 89(1).

[70]Bekou and Shah (2006), p. 525.

[71]Katz (2003), p. 28.

[72]Bassiouni (2013), pp. 500–502 (hereinafter 'Bassiouni *Intro to ICL*').

[73]Swart (2002), pp. 1639, 1652–1654.

[74]Ibid, 1653.

[75]Ibid.

requirement is the principle of speciality or specialty whereby the requesting state can only prosecute the surrendered person for the specific crimes for which extradition was granted.[76] Other procedural impediments to extradition include statutes of limitation and immunities.[77] These considerations are irrelevant under the Rome Statute because, first, the Statute uses the word 'surrender' and not extradition and second, inhibitions such as immunities and statutes of limitations have been conspicuously removed.[78]

Article 59 of the Rome Statute provides for arrest and surrender proceedings in the custodial state.[79] During the negotiations in Rome, three different terms were considered to achieve the handing over of an alleged perpetrator to the ICC; these were extradition, transfer or surrender. However, 'extradition' was rejected by some states during the Rome Conference because of constitutional restrictions on the extradition of nationals.[80] Similarly, the concept of 'transfer',[81] where a person sought is merely arrested and sent to the ICC, was rejected because the usual safeguards contained in the extradition process concerning the curtailment of liberty were absent.[82]

As a compromise, the term 'surrender' was adopted.[83] For the purposes of the Statute, Article 102 defines surrender as the delivering up of a person by a state to the Court pursuant to the Statute.[84] Extradition means the handing over of a person by one state to another as provided by treaty, convention or national legislation.[85] Thus, the surrender of a person to the ICC is fundamentally different from the handing over of a person within the framework of extradition between states,[86] because it does not rest on reciprocity. Although this may not be fundamentally different in practice, it is recommended that for the full cooperation required under the Rome Statute, states should not rely on their extradition laws for the purposes of arrest and surrender of alleged perpetrators to the ICC.

Second, similar to the *ad hoc* tribunals, the ICC cannot enforce its own decisions; it cannot execute arrest warrants in the territory of states and does not have its

---

[76]Bassiouni *Intro to ICL* Ibid, 501.

[77]Swart, 1653.

[78]Rome Statute, Articles 27 & 29. See also Swart 1657.

[79]See Rome Statute, art 59 (2). Other relevant provisions on surrender include articles 58, 86, 101, 102.

[80]States with civil law tradition (such as Germany, France, Spain and Italy) as opposed to a common law tradition do not as a rule extradite their own citizens.

[81]'Transfer' was the expression used by the ILC in its 1994 Draft Statute. In Part 10 of the Rome Statute, the term 'transfer' is now used in relation to persons serving a sentence of imprisonment imposed by the Court.

[82]Robinson (2002), p. 1852.

[83]Cassese et al. (2002), pp. 1664, 1676–1684.

[84]See Rome Statute, art 102 (a).

[85]See Rome Statute, art 102 (b).

[86]Cassese et al. 1678.

own police force.[87] As noted by the Appeals Chamber of the ICTY in the *Blaskic*[88] case, 'enforcement powers must be expressly provided and cannot be regarded as inherent in an international tribunal'.[89] From this perspective, there is no direct enforcement of international criminal law because the organs in charge of implementation depend on indirect enforcement in order to function properly.[90]

The cooperation regime of the *ad hoc* tribunals and states could be described as vertical, which is distinct from horizontal cooperation between states.[91] With the latter, there is no legal obligation to cooperate. Rather such cooperation depends on the sovereign decision of the state concerned.[92] The only precondition which may act as an impediment is the requirement of the principle of reciprocity.[93] On the other hand, vertical cooperation is not inhibited by such an obstacle because the state's cooperation is not theoretically dependent on the sovereign decision of the state, but rather on a general and international obligation to cooperate.[94]

Consequently, the cooperation regime set out in the ICTY and ICTR Statutes is binding on all member states of the United Nations by virtue of Chapter VII of the United Nations Charter and it contains no qualifications and no exceptions.[95] This is what makes it truly vertical, as the cooperation regimes were construed in a one-sided fashion; namely, entailing assistance and support from states to the tribunals.[96] National rules and other international obligations which are opposed to obligations towards the tribunals cannot, in principle, be raised as grounds for refusal to cooperate. Therefore, noncompliance with the duty to cooperate could be met with Security Council sanctions on the violating state.

Conversely, the Rome Statute favours a cooperation regime based on the traditional horizontal law of mutual assistance. At the same time, the

[87]Cryer *et al, An Intro to ICL* (Text to n 2 in Ch 2) 509; Ambos (2008), pp. 181–198 (noting that as a rule international tribunals depend on the cooperation with national jurisdictions not only for the arrest, investigation and prosecution of core international crimes but also for the execution of sentences).

[88]*Prosecutor v Tihomir Blaskic* ICTY Case No. IT-95-14-AR108*bis* Appeals Chamber decision of 29 October 1997 (*Blaskic* case).

[89]Ibid para. 25.

[90]Bassiouni (2013), p. 22. See also Harmon and Gaynor (2004), p. 403; Gamarra and Vicente (2008), p. 627.

[91]*Blaskic* case, paras 47 & 54.

[92]Bassiouni (2013), p. 24.

[93]Sluiter (2002), pp. 82–88.

[94]Cryer *et al, An Intro to ICL,* 510.

[95]See Articles 28 and 29 ICTY and ICTR Statutes respectively, which derive their authority from Security Council Resolutions 927 (1993) and 955 (1994). According to the provisions, the tribunals may issue an 'order' or 'request' both being equally binding on states. See Sluiter (2002), pp. 147–150.

[96]Stahn (2008), pp. 87–113.

'like-minded'[97] states proposed a new form of cooperation which takes into account the *sui generis* nature of the ICC.[98] As a result, the Rome Statute contains a mixed regime of cooperation that is, on the one hand, less vertical than the one of the *ad hoc* Tribunals but on the other hand, goes beyond merely horizontal cooperation.[99] This is because the ICC cooperation regime is treaty-based, and must therefore reconcile conflicting interests. In principle, the duty to cooperate presupposes the full cooperation of state parties upon ratification of the Statute,[100] and at least a conclusion of an *ad hoc* agreement with non-state parties in accordance with Article 87(5).[101] Therefore, there is a distinction between the general duty of states parties and the limited one of non-party states to cooperate.

Third, in addition to the mixed cooperation regime of the ICC, the Rome Statute's formulation of cooperation foresees the option of 'reverse' cooperation.[102] This means that the ICC is expected to provide assistance and support to domestic jurisdictions for the purposes of investigating and carrying out prosecutions under Article 93(10).[103] The proactive complementarity model proposed in the preceding chapter implies that where cooperation legislation is in place, states would be able to request assistance from the ICC in their domestic efforts. This distinctive provision in the Rome Statute is not only an advantage to states and the ICC, it is also a basis for a mutually inclusive interpretation and application of complementarity.

Moving from the theoretical framework to the practical questions involved, the first imperative is for the Prosecutor to know with whom to cooperate. This question should, among others, be dealt with in national cooperation laws of states parties.[104] The importance of determining who to cooperate with in national legislation is underscored by the withdrawal of the charges against Mr Muthaura in the *Muthaura et al*[105] case. The Prosecutor noted that a major challenge in the case and one of the reasons for the withdrawal was 'the disappointing fact that the Government of

---

[97]The 'like-minded' states were a group of states who shared the objective of establishing a strong ICC. They included Canada, Australia, and most African and European states with the exception of France, Argentina and Costa Rica. See Bedont and Matas (1998), p. 21. Available at http://peacemagazine.org/archive/v14n5p21.htm (Accessed 11 April 2013).

[98]Mochochoko (1999), p. 305.

[99]Ambos (2008).

[100]Rome Statute, Art 86.

[101]Art. 87(5) allows the ICC to request non-party state to the Statute to provide assistance on the basis of an *ad hoc* arrangement, an agreement with such state or any other appropriate basis. See Rastan (2008), p. 441.

[102]Gioia (2011), pp. 807–828.

[103]*Ibid.*

[104]Bekou and Shah (2006).

[105]*Prosecutor v. Francis Kirimi Muthaura and Uhuru Muigai Kenyatta* Case No ICC-01/09-02/11 (Prosecution notification of withdrawal of Charges against Francis Kirimi Muthaura). Available at http://www.icc-cpi.int/iccdocs/doc/ICC-01-09-02-11-687.pdf (Assessed 11 April 2013).

Kenya failed to provide my Office with important evidence and failed to facilitate our access to critical witnesses...'[106] This is irrespective of the decision on the confirmation of charges on the basis of a 'thorough review'[107] by the Pre-Trial Chamber in January 2012.[108]

Cooperation legislation therefore, could have the effect of eliminating confusion and streamlining the state's action by indicating which authority is empowered to provide the cooperation required by the ICC.[109] In practical terms, cooperation legislation has been enacted by a few states and, only by states where, frankly, the commission of international crimes is very unlikely.[110] This accounts for the inability of the Prosecutor in the cases currently before the ICC to obtain suspects, necessary witnesses and evidence, particularly concerning the indictments of alleged perpetrators in Sudan and Uganda.

The reasons advanced above in favour of states adopting cooperation legislation are by no means exhaustive. However, they demonstrate the distinctive cooperation regime under the Rome Statute. Without cooperation legislation at the domestic level, the ICC will not be effective. As noted, the Rome Statute is explicit on the need for states to cooperate fully with the ICC. However, the mechanisms of ensuring full cooperation are left entirely in the hands of individual states. Therefore it is imperative for states not to rely on existing cooperation or extradition rules, but to adopt cooperation legislation in line with the Rome Statute. There is yet further debate, particularly regarding complementarity legislation, because the Rome Statute does not specifically mandate the adoption of such legislation. Consequently, the next section discusses what complementarity legislation is and how states may incorporate the Rome Statute crimes into their domestic criminal law.

---

[106]'Statement by ICC Prosecutor on the Notice to Withdraw Charges against Mr Muthaura' 11 March 2013. Available at http://www.icc-cpi.int/en_menus/icc/press%20and%20media/press%20releases/Pages/OTP-statement-11-03-2013.aspx (Accessed 11 April 2013).

[107]See Summary of decision in the two Kenya Cases, 23 January 2012. Available at http://www.icc-cpi.int/en_menus/icc/press%20and%20media/press%20releases/news%20and%20highlights/Pages/summary%20of%20decision%20in%20the%20two%20kenya%20cases.aspx (Assessed 11 April 2013).

[108]See *Prosecutor v. Francis Kirimi Muthaura, Uhuru Muigai Kenyatta and Mohammed Hussein Ali* Case No: ICC-01/09-02/11 http://www.icc-cpi.int/iccdocs/doc/doc1314543.pdf (Decision on the Confirmation of Charges Pursuant to Article 61(7) (a) and (b) of the Rome Statute). The Prosecutor charged Muthaura and others with crimes against humanity of murder, deportation or forcible transfer, rape and other forms of sexual violence, other inhumane acts and persecution. Muthaura and Kenyatta were charged as indirect co-perpetrators pursuant to Article 25(3)(a) of the Rome Statute while Ali was charged as having contributed to the alleged crimes.

[109]Bekou and Shah (2006).

[110]See Amnesty International (2012a, b) (Noting that of the 111 state parties to the Rome Statute in 2010 only 33 states have enacted both complementarity and cooperation legislations); National Implementing Legislation Database University of Nottingham Human Rights Law Centre. Available at http://www.nottingham.ac.uk/hrlc/newsholding/news2009/nationalimplementinglegislationdatabaselaunchedoniccwebsite.aspx (Assessed 5 April 2013).

## 3.3 Complementarity Legislation

Complementarity legislation is the legislation required at the domestic level which should incorporate the Rome Statute's substantive crimes, their definitions, elements and the penalties attached thereto. It is anticipated that this would provide a legal basis for states to prosecute international crimes as such. This is important because intentions to prosecute international crimes on the basis of ordinary crimes such as murder, rape and theft without the international classification, could imply that the state is not equipped to prosecute international crimes.[111] In order to ensure that states are willing and genuinely able to prosecute international crimes as such, it is argued in this section that complementarity legislation is imperative. The section further contains an examination of the different methods by which the Rome Statute crimes may be reflected in domestic criminal law.

The justification for complementarity legislation has been discussed in the first part of this chapter. In addition, it is submitted that the argument is founded on the principle that criminal law must be written prospectively, as clarity and non-retroactivity are key components of the principle of legality, *nullum crimen sine lege* (no crime without law).[112] The principle of legality promotes a legal system's legitimacy by limiting the interventions of its criminal process to those clearly prescribed in advance by law.[113] Therefore, complementarity legislation gives states the opportunity to proscribe in advance the crimes in the Rome Statute within their domestic criminal laws. This would avoid a potential challenge to the exercise of jurisdiction on the grounds that the crimes were not known to domestic law. The Rome Statute does not allow retroactivity of criminal law,[114] and it is argued that states should conform to the same standard in view of the nature and gravity of the crimes concerned, as well as in keeping with this fundamental principle of criminal law.

Furthermore, the crimes listed in the Rome Statute have been recognised as having attained the status of *jus cogens*.[115] The *jus cogens* nature of the crimes imposes a duty on all states, irrespective of their ratification,.to ensure that they are

[111]See arguments on the *Saif Al-Islam* case (notes 24–40), Turns (2004); Kleffner (2003).

[112]Broomhall (2010), p. 26. (the *nullum crimen sine lege* principle is recognised under Art 22 of the Rome Statute).

[113]Ibid.

[114]See Rome Statute; art 11 on the temporal jurisdiction of the ICC (Stating that the ICC has jurisdiction only with respect to crimes committed after the coming into force of the Rome Statute).

[115]*Jus cogens* is the body of 'peremptory norm of general international law... from which no derogation is permitted and which can be modified only by a subsequent norm of general international law having the same character' (See art 53 Vienna Convention on the Law of Treaties 23 May 1969 1155 UNTS 331).

proscribed under domestic law.[116] Thus, the principle *aut dedere aut judicare* (duty to extradite or prosecute), considered not just as a rule of customary international law,[117] but also of *jus cogens*[118] means that states are obliged to either extradite or prosecute perpetrators of international crimes. The focus of complementarity is, however, on the latter.

The duty to prosecute international crimes under the Rome Statute entails a twofold requirement of national preparedness. First, states are expected to develop the legislative competence to prosecute core international crimes in their courts. This includes ensuring that there are provisions in the national criminal law explicitly criminalising genocide, crimes against humanity and war crimes.[119] Without such crimes in national criminal law, it may not be possible to bring cases with the proper international legal classification.[120] This may force prosecutors and judges to fall back on ordinary crimes which may not be adequate for the severity of international crimes.[121] Second, states should have the institutional capacity to investigate and prosecute international crimes domestically. Thus, states are expected to ensure that some members of the criminal justice system develop expertise in this area through suitable capacity building measures, including training and access to specialised electronic resources.[122]

Complementarity legislation is achieved through the process of incorporating core international crimes into national criminal law, thereby ensuring that crimes of such magnitude are proscribed by domestic law. To this end, there are different methods a state may adopt. They include; the minimalist, the express criminalisation approaches and the hybrid method. The next subsection discusses these methods in detail because it is in states' interest to integrate the Rome Statute crimes into their domestic criminal law.

### 3.3.1 The Minimalist Approach

The minimalist approach is a method by which states apply military or ordinary civilian criminal law, already in force and relying on domestic crimes, such as

---

[116] Bassiouni (2013), pp. 137–140; Broomhall (2010), pp. 41–42. See also the Trial Chamber of the ICTY in *Prosecutor v. Anto Furundzija* Case No: IT-95-17/1-T Judgment of 10 December 1998 paras 153–157 (Noting for example that torture is derived from the force of *jus cogens*).

[117] Bassiouni, 487–499. See also Radosavljevic (2007), pp. 96–114.

[118] Broomhall (2010), p. 41; ICJ's decision of 20 July 2012 (n 11) paras 71–75 & 99.

[119] Bergsmo et al. (2007) Forum for International Criminal Justice and Conflict (FICJC) International Peace Research Institute, Oslo (PRIO) http://www.prio.no/ficjc (hereinafter Bergsmo *et al* 'Importing Core International Crimes').

[120] See submission in the *Saif Al-Islam* case (section on 'Rationale for Implementing Legislation').

[121] Ibid.

[122] Bergsmo et al. (2007).

murder, theft and rape, which are closely related to the conduct in question.[123] In this approach, the domestic criminal law does not integrate international crimes but merely applies its categorisations to the conduct. Libya relied on this approach in its admissibility challenge, as analysed in the first section, and the result was a decision by the PTCI that Libya was unable to investigate and prosecute Saif Al-Islam Gaddafi.

Similarly, in April 2009, the Peruvian Supreme Court sentenced former President Alberto Fujimori for murder, serious bodily harm and kidnapping. The court recognised that the acts he was accused of committing could have fallen under the international definition of crimes against humanity but it could only sentence him for the ordinary crime of murder, because crimes against humanity was not known to Peruvian domestic criminal law at the time.[124]

This method is advocated by the so-called dualist states, i.e. those whose constitutions or domestic laws do not allow direct application of international law. Denmark, for example, applies a combination of regular criminal law provisions for substantive crimes, such as murder or torture, and a harsher sentencing regime to take into account the international character of the crimes.[125] However, a harsher sentencing regime may only reflect the seriousness of the crime under consideration; it does not reflect the scale, manner and pattern of the atrocity committed. Moreover, the stigma attached to a longer sentence for murder is not the same as a similar or even shorter sentence for an international crime.[126] Therefore a major criticism of this approach is that the crimes and their requirements together with the penalty conform only minimally to international standards. Consequently, the minimalist approach may not serve the best interests of states as it does not provide the opportunity to import international crimes into their domestic criminal law.

### 3.3.2 The Express Criminalisation Approach

A second method is that international crimes may be the subject of express criminalisation in domestic law, which involves specific incorporation through a general and open-ended reference to the Rome Statute. Two types of express criminalisation are considered here; the static or literal transcription approach and the dynamic criminalisation approach.

The static approach involves a transcription of the international crimes into domestic law in such a way that it repeats the definitions of genocide, crimes

---

[123] Sluiter (2010), pp. 459, 474. (Sluiter, Appearance of Witnesses).

[124] Corte Suprema de Justicia de la Republica, *Alberto Fujimori Fujimori* 7 April 2009 Exp No. A. V.19-2001 cited by Sluiter (2010), p. 475.

[125] See Bergsmo et al. (2007).

[126] Rikhof (2009), pp. 1–51.

against humanity and war crimes as set out in Articles 6, 7 and 8 of the Rome Statute.[127] The legislation uses identical wordings to those of the Rome Statute and sets out the penalties applicable to the crimes in question.[128] The United Kingdom,[129] Malta, Jordan,[130] and South Africa,[131] amongst others, have adopted this method in enacting complementarity legislation.

The static transcription approach accords with the principle of legality because it sets out clearly and predictably which conduct is considered an international crime and what punishment is envisaged thereto.[132] It also facilitates the task of those responsible for applying the law. By using the exact words of the Statute in domestic legislation, guidance with respect to the essential elements of international crimes as contained in the Rome Statute is provided. The disadvantage, however, is that it may not take into account new developments in international criminal law.[133] Therefore amendments would have to be made to reflect new developments.

A variation on the static transcription method is where states do not reproduce the text of the three articles of the Rome Statute but only make reference to them. This can be found in the legislation of New Zealand,[134] Uganda and Kenya.[135] Another variant on the approach can be found in Australia, where in importing core international crimes, it is not only the text of the three articles of the Rome Statute that is reproduced but also the full details set out in the ICC Elements of Crime document.[136]

On the other hand, the dynamic criminalisation approach is one in which the conduct criminalised in the Rome Statute is reformulated, rephrased and redrafted either to provide a better connection to existing criminal provisions in the domestic

---

[127]Bekou and Shah (2006), p. 508.

[128]Bergsmo et al. (2007).

[129]Cryer and Bekou (2007), pp. 441–459; Turns (2004), pp. 337–342.

[130]Malta and Jordan ratified the Rome statute in 2002. The International Criminal Court Act (Cap 452 Act XXIV of 2002) of Malta specifically defines international crimes in the exact terms of the Rome Statute. Available at http://www.iccwomen.org/whatwedo/projects/docs/Overview_Implementing_Legislation.pdf.

[131]Du Plessis (2007), pp. 460–479.

[132]Sluiter (2010).

[133]Sluiter (2010), p. 476.

[134]New Zealand, the International Crimes and International Criminal Court (Amendment) Act 2002. Articles 9, 10 and 11 define international crimes by reference to the Rome Statute.

[135]Uganda and Kenya ratified the Rome Statute 2002 and 2005 respectively. The International Criminal Court Bill 2005 of Uganda makes reference to the Rome Statute and the International Crimes Act 2008 of Kenya also defines international crimes by reference to the Rome Statute.

[136]Australia, the International Criminal Court Act (Consequential Amendment) 202, No 42 (2002) section 268.4 broadens the definition of genocide to include sexual violence. See http://www.iccwomen.org/whatwedo/projects/docs/Overview_Implementing_Legislation.pdf; Argentina, Law No. 26/200 on the Implementation of the ICC Statute (2007); Samoa, International Criminal Court Act 2007; Burundi Law No. 1/004, 08 May 2003; UK, International Criminal Court Act 2001; Trinidad and Tobago, International criminal Court Act 2006.

legislation or to clarify some of the Rome Statute concepts.[137] Such clarifications are especially used in instances where the definition of crimes under the Statute appears imprecise as a result of the incorporation of existing notions of customary international law. While the dynamic criminalisation approach may enable the legislator to complement the definitions of the Rome Statute in consideration of the lists and wordings of crimes in related international instruments,[138] it may also prove a major task for legislators and entail an extensive review of domestic criminal law.

Another approach categorised as an express criminalisation method could be termed a hybrid of the static and dynamic criminalisation. The hybrid approach combines both methods in order to facilitate the transcription of certain international crimes, with a generic or residual clause covering other grave violations of international humanitarian law or treaties to which the state is party.[139] Reforms in Finish criminal law may be considered a mixed or hybrid approach, as it is one in which some international crimes are expressly defined,[140] whereas others are incorporated through an open-ended reference to Finland's international obligations. This takes the form of an express prohibition of any acts which 'otherwise violate the provisions of an international agreement on warfare binding upon Finland or the generally acknowledged and established rules and customs of war under public international law.'[141]

From the above analysis of the different methods, it appears that the most straightforward approach compatible with the Rome Statute is the express (static) criminalisation method. This is because it repeats the Rome Statute crimes both in their definitions and penalties. However, whatever method is adopted, it is imperative that states are rightly positioned to benefit from the complementarity regime and to enable their domestic courts to assert jurisdiction accordingly.

This section has analysed the different approaches that states have taken or may take to incorporate international crimes into their domestic criminal codes. Having discussed the importance of implementing legislation, it is imperative to now examine how African states have incorporated international crimes into their national criminal law. The significance of this lies in the fact that, as noted earlier, all situations and cases, save Georgia, before the ICC to date have come from the African region, and most of them were referred by the respective states. It may be

---

[137] Sluiter, Appearances of Witnesses, 476.

[138] Examples of other related instruments are the Four Geneva Conventions of 1949 and their Additional Protocols I & II of 1977, the United Nations Convention on the Prevention and Punishment of the Crime of Genocide 1948, the Convention Against Torture 1984.

[139] See Bergsmo et al. (2007).

[140] An Act on the Implementation of the Provisions of a Legislative Nature of the Rome Statute of the International Criminal Court and on the Application of the Statute. No 1284/2000 Issued in Helsinki 28 December 2000. Available at http://www.finlex.fi/en/laki/kaannokset/2000/en20001284.pdf (the Finnish Criminal Code contains a Chapter 13 on war crimes and crimes against humanity).

[141] Ibid.

logical to conclude that the reason for this is both a lack of understanding of the implications of complementarity on the part of the states, and the lack of will and ability.

In addition, and as has been noted earlier the starting point for establishing willingness and ability is enacting implementing legislation. Therefore, for African states to demonstrate the willingness and the ability to investigate and prosecute international crimes domestically, it is proposed that the adoption of implementing legislation is important. The next section examines how South Africa enacted its implementing legislation.

## 3.4 States' Implementing Legislation

With a special focus on the implementation of the Rome Statute in national jurisdictions, some scholars have done detailed research on the need for implementing legislation and on how states have imported the core crimes in the Rome Statute into their domestic criminal law.[142] As a consequence, states from both the common law and civil law traditions have enacted implementing legislation using different approaches.[143]

According to Amnesty International, as of 2010, a total of 33 states have adopted implementing legislation.[144] For the purposes of analysis in this book, the procedure adopted by the United Kingdom appears to be the most appropriate approach and is in line with complementarity because the United Kingdom adopted its implementing legislation before it submitted its instrument of ratification.[145] While this approach is not strictly required under the Rome Statute, it is submitted that complementarity imposes an implied duty on states to look into their laws, revise them accordingly and enact implementing legislation to define how it would implement the Rome Statute before the coming into force of the Statute.

However, since the focus of this book is on African states, this section will examine how South Africa enacted its implementing legislation because South Africa is the only African state that adopted implementing legislation well

[142]See for example Kai Ambos and Ignaz Stegmiller, 'Prosecuting International Crimes at the International Criminal Court: Is there a Coherent and Comprehensive Prosecution Strategy?' (2012) *Crime Law Soc Change Springer link*; 'Ambos and Stegmiller (2008), pp. 181–198; Du Plessis and Ford (2008); Kress et al. (2005); Bekou and Shah (2006); Turns (2004); Cryer et al. (2010).

[143]See Implementation Report Card and the National Implementing Legislation Data Base (2012b).

[144]Amnesty International (2012).

[145]The UK International Criminal Court Act 2001, 2001 Ch 17 was passed on 24 September 2001. UK's instrument of ratification was deposited on 4 October 2001 after the implementing legislation had been passed. The UK ICC Act entered into force on 17 December 2001.

in advance.[146] It is important to note however, that subsequently, other African states, namely; Kenya,[147] Senegal and Uganda,[148] enacted implementing legislation. Consequently, references will also be made to the implementing legislation of Kenya and Uganda.

### *3.4.1 Procedures for South Africa's Implementing Legislation*

South Africa enacted its International Criminal Court Act No 27 of 2002 in July 2002.[149] The Act came into force in August 2002, barely a month after the entering into force of the Rome Statute itself. This reflected an understanding of South Africa's obligations under the complementarity regime of the Rome Statute and signalled a deep commitment to its implementation domestically. South Africa signed the Rome Statute on 17 July 1998 and deposited its instrument of ratification on 27 November 2000. The South African Parliament passed its implementing legislation on 18 July 2002.

In contrast, Kenya's International Crimes Act was passed in 2008 even though it had ratified the Rome Statute in 2005.[150] Kenya's ICC Act entered into force on 1 January 2009, approximately two years after the Chief Prosecutor's investigations into its 2007 post-election violence had resulted in six of its nationals standing trial before the ICC. Similarly, Uganda's ICC Act came into force in June 2010,[151] over 5 years after Uganda referred situations in its territory to the ICC and irrespective of the fact that Uganda had signed and ratified the Rome Statute in 1999 and 2002, respectively. Arguably, adopting implementing legislation 8 years after its ratification was only in a bid to secure the hosting of the First Review Conference of the Rome Statute, which was held in Kampala, Uganda in May and June of the same

[146]Bekou and Shah (2006), p. 501. (Lamenting the slow pace at which African states have adopted implementing legislations, Bekou and Shah noted that despite the many ratifications, only South Africa has enacted specific legislation regarding the ICC. See also Du Plessis and Ford (2008), pp. 3–4.

[147]See Kenya International Crimes Act 2008 (n 10).

[148]The International Criminal Court Act 2010 Act 11 (Act Supplement No 6 Act to the Uganda Gazette No 39 Vol CIII) 25 June 2010. Available at http://www.issafrica.org/anicj/uploads/Uganda_ICC_Act_2010.pdf (Accessed 30 June 2013).

[149]See South Africa ICC Act (above n 9).

[150]Kenya signed and ratified the Rome Statute on 11 August 1999 and 15 March 2005 respectively. See CICC at http://www.iccnow.org/?mod=country&iduct=89 (Accessed 30 June 2013).

[151]See the Ugandan ICC Act 2010 (n 148).

year.[152] It is for these reasons that the implementing legislation adopted by both Kenya and Uganda is regarded as late; i.e. coming only after cases involving their nationals were already before the ICC, and hence South Africa is used as a model.

Chapter 1 of the South African ICC Act states that the general objectives are to create a framework to ensure that the Statute is effectively implemented in South Africa, to ensure that the Act conforms with the obligations of South Africa under the Statute, to proscribe the crimes in the Rome Statute in South Africa and to enable South African courts to assume jurisdiction to investigate and prosecute the crimes.[153] Other aims include ensuring that South Africa cooperates with the ICC. The passing of the South African ICC Act has been described as momentous as it was the first implementing legislation by an African state.[154]

Prior to the adoption of the South African ICC Act, South Africa had no legislation on war crimes or crimes against humanity. Therefore no domestic prosecution of international crimes was contemplated in South Africa. Although customary international law forms part of South African law,[155] South African courts could not prosecute international crimes because of the *nullum crimen sine lege* (no law no crime) maxim.[156] Similarly, South Africa had not incorporated the Geneva Conventions of 1949 into its domestic criminal law and so it could not prosecute or punish grave breaches.[157]

The gap in South African law also exists in most states of Africa, as international crimes are not generally known to domestic legal codes. Clearly, it is important to examine how South Africa adopted its implementing legislation and to recommend that all African states, should follow the example. This is because the mutually inclusive and proactive complementarity model proposed in the previous chapter obliges states to engage in national construction and capacity building in preparation to assume primary jurisdiction if and when the need arises.

---

[152]The First Review Conference of the Rome Statute of the International Criminal Court was held in Kampala Uganda 31 May to 11 June 2010. (Arguably, it was important that the host country for such a review should not only have been the first state to activate the jurisdiction of the ICC but must demonstrate its willingness and ability to investigate and prosecute international crimes and cooperate with the ICC by adopting its implementing legislation).

[153]South African ICC Act, Chapter 1 sections 1–3.

[154]Du Plessis (2013).

[155]See section 232 of the Constitution of the Republic of South Africa 1996 (Act No 108 1996) adopted 8 May 1996 as amended by Notice No 78 in Government Gazette No 33899 of 24 December 2010. Available at http://www.info.gov.za/documents/constitution/1996/a108-96.pdf ('customary international law is law in the Republic unless it is inconsistent with the Constitution or an Act of Parliament').

[156]John Dugard, *International Law: A South African Perspective* (2nd edn 2000) 142.

[157]Ibid.

### 3.4.2 South Africa's Complementarity Legislation

South Africa has employed the static criminalisation method, meaning that the Rome Statute crimes have been expressly adopted into its law. Recognising its complementarity obligations, the South African ICC Act provides a framework to ensure the effective implementation of the Rome Statute in South Africa and to ensure that South African courts are able to prosecute persons accused of having committed those crimes.[158]

The South African ICC Act incorporates the Rome Statute definitions of the crimes of genocide, war crimes and crimes against humanity directly into South African law according to a schedule appended to the Act.[159] In this regard, Part 1 of Schedule 1 took the exact wording of Article 6 of the Rome Statute in relation to genocide, Part 2 of the Schedule mirrors Article 7 of the Statute with respect to crimes against humanity and Part 3 does the same for war crimes, as set out in Article 8 of the Rome Statute.[160]

Clearly the objective of criminalising the Rome Statute crimes domestically was met by the South African ICC Act, particularly as Section 4(1) of the Act provides that, notwithstanding anything to the contrary in any other law in South Africa, any person who allegedly commits these crimes shall be prosecuted.[161] Conversely, the Kenyan and Ugandan ICC Acts merely made references to the Statute's definitions of the crimes in their implementing legislation, without expressly using the exact wording of the Statute.[162]

The South African ICC Act did not only import the exact wordings of the Rome Statute in the definition of crimes, but it also made some amendments to its existing laws to bring them into conformity with other provisions of the Statute.[163] In this regard, section 18 of the Criminal Procedure Act of 1977 was amended by adding a paragraph (g) to include international crimes as defined in the Act.[164] Similarly, section 3 of the Military Disciplinary Supplementary Measures Act of 1999 was amended by adding a subsection (3) to expand the scope of jurisdiction to include military officials who may be perpetrators of international crimes.[165]

[158] South African ICC Act, para 1 of the preamble.

[159] Stone (2011), pp. 305–330, 310. See also Du Plessis (2008), p. 157.

[160] Du Plessis (2007), p. 463.

[161] South African ICC Act, section 4(1).

[162] See section 6 of the Kenya International Crimes Act and sections 7, 8 and 9 of the Ugandan ICC Act which made references to genocide, crimes against humanity and war crimes as defined in the Rome Statute.

[163] South African ICC Act, Schedule 2 relating to South African Laws Amended as a consequence of the Act.

[164] See Criminal Procedure Act of the Republic of South Africa, Act 51 of 1977, section 18(g) as amended.

[165] See Military Discipline Supplementary Measures Act of the Republic of South Africa, Act 16 of 1999, section 3(3) as amended.

By expressly criminalising the Rome Statute crimes domestically and amending existing laws, South Africa is not likely to fall into the dilemma of being found unable or unwilling to carry out domestic prosecution of such crimes should the situation arise. Arguably, the likelihood of being denied an admissibility challenge before the ICC as Libya was, as analysed above, would be almost non-existent. The reason is not far-fetched. The international categorisation of the crimes would allow South Africa to pass the 'same person same conduct' test, as its investigation would further meet the 'specificity and probative value' requirement of the PTCI in the *Saif Al-Islam* case.

In addition, the South African ICC Act expressly provides procedures for the institution of domestic prosecutions in South African courts.[166] First, the Act requires that the consent of the National Director of Public Prosecution (NDPP) be obtained before any prosecution may be initiated against any person accused of the crimes.[167] In reaching a decision whether to authorise a prosecution or not, the NDPP is guided by South Africa's primary obligation under complementarity to institute prosecution domestically.[168] South Africa's responsibility to prosecute is further emphasised by the fact that the NDPP is allowed to decline to authorise a prosecution only if the crimes were committed before the ICC Act entered into force.[169] The South African implementing legislation also provides for the designation of 'an appropriate High Court in which to conduct prosecution' of alleged perpetrators.[170]

Theoretically, the obligation and power to prosecute given under the South African ICC Act is not hindered by any considerations of immunity. In this regard, section 4(2)(a) of the South African ICC Act provides that, notwithstanding any other law to the contrary, including customary and conventional international law, the fact that a person is or was a head of state or government, a member of a government or parliament, an elected representative or a government official is neither (1) a defence for a crime, nor (2) a ground for any possible sentence reduction once the person has been convicted of a crime.[171]

Consequently, Du Plessis asserts that in terms of the Act, South African courts acting under complementarity are thus accorded the same power to 'trump' the immunity afforded to government officials in the same way as the ICC is by virtue of Article 27 of the Rome Statute.[172] In agreement, Dugard and Abraham noted that 'section 4(2)(a) of the South African ICC Act represents a wise choice by the South African legislature...'[173]

---

[166] South African ICC Act, section 5.

[167] Ibid, section 5(1).

[168] Ibid, section 5(3).

[169] Ibid, section 5(2).

[170] Ibid, sections 5(4) and 5(5).

[171] Ibid Section 4(2)(a)(i)&(ii).

[172] Du Plessis (2007), p. 474.

[173] See Dugard and Abraham (2002), p. 140, 166 cited in Du Plessis, Ibid.

Section 27 of Kenya's Act appears to have removed immunity but made the provisions subject to sections 62 and 115.[174] Sections 62 and 115 of the Kenyan Act relate to Article 98 of the Rome Statute, which provides for respect for bilateral immunity agreements between states. Consequently, the exact extent of the removal of immunity stipulated in section 27 in the Kenya International Crimes Act is unclear. However, Article 143(4) of Kenya's Constitution removes immunity for the President regarding international crimes.[175] By virtue of section 2(4), the Constitution is the supreme law of the land and it prevails over any other law that is inconsistent with its provisions.[176] Therefore like South Africa, immunity is not a hindrance to Kenya's implementing legislation.

Unlike the legislation of Kenya and South Africa, which explicitly remove immunity in line with the Rome Statute, the Uganda ICC Act seems to retain immunity.[177] Although section 25 of the Uganda ICC Act provides that the existence of any immunity is not a bar,[178] Article 98(4) of the Constitution provides for immunity for the President.[179] This position remains unchanged even though the Ugandan Constitution has undergone several amendments.[180] By virtue of the supremacy of the Ugandan Constitution over any other law,[181] the purported removal of immunity in its implementing legislation appears cosmetic.

### *3.4.3 South Africa's Cooperation Legislation*

The ICC lacks mechanisms to gain custody of suspects and ensure their attendance at proceedings taking place in The Hague. Since this is crucial, as the ICC cannot prosecute in *absentia*, the South African implementing legislation includes a broad cooperation regime by which certain government officials are empowered to

174 See section 27(1) & (2) Kenya International Crimes Act. See also Ford (2008), pp. 70–71 (Noting that there is a strong reluctance among the MPs in Kenya to implement a law removing immunities from state officials).

175 See section 143(4) Constitution of the Federal Republic of Kenya 2010 Available at http://kenyahighcommission.ca/wp-content/uploads/2013/04/constitution-of-kenya-2010.pdf (the subsection provides that the immunity of the President shall not extend to a crime for which the President may be prosecuted under any treaty to which Kenya is party and which prohibits such immunity).

176 Constitution of Kenya 2010, section 2(4).

177 See section 19 Ugandan ICC Act which provides for the general principles of criminal law but omits provisions relating to immunity).

178 See section 25 Ugandan ICC Act 2010.

179 See Article 98(4) of the Constitution of the Republic of Uganda 1995. Available at http://www.ugandalawlibrary.com/ull/files/constitution/constitution_1995.pdf (Accessed 30 June 2013). See also Afako (2008), pp. 93, 112.

180 See Uganda Constitution Amendment Act 2005 and Constitution Amendment (No 2) Act 2005.

181 See Constitution of Ugandan 1995, Article 2(2).

facilitate cooperation between South Africa and the ICC.[182] The Act stipulates how the South African government is to execute arrest warrants issued by the ICC under existing South African law.[183] However, the South African ICC Act does not rely on its existing law alone to ensure the execution of arrest warrants and surrender, but it further provides a detailed procedure which specifies the particular office and department that is responsible to ensure cooperation with the ICC.

Consequently, the office of the Director-General of Justice and Constitutional Development is tasked with dealing with such issues as regards the arrest and surrender of suspects to the ICC.[184] The Director General is responsible for forwarding the warrant to a magistrate who must endorse the ICC's arrest warrant for execution in any part of the Republic.[185] When an arrest has been executed pursuant to an ICC arrest warrant, the suspect is taken to the magistrate in whose jurisdiction the suspect has been arrested or detained.[186]

In line with due process guarantees and safeguards of the rights of the suspect, the South African Act provides that such suspect must be brought before the magistrate within 48 hours of their arrest.[187] Further safeguards of the rights of the suspect are provided for in section 10 of the ICC Act. This section mandates that the presiding magistrate ensures that the warrant relates to the suspect,[188] that the suspect has been arrested in accordance with the procedures outlined in the ICC Act[189] and that the rights of the suspect have been respected.[190] It is argued that with these procedures properly outlined in the South African ICC Act, actual cooperation between South Africa and the ICC will be enhanced in practice.

In addition, when the South African authorities have taken a suspect into custody, the country is then in a position to surrender the suspect to the ICC. The procedure for the surrender of a suspect, which includes a committal order, is outlined in the ICC Act.[191] The magistrate is mandated to ensure that the suspect is the same as named in the warrant and that the process is carried out in accordance with the provisions of the Act.

The procedure makes clear that surrender to the ICC is different from extradition proceedings. First, there is no condition of double criminality and second, there is no requirement that a *prima facie* case be made against the suspect.[192] The Act further provides that the magistrate must be satisfied that the three requirements in

---

[182]South Africa ICC Act, section 8.

[183]South African ICC Act, section 9(3).

[184]South African ICC Act, section 8(1).

[185]Ibid, section 8(2).

[186]Ibid, section 10.

[187]Ibid, section 10(1).

[188]Ibid, section 10(1)(a).

[189]Ibid, section 10(1)(b).

[190]Ibid, section 10(1)(c).

[191]Ibid, sections 10–13.

[192]Du Plessis (2007) 468.

section 10(1)(a), (b) and (c) are met before the issuance of an order committing the suspect to prison pending their surrender to the ICC.[193]

It is important to note however, that the South African ICC Act is not a perfect example of implementing legislation because it does not contain provisions relating to Article 9 of the Rome Statute on the Elements of Crimes.[194] In this regard, however, Du Plessis argues that there is nothing which prevents a South African court from referring to the Elements of Crimes when involved in a domestic prosecution.[195] This argument appears valid because ratification of the Statute by a state constitutes acceptance of the Rules of Procedure and Evidence (RPE) together with the Elements of Crimes.[196]

The South African Act does not also reflect Part 3 (Articles 22–33) of the Rome Statute which specifies the general principles of criminal law. Du Plessis further maintains that the general principles of criminal law will find application in any domestic trial under the ICC Act.[197] While this may be true, it is submitted that the absence of these provisions may be prejudicial to South Africa's domestic prosecution based on complementarity, as due process considerations are necessary for determining the admissibility of cases before the ICC under Article 17 of the Rome Statute.

Notwithstanding this apparent omission, the South African ICC Act remains an example for African States. Not only did the Act incorporate the Rome Statute crimes expressly, it also grants jurisdiction to South African courts on the basis of the crimes. It also contains elaborate cooperation regime which would ensure the effective functioning of the ICC. Arguably, with its implementing legislation adopted in advance, South Africa's willingness and genuine ability to exercise jurisdiction is not in doubt. This contrasts sharply with the implementing legislation of Kenya and Uganda, which were adopted only after cases involving their nationals were already brought before the ICC.

## 3.5 Conclusion

This chapter focused primarily on the legislative implications for states parties to the Rome Statute. Although not expressly required by the Statute, several arguments have been advanced in favour of the need for states to adopt implementing

[193]South Africa ICC Act, section 10(5).

[194]Elements of Crimes, adopted by the Assembly of States Parties in New York, on 9 September 2002 and entered into force on the same date (ICC-ASP/1/3) (the Elements of Crimes were adopted in order to assist the Court in interpreting and applying Articles 6, 7 and 8 of the Rome Statute; Available at http://www.icc-cpi.int/NR/rdonlyres/9CAEE830-38CF-41D6-AB0B-68E5F9082543/0/Element_of_Crimes_English.pdf.

[195]Du Plessis (2007), p. 464.

[196]Rome Statute, Article 51.

[197]Du Plessis, Ibid.

legislation. First, embedded in complementarity is the notion that measures must be taken by individual states to prosecute international crimes domestically on behalf of the international community. Second, there must be mechanisms in place at the national level to arrest and surrender to the ICC suspects that it seeks to prosecute and who happen to be in a particular state's jurisdiction. These procedures are critical to the effective functioning of the ICC and to the implementation of complementarity.

In addition, the critical analysis of the PTCI decision of 31 May 2013 regarding the Libyan admissibility challenge in the *Saif Al-Islam Gaddafi* case reveals that implementing legislation is imperative for states to assert their criminal jurisdiction. Although the PTCI admitted that Libya could investigate and prosecute *Saif Al-Islam* based on its domestic criminal law, the conclusion reached by the Chamber was different. Thus, implicit in the Chamber's reasoning was the underlying inability based on the failure of Libya to pass the 'same conduct' limb of the 'same person same conduct' test, which Libya could have passed had it applied the international categorisation of the crimes. However, Libya, not being a party to the Rome Statute, did not have any implementing legislation and the crimes against humanity of murder and persecution were not known to its domestic Law.

Based on the premise that complementarity commits states to investigate and prosecute international crimes domestically, it was further argued that although not expressly stated in the Statute, it could be implied that adopting implementing legislation is a necessary step for states to fulfil their obligations. The combined effect of the dominant themes, complementarity and cooperation, which run through the Statute, means that states parties are meant to do much more than mere ratification.

Certainly, ratification of the Rome Statute clearly demonstrates a state's abhorrence of the crimes contained therein and its commitment to joining the international community's efforts to combat impunity.[198] African states' efforts in this regard are indisputable. This is reflected in the number of ratifications and self-referrals to the ICC. It is submitted however, that mere ratification cannot drive the complementarity regime of the Rome Statute. Nor is it the objective of the Statute that all cases and situations be referred to the ICC. In fact, it is submitted that self-referrals, if continued, could arguably defeat the object and purpose of the Statute, which focuses on state authorities as the primary mechanism to ensure accountability. The purpose of the ICC is only to fill in the gaps where and when necessary.

Consequently, in order for the ICC to truly function as a 'complement', it is submitted that African states should adopt the two prong components of the complementarity regime, namely; cooperation and complementarity legislation. As observed, African states' rapid ratification of the Rome Statute has not been matched with corresponding legislative action. Whilst the absence of implementing legislation may not be the only reasons for the inability of African states to investigate and prosecute international crimes domestically, adopting the

[198] Robinson (2002) in Cassese *et al* (n 22) 1849, 1867.

legislation is an appropriate starting point which would demonstrate both the willingness and the ability to act. As a mechanism designed by states and to be operated by states, complementarity can benefit African states when states of the continent integrate the Rome Statute crimes into their domestic criminal law.

Admittedly, there are significant challenges faced by African states in adopting complementarity and cooperation legislation. These include; the time involved in the process of integrating the crimes, the difficulty in accessing experts in the field, not taking the issue as a priority and the lack of political will.[199] Other challenges are corruption and the desire to preserve perpetuity in power by some African leaders. In view of these challenges, the express criminalisation approach has been advocated.

It is important to note that a few African states are involved in domestic prosecution of conduct that may qualify as crimes against humanity, whether as ordinary domestic crimes or as international crimes. This raises the question of whether national prosecution of ordinary domestic crimes instead of their international classification accords with the complementarity regime of the Rome Statute. In other words, could on-going prosecutions in some African states be categorised as realising the complementarity regime? The next chapter examines this question in light of the domestic prosecutions in Kenya, the DRC, Uganda and Sudan.

## References

Afako B (2008) Country study V: Uganda. In: du Plessis M, Ford J (eds) Unable or unwilling? Case studies on domestic implementation of the ICC Statute in selected African countries, ISS Monograph Series No 141, p 93

AI (2012) International Criminal Court: Rome Statute Implementation Report Card Part One. http://www.amnesty.org/fr/library/asset/IOR53/011/2010/fr/22fab440-cf1e-4ac2-a1ff-2a4ad9527b87/ior530112010en.pdf. Accessed 20 Dec 2012

Ambos K (2008) Prosecuting international crimes at the national and international level: between justice and real politik. CLF 19:181–198

Ambos K, Stegmiller I (2008) German research on international criminal law with a special focus on the implementation of the ICC Statute in national jurisdictions. CLF 19:181–198

Aranburu X (2013) Prosecuting the most responsible for the international crimes: dilemmas of definition and prosecutorial discretion. Available at http://s3.amazonaws.com/academia.edu.documents/30582797/100106_Xabier_AGIRRE_ARANBURU_Prosecuting_Most_Responsible.pdf?AWSAccessKeyId=AKIAJ56TQJRTWSMTNPEA&Expires=1389181216&Signature=7CteHoAGmmm9S6INTg07kQeo4ps%3D&response-content-disposition=inline. Accessed 6 Nov 2013

Arbia S (2009) No peace without justice: roundtable on implementing legislation, 17 July 2009, Rome, Italy. Available at http://www.icc-cpi.int/NR/rdonlyres/9EA855BC-A495-40AA-B5F8-92F44E08D695/280578/Statement_Registar2.pdf. Accessed 2 Mar 2013

Arbia S, Bassy G (2011) Proactive complementarity: a registrar's perspective and plans. In: Stahn C, ElZeidy M (eds) Complementarity from theory to practice. CUP, p 65

[199] Bekou and Shah (2006).

Bassiouni MC (2013) Introduction to international criminal law, 2nd edn. Martinus Nijhoff Publishers, Leiden

Bedont B, Matas D (1998) Negotiating for an international criminal court. Peace Magazine, Sept–Oct 1998, 21. Available at http://peacemagazine.org/archive/v14n5p21.htm. Accessed 11 Apr 2013

Bekou O (2011) In the hands of the state: implementing legislation and complementarity. In: Stahn C, ElZeidy M (eds) The international criminal court and complementarity: from theory to practice, vol 1. CUP, pp 830–852

Bekou O, Shah S (2006) Realising the potential of the international criminal court: the African experience. HRLR 6:499–544

Bergsmo M, Harlem M, Hayashi N (2007) Importing core international crimes into national criminal law. Forum for International Criminal Justice and Conflict (FICJC) International Peace Research Institute, Oslo (PRIO). http://www.prio.no/ficjc. Accessed 2 Feb 2009

Broomhall B (2010) International justice and the international criminal court: between sovereignty and the rule of law. Oxford Scholarship Online, p 26

Cassese et al (2002) Surrender and transfer under the statutes of the *ad hoc* international criminal tribunals for the former Yugoslavia and Rwanda. In: Cassese et al (eds) The Rome Statute of the international criminal court, vol 2. OUP, pp 1664–1684

Commonwealth Expert Group on Review of the Implementing Legislation for the Rome Statute' 23–25 February 2011 (Proposing a model law on the implementation of the Rome Statute by Commonwealth member states). Available at http://www.thecommonwealth.org/files/238381/FileName/LMM(11)17PICCStatuteandImplementationoftheGenevaConventions.pdf. Assessed 8 Apr 2013

Cryer R, Bekou O (2007) International crimes and ICC cooperation in England and Wales. JICJ 441–459

Cryer R, Friman H, Robinson D, Wilmshurst E (2010) An introduction to international criminal law and procedure, 2nd edn. CUP, p 509

Doherty K, McCormack T (1999) Complementarity as a catalyst for comprehensive domestic penal legislation. UC Davis J. Int'l L & Policy 5:147–180

Du Plessis M (2007) South Africa's implementation of the ICC Statute: an African example. JICJ 5:460–479

Du Plessis M (2008) Complementarity and Africa: the promises and problems of international criminal justice. ASR 17:157

Du Plessis M (2013) An African example: South Africa's implementation of the Rome Statute of the international criminal court. Available at http://www.issafrica.org/anicj/uploads/Du_Plessis_An_African_example.pdf. Accessed 28 June 2013

Du Plessis M, Ford J (2008) Unable or unwilling? Case studies on domestic implementation of the ICC Statute in selected African countries, ISS Monograph Series No 141, March 2008

Dugard J, Abraham G (2002) Public international law. Ann Surv South Afr Law 140:166

Ford J (2008) Country study III: Kenya. In: Du Plessis M, Ford J (eds) Unable or unwilling? Case studies on domestic implementation of the ICC Statute in selected African countries, ISS Monograph Series No 141 March 2008, pp 70–71

Gaeta P (2002) Official capacity and immunities. In: Cassese A, Gaeta P, Jones J (eds) The Rome Statute of the international criminal court. OUP, pp 975–1002

Gamarra Y, Vicente A (2008) United Nations' Member States' obligations towards the ICTY: arresting and transferring Lukic, Gotovina and Zelemenovic. ICLR 8:627

Garapon A (2012) What does complementarity commit us to? In: Tenth anniversary of the international criminal court: the challenges of complementarity. Politorbis Nr 54-2, 21

Gioia F (2011) Complementarity and reverse cooperation. In: Stahn C, ElZeidy M (eds) The international criminal court and complementarity: from theory to practice, vol 1. CUP, pp 807–828

Greppi E (2008) Inability to investigate and prosecute under article 17. In: Politi M, Gioia F (eds) The international criminal court and national jurisdictions. Ashgate, p 69

Harmon M, Gaynor F (2004) Prosecuting massive crimes with primitive tools: three difficulties encountered by prosecutors in international criminal proceedings. JICJ 2:403

International Centre for Criminal Law Reform and Criminal Justice Policy (ICCLR) (2012) Rights and Democracy, 'International Criminal Court Manual for the Ratification and Implementation of the Rome Statute'. Available at http://iccnow.org/documents/RightsDem&ICCLR_Manual_Eng.pdf. Accessed 10 July 2012

Katz A (2003) An act of transformation: the incorporation of the Rome Statute of the ICC into National Law in South Africa. ASR 12(4):25–30

Kleffner JK (2003) The impact of complementarity on national implementation of the substantive international criminal law. JICJ 1:86–113

Kress C, Broomhall B, Lattanzi F, Santori V (eds) (2005) The Rome Statute and domestic legal orders vol II: constitutional issues, cooperation and enforcement. Nomos Verlagsgesellschaft, Baden-Baden

Lattanzi F (2001) The international criminal court and national jurisdictions. In: Mauro Politi M, Nesi G (eds) The Rome Statute of the international criminal court: a challenge to impunity. Ashgate, pp 181–182

Mégret F (2011) Too much of a good thing? Implementation and the uses of complementarity. In: Stahn C, ElZeidy M (eds) The international criminal court and complementarity: from theory to practice, vol I. CUP, pp 361–390

Mochochoko P (1999) International cooperation and judicial assistance. In: Lee RS (ed) The international criminal court: the making of the Rome Statute. Issues. Negotiations. Results. Kluwer International Law, p 305

Nouwen S (2011) Complementarity in Uganda: domestic diversity or international imposition? In: Stahn C, ElZeidy M (eds) The international criminal court and complementarity: from theory to practice, vol 2. CUP, p 1127

Radosavljevic D (2007) An overview of the ICC complementarity regime. Rev. I L &P 3 (10):96–114

Rastan R (2008) Testing co-operation: the international criminal court and national authorities. LJIL 21(2):431–456

Rikhof J (2009) Fewer places to hide? The impact of domestic war crimes prosecutions on international impunity. CLF 20:1–51

Robinson D (2002) The Rome Statute and its impact on national law. In: Cassese A, Gaeta P, Jones J (eds) The Rome Statute of the international criminal court, vol 2. OUP, p 1849

Sluiter G (2002) International criminal adjudication and the collection of evidence: obligations of states. Antwerp

Sluiter G (2010) Appearance of witnesses and unavailability of subpoena powers for the court. In: Bellelli R (ed) International criminal justice: law and practice from the Rome Statute to its review. Ashgate, p 459

Stahn C (2008) Complementarity: a tale of two notions. CLF 19:87–113

Stone L (2011) Implementation of the Rome Statute of the international criminal court in South Africa. In: Murungu C, Biegon J (eds) Prosecuting international crimes in Africa. University of Pretoria Press, pp 305–330

Swart B (2002) Arrest and surrender. In: Cassese A, Gaeta P, Jones J (eds) The Rome Statute of the international criminal court, vol 2. OUP, pp 1639–1654

Triffterer O (2008) Preamble. In Otto T (ed) Commentary on the Rome Statute of the international criminal court: observers, notes article by article, 2nd edn. Nomos Oxford Hart, Baden-Baden, pp 1–16

Triponel A, Pearson S (2010) African states and the international criminal court: a silent revolution in international criminal law. J. L & Soc. Cha. 12:65–106

Turns D (2004) Aspects of national implementation of the Rome Statute: the United Kingdom and selected other states. In: McGoldrick D, Rowe P, Donnelly E (eds) The permanent international criminal court: legal and policy issues. Hart Publishing, Oxford, p 337

Yang L (2005) On the principle of complementarity in the Rome Statute of the international criminal court. Chi J Int'l L 4:121–132

# Chapter 4
# Domestic Prosecutions in Africa Under the Complementarity Regime of the Rome Statute: A Practical Approach

**Abstract** States have often criminalised conducts and have set up the criminal justice system at the domestic level to prevent the commission of crimes, as well as mechanisms to investigate, prosecute and punish any alleged criminal. However, these crimes are ordinary domestic crimes, which do not have the same definition, elements, impact and magnitude, as international crimes. The argument in this chapter is focused on the domestic prosecutions that are on-going in a few African states, namely, the DRC, Kenya, Uganda and Sudan, and to examine whether these prosecutions satisfy the requirement of complementarity. Granted that these prosecutions, may appear to close impunity gaps, it is argued that domestic prosecution of ordinary domestic crimes does not approximate complementarity-based prosecution because prosecuting on the basis of ordinary domestic crimes is not the same as prosecuting international crimes.

The ultimate aim of complementarity is for states to undertake the investigation and prosecution of international crimes domestically. This has begun in a few African states, namely: the Democratic Republic of the Congo (DRC), Uganda, Kenya and Sudan. The question of whether these prosecutions meet the requirements of complementarity under the Rome Statute is the focus of this chapter. It is argued that not all domestic prosecutions can be classified as realising the complementarity regime of the Rome Statute. This is because interpreting and applying complementarity as a mutually inclusive concept implies that adopting implementing legislation should precede any domestic prosecution based on complementarity.

Although not expressly mandated by the Rome Statute, cooperation and complementarity legislation are nevertheless necessary for states to implement the Rome Statute domestically. The purpose of such legislation is to ensure that domestic prosecutions are carried out in line with the provisions of the Rome Statute. Consequently, two types of domestic prosecutions and the difference between them are discussed in this chapter. The first type is domestic prosecutions ostensibly of international crimes but based on the ordinary domestic crimes of murder, theft and rape. The second is complementarity-based prosecution which is domestic prosecution carried out on the basis of international crimes categorised and defined as such.

Complementarity-based prosecution is preferable, as it arguably accords with the complementarity regime. This is due to the fact that international crimes are

 
O.C. Imoedemhe, *The Complementarity Regime of the International Criminal Court*, DOI 10.1007/978-3-319-46780-1_4

different from domestic crimes because they are more serious. Thus, it is argued that to treat international crimes as ordinary domestic crimes is to be unresponsive to the experience of mass criminality.[1] It also undermines the gravity and impact of international crimes and the entire complementarity regime of the Rome Statute.

This chapter is divided into three parts. The first part discusses domestic prosecutions in selected African states, namely: the DRC, Kenya, Sudan and Uganda. Domestic prosecutions in these states are discussed because they represent African states whose situations have been referred to the ICC either by self-referrals (DRC and Uganda),[2] Security Council referral (Sudan)[3] or the chief Prosecutor's *proprio motu* action (Kenya).[4] Consequently, they constitute four of the African states which are currently subject to ICC investigations and prosecutions. While some of these states have accepted the jurisdiction of the ICC, others have challenged it. The Sudanese government, for example, argued that it could not be deemed to be unwilling or unable to carry out domestic prosecutions since it had established a Special Criminal Court for the Event in Darfur (SCCED). Therefore, in line with the complementarity principle the ICC could not assert jurisdiction.[5]

Using the domestic prosecution in the United Kingdom as a model, the second part of this chapter discusses complementarity-based prosecution. The United Kingdom is used as a model for complementarity-based prosecution because though not mandated by the Rome Statute, the UK passed implementing legislation before its ratification of the Rome Statute in 2001. This is imperative because without implementing legislation in conformity with the Rome Statute domestic prosecution will inevitably be carried out based on ordinary crimes. The domestic prosecution that was carried out by the UK was thus based on the international categorisation of the crimes as recognised in the UK implementing laws, which flowed from the Rome Statute.

In the third part, the differences between the two types of prosecutions; domestic prosecution based on ordinary crimes and complementarity prosecution based on international crimes, are delineated. The crimes of genocide and crimes against humanity are analysed and it is observed that these crimes cannot be prosecuted as ordinary domestic crimes because they are different from the point of view of their definitions, elements, scale and overall impact. Although not a party to the Rome Statute, Rwanda is given as an example. The jurisdictional interaction between the International Criminal Tribunal for Rwanda (ICTR) and Rwandan national courts is

---

[1] Simpson (2007), pp. 340–355.

[2] The Situations in the DRC and Uganda were referred by the respective governments on 19 April 2004 and 29 January 2004 respectively. Available at http://www.icc-cpi.int/Menus/ICC/Situations+and+Cases/Situations/.

[3] By Security Council Resolution 1593 the situation in Darfur Sudan was referred to the ICC on 31 March 2005.

[4] The Chief Prosecutor's *proprio motu* action in the situation in Kenya was authorised by the Pre-Trial Chamber on 31 March 2010.

[5] Nouwen (2007). http://www.allacademic.com/meta/p178592_index.html. Accessed 12 January 2010.

cited because the transfer of cases from the former to the latter was only possible after the ICTR was convinced that Rwanda had passed legislation incorporating the crimes in the ICTR Statute into its domestic criminal law. It is argued that the transfer of cases is instructive to both the ICC and states in ensuring that domestic prosecution is in line with the complementarity regime.

The analysis in the chapter exposes the divergences of opinion amongst scholars on domestic prosecutions of international crimes and whether such prosecutions by states meet the standards of complementarity. It is argued that though attempts to prosecute domestically are being made by a few African states, these prosecutions may not be classified as complementarity-based prosecutions. The on-going debate regarding the domestic prosecution of international crimes is outlined first, in order to situate the argument within the context of the complementarity regime of the Rome Statute.

## 4.1 Domestic Prosecutions of International Crimes in Selected African States

The debate on the domestic prosecution of international crimes is on-going. Whilst some argue in its favour,[6] others think that international prosecution is better for the reason that domestic courts cannot be trusted with the effective prosecution of international crimes.[7] This is because, more often than not, there is direct or indirect involvement of state authorities in the commission of these crimes, which results not only in the collapse or malfunctioning of the judicial system,[8] but it also makes domestic prosecution a sham.

As a consequence, international crimes raise intrinsic questions that go far beyond the usual tasks of judges and prosecutors in a domestic setting.[9] Moreover, since the crimes are designated 'international', it follows that their prosecutions should be by an international institution established by the international community.[10] Nevertheless, the obstacles to international prosecution include limited resources and absolute dependence on the cooperation of states. These difficulties ultimately strengthen the argument for domestic prosecution.

The domestic prosecutions of international crimes in certain African states are discussed in this section. Prior to an analysis of the domestic prosecutions, it is important to note that two approaches to prosecuting international crimes domestically seem to have emerged. The first approach allows states to carry out such

[6]Elvarez (1999), p. 365; Broomhall, (Text to note 112 in Ch 2), pp. 23–24; Schabas (2007), p. 60, 175; Kleffner (2009), p. 2. See also Jurdi (2011), p. 34.

[7]Bickley (2000), pp. 213, 272–275; Sadat and Carden (2000), pp. 381, 383.

[8]Kleffner (2009).

[9]Jessberger (2010), pp. 209, 214; Cassese (2010), pp. 123, 127.

[10]Jessberger (2010).

prosecutions using domestic criminal law provisions for ordinary crimes.[11] This approach suggests that states should be permitted to prosecute the crimes of genocide, crimes against humanity and war crimes as the ordinary crimes of murder, theft and rape. Adapting Fédéric Mégrét's propositions,[12] Kevin Jon Heller stated that allowing states to prosecute international crimes as ordinary crimes could be termed the 'soft mirror thesis'.[13] The soft mirror thesis maintains that as long as the offenders are tried for correspondingly grave domestic crimes, it does not matter whether the trial was based on the international categorisation or not.[14]

The rationale behind this approach is that states are more familiar with domestic crimes and will not require additional expertise to handle their investigation and prosecution. In addition, it has been argued that requesting states to prosecute international crimes categorised as such may significantly increase the likelihood that domestic prosecutions will be unsuccessful.[15] This is because international crimes are far more difficult to investigate and prove than ordinary crimes, because their investigation and prosecution require better-trained personnel and significantly more financial resources.[16]

The foregoing argument for the soft mirror thesis that states may prosecute international crimes as ordinary crimes, implies that states do not have to ratify the Rome Statute. States may also not be required to enact domestic legislation incorporating the Rome Statute crimes into their domestic criminal law. Ultimately, the justification for the soft mirror thesis could mean that the Rome Statute has little relevance.

However, Jann Kleffner proposes that states should incorporate the substantive provisions of the Rome Statute, because to meet the complementarity criteria, it is better for states to prosecute international crimes as such rather than as ordinary crimes.[17] Significantly, international crimes are different from ordinary crimes; the context in which they are committed, the nature, scale, gravity and the overall impact are usually greater than for ordinary crimes. Crimes against humanity, for example, must be committed within the context of an attack that is characterised as 'widespread or systematic', directed against a civilian population, and the accused must have had knowledge of the attack.[18] Therefore, murder as crime against humanity, for example, cannot be the same as the ordinary crime of murder under domestic criminal law.[19]

---

[11]Nouwen (2011), p. 1127; Mégret (2011), pp. 363, 372.

[12]Mégrét, 372.

[13]Jon Heller (2012), pp. 86–134, 87.

[14]Ibid.

[15]OSJI (2010), p. 2.

[16]OSJI (2010).

[17]Kleffner (2003), p. 98. See also Seman (2010), pp. 259, 266.

[18]Rome Statute, art 7.

[19]Greppi (2008).

In line with this argument, the second approach proposes that domestic prosecution must be based on international crimes, categorised and defined as such, rather than on ordinary crimes.[20] Proponents of this approach argue that it is only by such prosecution that states can avoid the possibility of being considered 'unwilling' or 'unable', which facilitates intervention by the ICC.[21] Jon Heller classifies this approach as the 'hard mirror thesis'.[22]

Prosecuting international crimes as ordinary domestic crimes undermines the fundamental concept on which the international criminal justice system is founded. This is because while prosecuting for ordinary crimes may fulfil the objective of closing impunity gaps, such prosecutions risk the danger of being perceived as 'sham' trials, which effectively shields perpetrators from criminal responsibility.[23]

Contrary to this argument, Mégrét asserts, that the intermediary position of 'sham' trials seems unlikely.[24] He notes that if a state is unwilling, it will always be unwilling all the way as it can hardly be imagined that the Sudanese authorities would provide Al-Bashir even a lenient trial.[25] Accordingly, he argues that it is unlikely that the ICC would undertake sophisticated qualitative analysis of domestic trials to see if they constitute 'genuine' proceedings or not.[26]

Nevertheless, it is precisely the reason put forward by Mégrét that accounts for why the trials being conducted by the SCCED could be regarded as 'sham' trials. As Sudan is not a party to the Rome Statute, its criminal laws do not reflect the Rome Statute crimes. This means that domestic trials in Sudan could only be based on ordinary crimes. Furthermore, the President himself is one of the indictees and therefore domestic prosecution in Sudan does not accord with complementarity, because arguably, by virtue of the ICC's jurisprudence to prosecute those who bear the highest responsibility for the gravest crimes, the Sudanese President ought to be standing trial at The Hague. However, to date he has not been arrested and surrendered to the ICC for prosecution; this is one of the dilemmas of complementarity mentioned earlier, namely, how can a government that is complicit in

[20]Terracino (2007), pp. 421, 439; Philippe (2006), pp. 375, 390; see also Ellis (2003), pp. 224–225 (arguing that states 'must also ensure that all ICC crimes are incorporated into national legislation' because 'the crime of murder found in national law is not the same as a crime against humanity...'); Zahar and Sluiter (2008), p. 489; Halling (2010), p. 827.

[21]See Ellis (2003), p. 225; See also Ambos and Stegmiller (2012).

[22]Jon Heller (2012), pp. 87–89. (Noting that complementarity does not require that domestic prosecutions must be carried out in precise accord with the legal regime of the Rome Statute).

[23]See Zahar and Sluiter (2008), p. 489 (arguing that, 'the crimes set out in the Statute... must be implemented in domestic law as international crimes because prosecuting such crimes as ordinary crimes 'will in all likelihood result in an inability determination'); Halling, 839 (Noting that complementarity requires that states prosecute crimes as they are spelled out in the Rome Statute; the prosecutions have to be for 'crimes against humanity,' not the murders, rapes, and so on that underlie the charge of crimes against humanity').

[24]Mégret (2011), p. 376.

[25]Ibid 376–377.

[26]Ibid. See also Nouwen, (Text to note 45 in Ch 3) 1129.

international crimes prosecute itself or how can the government cooperate with the ICC?

There is yet a third approach; 'a sentence-based theory of complementarity', suggested by Jon Heller.[27] Discounting the earlier approaches, Jon Heller advanced a critique of both domestic prosecution based on ordinary crimes (soft mirror thesis) and domestic prosecutions based on international crimes (hard mirror thesis).[28] He proposed replacing both approaches with one focused exclusively on the sentence.[29] Rather than engage in the argument of the categorisation of the crimes concerned whether 'ordinary' or 'international', the outcome, which is the sentence, should be the focus. According to him, when a domestic prosecution ends with a sentence that is the same or higher than what is prescribed by the Rome Statute or what the ICC would have given in the same case, then domestic prosecution can be accepted regardless of the categorisation of the crime.[30]

It is submitted that proposing a sentence-based approach to complementarity that focuses exclusively on the severity of the sentence is not only contrary to the provisions of the Rome Statute,[31] but it may also present certain difficulties. The first is that a sentence-based approach does not reflect the differences in the crimes. Prosecuting international crimes as the ordinary crimes of murder or rape, rather than as their international counterparts, is not desirable, since ordinary crimes do not capture the scope, scale and gravity of the conduct.[32]

Moreover, the sentence-based approach does not take into consideration that a domestic prosecution could end up in acquittal.[33] Acquittal may well be the appropriate outcome of a domestic prosecution and yet, where an accused is acquitted, there is of course no sentence, and it is therefore impossible to compare with the Rome Statute. The sentence-based approach also implies that one must wait until the end of the prosecution to determine the acceptability of the prosecution, in which case the ICC would be barred by the *ne bis in idem* rule.[34] Other questions that the sentence-based approach fails to answer are; does the approach include traditional justice mechanisms? To what extent could high sentences

---

[27]Jon Heller (2012).

[28]Ibid, 88–107.

[29]Ibid, 107–130.

[30]Ibid.

[31]Implicitly, the sentence-based theory allows the death sentence which some states apply as the maximum sentence in consideration of the gravity of particular crimes. On the contrary, the maximum penalty under the Statute is life imprisonment, although it could be argued that article 80 which appears as a compromise allows states to apply the death penalty. See Schabas (2002), p. 1505.

[32]Bergsmo et al. (2010), pp. 791–811, 801.

[33]Robinson (2012b), p. 165. http://www.harvardilj.org/2012/04/online_53_robinson/. Accessed 28 June 2012.

[34]See Rome Statute, articles 17(1)(c) & 20 (the rule against double jeopardy which states that no person shall be tried twice for the same conduct.

achieved by alternative means in a domestic setting accord with the complementarity regime?

Thus, the complementarity-based prosecution which is proposed in this book is a holistic and proactive approach which requires that states should first incorporate international crimes that conform to Rome Statute definitions into their domestic criminal law. It is also a practical way of avoiding a scenario in which a crime occurs that is not covered under domestic law. A typical example is the rejection of the Pre-Trial Chamber I of the admissibility challenge by Libya in the *Saif Al-Islam Gaddafi*[35] case. As observed, the crime against humanity of persecution was absent in the Libyan Criminal Code and a proposed higher sentence by Libya was rejected by the Chamber.[36]

In response to Jon Heller's sentence-based theory, Darryl Robinson proposed a 'process-based' approach; stating that the genuineness of the process rather than its outcome should be the focus.[37] For Robinson, once it is shown that a state is carrying out or has carried out prosecutions in relation to a case,[38] the question should be whether the state is carrying out those prosecutions 'genuinely'.[39] Thus, in the context of Articles 17(2) and (3), 'genuinely' could be interpreted in two ways; in terms of the sincerity of the process, and in terms of exhibiting a rudimentary level of capacity.[40] Robinson suggests that 'process' is the master theory and that charges and sentences could be looked into insofar as they reveal something about the genuineness of the process.[41] Again, the process-based theory does not take into account the nature of the crimes.

The foregoing discussion is necessary to understand why a particular domestic prosecution may not meet the complementarity threshold. The next section will discuss domestic prosecutions in the DRC, Kenya, Sudan and Uganda, which were or are being conducted on the basis of ordinary crimes. Although the military tribunals in the DRC made references to the Rome Statute, the prosecutions could not be considered as complementarity-based because of the lack of implementing legislation and the use of mobile courts. It is maintained that for domestic prosecution to be considered complementarity-based, the Rome Statute crimes must have been incorporated into the domestic criminal law and must form the basis of such prosecution.

[35]*Saif Al-Islam* Case (Text to note 94 in Ch 2).

[36]Ibid, paras 111, 112 & 113.

[37]Robinson (2012a).

[38]See Rome Statute, art 17(1)(a)-(c).

[39]Rome Statute, arts 17(1) (a) & (b) 20.

[40]Informal Expert Paper 2009, (Text to 114 in Ch 2) 8; Holmes (2002), p. 667.

[41]Robinson.

### *4.1.1 Domestic Prosecution in the Democratic Republic of Congo (DRC)*

The DRC is a monist state,[42] meaning that international treaties carry the same weight as constitutional law and can be applied directly.[43] The DRC ratified the Rome Statute in March 2002,[44] and thus, in principle, the Statute should be applicable domestically.[45] Constitutions adopted successively since 1994 in the DRC provide that treaties and international agreements have higher authority than national laws upon publication.[46] Article 215 of the 2006 Constitution adopted the same monist view giving treaties primacy over domestic laws.[47]

In 2002 the DRC adopted a new Military Penal Code.[48] Title V of the Congolese Code specifically proscribes genocide, war crimes and crimes against humanity.[49] Although the Military Penal Code recognises and criminalises international crimes, there are gaps and inadequacies such that they do not conform to the definitions of

---

[42]Conversely in a dualist state, domestic and international law are two distinct legal systems and transposition of the contents of the treaty by a law is necessary for its incorporation into the domestic legal system. See Cassese (2005), pp. 213–217.

[43]The DRC Constitution of 18 February 2006, *Journal Officiel,* special edition of 18 February 2006 (DRC Constitution of 2006) states that civilian and military courts may apply ratified treaties provided they are consistent with the laws. See articles 153 & 215. The Constitution is available (in French) at: http://democratie.francophonie.org/IMG/pdf/Constitution_de_la_RDC.pdf (Accessed 28 June 2012). For an analysis of the legal basis for application of the Rome Statute in the DRC, see Avocats sans Frontières (ASF), 'Case Study: The Application of the Rome Statute of the International Criminal Court by the Courts of the Democratic Republic of Congo' March 2009 9-20 available at: http://www.asf.be/publications/ASF_CaseStudy_RomeStatute_Light_PagePerPage.pdf (Accessed 28 June 2012).

[44]The Rome Statute was signed by the DRC on 8 September 2000 and the Legislative Decree no. 003/2002 of 30 March 2002 authorised the ratification of the Rome Statute, *Journal Officiel* of 5 December 2002 (special edition 'International and Regional Instruments Relating to Human Rights Ratified by the Democratic Republic of Congo'). Ratification instrument was deposited on 11 April 2002 http://www.icc-cpi.int/asp/statesparties/country&id=5.html (Accessed 28 June 2012).

[45]OSJI (2011).

[46]Article 112 of the Constitutional Act of Transition (1994), Article 193 of the Transitional Constitution of the Democratic Republic of Congo of 4 April 2003, *Journal Officiel,* special edition of 5 April 2003 (Constitution of 2003), Article 216 of the Constitution of the Democratic Republic of Congo of 2006.

[47]The DRC Constitution of 2006, Article 215 provides that 'duly concluded treaties and international agreements have, upon publication, a higher authority than laws subject, for each treaty or agreement, by its application by the other party'.

[48]Loi 023/2002 of 18 November 2002 Portant Code judiciaire militaire (Military Code) http://www.leganet.cd/Legislation/Droit%20Judiciaire/Loi.023.2002.18.11.2002.pdf and Loi 024/2002 of November 2002 Portant Code Penal Militaire (Military Penal Code) http://www.leganet.cd/Legislation/Droit%20Judiciaire/Loi.024.2002.18.11.2002.pdf (Assessed 2 November 2012).

[49]*Ibid.*

crimes in the Rome Statute.[50] For example, the Code provides for the death penalty, making it incongruous with the Rome Statute.[51] In addition, gaps exist in the definitions of the crimes of 'rape' or 'sexual violence' concerning the prevention and punishment of the crime, protection of vulnerable groups, compensation of victims and the treatment of evidence.[52] The *Songo Mboyo,*[53] the *Kibibi*[54] and the *Bongi*[55] cases discussed below illustrate these gaps.

In the Congolese civil court system, *Tribunal de Grande Instance* (General Tribunal) is the competent court with jurisdiction over international crimes.[56] However, under the 2002 Penal Code, the *Tribunal Militaire de Garrison* TMG (Military Tribunals) have exclusive jurisdiction over these crimes.[57] In fact, most of the domestic prosecutions in the DRC have been carried out by the TMG, thereby depriving civil courts from exercising jurisdiction even though the civil court system is responsible for guaranteeing the rights and liberties of Congolese citizens.[58]

In the *Songo Mboyo* case, a Captain in the Congolese army stole the salaries of the soldiers under his command in December 2003 and this led to mutiny in Songo Mboyo in the northwest province of Equateur.[59] A reprisal by soldiers who were former rebels awaiting formal reintegration into the army in accordance with a 'global agreement',[60] led to the looting of property and the rape of 30 women, including a man. The violence led to the death of one of the women. Thirteen of the rape survivors instituted proceedings at the TMG of Mbandaka. The Military Prosecutor, on behalf of the victims, charged the soldiers with the crime against

[50] Mansfield (2009), pp. 367–408; International Centre for Transitional Justice (ICTJ) (2010).

[51] See arts 167–169 Military Penal Code 2002.

[52] Zongwe (2012), pp. 37, 42–45.

[53] TMG de Mbandaka, Affaire *Songo Mboyo*, 12 April 2006, RP 084/05; CM de l'Equateur, Affaire *Songo Mboyo* 7 June 2006, RPA 014/06. Also cited as *Military Prosecutor v Eliwo Ngoy & Ors* RP 084/2006 12 April 2006.

[54] TMG de l'Ituri, Affaire *Kibibi*, 19 February 2011, RP 101/11.

[55] TMG de l'Ituri, Affaire *Bongi*, 24 March 2006, RP 018/06.

[56] ICTJ, ibid.

[57] See art 161 Military Penal Code 2002 (note 48); Mansfield, ibid; Where the perpetrators were civilians, the General Tribunal applied the July 2006 amendments to the Penal Code which the Swahili called *vitendo vya haya*, 'the law of shameful acts'.

[58] ICTJ, ibid.

[59] Zongwe (2012).

[60] The war in the DRC has been described as 'Africa's World War', presumably because about eight countries (Angola, Burundi, Chad, Libya, Namibia, Rwanda, Uganda and Zimbabwe) were allegedly involved in it at different times. The conflict is divided into three eras. The first was 1996–1997 inter-tribal, the second 1998–2003 national and the third 2003 to date regional. In December 2002, former Congolese President Joseph Kabila signed a peace agreement with other belligerents, the *Accord Global Inclusif* (the Inclusive Global Agreement), which officially brought the war to an end. See Zongwe. See also Breton-Le Goff (2010). Available at http://ui04e.moit.tufts.edu/forum/archives/pdfs/34-1pdfs/34-1_Breton-LeGoff.pdf. (Assessed 2 November 2012).

humanity of rape. The Penal Code of 2002 does not define rape; rather, it merely states that the crime against humanity of rape comprises any form of sexual violence of comparable gravity knowingly committed in peacetime or wartime in the context of a systematic and widespread attack against a civilian population.[61] Notwithstanding the deficiency in the definition of rape in the penal code, the Military Tribunal relied on the Rome Statute definition of the crime against humanity of rape and found the soldiers guilty of the crime.

The broad definition found in Congolese laws stipulates that rape meant the act by which a man engages in sexual intercourse with a woman without her permission, either because she did not give her consent, because of physical or psychological violence or because of the element of surprise or other coercive means.[62] The defence relied on this definition in the *Songo Mboyo* case and argued that the crime of rape could not be committed against a man.

However, the TMG circumvented the defects in the Congolese law on rape and applied the Rome Statute definition, according to which both men and women can be victims of rape. Consequently, the Elements of Crimes together with Article 7 of the Rome Statute were used to fill gaps within the DRC military penal code by the TMG of Mbandaka in the *Songo Mboyo*[63] case.

In the *Kibibi*[64] case, a group from the Armed Forces of the Democratic Republic of the Congo (FARDC) carried out a reprisal attack on the town of Fizi south of Kivu, following the killing of a soldier. The attack in January 2011 resulted in the pillaging of property, inhumane and degrading treatment of a large number of the population, displacement and mass rape. The attack was allegedly instigated by *Colonel Kibibi Mutware* who was eventually arrested along with 11 others. His trial commenced on 11 February 2011 in the town of Baraka near Fizi and on 21 February 2011, he and three others were sentenced to 20 years' imprisonment for crimes against humanity.[65] Arguably, the summary judgement meant that due process may not have been followed and the accused persons' rights may not have been safeguarded during the trial.

Furthermore, the military penal code was found to be lacking with respect to the crime of pillaging,[66] as the constitutive ėlement of pillaging in the Military Code includes the requirement that the conduct must have taken place in the context of an

---

[61]Military Penal Code 2002, article 169(7).

[62]Military Penal Code 2002, art 170.

[63]TMG Mbandaka, Affaire *Songo Mboyo*, (note 53) 28.

[64]*Military Prosecutor v Lieutenant Colonel Kibibi Mutware et al* (note 54).

[65]Amnesty International (2011), 23 February 2011. See also 'DR Congo Colonel Kibibi Mutware Jailed for Mass Rape' *BBC News* 21 February 2011 Available at http://www.adh-geneva.ch/RULAC/national_judical_decitions.php?id_state=178. See also 'Congo Army Colonel guilty of Ordering Mass Rape on New Year's Day: Colonel and Subordinates Escape Death Penalty for Atrocity at Fizi in which 62 women were attacked'. Available at http://www.guardian.co.uk/society/2011/feb/21/congo-rape-trial (Accessed 28 May 2012).

[66]See Military Pena Code 2002, arts 162, 173–175.

international armed conflict.[67] However, the crime in question occurred during an internal conflict between two armed groups; the FADRC and the Front for the Patriotic Resistance in Ituri (FRPI) thus lacking in international character. Therefore, in the *Bongi* case,[68] the military court in Bunia Ituri applied the provisions of the Rome Statute on the war crime of pillaging, including sentencing provisions,[69] which the military code also lacked, with the result that Blaise Bongi Massaba was sentenced to life imprisonment. The tribunal thus applied provisions of the Rome Statute to meet the objectives of the ratification of the Treaty by the DRC.[70]

Whilst such a move may appear proactive, the tribunal is still susceptible to challenges due to the use of mobile-military courts. The DRC's military justice reform was not accompanied by a similar reform of the civilian justice system. Consequently, criminal justice was militarised to the extent that the most serious crimes committed during the armed conflicts were and are being prosecuted exclusively by mobile courts.[71] Granted that the prosecution of members of the armed forces in the DRC appears to be in line with domestic accountability efforts, the question as to how civilian perpetrators are to be held accountable is left unanswered. The DRC's Constitution of 2006 rightly limits the jurisdiction of the military courts to members of the armed forces.[72] As a result, it appears that selectivity will continue to pose a challenge to the emerging criminal justice system both at the domestic and international level.[73]

Moreover, the military reform of 2002 seems inadequate as it lacked provisions ensuring fair trial guarantees recognised by the Constitution of 2006 and other regional instruments.[74] In the *Kibibi*[75] trial, for example, the proceedings lasted only 10 days. Arguably, fair trial guarantees were compromised by such a short process.

It is argued that the use of military penal code and mobile courts in the domestic prosecutions in the DRC makes the prosecutions fall short of complementarity-based prosecution. This is because the prosecutions do not capture the conduct

---

[67]Military Penal Code (note 48) Arts 161–175 provide for genocide, war crimes and crimes against humanity. See ICRC Customary IHL, Democratic Republic of Congo Practice Relating to Rule 52.

[68]*Military Prosecutor v Blaise Bongi* TMG de I'Ituri, Affaire Bongi, 24 March 200610-11. Available at http://www.adh-geneva.ch/RULAC/national_judical_decitions.php?id_state=178 (Accessed 28 May 2012).

[69]Articles 8 & 77 of the Rome Statute on war crimes and penalties respectively were specifically applied.

[70]Article 153 of the Congolese Constitution of 2006 states that civil and military courts can implement duly ratified international treaties.

[71]Domestic prosecutions have been conducted before the following courts: military garrison tribunals (MTG) of Bunia, Songo Mboyo, Mbandaka, Gbadolite, Beni, and Katanga.

[72]DRC Constitution (note 43) (Article 156 limits the jurisdiction of military courts to members of the armed forces and the police).

[73]Cryer (2005), pp. 191–231.

[74]The right to a fair trial are stated in Articles 19 to 21 of the 2006 Constitution and in Article 7 of the African Charter on Human and Peoples' Rights.

[75]Trials started on 11 February and Kibibi was sentenced on 21 February 2011.

criminalised in the Rome Statute nor do they follow due process as recognised by international law. For instance, the use of mobile courts was not contemplated under the Rome Statute. Therefore, in order for the domestic prosecutions in the DRC to demonstrate effectiveness and genuineness, they ought to encompass the Rome Statute crimes by adopting implementing legislation and also follow due process as envisioned by the complementarity regime. Only by applying the Rome Statute definitions of crimes such as rape and pillaging was the military tribunal able to overcome the deficiencies in the Military Penal Code.

In other African states where domestic prosecution on the basis of complementarity has been proposed, it has come shortly after a referral of a situation concerning that state. At other times, an attempt at domestic prosecution has come after the announcement of a preliminary investigation by the Chief Prosecutor of the ICC in relation to a situation in the state concerned.

### *4.1.2 Domestic Prosecution in Kenya*

In Kenya, the announcement of the results of the December 2007 Presidential election led to inter-ethnic violence that culminated in the loss of about 1133 lives, accompanied by the displacement of several others and the destruction of property.[76] As the violence escalated, a mediation process was initiated by the former Secretary-General of the United Nations, Kofi Annan. A National Accord and Reconciliation Committee was constituted and charged with the task of finding a solution.[77] The outcome of the Committee's deliberations was the formation of a grand coalition government led by President Mwai Kibaki[78] with opposition leader Raila Odinga appointed as the Prime Minister.[79] Amongst other things, the Committee set up a Commission of Inquiry into the post-election violence that was mandated to investigate the circumstances surrounding the violence and to make recommendations.[80]

On 15 October 2008, the Commission of Inquiry, chaired by a judge of the Court of Appeals, Justice Philip Waki, issued its report (the 'Waki Report'). The Waki Report determined that crimes against humanity had been committed during the

---

[76]Findings of the Commission of Inquiry into the Post-Election Violence in Kenya. Available at http://www.kenyalaw.org/Downloads/Reports/Commission_ofInquiry_into_Post_Election_Violence.pdf. 345–346. (Accessed 13 December 2011).

[77]Okuta (2009), pp. 1063–1076.

[78]Mwai Kibaki was the third President of the Republic of Kenya. He was first sworn in on 30 December 2002, when he took over from Daniel Arap Moi. He served a second term in office from December 2007 to April 2013.

[79]The Constitution had to be amended to provide for the office of the Prime Minister; see the amendment Act http://www.kenyalaw.org/Downloads/Bills/2008/The_Constitution_of_Kenya (Amendment)_Bill_2008.pdf. (Accessed 13 December 2011).

[80]An Independent Review Committee (the IREC) was also set up and mandated to investigate all aspects of the 2007 Presidential Election and make findings and recommendations to improve the electoral process.

post-election violence and recommended the creation of a Special Tribunal for Kenya with the mandate to prosecute those bearing the greatest responsibility for these crimes.[81]

The Commission further noted that if the recommended Special Tribunal was not established or if it was established but failed to carry out its mission, a list containing the names of those suspected of bearing the greatest responsibility for crimes falling within the jurisdiction of the proposed Special Tribunal should be forwarded to the Prosecutor of the ICC. This was to be accompanied by a request for the Prosecutor to proceed with an investigation and prosecution of the suspects. The Commission handed over the list of names in a sealed envelope to Kofi Annan.[82]

Kenya was thus faced with the dilemma of either prosecuting those responsible or have the situation referred to the ICC. This development brought into focus Kenya's national legislation, as well as Kenya's capacity to handle the investigation and prosecution of international crimes. Apparently, Kenya lacked capacity to carry out domestic prosecution effectively because its implementing legislation for the Rome Statute was not yet passed into law. The Kenyan Penal Code, which lays down Kenya's criminal law, did not contain provisions for international crimes.[83] Similarly, the Armed Forces Act,[84] which provides for the establishment, regulation and discipline of the Kenyan armed forces, did not contain provisions concerning international crimes.

The only exception was the Geneva Conventions Act,[85] which criminalises grave breaches, including wilful killing, and prescribes penalties of life imprisonment and in some cases 14 years imprisonment for violators.[86] As a consequence, in the *Muthaura et al.*[87] case, the Pre-Trial Chamber II dismissed the admissibility challenge by Kenya on the grounds that Kenya's investigation failed the 'same person *same conduct*' test.[88]

---

[81]Okuta (2009), p. 1071.

[82]The list contained the names and information on those who were suspected to bear the greatest responsibility in the post-election violence. Kofi Annan handed the sealed envelope to the Chief Prosecutor of the ICC when the government of Kenya failed to set up the Special Tribunal.

[83]Chapter 63 Laws of Kenya, available at http://www.kenyalaw.org/kenyalaw/klr_app/frames.php (Accessed 13 December 2011).

[84]Armed Forces Act (Chapter 199) Laws of Kenya, available online at http://www.kenyalaw.org/kenyalaw/klr_app/frames.php (Accessed 13 December 2011).

[85]Kenya ratified the 1949 Geneva Conventions and their 1977 Additional Protocols on 23 February 1999. The Additional Protocols have not yet been incorporated through domestic legislation. The Geneva Conventions Act, 1968 (Chapter 198 Laws of Kenya) is available online at http://www.kenyalaw.org/kenyalaw/klr_app/frames.php. (Accessed 13 December 2011).

[86]Geneva Conventions Act 1968 Ibid; section 3(1).

[87]*The Prosecutor v. Francis Kirimi Muthaura, Uhuru Muigai Kenyatta and Mohammed Hussein Ali* ICC-01/09-02/11 (The decision of Pre-Trial Chamber II of 30 May 2011 on the Application by the Government of Kenya Challenging the Admissibility of the Case Pursuant to Article 19(2)(b) of the Statute). Available at http://icc-cpi.int/iccdocs/doc/doc1078823.pdf (Accessed 10 January 2012).

[88]Ibid, paras 49–53 (emphasis added).

The Geneva Conventions Act could not be used in the context of the post-election violence of 2007 because the crimes were not committed in the context of an international armed conflict. Granted that Common Article 3 of the Geneva Conventions and Additional Protocol II relate to non-international armed conflicts, still the post-election violence in Kenya did not meet the threshold. The conflict could only be classified as OSV (other situations of violence), to which the Geneva Conventions and their Additional Protocols do not apply. Arguably, the violence amounts to crimes against humanity on account of its widespread or systematic character.[89] However, the dissenting judgement of Hans-Peter Kaul appears to show a lack of organisational policy by the government,[90] which is an important element in the definition of crimes against humanity, and therefore this point is contested.

The domestic prosecution of the 2007 post-election violence was thus fraught with obstacles due to the lack of domestic implementing legislation at the time.[91] Consequently, upon authorisation by the Pre-Trial Chamber II in 2010, six Kenyan citizens voluntarily appeared before the ICC.[92] The 'Ocampo Six',[93] as they were frequently called, were charged with crimes against humanity. Arguably, had the crimes been known to the domestic criminal law of Kenya, or had the Kenya implementing legislation been passed before the violence, Kenya might have been rightly positioned to assert jurisdiction to prosecute the alleged perpetrators domestically.

Admittedly, this argument is significantly flawed because the indictees were top government officials including the president of Kenya. It could therefore to be conceded that for the Kenya cases, the ICC is the best forum to prosecute. However, the constraints of insufficient evidence resulting from the lack of cooperation from the Kenyan government, has resulted in all the cases being withdrawn and closed. This exemplifies the complementarity paradox articulated by Benvenuti.

However, Kenya's implementing legislation—The International Crimes Act of 2008—entered into force in January 2009,[94] after the Waki Report was released. While it represents a significant milestone towards Kenya's preparedness to ensure

---

[89]See ICTY, *Prosecutor v Tadic*, Appeals Chamber, 2 October 1995, para 141.

[90]See Dissenting Opinion by Judge Hans-Peter Kaul in the *Muthaura et al* Case No: ICC-01/09-02/11 (The Decision on the Confirmation of Charges Pursuant to Article 61(7)(a)&(b) of the Rome Statute) 156–193 23 January 2012. Available at http://www.icc-cpi.int/iccdocs/doc/doc1314543.pdf. (Accessed 10 January 2012).

[91]Brown and Sriram (2012), pp. 244–260.

[92]On 31 March 2010, Pre-Trial Chamber II granted the Prosecutor's Request to open an investigation *proprio motu* in the situation in Kenya. This culminated in the two Kenyan cases before the PTCII: *The Prosecutor v William Samoei Ruto, Henry Kiprono Kosgey and Joshua Arap Sang* Case No : ICC-01/09-01/11 and *The Prosecutor v. Francis Kirimi Muthaura and Uhuru Kenyatta and Mohammed Hussein Ali* Case No: ICC-01/09-02/11.

[93]The charges against Ali and Kosgey were not confirmed and those against Muthaura were withdrawn by the Chief Prosecutor for lack of cooperation from the Kenya authorities. Similarly, on 5 April 2016, the case against William Samoei Ruto and Joshua Arap Song were terminated. In addition, the case against President Uhuru Muigai Kenyatta was closed due to insufficient evidence.

[94]Kenya's International Crimes Act 2009 available at http://www.kenyalaw.org/kenyalaw/klr_app/frames.php (Accessed 12 December 2011).

domestic accountability,[95] the Act could not be used to prosecute perpetrators of the 2007 post-election violence because it was passed 2 years after the crimes were committed.[96] It may yet be a vital tool for Kenya in dealing with international crimes in the future. This point underscores the importance of states parties to the Rome Statute not stopping at ratification of the Rome Statute, but also taking a step further by ensuring enactment of implementing legislation to enable them handle domestic prosecutions should the need arise.

### *4.1.3 Domestic Prosecution in Sudan*

Since February 2003 the people of Darfur in Western Sudan have been victims of a systematic extermination campaign. The violence has claimed over 400,000 lives, mostly civilians, and has left over three million displaced within Sudan and to neighbouring Chad.[97] In response to protests by the Sudanese People's Liberation Movement (SPLM) and the Justice and Equality Movement (JEM), which demanded proportional political representation and equitable access to the country's economic resources, the Government of Sudan launched a violent campaign against the people of Darfur.[98] The governing party of Khartoum, known as the National Islamic Front (NIF), along with a government-sponsored Arab militia called the '*Janjaweed*' (militiamen on horseback), were allegedly linked to the rapes, killings and other human rights abuses in Darfur.[99] Amnesty International accused the Sudanese military of the 'use of rape as a tool for humiliation and intimidation.'[100]

The report[101] of the subsequent International Commission of Inquiry revealed that both 'the Government of Sudan and the *Janjaweed* were responsible for serious violations of international human rights and humanitarian law amounting to crimes under international law.'[102] This resulted in the referral of the situation in Darfur to the ICC by the United Nations Security Council under Article 13(b) of the Rome Statute.[103]

Having satisfied the requirement of the Rome Statute of a 'reasonable basis' to proceed,[104] the Prosecutor announced his intention of opening an investigation into the situation in Darfur on 6 June 2005, and the next day, the government of Sudan

---

[95] Okuta (2009); See also Alai and Mue (2011), pp. 1222, 1231.

[96] Brown and Sriram (2012).

[97] Darfur Australia Network, 'The Situation in Darfur' Available at http://www.darfuraustralia.org/darfur/background (Accessed 13 February 2012); Udombana (2005), pp. 1149, 1159.

[98] Ibid.

[99] Lipscomb (2006), pp. 218–212.

[100] Amnesty International Report (2004).

[101] Report of the International Commission of Inquiry on Darfur to the United Nations Secretary-General 25 January 2005 available at http://www.un.org/news/dh/sudan/com_inq_darfur.pdf (Accessed 13 February 2012).

[102] Fletcher and Ohlin (2005), pp. 539–561.

[103] UNSC Resolution 1593 UN DOC S/RES/1593 (2005); although 11 members of the Security Council voted in favour of the resolution and none voted against it, Algeria, Brazil, China, and the United States abstained.

[104] Article 53 Rome Statute stipulates the general procedure for the initiation of investigation.

promulgated a decree establishing the Special Criminal Court on the Events in Darfur (SCCED).[105] The SCCED was given jurisdiction over Darfur in relation to crimes under Sudanese Law. The government of Sudan noted that at least 160 cases would be brought before the court. However, only 13 cases were prosecuted between June 2006 and January 2013, the SCCED has not charged any Khartoum government official involved in the Darfur crisis.[106] Furthermore, the SCCED charged two intelligence officers allegedly involved in a mass killing with looting instead of murder.[107]

As the ICC was established to step in and ensure accountability where there is an apparent failure on the part of a state to do so, it is argued that the ICC is the best forum to prosecute in the Darfur, Sudan cases. This is because those indicted in Sudan are top government officials, including the president, Omar Al-Bashir. As Sudan is not a party to the Rome Statute, and international crimes are not known to its criminal laws, the Sudanese domestic prosecution by the SCCED does not meet the complementarity threshold.

### *4.1.4 Domestic Prosecution in Uganda*

The government of Uganda was the first to trigger the jurisdiction of the ICC when it referred the situation concerning the Lord's Resistance Army (LRA) to the ICC in December 2003.[108] This was a surprise because few people anticipated that a state would refer a situation on its own territory and concerning its own nationals to the Court.[109] It had been assumed that states would consider such intervention as costly to their sovereignty and reputation.[110] However, President Museveni's government may have perceived the referral as a strategy to defeat the LRA.[111]

Whatever the merits of self-referral, the Chief Prosecutor of the ICC commenced an investigation into crimes committed by the LRA in northern Uganda. The same government which referred the situation and further, in February 2008, established

[105]Sudan: Special Criminal Court on the Events in Darfur (SCCED). Available at http://www.justiceinperspective.org.za/africa/sudan/special-criminal-court-on-the-events-in-darfur.html (Accessed 13 February 2012).

[106]Sudanese SCCED.

[107]See Human Rights Watch Briefing Paper, 'Lack of Conviction: The Special Criminal Court on the Events in Darfur' (June 2006) 13–14.

[108]ICC, 'President of Uganda Refers Situation Concerning the Lord's Resistance Army (LRA) to the ICC' ICC-20040129-44-En, 29 January 2004.

[109]Nouwen and Werner (2010), pp. 941–965 (Nouwen & Werner).

[110]See Williams and Schabas (2008), pp. 547–561, 560; Akhavan (2003), pp. 712, 716; Schabas (2001), pp. 197, 204.

[111]Nouwen and Werner, 948–949.

a War Crimes Division, also called International Crimes Division (ICD),[112] nevertheless appeared to go to great lengths to defeat the purpose of the ICD and obstruct the functioning of the ICC particularly through the use of amnesty. The Ugandan Amnesty Act allows anyone who renounces violence, regardless of rank, to return to his community without fear of prosecution.[113]

According to this Act, amnesty means pardon, forgiveness, exemption or discharge from criminal prosecution or other forms of punishment by the state.[114] Its significance is that it confers on the beneficiaries an irrevocable legal immunity from prosecution or punishment and covers all insurgency-related offences ranging from combat to collaboration and aiding rebellion. It was reported that over 4000 persons applied for amnesty under the Amnesty Act.[115]

An illustrative case is that of *Thomas Kwoyelo,*[116] a member of the LRA, who was arrested in the DRC in 2009 and charged with 53 counts of murder, wilful killing, kidnapping, aggravated robbery and destruction of property during the conflict that began in 1986.[117] It is submitted that the conducts for which Kwoyelo was charged constitute crimes against humanity. However, since there was no implementing legislation at the time, that recognised and defined crimes against humanity in Uganda, Kwoyelo was initially charged with war crimes under Uganda's Geneva Conventions Act of 1964,[118] even though that Act does not apply to non-international armed conflicts.[119] The prosecution was the first con-

[112]Agreement on Accountability and Reconciliation between the Government of Uganda and the Lord's Resistance Army/Movement (LRA) Juba, Sudan 29 June 2007, paras 4 & 6; Annex to the Agreement 19 February 2008, paras 7, 10–14. Available at http://www.iccnow.org/documents/Annexure_to_agreement_on_Accountability_signed_today.pdf. See also Judiciary of the Republic of Uganda, 'High Court Divisions: International Crimes Division'. Available at http://www.judicature.go.ug/index.php?option=com_content&task=view&id=117&Itemid=154. (Accessed 14 June 2012).

[113]Uganda: Laws of Uganda Amnesty Act 2000 (Cap 294); Article 3. Available at http://www.ulii.org/ug/legis/consol_act/aa2000111/ (Accessed 24 March 2012). See also Greenawalt (2009), pp. 108–159, 113.

[114]Amnesty Act, Ibid, sec. 3(1)(b).

[115]Afako (2002) ACORD 64–67. See also HRW (2012). Available at http://www.hrw.org/sites/default/files/reports/uganda0112ForUpload_0.pdf.

[116]Justice in Conflict (2012).

[117]Amnesty International, 'Uganda's Amnesty for LRA Commander a 'Setback' for Justice' Available at http://www.twylah.com/amnestyonline/tweets/117279987211571201 (Accessed 16 March 2012).

[118]Geneva Conventions Act (Ch 363) 16 October 1964 http://www.ulii.org/ug/legis/consol_act/gca1964208/ Article 2 (Accessed 14 June 2012).

[119]*See* HRW, 'Uganda: Q&A on the Trial of Thomas Kwoyelo' Human Rights Watch 7 July 2011. Available at http://www.hrw.org/en/news/2011/07/07/uganda-qa-trial-thomas-kwoyelo; 'Justice for Serious Crimes before National Courts: Uganda's International Crimes Division' January 2012. http://www.hrw.org.

cluded by the ICD and it culminated in the acquittal of Kwoyelo, on the basis of his application for amnesty.[120]

Although the five-judge panel ultimately ruled that Thomas Kwoyelo was entitled to amnesty for all crimes committed by him during the conflict and was therefore acquitted, they initially refused to grant amnesty, leading Kwoyelo's lawyers to appeal. The ICD then referred the case to the Constitutional Court which found that the only way by which an alleged criminal could be excluded from amnesty was by a statement issued by the Minister of Internal Affairs.[121] Consequently, the Constitutional Court granted amnesty on the grounds that such a statement had not been issued by the minister and considering that Kwoyelo had not been granted amnesty prior to the case.[122]

The Court thereafter ordered the ICD to terminate the case against Kwoyelo.[123] Indeed, such prosecution could be categorised as proceedings undertaken for the purpose of 'shielding the person concerned from criminal responsibility'.[124] While the Amnesty Act enjoins the Amnesty Commission[125] to promote appropriate mechanisms for reconciliation,[126] it is argued that it actually undermines efforts towards accountability and leads to impunity.

The involvement of the ICC has been criticised as tantamount to a breach of the Amnesty Act and an impediment to Uganda's peace process.[127] However, it is argued that the grant of amnesty to individuals allegedly accused of international crimes and who are subject to the jurisdiction of the ICC compromises the complementarity regime.[128] The international community recognises that amnesty is an accepted legal concept and a gesture of peace and reconciliation at the end of an internal armed conflict. However, the United Nations notes that amnesty cannot be granted with respect to international crimes.[129]

Besides the Amnesty Act, the lack of implementing legislation led to the application of alternative justice mechanisms in Uganda. These include the mediation of traditional chiefs (*rwodi*) through which many offences are

---

[120]The Statutory basis for the International Crimes Division (ICD) was the legal notice issued by the Uganda's Chief Justice, 'ICD Practice Directions' Legal Notice No 10 of 2011. Legal Notice Supplement, Uganda Gazette No 38 vol CIV 31 May 2011.

[121]By virtue of an amendment to the Amnesty Act in 2006, the Minister of Internal Affairs with approval by the Ugandan Parliament could exclude certain individuals from receiving amnesty.

[122]Wegner (2011). Available at http://justiceinconflict.org/2011/09/12/squashing-the-amnesty-law-in-uganda-possible-implications-of-the-kwoyelo-trial/. (Accessed 24 March 2012).

[123]Kersten (2011).

[124]See article 17(2)(a) Rome Statute.

[125]An Amnesty Commission and Demobilisation and Resettlement Team (DRT) were established by the Act to oversee amnesty processes. Their functions include promoting dialogue, sensitisation, drawing up programmes for decommissioning of weapons and resettlement of returnees.

[126]See section 9C Amnesty Act.

[127]Klein (2010), pp. 669, 676; Jennings (2011).

[128]Robinson (2003), pp. 481–505, 484; Clark (2010), pp. 141–160.

[129]Report of the United Nations Secretary-General UN Doc.S/2000/915 (2000), para. 22.

routinely resolved by reconciliation. Whenever a crime occurs, for example, homicide, the *rwodi* intervenes to offer mediation and a reconciliation process known as *mato oput*.[130] The *mato oput* is a ceremony of clan and family-centred reconciliation which incorporates the acknowledgment of wrongdoing or confession, the offering of compensation by the offender and the sharing of a symbolic drink.[131] It is believed to bring true healing in a way that the formal justice system does not. Other traditional justice mechanisms include individual cleansing rituals, which routinely take place whenever former LRA members return to the community.

The analysis in this part has indicated that although there seems to be domestic prosecutions taking place in the DRC, Kenya, Sudan and Uganda, such prosecutions do not meet the requirements of complementarity for various reasons. Kenya's International Crimes Act was passed 2 years after the violence and therefore could not be applied retroactively. Sudan is not a party to the Rome Statute, and the legal basis for its SCCED and domestic trials is therefore doubtful. This point is underscored by the fact that alleged perpetrators can only be charged with crimes that are known to Sudanese law, which does not incorporate international crimes.

Moreover, the indictees in the Kenyan and Sudanese cases are top government officials including the presidents of both states. Therefore, the ICC is the appropriate forum for their prosecution and any purported domestic prosecution is arguably a sham. Although President Uhuru Kenyatta of Kenya voluntarily appeared before the ICC, the case against him and all six indictees, which are top officials of his government have been closed for want of sufficient evidence. Al-Bashir of Sudan has refused to submit to the ICC's prosecution.

Domestic prosecution is vital to the success of the ICC and therefore domestic implementing legislation and institutional preparedness are necessary to catalyse the process. The unsuccessful attempts by the selected African states to carry out complementarity-based prosecution were partly due to the lack of implementing legislation. The next part discusses complementarity-based prosecution using the United Kingdom as a model.

## 4.2 Complementarity-Based Prosecution in the United Kingdom

Complementarity-based prosecutions are prosecutions of international crimes conducted by states domestically, with the provisions of the Rome Statute underpinning the process. Such domestic prosecutions aim at ensuring conformity with the Rome Statute both in the legal framework and in the institutional preparedness of states to take on the primary responsibility to prosecute international crimes. The United Kingdom is used here as a model of complementarity-based prosecution because it carried out a domestic prosecution on the basis of its implementing

[130] Afako (2002).

[131] Ibid.

legislation with the proper classification of international crimes as defined in the Rome Statute.

The legal system in the United Kingdom is dualistic in relation to treaties.[132] Consequently, parliament passed the International Criminal Court Act in 2001(the ICC Act), which entered into force on 1 September 2001.[133] This was necessary to incorporate international crimes into the British legal system. Referring to a similar Act passed in Scotland, Baroness Scotland declared that these Acts sought to 'provide a robust regime which will prevent the United Kingdom [from] being, or being seen as, a safe haven for war criminals'.[134] Prior to the ICC Act, legislative provisions incorporating international crimes into the British criminal justice system consisted of three Acts: the Geneva Conventions Act of 1957,[135] the Genocide Act of 1969[136] and the War Crimes Act of 1991.[137] The first two Acts remained largely unused,[138] whilst the use of the War Crimes Act culminated in one conviction.[139]

In conformity with the Rome Statute, Part 5 of the ICC Act relates to international crimes. Specifically, Section 51(1) of the ICC Act provides that 'it is an offence against the law of England and Wales for a person to commit genocide, a crime against humanity or a war crime'.[140] Pursuant to section 51(2), the ICC Act grants jurisdiction to courts in England and Wales over these crimes where they are committed in England and Wales and under Section 51(2)(b) when they are committed 'outside the United Kingdom by a United Kingdom national, a United Kingdom resident or a person subject to United Kingdom service jurisdiction.'[141]

The ICC Act has already been used to sustain domestic prosecutions in the United Kingdom. For example in 2007, *Donald Payne,*[142] a member of the British Armed Forces, became the first citizen to be convicted of war crimes in relation to

[132]See Shaw (2008), pp. 129–143.

[133]The United Kingdom enacted local implementing legislation before the ratification of the Rome Statute on 4 October 2001. The International Criminal Court Act 2001c.17, (2001) 1 Law Reports: Statutes 1367 (ICC Act) the Act also covers Northern Ireland.

[134]Scotland being governed by its system of criminal law, the Scottish Parliament brought in similar legislation at approximately the same time. This Act was passed on 24 September 2001, and entered into force on 17 December 2001. International Criminal Court (Scotland) Act 2001, 2001 ASP 13 House of Lords Hansard, Vol. 623, cols 418–419.

[135]See C.53(1957) Law Reports: Statutes 543 as amended by the Geneva Conventions (Amendment) Act 1995, C.27.

[136]C.12 (1969) Law Reports: Statutes 75.

[137]C.13 [1991] 1 Law Reports: Statutes 101. See Turns (1998), pp. 1–39.

[138]Cryer and Bekou (2007).

[139]The conviction concerned the matter of Andrei Sawoniuk. *R. v. Sawoniuk* [2000] 2 Criminal Appeal Reports 220. A second prosecution, concerning the matter of Simon Serafinowicz, was abandoned owing to the accused's ailment.

[140]See ICC Act 2001, Part 5; sections 50-69.

[141]ICC Act 2001, section 51(2)(b).

[142]*R v Payne,* General Court Martial Charge Sheet (2006), available at http://www.army.mod.uk/apa/courtsmartial-trials. (Accessed 18 October 2007).

atrocities committed by members of the British Armed forces in Iraq in 2003.[143] British forces in Basra, Iraq, arrested Baha Mousa along with nine other Iraqis in 2003. Mousa and the nine others were assaulted by British soldiers while in British custody. As a consequence, Mousa was reported to have died from the cumulative effects of 93 different injuries.[144] Then British Defence Secretary Liam Fox noted that Mousa's death and the abuse of other detainees in British custody was 'deplorable, shocking and shameful'.[145]

Consequently, Donald Payne was charged with manslaughter, inhumane treatment of persons and perverting the course of justice. He pleaded guilty for the crime of inhumane treatment and was convicted on that basis and sentenced to one year imprisonment. Others charged with him were acquitted, although of lesser crimes.[146] While the prosecution may be hailed as constituting domestic prosecution under complementarity, the conviction for the lesser crime of inhumane treatment and the penalty of one year imprisonment is questionable. Even more questionable is the acquittal of the others who were charged with Donald Payne. Colonel Jorge Mendonca, for example, who was commander of the 1st Battalion Queen's Lancashire Regiment (1QLR) in which Payne served, was acquitted.[147] Arguably, a charge and conviction as a co-perpetrator or an indirect perpetrator could have been sustained against Mendonca as the commander bearing responsibility.

Nevertheless, the case represents a ready example of complementarity-based prosecution because the crimes for which Donald Payne and others were prosecuted had already been proscribed and their penalties explicitly provided for before the crimes were committed. It was therefore easy to carry out domestic prosecution based on the international categorisation of the crimes. Other prosecutions including those analysed above fall short of the requirement of complementarity because of the deficiencies described previously, such as being based on ordinary crimes.

Until implementing legislation which conforms to the Rome Statute is enacted domestically and in force, domestic prosecution could be challenged on the basis of the non-retroactivity of criminal law. Moreover, such domestic prosecutions may

---

[143]Members of the British Armed Forces had employed the use of controversial interrogation techniques which had been banned over 30 years ago.

[144]Baha Mousa was a 26-year-old father of two and a hotel receptionist. He was one of the men rounded up after wrongly being identified as insurgents in 2003. He was detained in British custody and later died of 93 injuries from inhumane treatment. *BBC News* 19 September 2006 http://news.bbc.co.uk/1/hi/5360432.stm See also Raymond Whitaker, '93 Injuries, One Killing, No Justice' *The Independence* 18 March 2007, 19 London.

[145]Fox stressed that Baha Mousa's death occurred as a detainee in British custody, it was avoidable and preventable and there can be no excuses. *Mail Online* 8 September 2011. http://www.dailymail.co.uk/news/article-2035029/Baha-Mousa-inquiry-Army-condemned-gratuitous-violence.html#ixzz1jpZSdvLd.

[146]Wayne Crowcroft (inhumane treatment of persons), Darren Fallon (inhumane treatment of persons) Kelvin Stacey (actual bodily harm, alternatively assault), Mark Davies (negligently performing a duty) Michael Peebles (negligently performing a duty), Jorge Mendonca (negligently performing a duty) http://www.upi.com/Top_News/Special/2011/09/08/No-excuse-for-Iraqi-detainee-death/UPI-66021315494062/#ixzz1jpPr9v6k.

[147]Doyle (2011). Although, the inquiry found he had no knowledge of the abuse, the report said that as commanding officer he bears a 'heavy responsibility' for the tragedy.

be perceived as sham trials with the purpose of shielding perpetrators from criminal responsibility and may be susceptible to being used as a tool of revenge. In order to illustrate the difference between the two types of domestic prosecution discussed, the key features of the crime of genocide and crimes against humanity are analysed, in the next part, to explain why they cannot be prosecuted as ordinary domestic crime. The part further includes a discussion of the transfer of cases from the ICTR to Rwandan national courts as an example that may be instructive for states in the performance of their duties as required by the complementarity regime.

## 4.3 The Differences Between Domestic Prosecution and Complementarity-Based Prosecution

### *4.3.1 The Differences Between International and Domestic Crimes*

Both the high threshold set for the act and the mental element required for proof of international crimes such as genocide and crimes against humanity remove them from the realm of ordinary crimes.[148] This section comprises an analysis of the crimes of genocide and crimes against humanity in order to demonstrate that prosecuting them as the ordinary domestic crimes of murder, rape and theft does not meet the objectives of the Rome Statute.

The definition of the crime of genocide in the Rome Statute is comparable to the definition in Article II of the 1948 Convention on the Prevention and Punishment of the Crime of Genocide.[149] According to William Schabas, replicating the definition of Genocide in the Rome Statute represents a codification of customary international law.[150] The Statute defines the crime of genocide as

> any of the following acts committed with an intent to destroy, in whole or in part, a national, ethnical, racial or religious group as such: (a) killing members of the group (b) causing serious bodily or mental harm to members of the group, (c) deliberately inflicting on the group conditions of life calculated to bring about its physical destruction in whole or in part (d) imposing measures intended to prevent births within the group and (e) forcibly transferring children of the group to another group.[151]

Two components of the crime of genocide are readily apparent. The first is the specific intent (the *mens rea* or mental element) to destroy in whole or in part a national, ethnical, racial or religious group. There must be a psychological nexus

---

[148]Brandon and Plessis (2005), p. 35.

[149]The Convention on the Prevention and Punishment of the Crime of Genocide 9 December 1948 78 UNTS 277 28 ILM 763 art II.

[150]Schabas (2011), pp. 93–94. See also Lee, *The Making of the Rome Statute* (Text to note 13 in Ch 1) 122–126 (demonstrating that the crime of genocide is identical to the definition laid out in the Genocide Convention of 1948 whereas the definition of crimes against humanity and war crimes codify existing developments in international criminal law); Kress (2009), pp. 143, 148.

[151]Rome Statute, art 6.

between the physical result and the mental state of the perpetrator.[152] The mental element of the crime is important in determining whether or not an act constitutes genocide.[153] The Trial Chamber in the *Akayesu*[154] case held that

> genocide is distinct from other crimes in as much as it embodies a special intent or *dolus speclialis*. Special intent of a crime is the specific intention required as a constitutive element of the crime, which demands that the perpetrator clearly seeks to produce the act charged. Thus the special intent in the crime of genocide lies in the intent to destroy in whole or in part a national, ethnical, racial or religious group.[155]

Consequently, genocide is described as the crime of crimes.[156] This is because in the absence of direct evidence relating to *mens rea,* the ICTR held in the *Nshamihigo*[157] case that '...the overall context in which the crime occurred, the systematic targeting of the victims on account of their membership in a protected group, the scale and scope of the atrocities and the frequency of the destructive and discriminatory act...'[158] indicate the specific intent.

Therefore, although in the *Jelisic*[159] case, the ICTY held that the specific intent to destroy in whole or in part must be found in order to justify a conviction for the crime of genocide, the genocidal intent may be shown in two forms. The first is the desire to exterminate a large number of a protected group and the second is the desire to destroy a more limited number of members of such a group who are selected because of the potential impact of their destruction on the survival of the group.[160]

Similarly, the second constituent element of the crime of genocide is the *actus reus,* which is the commission of one or more of the five enumerated acts,[161] and which takes it far from the realm of ordinary crime. Furthermore, as decided in the *Kambanda*[162] case, the failure to act to stop genocide may itself constitute genocide. In this case, the ICTR found Jean Kambanda guilty of genocide on account of his failure as Prime Minister of Rwanda at the time to take action to stop the

---

[152]Bassiouni (2013), pp. 153–156. See also Kittichaisaree (2000), pp. 498–529, 512.

[153]Garuka (2011), pp. 221, 227–228.

[154]*Prosecutor v Jean-Paul Akayesu* (Case ICTR-96-4-T) ICTR Trial Chamber 1, 2 September 1998.

[155]Ibid para 498–520.

[156]Schabas (2012), p. 105.

[157]*Prosecutor v Simeon Nshamihigo* (Case ICTR-01-63-T).

[158]Ibid, para 331. See also *Prosecutor v Micah Muhimana* (Case ICTR-95-1B-T) para 496 (noting that the perpetrator's specific genocidal intent may be inferred from the general context of the perpetration, in consideration of the factors such as the systematic manner of killing).

[159]*Prosecutor v Goran Jelisic* Case No IT-95-10 Trial Chamber 1 of the ICTY, Oral Judgement of 19 October 1999. (*Jelisic* case).

[160]*Jelisic*, para 81–81, *Akayesu* para 520. See also Kittichaisaree (2000), pp. 512–513.

[161]Rome Statute, Article 6; See also *Akayesu,* (note 154).

[162]*The Prosecutor v. Jean Kambanda* (ICTR Case no 97-23-S) Para 40(1)-(4). Jean Kambanda was the first Prime Minister to be convicted of the crime of genocide. He was PM of the interim government of Rwanda established 8 April 1994 during the Rwandan genocide. He was arrested in Nairobi Kenya and transferred to the ICTR Detention Camp in Arusha. Kambanda was subsequently tried and convicted for genocide, conspiracy to commit genocide and complicity in genocide in 1998.

on-going exterminations, which he was aware of, and for his failure to protect the entire population from being destroyed.[163]

Furthermore, culpability stems from the fact that the perpetrator knew or should have known that the act committed would destroy a group in whole or in part.[164] In the *Al-Bashir*[165] case, the PTCI noted that pursuant to the case law of the *ad hoc* tribunals, 'the crime of genocide is completed by *inter alia*, killing or causing serious bodily harm to a single individual with the intent to destroy in whole or in part the group to which such individual belongs.'[166] The crime of genocide may thus be committed during armed conflict or peacetime and therefore is punishable regardless of the context.[167]

Similarly, crimes against humanity require the intent to commit the crime together with the knowledge that the crime is being committed within the context of a widespread or systematic attack.[168] Not only is the definition of crimes against humanity in the Rome Statute more detailed than previous definitions,[169] the requirement of a nexus to armed conflict or proof of a discriminatory motive is absent.[170] This means that crimes against humanity can occur, not only in the course of armed conflict or civil strife but also during times of peace.[171] This is one of the reasons the 2007 post-election violence in Kenya qualified for investigation and prosecution by the ICC. Also, a discriminatory motive is not required for crimes against humanity except for the specific crime of persecution, as discrimination is the essence of that crime.[172]

For an act to constitute a crime against humanity, the specific element requiring that such acts be committed in the context of a widespread or systematic attack must be present. In analysing the underlying acts constituting murder as a crime against humanity, the OTP observed that the *actus reus* requires that the perpetrator killed one or more persons and that the conduct was committed as part of a widespread or systematic attack directed against a civilian population.[173]

---

[163] *Kambanda* case.

[164] Ibid.

[165] *The Prosecutor v. Al-Bashir* Case No ICC-02/05-01/09. Decision on the Prosecution's Application for a Warrant of Arrest agasint Omar Hassan Al-Bashir 4 March 2009. (*Al-Bashir* case).

[166] *Al-Bashir* case, para 119.

[167] Triponel and Pearson (2010), p. 79.

[168] See Rome Statute, art 7.

[169] The ICTY and ICTR Statutes (arts 5 & 3 respectively) listed 9 crimes constituting crimes against humanity whereas the Rome Statute (art 7) has 11 crimes listed under crimes against humanity.

[170] Schabas (2012), pp. 110–111.

[171] Mahnoush Arsanjani (1999), pp. 43–57.

[172] Discriminatory motive was a requirement in the ICTR Statute and although the ICTY Statute contains no such requirement, it was applied by the ICTY in the *Tadic* case. See *Prosecutor v. Tadic* Opinion and Judgement No IT-94-1-T para 652 (7 May 1997).

[173] See Report of the OTP, 'Situation in Nigeria Article 5 Report' 5 August 2013. (Article 5 Report on Nigeria 5 August 2013 on Nigeria) Available at http://www.icc-cpi.int/iccdocs/PIDS/docs/SAS%20-%20NGA%20-%20Public%20version%20Article%205%20Report%20-%2005%20August%202013.PDF (Accessed 29 November 2013) para 91.

The condition of a 'widespread or systematic attack' distinguishes crimes against humanity from ordinary crime. The threshold of 'widespread' was defined by the ICTR as denoting a substantial number of victims, with massive, frequent and large-scale action carried out collectively against a multiplicity of victims.[174] Also, 'systematic' comprises a thoroughly organised and following a regular pattern on the basis of a common policy involving considerable public or private resources.[175] Thus, prosecuting crimes against humanity as ordinary crimes makes light of the gamut of international crimes.

Furthermore, the contextual elements of crimes against humanity include; first that the attack must be targeted against a civilian population[176]; second the attack must involve a state or organisational policy[177]; third, it must be of a widespread or systematic nature[178]; and fourth, there must be an established nexus between the individual act and the attack and the accused must have knowledge of the attack.[179] Thus an accused must know that the attack is directed against a civilian population and that his criminal act comprises part of that attack or at least risks being part of that attack.[180] In addition to the distinction between ordinary domestic crimes and international crimes, the modalities for the transfer of cases from the ICTR to Rwandan domestic courts as the next subsection demonstrates, imply that under the complementarity regime, it is not ideal to equate ordinary crimes with international crimes.

### 4.3.2 The Transfer of Cases from the ICTR to Rwandan National Courts

Rwanda is not a party to the Rome Statute. However, points of interaction between the ICTR and Rwandan national courts in the transfer of cases from the former to the latter make the analysis relevant to the complementarity regime of the Rome statute. The purpose is not necessarily to anticipate the transfer of cases from the ICC to states, although that is permissible and envisaged under the Rome Statute. Rather, it is to derive lessons from the example, to the effect that the legal

---

[174] *Prosecutor v. Akayesu Judgment* No ICTR-96-4-T 2 September 1998. Available at http://www.unictr.org/Portals/0/Case/English/Akayesu/judgement/akay001.pdf paras 579–581.

[175] There must be an element or evidence of organisational policy; see Hans-Peter Kaul dissenting opinion in the *Muthaura et al* case (note 90).

[176] Ibid; Article 5 Report on Nigeria, 5 August 2013, para 79.

[177] Ibid, paras 82–89.

[178] Article 5 Report on Nigeria, 5 August 2013 (note 173) paras 80 & 81.

[179] Ibid, para 35. See also Situation in the Republic of Cote D'Ivoire, 'Decision Pursuant to Article 15 of the Rome Statute on the Authorisation of an Investigation into the Situation in the Republic of Cote d'Ivoire' 3 October 2011 (notified on 15 November 2011), ICC-02/11-14-Corr, para 29.

[180] See *Prosecutor* v *Kunarac et al.* (IT-96-23 & 23/1) 'Foca' Appeals Chamber Judgement of 12 June 2002.

framework of states and their institutional preparedness in conformity with the Rome Statute is critical to their exercise of jurisdictional primacy to investigate and prosecute international crimes.

In pursuit of justice and reconciliation in post-genocide Rwanda, three transitional justice processes were instituted. The first was the International Criminal Tribunal for Rwanda (ICTR), the second was the National Genocide Trials and the third was the *gacaca* proceedings.[181] While the three institutions each aimed at ensuring accountability for those responsible for the genocide, there were significant differences in the methods they employed. However, it is not within the scope of this chapter to analyse prosecutions by these institutions but only to highlight the points of interaction between the ICTR and Rwandan national courts.

Rule 11*bis* of the Rules of Procedure and Evidence (RPE) of the ICTR[182] and the completion strategy formed the basis for the transfer of cases from the ICTR to Rwandan courts.[183] Through the completion strategy, the ICTR was mandated by the Security Council to transfer intermediate and lower-level accused persons to national courts. This was to ensure that the Tribunal focused on those who bore the greatest responsibility for the crimes in order to finish its work within the time designated by the Security Council.

Rule 11*bis* allows a trial chamber to refer a case to a state in whose territory the crime has been committed and in which the accused is arrested provided that the state is willing and adequately prepared to accept the case. In assessing whether a state is competent according to Rule 11*bis* to accept a case from the tribunal, the designated trial chamber must consider whether the state has a legal framework that criminalises the alleged conduct and provides an adequate penalty structure.[184]

However, the Rwandan government was not able to secure the transfer of any cases until June 2011. Prior to transfer, the Rwandan authorities had to ensure that the parliament enacted a Transfer Law (Organic Law No. 11/2007) to comply with the legislative requirements of Rule 11*bis*.[185] Even after the enactment of the Organic Law, Rwanda lacked facilities and had to embark on the building of

[181]Apuuli (2009), pp. 11–30.

[182]RPE Rule 11*bis* (A). (Rule 11*bis* was first introduced into the ICTR RPE in 2002 during the twelfth plenary session of judges (ICTR 12th Plenary Session of 5-6 July 2002 Amendments Adopted at the Plenary Session of Judges Rules of Procedure and Evidence). Rule 11*bis*: Suspension of Indictment in case of Proceedings before National Courts Available at http://ictr-archive09.library.cornell.edu/ENGLISH/rules/050702/amend12.html Accessed 9 June 2012.

[183]See Completion Strategy for the ICTR, United Nations Security Council Resolution 1503 of 2003; Joensen (2013).

[184]Rule 11*bis*(A).

[185]Organic Law No 11/2007 of 16 March 2007 Concerning Transfer of Cases to the Republic of Rwanda from the International Criminal Tribunal for Rwanda (ICTR) and from Other States. Available at http://www.refworld.org/docid/476644652.html (accessed 26 August 2013).

prisons[186] and the training of lawyers before it was found ready to handle the cases.[187] Consequently, the Rwandan national courts only began to receive cases from the ICTR several years after the enactment of the law.

Thus, the *Bosco Uwinkindi*[188] case was the first time the Appeals Chamber of the ICTR judged in favour of transferring a case to Rwandan courts for prosecution. Hitherto, in the *Kanyarukiga*,[189] the *Hategikimana*[190] and the *Munyakazi*[191] cases the Appeals Chamber decided against the transfer to Rwandan national courts because Rwandan laws and fair trial guarantees failed to meet the requirements of Rule 11*bis*.[192] In these cases, the Trial Chambers looked beyond the relevant legislation to the practices of Rwandan courts, thereby coming to perceive the legislation as cosmetic.[193] Another problem was the legal ambiguity between the law and the imposition of the death penalty,[194] which was addressed through an amendment establishing life imprisonment as the maximum sentence for transferred cases.[195]

The lack of an appropriate legal framework in Rwanda effectively militated against the transfer of cases to Rwandan national courts. This is instructive for the complementarity regime because domestic prosecution could only be considered complementarity-based when the state carrying out such prosecution has laws criminalising genocide, crimes against humanity and war crimes as defined in the

---

[186]'Mpanga, A Stronghold for the UN in Rwanda' *International Justice Tribune* 5 May 2008. Available at http://www.rnw.nl/international-justice/article/mpanga-stronghold-un-rwanda (The Rwandan government built the Mpanga Prison near Nyanza in South-Western Rwanda and with financial support from The Netherlands embarked on its reconstruction in February 2008. It contained a 'UN block' designated to meet standards equivalent to the UN Detention Facility in Arusha).

[187]Palmer (2012), pp. 1–21, 13–14.

[188]*The Prosecutor v Jean-Bosco Uwinkindi* ICTR-2001-75-R11*bis* T Ch (Decision on the Prosecutor's Request for Referral to the Republic of Rwanda) 28 June 2011 http://www.unhcr.org/refworld/pdfid/4e5602ca2.pdf Accessed 28 June 2012.

[189]*The Prosecutor v. Gasper Kanyarukiga* Case No. ICTR-2002-78-R11*bis* (Decision on the Prosecutor's Appeal Against Decision on Referral Under Rule 11*bis*) 30 October 2008.

[190]*The Prosecutor v. Ildephonse Hategekimana* ICTR-00-55-R11*bis* AC (Decision on the Prosecutor's Appeal against the Decision on the Transfer under Rule 11*bis*) 4 December 2008.

[191]*The Prosecutor v. Yusuf Munyakazi* (Judgement and Sentence) ICTR-97-36A-T ICTR 5 July 2010. Available at http://www/unhcr.org/refworld/docid/4c722d350.html (Accessed 22 October 2012).

[192]Other cases include *The Prosecutor v Yusuf Munyakazi* ICTR-97-36-R11*bis*AC (Decision on the Prosecutor's Appeal against Decision on Transfer under Rule 11*bis*) 8 October 2008; *The Prosecutor v Jean-Baptiste Gatete* ICTR-2000-61-1 TCI (Decision on the Prosecutor's Request for transfer to the Republic of Rwanda 17 November 2008. (The transfer of Jean-Baptiste Gatete was also refused but was not appealed).

[193]Palmer (2012), p. 10. See also Melman (2011), pp. 1271, 188–1289.

[194]Organic Law, No. 31/2007 of 25 July 2007 Relating to the Abolition of the Death Penalty (Official Gazette of the Republic of Rwanda. Year 46, no. special, 25 July 2007).

[195]Rwanda's Organic Law No. 66/2008 of 21 November 2008 which modified Organic Law No. 31/2007 of 25 July 2007 relating to the Abolition of the Death Penalty.

Rome Statute. It may be argued that the complementarity regime accepts domestic prosecutorial efforts that are far from comprehensive as against the primacy of the *ad hoc* tribunals.[196] Nevertheless, it is submitted that if the ICC and states parties are to draw on the jurisprudence of the *ad hoc* tribunals,[197] then it is necessary to avoid their pitfalls and establish a pragmatic approach to the domestic prosecution of international crimes.

## 4.4 Conclusion

The Rome Statute outlines a set of obligations for individuals who fall within the jurisdiction of the ICC.[198] To the extent that this branch of international law focuses on individuals, it represents a departure from classical international law, which focused on states.[199] However, in constructing the regime of the ICC, it has not proved possible to discount the role of the state completely.[200] Thus, the Rome Statute hinges international criminal justice on the ability and willingness of states to investigate and prosecute international crimes domestically.

Domestic prosecutions represent the new frontline of criminal justice for international crimes, and complementarity as intended in the Rome Statute is meant to first activate the jurisdictions of domestic courts before that of the ICC. African states represent the largest regional support for the ICC in terms of number of ratifications of the Rome Statute. Paradoxically, they appear to be the least prepared to prosecute international crimes domestically, resulting in self-referrals and ultimately in the complex application of the complementarity regime in practical terms.

The domestic prosecutions in the African states discussed in this chapter were based on ordinary crimes as defined by the respective states' domestic statutes, which makes them fall short of the requirements of complementarity. In addition, the states' domestic prosecutions were a reaction to situations in their territories, after the situations were referred to the ICC. Admittedly, there is nothing wrong with such prosecution, taking into consideration that the ICC prosecutes only those who bear the greatest responsibility while states must be involved in bringing the intermediate and lower-level perpetrators to justice. However, prosecutions in the

[196] Sarah Nouwen (Text to note 45 in Ch 3) 1146.

[197] Betts (2005), pp. 735–752, 741. (Noting that 'the ICTR has formed a substantial body of case law and... a solid foundation for the work of the ICC').

[198] Rome Statute, arts 1, 25, 27, 28 (essentially, the ICC has jurisdiction over individuals/persons and not states, but excludes persons under the age of 18 at the time of the alleged commission of a crime in article 26).

[199] Paola Gaeta, 'International Criminalization of Prohibited Conduct' in Antonio Cassese (ed) *The Oxford Companion to International Criminal Justice* (OUP 2010) 63–74. See also Mansell and Openshaw (2013), p. 126.

[200] Akande (2012), pp. 299–324.

states have thus far relied on domestic crimes and they appear to conflict with rather than complement the efforts of the ICC, particularly in Uganda where amnesty and other alternative justice mechanisms are being used.

The underlying assumption of the complementarity regime is that states would ensure transcription of the Rome Statute's crimes into domestic criminal law to allow for domestic prosecutions of those crimes. This argument is premised on the fact that complementarity cannot be based on two distinct bodies of laws. If existing domestic criminal laws were sufficient to deal with international crimes then the Rome Statute would not have been necessary. Thus, a mutually inclusive interpretation of complementarity implies that both the ICC and states will have the same legal basis to act. It may be argued that prosecutions in the DRC constitute complementarity-based prosecutions but the use of military courts makes the argument significantly flawed.

The test of what might constitute appropriate criteria for domestic prosecution in line with complementarity is ill-defined. This is because the complementarity regime of the Rome Statute is still evolving. The 'sentence-based'[201] and 'process-based'[202] theories of complementarity advanced by Jon Heller and Robinson, respectively, are steps towards achieving a practical approach to domestic prosecutions.

This chapter proposes complementarity-based prosecution that looks not only at the charges, process and sentence, as propounded by scholars, but is also holistic in terms of the legal and institutional preparedness of states. Jon Heller acknowledged this point when he noted that the sentence-based theory is not intended to be a permanent solution to the problems facing national criminal justice systems, and that in an ideal world, states would always prosecute international crimes as international crimes, but that the problem is lack of capacity on the part of states.[203]

The analysis of the crimes of genocide and crimes against humanity within the chapter highlights the fact that international crimes and ordinary domestic crimes are not the same and thus domestic prosecution based on ordinary crimes cannot meet the requirements of complementarity. The interaction between the ICTR and Rwanda national courts was further analysed to emphasise the point that a state's legal framework must incorporate international crimes stipulated in the Rome Statute for its domestic prosecution to qualify as complementarity-based. On this point, the domestic prosecution in the United Kingdom was used as a model of complementarity-based prosecution.

The inability of African states to carry out complementarity-based prosecutions is largely due to the lack of implementing legislation in conformity with the Rome Statute. Beyond the legal perspective however, there is also the capacity question. Should African states adopt implementing legislation, will they then have the institutional capacity to carry out complementarity-based prosecutions? The

---

[201] Jon Heller (2012).

[202] Robinson (2012a).

[203] Jon Heller, 133.

institutional preparedness of African states, particularly Nigeria, to carry out complementarity-based prosecution will be analysed subsequently, but first an analysis of the tension between the African Union and the ICC will be undertaken in the next chapter.

## References


Afako B (2002) Reconciliation and justice: *Mato Oput* and the amnesty act. ACORD 64–67. http://www.c-r.org/sites/c-r.org/files/Accord%2011_13Reconciliation%20and%20justice_2002_ENG.pdf. Accessed 15 Jan 2013

AI Report (2004) Darfur: rape as a weapon of war: sexual violence and its consequences, 19 July 2004. http://web.amnesty.org/library/index/ENGAFR540762004. Accessed 25 Apr 2009

Akande D (2012) The effect of security council resolutions and domestic proceedings on state obligations to cooperate with the ICC. JICJ 10:299–324

Akhavan P (2003) The international criminal court in context: mediating the global and local in the age of accountability. AJIL 97:712

Alai C, Mue N (2011) Complementarity and the impact of the Rome Statute and the international criminal court in Kenya. In: Stahn C, ElZeidy M (eds) The international criminal court and complementarity: from theory to practice, vol II. CUP, p 1222

Ambos K, Stegmiller I (2012) Prosecuting international crimes at the international criminal court: is there a Coherent and comprehensive prosecution strategy? Crime Law Soc Change Springer link

Apuuli KP (2009) Procedural due process and the prosecution of genocide suspects in Rwanda. J Genocide Res 11(1):11–30

Arsanjani MH (1999) Defining crimes against humanity at the Rome conference. AJIL 93 (1):43–57

Bassiouni MC (2013) Introduction to international criminal law, 2nd edn. Martinus Nijhoff Publishers, Leiden

Bergsmo M, Bekou O, Jones A (2010) Complementarity after Kampala: capacity building and the ICC's legal tools. Goe J Int'l L 2:791–811

Betts A (2005) Should approaches to post-conflict justice and reconciliation be determined globally, nationally or locally? Eur J Dev Res 17(4):735–752

Bickley LS (2000) US resistance to the international criminal court: is the Sword Mightier than the law? Emory Int Law Rev 14:213

Brandon B, Plessis MD (2005) The prosecution of international crimes: a practical guide to prosecuting ICC crimes in commonwealth. Commonwealth Secretariat, Marlborough House, United Kingdom

Breton-Le Goff G (2010) Ending sexual violence in the Democratic Republic of the Congo. The Fletcher Forum of World Affairs 34(1). Available at http://ui04e.moit.tufts.edu/forum/archives/pdfs/34-1pdfs/34-1_Breton-LeGoff.pdf. Accessed 20 Oct 2012

Brown S, Sriram CL (2012) The big fish wont fry themselves: criminal accountability for post-election violence in Kenya. Afr Aff 111/443:244–260

Cassese A (2005) International law, 2nd edn. OUP, pp 213–217

Cassese A (2010) The rationale for international criminal justice. In: Cassese A (ed) The Oxford companion to international criminal justice. OUP, p 123

Clark JN (2010) The ICC, Uganda and the LRA: re-framing the debate. Afr Stud 69:141–160

Congo Army Colonel guilty of Ordering Mass Rape on New Year's Day: Colonel and Sub-ordinates Escape Death Penalty for Atrocity at Fizi in which 62 women were attacked. Available at http://www.guardian.co.uk/society/2011/feb/21/congo-rape-trial. Accessed 28 May 2012

Cryer R (2005) Prosecuting international crimes: selectivity and the international criminal law regime. CUP

Cryer R, Bekou O (2007) International crimes and ICC cooperation in England and Wales. JICJ 441–459

Doyle J (2011) The men who disgraced the army. Mail Online, 8 September 2011. http://www.dailymail.co.uk/news/article-2035029/Baha-Mousa-inquiry-Army-condemned-gratuitous-violence.html. Accessed 30 Dec 2012

Ellis MS (2003) The international criminal court and its implication for domestic law and national capacity building. Fla. J Int'l L 15:215

Elvarez J (1999) Crimes of states/crimes of hate: lessons from Rwanda. YJIL 24:365. https://litigation-essentials.lexisnexis.com/webcd/app?action=DocumentDisplay&crawlid=1&doctype=cite&docid=24+Yale+J.+Int'l+L.+365&srctype=smi&srcid=3B15&key=863675bfe00f42c9c396d2735d9e2a67. Accessed 15 June 2013

Fletcher GP, Ohlin JD (2005) The commission of inquiry on Darfur and its follow-up: a critical view. JICJ 3:539–561

Garuka C (2011) Genocide as prosecuted by the international criminal tribunal for Rwanda and *Gacaca* Courts in Rwanda. In: Murungu C, Biegon J (eds) Prosecuting international crimes in Africa. Pretoria University Law Press, p 221. http://www.pulp.up.ac.za/pdf/2011_04/2011_04.pdf

Greenawalt AKA (2009) Complementarity in crisis: Uganda, alternative justice and the international criminal court. Va J. Int'l L 50(1):108–159, 113

Greppi E (2008) Inability to investigate and prosecute under article 17. In: Politi M, Gioia F (eds) The international criminal court and national jurisdictions. Ashgate, p 69

Halling M (2010) Push the envelope-watch it bend: removing the policy requirement and extending crimes against humanity. LJIL 23:827

Holmes JT (2002) Complementarity: national courts *versus* the ICC. In: Cassese A et al (eds) The Rome Statute of the international criminal court. OUP, p 667

International and Regional Instruments Relating to Human Rights Ratified by the Democratic Republic of Congo. http://www.icc-cpi.int/asp/statesparties/country&id=5.html. Accessed 28 June 2012

Jennings S (2011) Ugandan war crimes trial hangs in balance. Institute for War & Peace Reporting, 25 August 2011. Available at http://iwpr.net/report-news/ugandan-war-crimes-trial-hangs-balance. Accessed 21 May 2012

Jessberger F (2010) International v. National Prosecution of International Crimes. In: Cassese A (ed) The Oxford companion to international criminal justice. OUP, pp 209–214

Joensen JV (2013) Report on the completion strategy of the international criminal tribunal for Rwanda (as at 10 May 2013). S/2013/310. http://www.unictr.org/Portals/0/English/FactSheets/Completion_St/S-2013-310e.pdf

Jon Heller K (2012) A sentence-based theory of complementarity. Harv. Int'l LJ 53(1):86–134, 87. http://www.harvardilj.org/2012/01/issue_53-1_heller/. Accessed 2 May 2012

Jurdi NN (2011) The international criminal court and national courts: a contentious relationship. Ashgate

Justice for Serious Crimes before National Courts: Uganda's International Crimes Division, January 2012. http://www.hrw.org. Accessed 16 Mar 2012)

Kersten M (2011) Kwoyelo granted amnesty and set free but questions remain, 22 September 2011. Available at http://justiceinconflict.org/2011/09/22/kwoyelo-granted-amnesty-and-set-free-but-questions-remain/. Assessed 2 Nov 2012

Kittichaisaree K (2000) The Nato military action and the potential impact of the international criminal court. SJICL 4:498–529. Available at http://law.nus.edu.sg/sybil/downloads/articles/SJICL-2000-2/SJICL-2000-498.pdf. Accessed 20 Oct 2012

Kleffner JK (2003) The impact of complementarity on national implementation of the substantive international criminal law. JICJ 1:86–113

Kleffner JK (2009) Complementarity of the Rome Statute and National Criminal Jurisdictions. Oxford Scholarship Online, p 2. www.oxfordscholarshiponline.com. Accessed 15 Mar 2012
Klein S (2010) Uganda and the international criminal court review conference-some observations of the conference's impact in the 'Situation Country' Uganda. Goe J Int'l L 2:669
Kress C (2009) The international criminal court as a turning point in the history of international criminal justice. In: Cassese A (ed) The Oxford companion to international criminal justice. OUP, p 143
Lipscomb R (2006) Reconstructing the ICC framework to advance transitional justice: a search for a permanent solution in Sudan. CLR 106:218
Mansell W, Openshaw K (2013) International law: a critical introduction. Hart Publishing, p 126
Mansfield J (2009) Prosecuting sexual violence in the Eastern Democratic Republic of Congo: obstacles for survivors on the road to justice. Afr Hum Rights Law J 9:367–408
Mégret F (2011) Too much of a good thing? Implementation and the uses of complementarity. In: Stahn C, ElZeidy M (eds) The international criminal court and complementarity: from theory to practice, vol I. CUP, pp 361–390
Melman J (2011) The possibility of transfer(?): a comprehensive approach to the international criminal tribunal for Rwanda's rule 11bis to permit transfer to Rwandan domestic courts. Fordham Law Rev 79(3):1271
Nouwen S (2007) The ICC in Sudan: a first test for the complementarity principle. Paper presented at the annual meeting of the International Studies Association 48th Annual Convention, Hilton Chicago, Chicago, IL, USA, 28 February 2007. http://www.allacademic.com/meta/p178592_index.html
Nouwen S (2011) Complementarity in Uganda: domestic diversity or international imposition? In: Stahn C, ElZeidy M (eds) The international criminal court and complementarity: from theory to practice, vol 2. CUP, p 1127
Nouwen S, Werner W (2010) Doing justice to the political: the international criminal court in Ugandan and Sudan. EJIL 21:941–965
Okuta A (2009) National legislation for prosecution of international crimes in Kenya. JICJ 7:1063–1076
OSJI (2010) Promoting complementarity in practice-lessons from three ICC situation countries, 2. http://www.issafrica.org/anicj/uploads/OSJIComplementaritycasestudies.pdf. Accessed 10 March 2013
OSJI (2011) Putting complementarity into practice: domestic justice for international crimes in DRC, Uganda and Kenya, January 2011. Available at http://www.soros.org/reports/putting-complementarity-practice. Accessed 28 June 2012
Palmer N (2012) Transfer or transformation: a review of the rule 11bis decision of the international criminal tribunal for Rwanda. AJICL 20:1–21
Philippe X (2006) The principles of universal jurisdiction and complementarity: how do the two principles intermesh? IRRC 88:375
Report of the International Commission of Inquiry on Darfur to the United Nations Secretary-General 25 January 2005. Available at http://www.un.org/news/dh/sudan/com_inq_darfur.pdf. Accessed 13 Feb 2012
Robinson D (2003) Serving the interests of justice: amnesties, truth commissions and the international criminal court. EJIL 14(3):481–505
Robinson D (2012a) Three theories of complementarity: charge, sentence or process? HILJ 53:165–182
Robinson D (2012b) Three theories of complementarity: charge, sentence or process? Harv. Int'l L. J 53:165. http://www.harvardilj.org/2012/04/online_53_robinson/. Accessed 28 June 2012
Sadat LN, Carden R (2000) The new international criminal court: an uneasy revolution. Goe.J.Int'l L 88:381–383
Schabas WA (2001) The international criminal court jurisdiction, trigger mechanism and relationship to national jurisdictions. In: Politi M, Nesi G (eds) The Rome Statute of the international criminal court: a challenge to impunity, p 197

Schabas WA (2002) Penalties. In Cassese A et al (eds) The Rome Statute of the international criminal court, vol II. OUP, p 1505

Schabas WA (2007) An introduction to the international criminal court, 3rd edn. CUP

Schabas WA (2012) Unimaginable atrocities. OUP

Seman D (2010) Should the prosecution of ordinary crimes in domestic jurisdictions satisfy the complementarity principle? In: Stahn C, van den Herik L (eds) Future perspectives on international criminal justice. p 259

Shaw M (2008) International law, 6th edn. CUP, pp 487–490

Simpson G (2007) The death of Baha Mousa. Melb J Int Law 8:340–355. http://search.informit.com.au/documentSummary;dn=000235949649387;res=IELHSS. Accessed 30 June 2013

Terracino JB (2007) National implementation of ICC crimes: impact on national jurisdictions and the ICC. JICJ 5:421–440

Triponel A, Pearson S (2010) African states and the international criminal court: a silent revolution in international criminal law. J. L & Soc. Cha. 12:65–106

Turns D (1998) Prosecuting violations of international humanitarian law: the position in the United Kingdom. J Armed Confl Law 4:1–39

Udombana N (2005) When neutrality is a sin: the Darfur crisis and the crisis of humanitarian intervention in Sudan. HRQ 27:1149, 1159

Wegner P (2011) Squashing the Amnesty Law in Uganda? Possible implications of the Kwoyelo Trial, 12 September 2011. Available at http://justiceinconflict.org/2011/09/12/squashing-the-amnesty-law-in-uganda-possible-implications-of-the-kwoyelo-trial/. Accessed 20 Aug 2012

Zahar A, Sluiter G (2008) International criminal law: a critical introduction. OUP

Zongwe DP (2012) The new sexual violence legislation in the Congo: dressing indelible scars in human dignity. Afr Stud Rev 55(2):37, 42–45

# Chapter 5
# Unpacking the Tension Between the African Union and the ICC: The Way Forward

**Abstract** During the first decade of its operational phase, the ICC has investigated, prosecuted and secured convictions involving only Africans. With the exception of the situation in Georgia over which the Pre-Trial Chamber I authorised the OTP on 27 January 2016 to open *proprio motu* investigation, all situations and cases before the ICC to date are from the African region. This has prompted the perception that the ICC is anti-Africa. This chapter analyses the relationship between the ICC and African states. It situates the nuances of the relationship more accurately to find that the source of the seemingly antagonistic posture of the African Union against the ICC could be traced, not to the ICC itself, but to the United Nations Security Council. The analysis reveals that it is also not accurate to assert that the ICC is anti-Africa. Rather, with better understanding of the relationship as unpacked by the analysis in this chapter, African states and the ICC stand to gain from a mutually beneficial rapport if there is sincerity between the institutions. This chapter was published in the *African Journal of International and Comparative Law* (2015) 23 (1) 74–105.

It has been asserted that the international criminal justice regime anchored on the complementarity of the ICC could be undermined by distrust, much of which stems from Africa's historical experience with the slave trade and colonialism.[1] This contention seems well-founded, as the ICC is widely perceived as selective and biased against Africa.[2] The perception appears to be justified by the fact that, although the ICC has the potential to cover all states, whether they are party to the Rome Statute or not, it has only African cases before it, even after utilising all

This chapter was published in the *African Journal of International and Comparative Law* in 2015. ((2015)23(1) AJICL 74–105). ISSN: 9548890. Licence has been sought and granted from the Edinburgh University Press to Springer International Publishing AG on 4 July 2016.

[1] Jalloh (2009), pp. 445–499, 452.

[2] Ibid.



O.C. Imoedemhe, *The Complementarity Regime of the International Criminal Court*, DOI 10.1007/978-3-319-46780-1_5

the means by which it may be seized of jurisdiction.[3] As a result, Africans are portrayed as being exclusively responsible for all of humanity's inhumanity.[4]

In previous chapters, it has been proposed that a mutually inclusive interpretation and application of complementarity would be beneficial to both the ICC and states. Further, it has been argued that though not expressly stated in the Rome Statute, it is imperative for states to incorporate the crimes in the Statute into their domestic criminal law. Subsequently, domestic prosecutions in selected African states were analysed in the preceding chapter and it was proposed that for such prosecutions to meet the complementarity threshold, they should be based on international crimes and not on ordinary domestic crimes.

In this chapter, the relationship between the ICC and the African Union (AU) is analysed. The importance of this argument to the entire complementarity regime cannot be overemphasised because except for Georgia, all situations and cases before the ICC to date have come from Africa. This means that the success of the ICC in the investigation and prosecution of these cases will depend on the sustained support and cooperation of African states. Also, the ICC is only able to prosecute a few cases, therefore to close the gaps, African states need credible institutions, in addition to implementing legislation, in order to prosecute lower-level and intermediate perpetrators.

Relations between the two institutions deteriorated from cooperation to conflict following the indictment of President Omar Hassan Ahmad Al-Bashir of Sudan for crimes against humanity and genocide. Therefore, the chapter examines how the trajectory of this relationship can be enhanced for the mutual benefit of both bodies with a view to achieving the goal of complementarity. It is argued that the basis for the tension was the involvement of the United Nations Security Council in the referral of the situation in Darfur, Sudan to the ICC and its subsequent refusal to defer the case as requested by the AU.

This chapter is divided into four sections. The first section discusses the politics behind international criminal law. It analyses the characteristics of selectivity and the 'scapegoat' thesis and argues that, although selectivity features in every criminal justice system, the assertion that the ICC targets African states may not be supported by the facts—particularly because five out of the ten situation countries currently before the ICC were referred by the respective African states' governments themselves.

The relationship between the ICC and the AU is analysed in the second section. In order to capture the essence of this relationship, the section includes a discussion of Africa's modern perspective on conflict and the desire among nations of the continent to achieve peace, security and stability. It is argued that relations between the ICC and the AU had hitherto been cordial and that the current conflict arose from the referral of the situation in Darfur. Therefore, although there might be good

[3] Bikundo (2012), pp. 21–41, 23. However, on 27 January 2016 Georgia was brought to the ICC as a situation country.

[4] Bikundo, 26–27.

reasons why some African leaders perceive the ICC as 'neo-imperialism masquerading as international rule of law',[5] it is proposed that the conflict is not between the AU and the ICC *per se* but rather, it is between the AU and the United Nations Security Council. It is further suggested that if there is sincerity, both the ICC and the AU would benefit from the investigations and prosecutions being carried out by the ICC in Africa.[6] It is therefore prudent for the two institutions to collaborate.

Based on the assertion that the present tension between the AU and the ICC is misplaced, the third section discusses the need to illuminate the tension between the two institutions by characterising the relations between them more accurately. To that end, some points of misunderstanding between the AU and the ICC; conceptualised into legal and political perspectives are identified as further sources of tension.

The legal misconstructions stem from the inaccurate interpretation and application of complementarity and other concepts, including the ICC's jurisdiction over nationals of non-party states and the irrelevance of immunities under the Rome Statute. The political perspective includes discussions on alternative justice mechanisms, discussed in the preceding chapter,[7] the uneven playing field and the United States' exceptionality, both of which are examined in this chapter. Clarifying these points is necessary for the national implementation of the complementarity regime of the Rome Statute in Africa.

It is acknowledged that international criminal law is not always applied equally, but argued nevertheless, that the perception that the ICC has an inappropriate fixation on Africa, to the exclusion of crimes committed elsewhere, amounts to assuming bias where in fact more benign explanations are likely. In support of this, the incidences of self-referrals, particularly of the most recent by another African state, Mali, in January 2012,[8] together with other points, are considered in the fourth section.

The Office of the Prosecutor (OTP) has received information regarding alleged atrocities in various situations all over the world.[9] Although the current crisis in

[5]Jalloh (2006).

[6]Jalloh (2009), pp. 451–452 (noting that both the ICC and the Africa continent needs each other and that if the relationship is properly harnessed, it could offer a 'win-win' prospect for both sides).

[7]See Afako (2002), (Text to notes 115, 128–130 in Ch 4).

[8]Also, on 14 May 2013, another African state, the Union of Comoros referred to the OTP the situation relating to the Israeli raid on the Humanitarian Aid Flotilla bound for Gaza Strip. However, on 6 November 2013, the Prosecutor closed preliminary examination because the situation did not meet the 'sufficient gravity' requirement for opening an investigation. Upon further request for review by the government of the Union of Comoros on 16 July 2015, the Appeals Chamber dismissed the case on 6 November 2015.

[9]The OTP has received information on alleged atrocities in Iraq, Venezuela, Palestine, Colombia, Honduras and Afghanistan, but it has decided not to open investigations into those situations but instead kept them under preliminary examination. See 'Africa Debate - Is the ICC Targeting Africa Inappropriately?' Available at http://iccforum.com/africa (Accessed 3 August 2013).

Syria and other crimes committed by nationals of the United States in Iraq and Guantanamo Bay may have met the gravity threshold, the Prosecutor is unlikely to invoke his or her *proprio-motu* powers to bring these states before the ICC, neither is it likely that the United Nations Security Council will ever refer these situations. This is because, although the first Prosecutor has insisted that he is only guided by legal considerations, the question of whether or not to refer a situation and to indict suspects is not merely legal; it is largely political.[10] Therefore an analysis of the politics of international criminal law and of the ICC is imperative.

## 5.1 The Politics Behind International Criminal Law

The first Chief Prosecutor of the ICC Luis Moreno-Ocampo once declared: 'I apply the law without political considerations. But the other actors have to adjust to the law'.[11] This statement implies that the ICC is an independent judicial institution, which must stay clear of politics. As a consequence, politics is portrayed as external to law, and as something that must be overcome by independent organs acting on the basis of rules.[12] Paradoxically, the ICC's fight against impunity is a fight against politics, with the aim of establishing individual criminal accountability before an independent court, which arguably, is not compromised by political considerations.[13]

Similarly, when asked whether he was 'becoming a politician at the ICC'? Moreno-Ocampo answered, 'on the contrary, I am putting a legal limit to the politicians. That is my job. I police the border-line and say, if you cross this you're no longer on the political side, you are on the criminal side. I am the border control'.[14] However, determining who is 'on the political side' or not is inherently political, especially when it involves the labelling of groups and individuals as international criminals.[15]

Three features of the ICC make it particularly susceptible to political considerations. The first is that, in contrast to its predecessors, post-World War II tribunals and the *ad hoc* tribunals, the ICC, with jurisdiction over on-going armed conflicts, operates in the midst of conflict. Thus, while the Nuremberg, Tokyo, former

---

[10]Udombana (2012).

[11]Luis Moreno-Ocampo, former Chief Prosecutor of the ICC, 'Keynote Address on the International Criminal Court to the Council on Foreign Relations' Washington DC 4 February 2010; 'Keynote Address at the Salzburg Law School at the 10th Anniversary of the Rome Statute of the International Criminal Court Salzburg Law School on International Humanitarian, Human Rights and Criminal Law' Salzburg August 2008.

[12]Nouwen and Werner (2010), pp. 941–965.

[13]Ibid.

[14]Smith (2009). Available at http://www.theafricareport.com/News-Analysis/interview-luis-moreno-ocampo-icc-prosecutor.html (Accessed 25 September 2013).

[15]Nouwen and Werner, 962.

Yugoslavia and Rwanda Tribunals dealt only with defeated antagonists in aftermath situations, the ICC can be used as an instrument for defeating enemies.[16] Consequently, when the ICC gets involved in continuing strife, it can be expected to end up in political struggles.

The second is that one of the trigger mechanisms of the ICC's jurisdiction is referral by the United Nations Security Council. The Security Council is a political body, and yet it is empowered to refer situations to a judicial institution. Such authority makes it difficult to separate the ICC from the politics of the Security Council, especially as the Security Council is further empowered to defer situations it has already referred.[17] Closely related to the power of the Security Council to refer situations to the ICC is the Prosecutor's discretionary powers on whether or not to proceed and who to indict or not in a particular situation. The exercise of these powers, described in Article 53, particularly that of the prosecutor's appraisal regarding whether the indictment of a certain person would serve the 'interest of justice',[18] necessarily involves political considerations.

The third feature is the ICC's absolute dependence on states' cooperation. Therefore, its institutional interests may politicise its sentiments, for example, by necessitating the consideration of whether a case is against rebel groups or against state officials and determinations based on the need to attract more cooperation.[19] The more the ICC's suspects are generally recognised as enemies of the state or of mankind as a whole,[20] the greater the likelihood that the state of which the suspects are nationals and other states will cooperate with the court by executing its arrest warrants.[21]

In view of the above, the politics of international criminal law are evident in distinction between when the ICC's jurisdiction is invoked to prosecute certain individuals and when it is not. The distinction does not necessarily imply that the ICC betrays justice or the rule of law. Nor does it mean that the 'ICC is the only site of political contestation'.[22] Rather, it requires the admission that the ICC is not a non-political oasis in a political world.[23]

Inherent in the complementarity regime is the fact that the jurisdiction of the ICC can be invoked to prosecute certain individuals. This is because in practical terms, the ICC can only prosecute a small number of perpetrators, namely, those who bear the greatest responsibility. However, prosecuting a select few is insufficient to serve

---

16 Crawford (2012), p. 682; Simpson (2007), p. 116.

17 Rome Statute, Art 16.

18 Jo Stigen (2011), p. 504.

19 Nouwen and Werner (2010), p. 963.

20 Simpson (2007), p. 75.

21 Nouwen and Werner, 963.

22 De Waal (2004), (noting how political opponents in Darfur have banked on international responses in taking their positions).

23 Clarke (2009), p. 237.

the purpose of preventing criminality,[24] and this has led to accusations of selectivity and the formulation of the scapegoat thesis.

### 5.1.1 Selectivity

Kenneth Davis describes selectivity as the situation in which an enforcement agency or officer chooses to use his discretionary power to do nothing about a case in which action would be clearly justified and expected.[25] Such power involves the selection of parties against whom the law is enforced.[26] According to Courtenay Griffiths, 'there is an unspoken truth about international criminal law as currently practiced. It is that certain individuals, from certain countries of origin will never find themselves indicted before an international criminal tribunal.'[27] Selectivity in relation to which suspects the international community is prepared to prosecute collectively is known as selectivity *ratione personae*.[28]

Analysis of selectivity *ratione personae* is found on the fact that political influences should not interfere with the equal application of the law.[29] Admittedly, selective enforcement of law is not inherently wrong because prosecutorial discretion is allowed in almost all legal systems.[30] This is because while equal application of the law is desirable, in practical terms, no criminal justice system has the capacity to prosecute all crimes no matter their gravity.[31] In this sense, all terrestrial justice is selective.[32] The question is therefore, not whether selective prosecution should occur, as it is almost impossible that it does not, but when selective enforcement is unacceptable.[33] Clearly, selective enforcement would be unacceptable when there is a duty to prosecute all crimes.[34]

There are two aspects of selectivity *ratione personae*. The first is legal-based and the second is legitimacy-based. The legal element of selectivity was explained by

[24]Tallgren (2002), p. 576.

[25]Davis (1969), p. 163.

[26]Ibid.

[27]Courtenay Griffiths (2012), (Griffiths was Counsel to former President Charles Taylor of Liberia during his trial by the Special Court for Sierra Leone).

[28]McCormack (1996–1997), pp. 681, 683. (McCormack also discusses selectivity *ratione materiae* i.e. selectivity in relation to the acts that the international community is prepared to characterise as 'war crimes').

[29]Cryer (2005), p. 192.

[30]Ibid.

[31]Ambos (2000), pp. 495, 525.

[32]Damaska (2008), pp. 347, 361. Also available at http://digitalcommons.law.yale.edu/fss_papers/1573.

[33]Davis (1969), pp. 167–168.

[34]Cryer, Ibid, 193.

the Appeals Chamber of the ICTY in the *Čelebići*[35] case. The Appeals Chamber noted that for a plea of selective enforcement to be accepted, there must be evidence establishing unlawful or improper motives and evidence that other similarly situated persons were not prosecuted.[36] This is a high threshold, as proving a motive is very difficult, although improper or unlawful motives may be demonstrated by showing that the prosecutor has violated his duty of impartiality.[37] Nevertheless, even where selectivity is established, the appropriate remedy does not include overturning a conviction.[38]

A legitimacy-based perspective on selectivity comprises an evaluation of international criminal law based on equal application. The legitimacy of criminal law is undermined when the law is neither general nor applied equally.[39] As argued by Robert Cryer, 'when a law is general and yet in practice is applied only against a certain group or groups, the effect is the same as if it were explicitly targeted at those groups by its terms'.[40] This is because it is insufficient to simply look at the law as it is written; 'we must consider the interaction between the law itself and the discretion in the criminal process if we are to understand the social reality of the criminal law.'[41]

Thomas Franck further explicates that legitimacy encompasses principles of coherence and consistency.[42] According to him, a rule is coherent when, in its application, similar cases are treated similarly, and when the rule relates, in a principled fashion, to other rules of the same system. Consistency requires that a rule, whatever its content, be applied in similar or applicable instances.[43]

Accusations of selective enforcement involve allegations that international crimes are ignored when it is considered politically expedient to do so; consequently, international criminal law has been criticised for being selective.[44] During the Nuremberg and Tokyo trials, for example, the law was applied only to the defeated powers. In his opening speech, Justice Jackson admitted that it was not ideal that the victors tried the vanquished,[45] but declared: '...let me make clear that while the law is first applied against the German aggressors, the law includes, and if it is to serve a useful purpose, it must condemn aggression by any other nations,

---

[35]*Prosecutor v Delalić, Mucić, Delić and Landžo* Judgement, IT-96-21-A 20 February 2001 (*Čelebići* case).

[36]*Čelebići* case, *para 611.*

[37]Ibid, paras 602–603.

[38]Ibid, para 618.

[39]Cryer (2005), p. 195.

[40]Ibid.

[41]Ashworth (2009), p. 9.

[42]Franck (1995), p. 35.

[43]Ibid 38.

[44]Cryer, 194–198.

[45]Justice Jackson in Trial 1, Trial of Major War Criminals Nuremberg 51. Available at http://law2.umkc.edu/faculty/projects/ftrials/nuremberg/jackson.html.

including those who sit here now in judgement.'[46] However, this statement did not assuage the 'victor's justice'[47] cliché for which the trials were and are known to date.

Selectivity was further observed in the creation of the *ad hoc* tribunals, the ICTY and the ICTR, although in a different dimension. Richard Goldstone highlighted selectivity in the establishment of the tribunals thus:

> The problem with the UNSC is that it says no in the case of Cambodia, Mozambique, Iraq and other places where terrible war crimes have been committed, but yes in the case of Yugoslavia and Rwanda. It is noteworthy that no *ad hoc* tribunals would ever be established to investigate war crimes committed by any of the five permanent members of the United Nations Security Council or those nations these powerful states might wish to protect.[48]

Consequently, like incidents are not being treated alike and as noted by the defendant and *amici curiae* in the *Milosevic*[49] case, '*ad hoc* reactions relating to one country corrupt justice and law'.[50] Similarly, the Security Council, albeit by agreement with Sierra Leone, established the Special Court for Sierra Leone (SCSL),[51] but it has not responded to other conflicts in a similar way.[52] In his submission, the defence counsel in the *Charles Taylor*[53] case noted:

> The Prosecution of Charles Taylor before the Special Court for Sierra Leone has been irregular, selective and vindictive from its inception. Examined from any vantage point imaginable, the case against Taylor has at its core political roots and motives and the inexorable determination of the United States and Great Britain to have Taylor removed and kept out of Liberia at any cost. Indeed this case directly raises the question of whether the judicial process can be fashioned into a political tool for use by powerful nations to remove democratically-elected leaders of other nations that refuse to serve as their handmaidens and footstools.[54]

---

[46]Trial 1, 85.

[47]Grandi (2013), pp. 1–17. Available at http://jpr.sagepub.com/content/early/2013/06/20/0022343313480202.full.pdf+html (accessed 15 August 2013).

[48]Goldstone (2013). Available at http://africanbusinessmagazine.com/special-reports/sector-reports/icc-vs-africa/icc-a-tool-to-recolonise-africa (Accessed 24 July 2013). See also Scharf (1995), pp. 167–174, 170.

[49]*Prosecutor v. Slobodan Milosevic* IT-99-37, Decision on Preliminary Motions 8 November 2001, paras 8–10.

[50]Ibid para 11.

[51]Agreement between the United Nations and the Government of Sierra Leone on the Establishment of the Special Court for Sierra Leone signed 16 January 2002 pursuant to Security Council resolution 1315 of 14 August 2000 wherein it expressed deep concern at the very serious crimes committed within the territory of Sierra Leone against the people of Sierra Leone.

[52]See Africa Debate (note 8); Soares (2013), pp. 319–338, 328.

[53]*Prosecutor v. Charles Ghankay Taylor* Case No SCSL-03-1-T (Judgment of 26 April 2012) (in a unanimous judgment, the Trial Chamber II of the SCSL found Charles Taylor guilty of aiding and abetting 11-count indictment for crimes against humanity of murder, rape, sexual slavery, enslavement and other inhumane acts.

[54]Courtenay Griffiths (2012).

Further to the above selectivity discourse, Gerry Simpson notes that ‘each war crime trial is an exercise in partial justice to the extent that it reminds us that the majority of war crimes remain unpunished. If Yugoslavia why not Somalia, if Rwanda why not Guatemala?’[55] Also, Alfred Rubin postulates that ‘unless the law can be seen to apply to George H.W. Bush [who ordered the invasion of Panama]...it will seem hypocritical again.’[56] Similarly, Ian Brownlie notes that ‘political considerations, power and patronage will continue to determine who is tried for international crimes and who is not.’[57]

It has been argued that selectivity is also demonstrated with respect to the ICC.[58] This is because even though the ICC has the potential to prosecute cases from all over the world, it has only African situations and cases before it, even after utilising all the trigger mechanisms in the Rome Statute.[59] Thus, it appears that it could be rightly asserted that the ICC has been selective in its prosecutions of African nationals on the basis that their states are weak or because they fail to enjoy the support of powerful countries. As argued by Damaska, when international prosecutors bring to justice only or mainly criminals from weak nations, the result is that they discriminate among human rights abusers on the basis of their citizenship.[60]

Arguably, the formulation of a prosecutorial strategy which allows for some exercise of discretion, ultimately has led to the accusation that the ICC targets only Africa and Africans. However, there are facts to the contrary which will be examined subsequently, but first, an analysis of the second aspect of the politics of international criminal law, the scapegoat thesis, is in order.

### 5.1.2 Is Africa Merely a Laboratory or a Scapegoat?

Jean Ping,[61] then Chairperson of the African Union Commission, once noted: ‘we are not against international justice, it seems that Africa has become a laboratory to test the new international law’.[62] Referring to the ICC as a ‘fraudulent institution’, Paul Kagame,[63] the President of Rwandan further observed; ‘Rwanda cannot be

[55] Simpson (1997), pp. 1, 8–9.

[56] Rubin (fall 1993), pp. 73, 74 Cited in Cryer (2005), p. 194.

[57] Brownlie (2003), p. 575.

[58] Bikundo (2012), p. 23.

[59] Ibid.

[60] Damaska (2008).

[61] Jean Ping was former Foreign Minister of Gabon who headed the AU from 2008–2012. He was succeeded by South Africa’s Minister of Home Affairs Nkosazana Dlamini-Zuma who became the first female head of the AU in July 2012. http://www.tesfanews.net/jean-ping-lost-au-chairmanship-to-dlamini-zuma/.

[62] BBC News, ‘Vow to Pursue Sudan over Crimes’ 27 September 2008. Available at http://news.bbc.co.uk/1/hi/world/africa/7639046.stm (Accessed 3 September 2013).

[63] Paul Kagame is President of Rwanda since April 2000 to date.

party to ICC for one simple reason…with ICC all the injustices of the past including colonialism, imperialism, keep coming back in different forms. They control you. As long as you are poor, weak there is always some rope to hang you. ICC is made for Africans and poor countries'.[64]

In a similar vein, Bikundo asserts that the arbitrariness of the selection of only Africans for prosecution by the ICC is revealed by the fact that those Africans neither have the monopoly on international criminality nor can they be regarded as the worst offenders.[65] Therefore, he proposes that 'the ICC starts with Africans in order to cut its teeth before promising to sink its talons on bigger prey'.[66] This buttresses the point that the ICC is yet to achieve legitimacy and respect and in seeking such credibility it has begun with the weakest and not necessarily the most criminal. This is the scapegoat thesis.

According to Jacques Derrida, a scapegoat is a being that simultaneously belongs and does not belong to a society.[67] This ambiguous status between being an 'insider' and an 'outsider' makes scapegoats more amenable to sacrifice for communal atonement or expiation[68]; they belong to the community enough to be associated with it but are just vulnerable enough within it to be picked as the victims of sacrifice.[69] The scapegoat therefore exemplifies a channel through which a social body figuratively expels evil, harm or wrongdoing from itself as a purification process.[70] Frazer and Fraser in their ethnographic study of the scapegoat, documented examples from all over the world, demonstrating the theory and practice of ritually transferring the guilt of a whole people onto an individual, animal or object.[71]

Thus, it has been asserted that by targeting Africa, the continent is being used as a scapegoat; a sacrifice in order to mollify the international community through criminal justice.[72] Admittedly, the scapegoat thesis and selectivity discourse lend credence to the assertion that Africa is inappropriately targeted by the ICC. However, there may be justifications for the fact that most of the situations and cases currently under investigation or prosecution happen to be in Africa.[73]

---

[64]Kezio-Musoke (2008) (Accessed 3 September 2013).

[65]Bikundo (2012), p. 28.

[66]Ibid.

[67]Derrida (1981), pp. 130–134.

[68]Bikundo, 35.

[69]Bikundo, 35.

[70]Ibid.

[71]Frazer and Fraser (2009), p. 557.

[72]Bikundo, 29.

[73]Kamari Clarke, 'Is the ICC Targeting Africa Inappropriately or are there Sound Reasons and Justifications for Why all of the Situations Currently Under Investigation or Prosecution happen to be in Africa?' in Africa Debate (note 9).

## 5.2 Africa and the ICC

The relationship between the ICC and Africa suggests that the ICC enjoys its largest support from the continent. This support is evident in the number of ratifications of the Rome Statute by African states, 34 to date, thus constituting the largest regional bloc among states parties.[74] Indeed the very first ratifications of the Rome Statute came from Africa.[75] In addition, active support for the ICC was reflected in African states' participation in the Rome Diplomatic Conference that negotiated the Statute establishing the ICC.[76] This suggests that African states contributed to the final wording of the document. Arguably, part of Africa's support for the ICC was the hosting of the first Review Conference of the Rome Statute in Kampala, Uganda in May and June 2010. As a prelude to the Conference, at the July 2009 AU Summit held in Libya, the AU urged its member states to prepare for it fully.[77]

Furthermore, states in the region have been described as the most 'frequent users'[78] and 'repeat customers'[79] of the ICC. It is postulated that this is due to the relatively high prevalence of conflicts, serious human rights violations and the general lack of a credible legal system to address them. The referrals of situations by some states' governments in the continent might also constitute manifestations of the cordial relationship.

However, the good will diminished with the indictment of the president of Sudan, Omar Hassan Al-Bashir. Identifying the reasons requires a brief discussion of Africa's more recent attempts towards realising peace and stability. It is argued that Africans cannot continue to blame their failings on their colonial past. Rather, Africa's approach to peace and stability, the indictment of Al-Bashir by the ICC and the consequent reaction of African governments will be examined. The importance of this analysis is to demonstrate that the relationship between the ICC and African

---

[74] 124 countries are states parties to the Rome Statute. Out of them 34 are African States, 19 are Asia-Pacific States, 18 are from Eastern Europe, 28 are from Latin American and Caribbean States and 25 are from Western European and other states. See Status of states parties to the Rome Statute at http://www.icc-cpi.int/en_menus/asp/states%20parties/african%20states/Pages/african%20states.aspx (Assessed 12 March 2016).

[75] Simmons and Danner (2010), pp. 225. (Senegal was the first to ratify the Rome Statute on 2 February 1999). See also Mills (2012), pp. 404–447, 409 (noting that of the 160 states in Rome only seven voted against the Statute including one African state; Libya).

[76] Keppler (2011). Available at http://allafrica.com/stories/201109200230.html (Assessed 13 March 2013).

[77] AU Assembly, 'Decision on the meeting of African States parties to the Rome Statute of the International Criminal Court. Doc. Assembly/AU/13(XIII)' in *Decisions and Declarations* of the 13th ordinary session of the AU Assembly: Assembly/AU/Dec. 245 (XIII) (Sirte, 3 July 2009) 7–8, para 8. Available at http://www.au.int/en/sites/default/files/ASSEMBLY_EN_1_3_JULY_2009_AUC_THIRTEENTH_ORDINARY_SESSION_DECISIONS_DECLARATIONS_%20MESSAGE_CONGRATULATIONS_MOTION_0.pdf (Accessed 25 July 2013).

[78] Jalloh (2009), p. 447.

[79] Igwe (2008), p. 294.

states could be enhanced for the purposes of establishing the credibility of the ICC and for helping the AU realise its goal of stable peace on the continent.

### 5.2.1 *Africa's Modern Perspective on Peace and Stability*

The 1950s and 1960s represent Africa's first years of political independence from colonialism.[80] The aspiration that independence would translate to greater stability, prosperity and development was not, however, realised in no small part because many African states began to exhibit traits of colonialism even among and within themselves, as a result of which several conflicts were recorded.[81]

According to the United Nations' report, well over 30 civil wars have been fought in Africa since 1970.[82] Of these, the majority were internal i.e., civil wars, as opposed to inter-state or international conflicts.[83] The continent was thus labelled the most conflict-ridden and conflict prone region in the world,[84] as 10 out of the 24 most war-ridden countries recorded between 1980 and 1994, were in Africa.[85] It is further alleged that over a decade later, as of 2007, the region retained majority of the world's conflicts.[86]

However, Paul Zeleza regards the above assertion as a distortion of facts calculated by the West to portray African conflicts as peculiar and pathological without rational explanations.[87] He argues that from a historical standpoint, Africa has been no more prone to violent conflicts than other regions. Indeed, Africa's share of the more than 180 million people who died from conflicts and atrocities during the twentieth century is relatively modest.[88] On the scale of sheer casualties, there is no equivalent in African history to Europe's First and Second World Wars, or to the civil wars and atrocities in revolutionary Russia and China.[89]

[80]Beginning with Sudan which had its independence in 1956, other African states immediately followed in regaining independence in the 1960s and 1970s.

[81]Kambudzi (2004), pp. 53–66.

[82]Report of the Secretary General to the United Nations Security Council: 'The Causes of Conflict and the Promotion of Durable Peace and Sustainable Development in Africa' 16 April 1998 para 4. UN doc.A/52/871-S/1998/318. See also Stockholm International Peace Research Institute (SIPRI) (2000).

[83]Ibid.

[84]Jalloh (2009) 475.

[85]Cabinet Sub-Committee on Conflict Prevention in Africa, 'Causes of Conflicts in Africa' Consultation Document March 2001 http://www.dfid.gov.uk/pubs/files/conflict-africa.pdf.

[86]Harbom and Wallensteen (2009), pp. 577–587 http://jpr.sagepub.com/content/46/4/577.full.pdf+html.

[87]Zeleza (2008), pp. 1–26, 1.

[88]Ibid.

[89]Ibid.

Zeleza's argument appears valid because in 2012, 32 conflicts in 30 different states and locations were recorded.[90] Although 13 of these occurred in Africa,[91] others which occurred in America,[92] Asia,[93] Europe[94] and the Middle East[95] were of greater intensity and gravity than those in Africa. The conflicts in Syria and Afghanistan ranked highest in gravity, while Somalia, Pakistan, Yemen and Sudan followed in intensity and number of battle-related deaths[96] in 2012.[97] Also, the Middle East saw the highest number of battle-related deaths in 2012.[98]

Be that as it may, the conflicts in Africa have led to the deaths of millions of Africans and to the displacement of thousands more.[99] Different conflicts have been attended with extreme sexual violence and the deliberate targeting of not just civilians but women and children.[100] States including Angola, Burundi, Congo, Liberia, Mozambique, Rwanda, Sierra Leone, Somalia, Sudan and Uganda were involved in conflicts of varying degrees, with some spilling over to neighbouring states.[101]

In the quest for peace and stability in the continent, the Organisation of African Unity (OAU) was established with the expectation that it would help foster accord on the continent.[102] However, the OAU's extreme interpretation of sovereignty and

---

90 Themnér and Wallensteen (2013), pp. 509–521. Available at http://jpr.sagepub.com/content/50/4/509.full.pdf+html (Accessed 15 August 2013).

91 These include Algeria, Central African Republic, Ethiopia, Ivory Coast, Libya, Mauritania, Nigeria, Rwanda, Senegal, Somalia, South Sudan, Sudan, Uganda. Out of these, the conflicts in Cote d'Ivoire, Libya, Mauritania and Uganda were no longer active in 2012.

92 Colombia and the United States of America.

93 Afghanistan, Cambodia, India, Myanmar, Pakistan, Philippines, Tajikistan and Thailand.

94 Russia.

95 Iran, Iraq, Israel, Syria, Turkey, Yemen. See generally UCDP at http://www.pcr.uu.se/research/ucdp/faq/.

96 Battle-related deaths are all deaths-military as well as civilian- related to combat in a conflict involving the armed forces of the warring parties which includes traditional battlefield fighting, guerrilla activities and all kinds of bombardments of military units, cities and villages. See Themnér and Wallensteen (2013), p. 520.

97 Themnér and Wallensteen, 510 (Noting that Syria had over 15,000 battle-related deaths in 2012 and that this is an exceptionally high figure).

98 In 2012, the number of battle-related deaths recorded in the Middle East was 34,754, Asia recorded 14,759 while Africa had 9379. Europe was 750 and Americas 618. See Themnér and Wallensteen, 512.

99 Clarke, 'Is ICC Targeting Africa Inappropriately?' (note 73).

100 See for example, African Union Peace and Security, 'Women and Children in Armed Conflicts/Gender Mainstreaming' Available at http://www.peaceau.org/en/topic/women-and-children-in-armed-conflicts-gender-mainstreaming; 'Women Targeted or Affected by Armed Conflict: What Role for Military Peacekeepers?' Being a Conference Summary of May 27–29 2008 Wilton Park, Sussex. http://www.stoprapenow.org/uploads/advocacyresources/1282164694.pdf.

101 Kambudzi (2004).

102 The Organisation of African Unity (OAU) was established on 25 May 1963 in Addis-Ababa Ethiopia to promote unity. See preamble and Articles II & III. Available at http://www.au.int/en/sites/default/files/OAU_Charter_1963_0.pdf (Accessed 30 August 2013).

the principle of non-intervention in the internal affairs of its member states militated against the achievement of its objective.[103] It did, however, achieve some successes in its support for national liberation, especially the fight against apartheid.

As a rebranded version of the OAU, the African Union (AU) came into existence in 2002, about 8 days after the coming into force of the ICC.[104] It was an attempt by states in the continent to create a more unified front to address Africa's problems. In this regard, the AU has pursued the 'African Renaissance', which entails a commitment to anti-colonialism, African solidarity, African responsibility for policies (commonly referred to as 'African solutions for African problems') and democracy.[105]

In order to realise the objectives of the African Renaissance, the AU established the African Peer Review Mechanism (APRM) and the Principle of 'non-indifference'. The APRM, headed by former South African President Thabo Mbeki, was intended to ensure that African states' human rights records were reviewed by a panel under the APRM with a view to stemming violence in the continent. The legal adviser of the AU explained the term 'non-indifference' as a form of active solidarity that conforms to the maxim in most African cultures that 'you do not fold your hands and just look on when your neighbour's house is on fire'.[106]

The AU's main objective is to promote peace, security and stability on the continent based on the understanding that Africa needs to protect the well-being of her peoples and their environment, as well as create conditions conducive for sustainable economic growth and development.[107] In furtherance of this objective, Article 4(h) empowers the AU to intervene in the internal affairs of member states where genocide, war crimes and crimes against humanity are being committed.[108]

In addition, the AU adopted the Protocol Relating to the Establishment of the Peace and Security Council of the African Union (the Protocol).[109] The Protocol created the Peace and Security Council (PSC) as the permanent mechanism for

---

[103] Mills (2012), p. 412.

[104] Swarns (2002).

[105] In January 2011, the AU Assembly further recognised these elements of the African Renaissance in a discussion on 'Shared Values'. See AU Summit, 'Towards Greater Unity and Integration Through Shared Values' 31 January 2011 AU Assembly 16th Ord. Sess. AU Doc Assembly/AU/Decl. 1 (XVI). See also Borer and Mills (2011), p. 76.

[106] Kioko (2003), pp. 807, 819–820. (Ben Kioko is Legal Counsel to the AU Commission).

[107] Constitutive Act of the African Union (AU) adopted 11 July 2000 and entered into force 26 May 2001, para 8 of the Preamble.

[108] Constitutive Act, Art 4(h) (stating the right to intervene in a member state pursuant to a decision of the Assembly in respect of grave circumstances; namely genocide, war crimes and crimes against humanity).

[109] Pursuant to Article 5(2) of the Constitutive Act, the Protocol for the Establishment of the Peace and Security Council of the African Union was adopted by the 1st Ordinary Session of the Assembly of the African Union in Durban, 9 July 2002. (the Protocol) Available at http://www.africa-union.org/root/au/organs/psc/Protocol_peace%20and%20security.pdf.

conflict prevention, management and resolution in the continent.[110] The AU's further commitment to undertaking the tasks of post-conflict reconstruction, peace building and revitalisation of state institutions in its members states experiencing conflict were outlined in the Protocol.[111]

Most significantly, Article 4(o) of the Constitutive Act provides for respect for the sanctity of human life, condemns impunity and political assassination, acts of terrorism and subversive activities.[112] The combined intention of the 'sanctity of human life' and 'rejection of impunity' is to protect the civilian population from atrocities. To this end, the AU has the right to unilaterally deploy the African Standby Force (ASF) in grave circumstances or, alternatively, to request an AU member state to restore stability in the territory of any other member state.[113] This makes Africa the first region in the world to provide a specific legal basis for military intervention during conflict in order to protect the civilian population.[114]

In order to realise its objectives, African leaders undertook, both in the Constitutive Act and in the Protocol, to engage other governments, civil societies, international organisations, for example, the United Nations, and other external entities.[115] In relation to the ICC, these instruments represent an avenue for mutually beneficial AU-ICC cooperation on issues ranging from technical assistance, cooperation and concrete measures towards ensuring peace, security and stability in Africa. Indeed, until recently, there had been discussions of forming a Memorandum of Understanding between the two institutions.[116] The indictment of Al-Bashir by the ICC halted these negotiations.

### *5.2.2 The Case against President Omar Hassan Ahmad Al-Bashir of Sudan*[117]

With the adoption of the Rome Statute, it was hoped that the ICC would help ensure greater consistency in the application of international criminal justice by removing

[110]Ibid, Art 2.

[111]Ibid, Arts 3(a)(Objectives) & 14(Peace Building).

[112]See Constitutive Act, Art 4(o).

[113]See Constitutive Act, Art 4(h) & (j) & The Protocol, Art 13.

[114]Jalloh (2009) 458.

[115]See Constitutive Act, Art 13(C) & The Protocol, Arts 17–20.

[116]Kambudzi (2007), pp. 35–37.

[117]Pre-Trial Chamber I, 'ICC issues a warrant of arrest for Omar Al-Bashir, President of Sudan'; Situation in Darfur, Sudan (ICC-02/05-157) 'Public Redacted Version of Prosecutor's Application under Article 58 filed on 28 July 2008'; *Prosecutor v. Omar Al-Bashir* (ICC-01/05-157), 'Decision on the Prosecution's Application for a Warrant of Arrest against Omar Hassan Ahmad Al-Bashir' 4 March 2009.

it from the vagaries of Security Council politics.[118] Unfortunately, that did not happen as a role was ultimately carved out in the Rome Statute for the body to refer and defer situations to the ICC.[119] It appears that the involvement of a political body in a judicial process haunts the ICC, as the Sudanese controversy demonstrates.

Following the Prosecutor's application for an arrest warrant for President Al-Bashir, the AU's Peace and Security Council immediately called on the United Nations Security Council to invoke Article 16 of the Rome Statute to defer the process initiated by the ICC.[120] The AU stated that, while it endorses criminal accountability for gross human rights violations, given the delicate nature of the processes in Sudan, the search for justice should be pursued in a way that complements rather than impedes efforts to secure lasting peace in the country.[121]

Two arrest warrants were nevertheless issued against President Al-Bashir, first in 2009 for war crimes and crimes against humanity, and then in 2010 for genocide.[122] On both occasions, the AU adopted resolutions, in its summits of 2009 and 2010.[123] In the July 2010 Summit in Kampala, Uganda, the AU expressed its disappointment that the United Nations Security Council had not acted upon its request to defer the proceedings against President Al-Bashir in accordance with Article 16.[124] Consequently, the AU called on its member states not to cooperate with the ICC in the arrest and surrender of Al-Bashir to The Hague.[125] The call not to cooperate was not new, as it only reiterated an earlier decision of the AU.[126] However, it is contrary to African states' obligations under the Rome Statute to cooperate fully with the ICC.

---

[118]Jalloh (2009), p. 561.

[119]Rome Statute, Articles 13(b) & 16.

[120]AU Peace and Security Council Decision (PSC/MIN/Comm CXLII) 21 July 2008 paras 3, 5, 9 & 11(i); AU Assembly Decision on the Application by the International Criminal Court Prosecutor for the Indictment of the President of the Republic of Sudan (Doc. 221 (XII) 3 February 2009 paras 2 & 3; Peace and Security Council Decision (PSC/PR/Comm CLXXV) 5 March 2009 paras 4–6. See also AU Press Statement, 'The Chairperson of the Commission Expresses Deep Concern at the Decision of the Pre-Trial Chamber of the International Criminal Court on Darfur' 4 March 2009.

[121]Ibid, AU PSC Decision 21 July 2008.

[122]See ICC, 'Darfur Sudan' available at http://www.icc-cpi/Menus/ICC/Situations+and+cases/Situations/Situaation+ICC+0205/ (Accessed 4 August 2013).

[123]AU Summit, 'Decision on the progress report of the Commission on the implementation of decision Assembly/AU/Dec.270 (XIV) on the second ministerial meeting on the Rome Statute of the International Court: Doc.Assembly/AU/10 (XV) in Decisions, Declarations, Resolution of the 15th ordinary session of the AU Assembly: Assembly /AU/Dec.296 (XV) (Kampala 27 July 2010) 24–25. Available at http://www.au.int/en/sites/default/files/ASSEMBLY_EN_25_27_July_2010_BCP_ASSEMBLY_OF_THE_AFRICAN_UNION_Fifteenth_Ordinary_Session.pdf (Accessed 25 July 2013).

[124]Ibid, para 4.

[125]Ibid, para 5.

[126]See AU Assembly, Decisions and Declarations of the 13th ordinary session (note 77) 7–8, paras 9 & 10.

Thus, it appears that some African states are more committed to the AU's call for non-cooperation than to observing their international obligations under the Rome Statute. As a result, Al-Bashir has freely visited several African states who are party to the Rome Statute without fear of being arrested and surrendered to the ICC. On 22 July 2010, President Al-Bashir travelled to Chad to attend a summit of the Community of Sahel-Saharan States and in August of the same year travelled to Kenya to attend the celebrations of a new constitution.[127] More recently, President Al-Bashir travelled to Nigeria to attend the AU Special Summit on HIV/Aids, Tuberculosis and Malaria on 16 July 2013.[128]

It may well be that the arrest warrant for Al-Bashir discomfited not just other African political leaders who dislike the precedent, but also those who fear the uncertainty of a new element in the already complex dynamics of international criminal justice.[129] With other cases before the ICC implicating high government officials in Kenya,[130] Libya[131] and Cote d'Ivoire,[132] African leaders seem to be afraid of 'whose turn would be next' and have begun to threaten withdrawal from the ICC, which they once actively and fully supported.

On account of Africa's conflicts and the desire to establish peace and stability in the continent, the cordial relationship between the ICC and the AU seemed entrenched. This is particularly demonstrated in the enabling instruments of both institutions which seek to ensure accountability for atrocious crimes in order to realise their respective goals. However, the amity gave way to conflict and this downturn originated with the referral of the situation in Sudan to the ICC by the United Nations Security Council.

[127] See *The Prosecutor v Omar Hassan Ahmad Al-Bashir* ICC case No ICC-02/05-01/09, 'Decision informing the United Nations Security Council and the Assembly of States Parties to the Rome Statute about Omar Al-Bashir's visit to Chad' (27 August 2010) available at http://www.icc-cpi.int/iccdocs/doc/doc931075.pdf (Accessed 30 August 2012).

[128] Darfur, Sudan, *The Prosecutor v. Omar Hassan Ahmad Al Bashir*, Case No ICC-02/05-01/09, ICC-CPI-20130716-PR932 Decision of the Pre-Trial Chamber II Regarding Omar Al Bashir's Visit to Nigeria) 15 July 2013.

[129] Comments of James Goldston, Executive Director, Open Society Justice Initiative at the United Nations/ICC Seminar on International Criminal Justice, New York 19 May 2009.

[130] Situation in Kenya No ICC-01/09 Decision on the Authorisation of an Investigation 31 March 2010 http://www.icc-cpi.int/iccdocs/doc/doc854287.pdf.

[131] Press Release, ICC Statement of the Prosecutor on the Opening of the Investigation into the Situation in Libya 3 March 2011 http://www.icc-cpi.int/NR/rdonlyres/035C3801-5C8D-4ABC-876B-C7D946B51F22/283045/StatementLibya_03032011.pdf.

[132] Situation in Cote d'Ivoire No ICC-02/02/11, Decision on the Authorisation of an Investigation into the Situation in the Republic of Cote d'Ivoire 3 October 20011 http://www.icc-cpi.int/iccdocs/doc/doc1240553.pdf.

## 5.3 Unpacking the Tension Between the ICC and the AU

Understanding the underlying reasoning behind the AU's call on its member states not to cooperate with the ICC would be valuable for achieving a more accurate portrayal of the relationship between the two institutions.[133] First, unpacking the tension underscores that many of the AU's expressed concerns *vis-à-vis* the ICC relate to the Security Council's actions or inactions and not to the ICC itself.[134] It is submitted that the premise of the AU's call for non-cooperation on the part of its member states with the ICC is the fact that the United Nations Security Council ignored its July 2008 request to defer the case against Al-Bashir.[135] This is arguably so because even among strong supporters of the ICC in Africa, the posture of the Security Council in failing to respond, either positively or negatively, to the AU's request was perceived as disrespectful.[136]

Second, the strain between the ICC and the AU may be attributed to the challenges that both institutions face in building a mutually beneficial relationship. These challenges could be broadly categorised as either legal or political, with some overlap.[137] It must be noted, however, that these hindrances are not unique to the ICC and its relationship with states in the African continent. Rather they relate to the nature of international criminal law and the development of the ICC as a permanent institution.

### *5.3.1 Legal Challenges*

Arguably, the current hostility between the ICC and the AU stems from new legal principles whose interpretation and implications remain unclear, though they are evolving. Fundamental to this ambiguity is the interpretation and implementation of complementarity, the application of which, as a mutually inclusive concept, would involve both national authorities and the ICC equally sharing the responsibility of prosecuting international crimes. However, certain legal issues arise from the complementarity regime; such as the ICC's jurisdiction over nationals of non-party states and the irrelevance of immunity. Clarifying these uncertainties will reduce the points of contention between the ICC and the AU.

[133]Keppler (2012), pp. 1–14.

[134]Ibid.

[135]Specifically, the AU expressed deep regrets that its request to the UN Security Council to defer the proceedings initiated against President Bashir has neither been heard nor acted upon. (See notes 77 & 123).

[136]Keppler (2012).

[137]Jalloh (2009).

#### 5.3.1.1 The ICC's Jurisdiction Over Nationals of States Not Party to the Rome Statute Without the Need for Consent

A primary rule of customary international and treaty law is that consent must precede a state's assumption of international obligations under a treaty.[138] It is quite significant that under the Rome Statute, this rule is not applicable because the Statute is held to bind nationals of all countries and indeed states themselves, whether they are party to it or not. This new legal position is founded upon the individualisation of criminal responsibility[139]; specifically in Article 25, which gives the ICC jurisdiction over individuals and not necessarily states, but requires enforcement and cooperation of states. The provision indicates that a person who commits a crime within the jurisdiction of the Court shall be individually responsible and liable to punishment.[140] Since the Rome Statute addresses the individual, the place of the consent of the state of which such an individual is a national has become of negligible consequence.

Further support for the irrelevance of states' consent is found in Article 12. As argued previously,[141] the trigger mechanism of the ICC implies that the ICC's jurisdiction can extend to nationals of a non-party state in three different circumstances.[142] The first is that the ICC has jurisdiction where crimes proscribed by the Rome Statute are committed within the territory of a state party, by a national of a non-party state.[143] The second is where a non-party state decides to lodge a declaration accepting the jurisdiction of the ICC, as happened with Cote d'Ivoire,[144] and the third is where the Security Council, acting under Chapter VII of the UN Charter, refers a non-party state to the ICC,[145] as was the case with Sudan and later, Libya.

David Scheffer, who led the United States delegation to the Rome Conference, conceded that under the Statute, nationals of non-party states would be subjected to the jurisdiction of the ICC under Article 12, but contended that this should not be applied more generally.[146] However, the overwhelming majority of nations could not agree to require the consent of the state of which a suspect is a citizen as a prerequisite for the Court's jurisdiction.[147] Consequently, the ICC may exercise

138 Vienna Convention on the Law of Treaties 23 May 1969 UNTS Vol 1155, p 331 entered into force 27 January 1980. Available at http://untreaty.un.org/ilc/texts/instruments/english/conventions/1_1_1969.pdf Articles 11–16 & 34.

139 Clarke (note 73).

140 Rome Statute, Articles 25(2), 25(3)(a), (b) & (c).

141 See 'Admissibility and Trigger Mechanism' (text to notes 76–81 in Ch 2).

142 Akande (2003), pp. 618–650.

143 Rome Statute, Art 12(2)(a).

144 Rome Statute, Art 12(3).

145 Rome Statute, Art 13(b).

146 Scheffer (1999), pp. 12, 18–20.

147 Kirsch and Holmes (1999), pp. 2, 9–10; Bassiouni (1999b), pp. 443, 458; Arsanjani (1999), pp. 22, 26.

jurisdiction over anyone anywhere in the world if either the state in whose territory the crime was committed or the state of which the accused is a national consents and thus the treaty exposes nationals of non-parties.[148]

Article 12(1) provides no further guidance, except that it states merely that 'if' a state becomes a party, it 'thereby accepts the jurisdiction of the court'. Thus, there is no requirement that a state be a party in order to accept the jurisdiction of the court and there is no requirement that the state of which the accused is a citizen be a party or accepts the jurisdiction of the ICC.[149] Article 12(3), which provides for the acceptance of jurisdiction signifies only that such acceptance may be the result of *ad hoc* declaration as for example, Cote d'Ivoire.

The above position is novel and it will take some time for states to appreciate the dynamics of the international criminal justice system envisioned by the Rome Statute which they have created and embraced. It is therefore not surprising that after the referral of the situation in Darfur, Sudan to the ICC, some states, including Sudan argued that the ICC's assertion of jurisdiction was a violation of Sudan's sovereignty since it is not a party and had not consented to be bound by the Rome Statute. Arguably, however, Sudan and all United Nations member states agreed to implement the decisions of the Security Council in view of the binding effect of Chapter VII and specifically, Articles 25 and 103 of the UN Charter. As the Security Council's referral was based on its Chapter VII authority, it is hardly comprehensible that the ICC should subsequently be criticised for this action.

#### 5.3.1.2 The ICC's Jurisdiction Over a Sitting Head of State and the Immunity Question

A second related legal question is whether the ICC is competent to issue an arrest warrant for a sitting president of a non-party like Sudan. The question of the consequences of the Security Council's referral and its implication for the immunity that accrues to President Al-Bashir has been discussed by a number of scholars.[150] Thus, it suffices to analyse the personal immunity of heads of state as recognised under international law as well as the Rome Statute's position on the subject.

The doctrine of head of state immunity in international law proposes that serving heads of state enjoy immunity *ratione personae* (personal immunity) for every act undertaken by them while in office, regardless of whether such acts are carried out in an official or private capacity.[151] This personal immunity is not limited to heads

[148]Paust (2000), pp. 1–16.

[149]Paust, 14.

[150]See for example Papillon (2010), pp. 275–288; Gaeta (2009), pp. 315–332; Akande (2009), pp. 333–352; Williams and Sherif (2009), pp. 71–92; Ciampi (2008), pp. 885–897; Gosnell (2008), pp. 841–851; Imoedemhe (2008), pp. 66–97.

[151]Wardle (2011), pp. 181–206, 183.

of state, but it also extends to all high-ranking state officials by virtue of the office they hold.[152] Also, former heads of state enjoy a reduced form of immunity *ratione materiae* (functional immunity), which offers immunity for acts carried out in pursuance of some official function, but not for those which are undertaken in a private capacity.[153]

In the *Arrest Warrant*[154] case, the International Court of Justice (ICJ) found that the issuance of the arrest warrant by the Belgian judicial authorities against the incumbent Minister of Foreign Affairs of the DRC breached international norms on personal immunity.[155] The ICJ held further that serving heads of state enjoy absolute immunity from prosecution in foreign courts,[156] but that they may be prosecuted by certain international courts.[157]

In contrast, the arrest warrant of Al-Bashir, did not emanate from a national court. Rather it is an international arrest warrant issued by the ICC.[158] On the question of whether the customary rules of international law on the immunity of heads of state, which prevent a domestic judicial authority from issuing an arrest warrant against such an individual equally applies to the ICC, the ICJ made a clear exception for international tribunals and particularly, the ICC.[159]

There are several justifications for this exception. First, since the personal immunity accorded to heads of state and state officials is informed by the principles of state equality and the desire to preserve the horizontal architecture of the international system, it may appear that such immunity should never be pleaded before truly international courts and tribunals.[160] This is because the ICC derives its mandate from the international community as a whole and accordingly, cannot depend on a principle that operates between sovereign states.[161] Consequently, Gaeta argued that the functions of inter-state relations have little bearing on the ICC.[162] She postulates:

> The very *rationale* for the rules on personal immunities is lacking when criminal jurisdiction is instead exercised by an international criminal court. While at the 'horizontal' level, there is a need to protect foreign state officials from the exercise or even abuse of

[152]Miglin (2007), p. 22.

[153]See Vienna Convention on Diplomatic Relations, done at Vienna 18 April 1961, 500 UNTS 95 entered into force 24 April 1964, Article 31(1).

[154]*Arrest Warrant of 11 April 2000 (Democratic Republic of Congo v. Belgium)*, ICJ decision 14 February 2002. (*Arrest Warrant* case).

[155]Ibid, para 70.

[156]Ibid, para 58.

[157]Ibid, para 61.

[158]Gaeta (2009), p. 318.

[159]*Arrest Warrant* case, para 61. The ICJ specifically referred to Article 27(2) of the Rome Statute which removes immunities that may attach to certain persons by reason of their official positions.

[160]Gaeta (2002), pp. 975, 991. (hereinafter, 'Gaeta, Official Capacity').

[161]Nouwen (2005), pp. 645, 650, 652.

[162]Gaeta (2009), p. 320. See also Decision on Immunity in *Prosecutor v. Taylor* SCSL-2003-01-1 Appeals Chamber 31 May 2004, para 51.

> jurisdiction by the receiving state, things are clearly different at [the] purely 'international' level. International criminal courts are not organs of a particular state; they act on behalf of the international community as a whole to protect collective or universal values and thus to repress very serious international crimes.[163]

Persuasive as the foregoing argument appears, it must be noted that the exercise of jurisdiction by the ICC can have serious consequences for the sovereign equality of states and the intercourse of international relations.[164] This is particularly manifested in the complementary jurisdiction of the ICC, on account of which it depends absolutely on the cooperation of states to investigate and prosecute cases before it. Therefore, to disconnect the jurisdiction of the ICC from the operation of domestic courts and the sovereignty of states posits an inherently artificial understanding of the international criminal jurisdiction.[165]

Article 27 of the Rome Statute stipulates that neither international nor domestic immunities nor special procedural rules will prevent the Court from exercising jurisdiction over any person.[166] This implies that the ICC can exercise jurisdiction over persons who enjoy immunity under customary international law, regardless of whether the state of which the alleged perpetrator is a national is a party to the Rome Statute or not. This provision differs from its corresponding provisions in the Statutes of the ICTY, ICTR and the SCSL in that it resolves to render both official capacity[167] and immunities[168] irrelevant before the ICC.

In contrast, the ICTY Statute stipulates that the official position of any accused person, whether head of state or government or a responsible government official, shall not relieve that person of criminal responsibility nor mitigate punishment.[169] This provision is replicated in both the ICTR and SCSL Statutes,[170] and it does not refer to immunity enjoyed by heads of state under customary international law presumably because the tribunals were created by the Security Council.

Consequently, the question of whether or not the tribunals violated the immunities of Slobodan Milosevic, Jean Kambada and Charles Taylor was not directly answered by reference to their enabling Statutes. However, Akande argues that immunity in those cases had been removed by the Security Council.[171] Supporting this view, Gaeta noted that no one has ever claimed that the ICTY violated Milosevic's immunity and that the absence of any challenge in that regard shows

---

163 Gaeta (2009), pp. 320–321.

164 Akande (2004).

165 Wardle (2011), pp. 186–187.

166 Rome Statute, Article 27.

167 Rome Statute, Art 27(1).

168 Rome Statute, Art 27(2).

169 ICTY Statute, Art 7(2).

170 Article 6(2) of both Statutes of the ICTR & the SCSL.

171 Akande (2009), p. 337.

that an international tribunal and the ICC are not circumscribed by such immunities.[172]

Be that as it may, it is important to note that neither the resolutions creating the tribunals nor their statutes contain provisions expressly removing personal immunity, let alone the immunities of serving heads of state. Accordingly, Gaeta argues that it is difficult to understand how the Security Council or the Statutes, could have derogated from the customary rules on personal immunity by simply remaining silent on the matter.[173] Clearly, it would not be sufficient to counter that this derogation is implicit because the Security Council has created an international tribunal vested with jurisdiction over persons responsible for international crimes. As the ICJ aptly noted in the *Arrest Warrant* case, the existence of jurisdiction does not imply the absence of immunity.[174]

As Sudan came under the jurisdiction of the ICC because of referral by the Security Council, the question was whether the referral, in effect, abrogates Bashir's immunity. Neither the resolution nor the Rome Statute provides an answer to this question. The Pre-Trial Chamber which approved the arrest warrant in March 2009 asserted that Bashir's current position as president or head of state does not constitute a bar to the Court's exercise of jurisdiction over his case.[175]

Two justifications have been advanced for this position. The first is that by the exercise of Chapter VII power, Al-Bashir's immunity was lifted through the specific provision in the referral resolution that the government of Sudan 'shall cooperate fully with the ICC'.[176] The second is the assertion by Akande that the mere referral of Sudan by the Security Council automatically bound Sudan as if it were a party to the Rome Statute, including the provisions abrogating immunities.[177] While the first condition is met by Article 27(2) which effectively removed the immunity accorded to state officials, the second might not because Sudan, to which the immunity is attached, insists on its immunity under customary international law.

Conversely, Charles Jalloh argues that the assertion that the United Nations Security Council Resolutions which created the tribunals abrogated immunities by virtue of Chapter VII of the United Nations Charter cannot be relied upon.[178] This is because the situations are slightly different in the Sudan scenario, particularly as Al-Bashir is still in power. Jalloh contends that this declaration could lead to some difficulties. The first is that a strong argument can be made that for the Security Council to revoke the immunity of a serving president, the referral resolution would

---

[172]Gaeta (2009), p. 321.

[173]Ibid.

[174]*Arrest Warrant* case, para 59.

[175]Decision on the Prosecution's Application for Al Bashir's Arrest Warrant 4 March 2009, paras 41–45.

[176]See Resolution 1593 of 31 March 2005, para 2.

[177]Akande, Legal Nature of Security Council Referral 340–341.

[178]Jalloh (2009), p. 484.

have to explicitly nullify the immunity, since immunity accrues to the state (Sudan) as opposed to the person occupying the presidential office (Al-Bashir).[179] This problem could then be resolved easily by the adoption of a subsequent resolution expressly removing Al-Bashir's immunity.

The second difficulty is that while the Security Council is competent to adopt measures aimed at restoring international peace and security, it does not possess the power to unilaterally impose treaty obligations upon a state.[180] The United Nations Charter does not expressly give it such powers.[181] Thus, it may be argued that the removal of Sudan's immunity is an implied power necessary for the performance of its functions.

Furthermore, Gaeta argues that Article 27(2) merely restates the already existing principle of customary international law, that no official immunity may be enforced before an international criminal court.[182] However, the provision of Article 98(1) of the Rome Statute renders this argument ineffective. Article 98(1) reads;

> The Court may not proceed with a request for surrender or assistance which would require the requested state to act inconsistently with its obligations under international law with respect to the state or diplomatic immunity of a person or property of a third state.[183]

Clearly, there is a problem with the reconciliation of these two seemingly contradictory provisions,[184] as Article 98 anticipates a situation of conflict between the provisions of the Rome Statute and existing international law norms. As argued by Wardle, if immunity is inapplicable before the Court, then why should such immunity be considered and respected in the course of requests for the surrender of persons indicted by the ICC?[185] Indeed, if all states parties to whom requests for arrest and surrender are directed were permitted to avoid compliance with such requests because of the immunity accruing to the accused individual, then Al-Bashir, who enjoys such immunity, would never be brought before the ICC. The result is that Article 27(2) would be meaningless.

To resolve these contradictions, Akande argued that Article 27(2) serves to remove immunities and that Article 98(1) cannot be interpreted as to allowing parties to rely on those same immunities.[186] The way forward, particularly to

---

[179] Jalloh, 484.

[180] Ibid.

[181] Ibid.

[182] Gaeta (2009), p. 322; Gaeta (2002), p. 991.

[183] Rome Statute, Art 98(1).

[184] It has been argued that the ambiguity in these provisions is as a result of the drafting history of Article 98, which was proposed at the final stages of the Rome Conference by a completely different working group to that which proposed and negotiated Article 27. See Saland (1999), p. 202; Claus Kress and Kimberly Prost, 'Article 98 Cooperation with Respect to Waiver of Immunity and Consent to Surrender' in Otto Triffterer (ed) *Commentary on the Rome Statute* 1601–1619, 1607.

[185] Wardle (2011), p. 188.

[186] Akande (2009), p. 337.

enhance the relationship between the AU and the ICC, and for the purpose of complementarity, may be to expunge Article 98 altogether from the Statute.

Ultimately, immunity is no longer relevant for international crimes. This is regardless of whether the alleged criminal is a past or incumbent head of state. Granted that immunity does not operate with respect to the crimes proscribed by the Rome Statute, the practicality of ensuring that states comply with this obligation is very unlikely, particularly taking into consideration that Article 98(1) seemingly contradicts Article 27 and has inhibited the functioning of the ICC, especially with the Al-Bashir case.

## 5.3.2 *Political Challenges*

Sharp criticism is sometimes directed at the United States and others for participating in the referral of situations to the ICC while at the same time refusing to ratify the Rome Statute themselves. This constitutes one aspect of the critical political challenges to relations between the ICC and the AU; these include an uneven playing field, Western complicity in Africa's conflicts and the exceptionality of the United States. Nevertheless, deriding the ICC as imperialistic only fuels the AU's hostility towards the ICC and ultimately inures perpetrators while leaving millions of African victims' claim to justice unaddressed.

### 5.3.2.1 An Uneven Playing Field, Western Complicity in Africa's Conflicts and the United States Exceptionality

It is difficult to deny that the implementation of international criminal justice faces some obstacles which are founded on the legitimate concerns of some states, whether party to the Rome Statute or not.[187] One of these impediments is the perception that citizens of some states are subject to such justice while those of others are not. As noted by a commentator with respect to the jurisdiction granted to the ICC in the Darfur referral, there is little chance that the ICC's jurisdiction will one day be imposed on the United States, China, Israel or Russia.[188] Similarly, Human Rights Watch once observed:

> The reality that justice unfolds on an uneven international landscape has generated genuine frustration. This is a landscape that needs to change, so that the leaders of the world's most powerful states as well as those from smaller, weaker states are subject to the reach of law for the worst crimes under international law.[189]

---

[187]Black (2009/2010), pp. 137, 144.

[188]Fabrice Weismann, 'Secourir les victim ou Collaborer avec la CPI...' (Rescue the Victims or Collaborate with the ICC) available at http://www.grotius.fr/rubrique/justice-internationale.

[189]Gagnon (2009).

Some African leaders have actively sought to exploit the disparities in the application of international justice to present the ICC as a new form of imperialism that should be opposed.[190] The insincere posture of some permanent members of the Security Council, who participate in referrals and yet are not parties to the Rome Statute themselves, seems to validate the disapproval.

In addition to the inequality of international criminal justice, it has been asserted that the flames of conflicts in Africa have been fanned to varying degrees by Western powers.[191] In this regard, Ifeonu Eberechi contends that the on-going resistance to the prosecution of Al-Bashir by the ICC is in part borne out of a legitimate feeling among some African states that the ICC is an institution controlled by those who are partly responsible for the conflicts in the continent.[192] Thus, from the AU point of view, an 'international community' which is complicit in the conflicts in Africa lacks the moral authority to enforce international criminal justice on the continent.[193]

The United Nations Charter affirms the 'equal rights of men and women and of nations large or small' and the principle of sovereign equality of all states.[194] The principle of equality, whether of individuals or of states, precludes arbitrary distinctions with respect to its application based on states' or individuals' social, wealth, moral or other status.

This principle is belied, however, by the exceptionality of the United States *vis-à-vis* the ICC, thereby piquing Africa's sense of justice.[195] In the words of Ramtane Lamamre, 'how could you refer the cases of others while you don't feel compelled to abide by the same rule?'[196] Although, the fact that the United States, China and Russia, are not parties to the Rome Statute has led to charges of hypocrisy, this charge is weakened in this case by the abstention of the first two from the vote which resulted in the referral of Sudan to the ICC.[197] However, it is nevertheless problematic that citizens of the United States are unlikely to ever face the Court themselves for war crimes that were committed in the context of hostilities in Afghanistan and Iraq in 2002 and 2003.[198] This state of affairs bolsters the

---

[190]See for example, 'AU Chief Chides ICC Prosecutor' 23 July 2010 News24.com. available at http://www.new24.com/Africa/News/AU-chief-chides-ICC-prosecutor-20100723; Rabkin (2010).

[191]Anghie and Chimni (2003), pp. 77, 90. See also Zeleza (2008), p. 22.

[192]Eberechi (2009), pp. 53–76, 55.

[193]Ibid, 56.

[194]See the preamble and Article 2(1) of the UN Charter.

[195]Schabas (2004), pp. 701–720.

[196]Lamamra (2013). Available at http://www.bbc.co.uk/news/world-africa-22681894 (Accessed 30 November 2013). (Mr Lamamre is the Head of the AU Peace and Security Council (PSC) since 2008).

[197]See Press Release, 'SC/8351 Security Council Refers Situation in Darfur, Sudan to the Prosecutor of the International Criminal Court Resolution 1593 (2005)' (There were four abstentions namely; Algeria, Brazil, China and the United States).

[198]Jalloh, 491.

position of those who, rightly or wrongly, argue that international criminal law is being used to discipline only citizens of weak and poor states.[199]

Moreover, the United States adopted a domestic legislation, The American Service-Members Protection Act (2002), precluding cooperation with the ICC.[200] In addition, the Act prohibits American military assistance to states who are parties to the Rome Statute,[201] and it provides a mechanism to penalise others, including through the use of military force, which would be so bold as to surrender a United States national to the ICC.[202] Yet the Court has not publicly expressed a position regarding the posture of the United States[203] While this is not to suggest that the ICC may not have its own misgivings about the posture of the United States, its silence on the issue has detrimental impact on the ICC, as it is being unfavourably interpreted by a number of African states.

Furthermore, during the George W. Bush administration, the United States coerced many developing countries to sign Article 98(2) Bilateral Immunity Agreements (BIA) wherein promises were made not to hand over American nationals to the ICC without first securing the consent of the United States. The countries were faced with the prospect of losing all financial, military and humanitarian aid if they failed to sign the BIA.[204] Over 36 states in Africa signed those agreements; the exceptions were South Africa and a few other larger states that refused to succumb to the pressure. However, they lost the much-needed American assistance as a result of their refusal.[205]

Notwithstanding these criticisms, it is suggested that Africa should enhance the support they once accorded and still accord the ICC. This is because the criticisms so far have been based on the involvement of the United Nations Security Council and the hypocritical stance of its permanent members and not on the ICC itself. In fact, it would appear that the accusation that the ICC is unfairly targeting Africans cannot be substantiated by the evidence.[206]

[199] Hoile, 'ICC, A Tool to Recolonise Africa?' (2013).

[200] See section 2004 of The American Service-Members Protection Act 2002, 26 July 2002. See also CICC, Press Release, 'US Congress Passes Anti-ICC Hague Invasion Act' 26 July 2002 at http://www.iccnow.org/documents/07.26.02ASPAthruCongress.pdf (Accessed 24 July 2013).

[201] The American Service-Members Protection Act 2002, s 2007.

[202] Ibid.

[203] Jalloh, 493.

[204] CICC, 'USA and the ICC: Bilateral Immunity Agreements' at http://www.iccnow.org/?mod=bia; Human Rights Watch, 'Briefing Paper on Bilateral Immunity Agreements' New York, 20 June 2003.

[205] Bekou and Shah (2006), p. 537.

[206] Keppler (2012).

## 5.4 The ICC: Unfairly Targeting Africa?

It is acknowledged that, to date, international justice has not been and may never be equally applied, for the reason that the ICC is less likely to prosecute leaders of powerful states and those that they protect. This is an important issue that should be addressed, but in a manner that extends, rather than curtails accountability, so that victims have recourse to justice no matter where the atrocities are committed.[207] Despite the shortcomings in international criminal justice, dismissing the ICC as a new form of imperialism targeting African states may not be accurate and is in any case counterproductive to the pursuit of justice. It is proposed that, rather than point to alleged perpetrators in other parts of the world that are not being prosecuted by the ICC, African states should focus on how the ICC's present prosecutions and investigations on the continent could help ensure accountability and create peace and stability in African countries.

The first reason why it is argued that the aforementioned assertion does not bear scrutiny is that five African states have engaged in self-referrals to the ICC, namely: Uganda, the Central African Republic (CAR) twice, the Democratic Republic of the Congo (DRC), Mali and the Union of Comoros. It has been argued that the first referrals by the governments of Uganda and the DRC occurred only under considerable pressure by the ICC prosecutor,[208] as the Prosecutor had publicly called on states to refer those situations to the ICC.[209] According to Akhavan, 'the referral was an attempt to engage an otherwise aloof international community by transforming the prosecution of LRA leaders into a litmus test for the much celebrated promise of global justice.'[210]

Nevertheless, it is submitted that self-referrals are a product of the lack of understanding of the obligations of both the ICC and states under complementarity because one of the reasons for the referral by the Ugandan government, for example, was its inability to arrest members of the LRA.[211] Absurdly, 8 years on, both the ICC and the Ugandan government have not been able to arrest any of the suspects. The question is: if the government of Uganda, on whose territory the crimes were committed and whose nationals (members of the LRA) are the perpetrators, is not able to arrest the alleged criminals, how can the ICC, without a police force, manage to achieve that?

Irrespective of the above argument, the first 10 years of the functioning of the ICC has been referred to as the 'teething' period and therefore neither the ICC nor

[207]Keppler (2012).

[208]Hoile (2012).

[209]Report of the Prosecutor of the ICC to the Second Assembly of States Parties to the Rome Statute of the International Criminal Court' 8 September 2003, 4.

[210]Akhavan (2005), pp. 403, 404.

[211]See Pre-Trial Chamber II, *Decision on the Admissibility of the Case Under 19(1) of the Statute* ICC-02/04-01/05-377, 10 March 2009, para 37. See also Rome Statute, art 17(3).

the states that referred situations in their territories are to blame.[212] Moreover, the self-referrals could be interpreted as a demonstration that the desire within the African region to promote international rule of law is not just a matter of principle, but of practice.[213] As articulated by Fatou Bensouda, the Chief Prosecutor of the ICC, the states of the continent realise that acting alone cannot protect their citizens from perpetrators of international crimes[214]; therefore, a realisation of the usefulness of collaboration may have prompted the self-referrals.

The self-referrals by the governments of Mali and Union of Comoros in 2012 2013 respectively, which made them the fourth and fifth African states to refer situations in their territories, arguably, reveal the support and confidence that African states continue to have in the ICC. Consequently, it cannot be said that the ICC is anti-Africa, any more than it can be said that these African states that have engaged in self-referrals are themselves anti-Africa.[215]

In the situations of Sudan and Libya, the ICC's investigation was triggered by referrals from the United Nations Security Council. Thus, the ICC has only utilised its *priopro motu* powers in two situations, namely; Kenya and Cote d'Ivoire, but again, these were, in the case of Kenya, based upon information received by the Prosecutor, and, in the case of Cote d'Ivoire, upon invitation of the government.

The second and most persuasive reason why the ICC cannot be accused of being biased against Africa is one which emanates from the nature of the victims-Africans- of the alleged crimes and not necessarily the perpetrators of the crimes or the interests of the states that defend them. In this regard, to the extent that the ICC's attention thus far has been focused on Africa, for the benefit of the victims, it should arguably be celebrated rather than criticised.[216]

As noted earlier, Africa has been the site of the commission of many, if not most, international crimes. Nevertheless, opposition to the ICC in Africa is led by the political interests of those who oppose the ICC's mission, who possibly have never reconciled themselves to the idea of legal accountability for mass atrocities.[217] Although the relevance of this point may be disputed, it does serve to highlight the fact that the controversy surrounding the ICC's record and activities has ignored the interests of a substantial number of victims.[218] What is certain, however, is that by working to render justice to African victims of mass crimes, one cannot simultaneously maintain that the ICC is biased against Africa.[219] The argument is that

[212]William Schabas, 'The ICC at Ten' and Antonio Cassese 'Is the ICC Still having Teething Problems? (Text to notes 61 & 230 in Ch 2).

[213]Eze (2012).

[214]Ibid.

[215]Black (2009/2010) 148.

[216]Black (2009/2010) 154.

[217]James Goldston, 'The International Criminal Court: Justice and Politics' *OpenDemocracy* available at http://www.opendemocracy.net (Accessed 30 January 2010).

[218]Black, ibid.

[219]Ibid.

where crimes are committed and perpetrators are made accountable and potential perpetrators are deterred from such conduct in the future, the victims (both actual and potential) are the beneficiaries. Denying justice to some victims because redress is not possible for all cultivates, rather than combats, the culture of impunity.[220]

A third reason which is closely linked with the benefit that accrues to victims of international crimes in Africa is the benefit of lasting peace and stability. The ultimate aim of ICC's investigations and prosecutions is to foster peace and stability on the continent through justice. In this regard, both the AU and the ICC share common objectives, as both the provisions of the Constitutive Act of the AU, the Peace and Security Protocol, and the Rome Statute demonstrate. For this reason, the AU should enhance its relationship with the ICC to ensure capacity building in its institutions in order to be able to prosecute and investigate international crimes domestically, thereby ensuring peace, security and stability.

## 5.5 Conclusion

Politics cannot be entirely divorced from law and this is particularly the case with international criminal law and the ICC. The scapegoat thesis and selectivity appear at first to buttress the assertion that Africa is inappropriately targeted for prosecution. However, closer examination reveals that the United Nations Security Council, which is a political body, is actually the source of some points of contention and that other points are unsound. In the event, proof of selectivity does not negate the carriage of justice against the individual who was selected for prosecution.[221]

Admittedly, the ICC is less likely to prosecute leaders of powerful states and those they protect, but this issue must be addressed in and of itself and should not be used to curtail the accountability of others. The ICC cannot be said to be unfairly targeting Africa, as the ultimate aim of both the AU and the ICC is to ensure accountability for serious crimes and foster peace, security and stability. This is irrespective of the point that such actions are not being taken in other parts of the world where equally serious crimes are being committed. The cumulative gain to Africa, in addition to ensuring peace, is also the deliverance of justice to victims of atrocities.

Thus, the shared goals of justice and peace reveal that there is accord between the objectives of the AU and the ICC. This is particularly demonstrated in the enabling instruments of both institutions, such as the Constitutive Act and the Protocol, which seek to ensure accountability for atrocious crimes in order to realise lasting peace and stability. Both the Constitutive Act and the Protocol encourage

---

[220] Gagnon (2009).

[221] See *Celebici* case, (note 35) paras 611 & 618.

relations and consultations with international institutions and organisations to ensure institutional capacity and peace building.[222]

Whiles it is conceded that the relationship between the ICC and the AU is strained, a more detailed analysis of the cause of the tension revealed, in fact, the strong support among African nations for the ICC. Therefore, unpacking the tension was necessary to situate an accurate portrayal of the AU/ICC relationship and to trace the cause of the conflict to the Security Council's referral of the Darfur situation and the subsequent indictment of the Sudanese President by the ICC.

Certainly, other areas of misunderstandings do exist between the two institutions, which arise from both political and legal sources. These include the issue of the ICC's jurisdiction over nationals of non-party states and irrelevance of immunities of heads of states, both of which were analysed as points of misconceptions that could exacerbate the tension between not only the AU and the ICC, but also between the ICC and other states parties and non-party states alike. It is suggested that Article 98 which is identified as a contradictory provision, should be removed from the Statute entirely. This will reduce confusion and points of conflicts in the functioning of the ICC.

With the institution of self-referrals, which African states alone have '*proprio-motu'* embarked upon, it is apparent that the AU cannot substantiate an argument that Africa is being unfairly targeted. Rather, it would be of immense benefit for the AU to find solutions to the tension. It would be for the mutual benefit of both the AU and the ICC to resume a cordial relationship, irrespective of the perceived selectivity and bias of the ICC with regards to Africa. The ultimate aim of such relationship will be to enhance African states' criminal justice systems to enable them investigate and prosecute international crimes domestically. Using Nigeria as a case study, the next chapter examines institutional preparedness of African states to implement complementarity.

## References

Afako B (2002) Reconciliation and justice: *Mato Oput* and the amnesty act. ACORD 64–67. http://www.c-r.org/sites/c-r.org/files/Accord%2011_13Reconciliation%20and%20justice_2002_ENG.pdf. Accessed 15 Jan 2013

Akande D (2003) The jurisdiction of the international criminal court over nationals of non-parties: legal basis and limits. JICJ 1:618–650

Akande D (2004) International law immunities and the international criminal court. AJIL 98(407): 417

Akande D (2009) The legal nature of security council referrals to the ICC and its impact on Al-Bashir's immunities. JICJ 7(2):333–352

[222]See Arts 4, 13 & 17 of the Constitutive Act of the AU and Arts 14 & 17 of the Peace and Security Protocol.

Akhavan P (2005) Developments at the international criminal court: the Lord's resistance army case: Uganda's submission of the first state referral to the international criminal court. AJIL 99: 403
Ambos K (2000) Comparative summary of the national reports. In: Arbour et al (eds) The prosecutor of a permanent international criminal court. Edition Iuscrim, Freiburg, p 495
Anghie A, Chimni BS (2003) Third world approaches to international law and individual responsibility in internal conflicts. Chi J Int'l L 2:77
Arsanjani MH (1999) The Rome Statute of the international criminal court. AJIL 93:22
Ashworth A (2009) Principles of criminal law, 6th edn. OUP, Oxford
AU Chief Chides ICC Prosecutor' 23 July 2010. News24.com. Available at http://www.new24.com/Africa/News/AU-chief-chides-ICC-prosecutor-20100723. Accessed 10 July 2012
Bassiouni C (1999) Negotiating the treaty of Rome on the establishment of an international criminal court. Cor Int'l L J 32:443
Bekou O, Shah S (2006) Realising the potential of the international criminal court: the African experience. HRLR 6:499–544
Bikundo E (2012) The international criminal court and Africa: exemplary justice. Law Crit 23(1): 21–41
Black C (2009/2010) Some reasons for considering why the ICC may not be considered as an anti-African institution. In: African year book of international humanitarian law. p 137
Borer TA, Mills K (2011) Explaining post-apartheid South African human rights foreign policy: unsettled identity and conflicting interests. J Hum Rights Law 10:76
Brownlie I (2003) Principles of international law, 6th edn. OUP
Ciampi A (2008) The proceedings against president Al-Bashir and the prospect of their suspension under Article 16 ICC Statute. JICJ 6(5):885–897
Clarke K (2009) Fictions of justice: the ICC and the challenge of legal pluralism in Sub-Saharan Africa. CUP
Courtenay Griffiths QC (2012) The politics of international criminal law. News Africa, 1 March 2012. http://www.newafricanmagazine.com/special-reports/sector-reports/icc-vs-africa/the-politics-of-international-criminal-law. Accessed 10 Dec 2012
Crawford J (2012) Brownlie's principles of public international law, 8th edn. OUP, Oxford
Cryer R (2005) Prosecuting international crimes: selectivity and the international criminal law regime. CUP
Damaska M (2008) What is the point of international criminal justice? Chicago-Kent Law Rev 83(1):347. Available at http://digitalcommons.law.yale.edu/fss_papers/1573. Accessed 20 May 2012
Davis KK (1969) Discretionary justice: a preliminary enquiry. Louisiana State University Press, Baton Rouge
De Waal (2004) Who are the Darfurians? Arab and African identities, violence and external engagement. SSRC, 10 December 2004. Available at http://conconflicts.ssrc.org/hornofafrica/dewaal. Accessed 20 May 2012
Derrida J (1981) Dissemination. Chicago University Press
Eberechi I (2009) Armed conflicts in Africa and Western complicity: a disincentive for African Union's cooperation with the ICC. Afr J Legal Stud 3:53–76
Eze M (2012) Fatou Bensouda: we are not against Africa but can she bring any real change to Africa-ICC relations? New Afr Mag
Franck T (1995) Fairness in international law and institutions. Clarendon Press, Oxford
Frazer J, Fraser R (2009) The golden bough: a study in magic and religion, Reissued edn. OUP
Gaeta P (2002) Official capacity and immunities. In: Cassese A, Gaeta P, Jones J (eds) The Rome Statute of the international criminal court. OUP, pp 975–1002
Gaeta P (2009) Does president Al Bashir enjoy immunity from arrest? JICJ 7(2):315–332
Gagnon G (2009) Letter to AU heads of State in advance of Libya Summit' human rights watch 25 June 2009. Available at http://www.hrw.org/news/2009/06/25/letter-au-heads-state-advance-libya-summit. Accessed 17 July 2010

Goldstone R (2013) In David Hoile, ICC, A Tool to Recolonise Africa. African Business, July 2013. Available at http://africanbusinessmagazine.com/special-reports/sector-reports/icc-vs-africa/icc-a-tool-to-recolonise-africa. Accessed 15 Dec 2013

Gosnell C (2008) The request for an arrest warrant in Al Bashir: idealistic posturing or calculated plan? JICJ 6(5):841–851

Grandi F (2013) Why do the victors kill the vanquished? Explaining political violence in post-world war II Italy. J Peace Res 1–17. Available at http://jpr.sagepub.com/content/early/2013/06/20/0022343313480202.full.pdf+html. Accessed 15 Aug 2013

Harbom L, Wallensteen P (2009) Uppsala conflict data program (UCDP), 'Armed Conflict, 1946–2008'. J Peace Res 46(4):577–587. http://jpr.sagepub.com/content/46/4/577.full.pdf+html. Accessed 12 Dec 2012

Hoile D (2012) The ICC, a tool to recolonise Africa? New African Magazine. Available at https://www.questia.com/magazine/1G1-283751284/icc-a-tool-to-recolonise-africa

Igwe C (2008) The ICC's favourite customer: Africa and international criminal law. Comp. & Int'l. L. J. Southern Afr. XLI(2):294

Imoedemhe O (2008) The indictment of president Omar Al-Bashir of Sudan by the ICC: from impunity to accountability. In: Lawrence Atsegbua L, Dimowo F (eds) Landmarks in law: essays in honour of justice omage. University of Benin Press, pp 66–97

Jalloh CC (2006) The law and politics of the Charles Taylor Case. Can Counc Int Law Web Bull. http://www.ccil.ca/index.php?option=com_content&task=view&id=165&Itemid=76. Accessed 12 Apr 2012

Jalloh CC (2009) Regionalizing international criminal law? ICLR 9:445–499

Kambudzi A (2004) Issues and problems in political renewal in Africa. In: Adesida O, Oteh A (eds) African voices African vision. Nordic African Institute, pp 53–66

Kambudzi A (2007) The international criminal court and Africa: the AU and the ICC. In: Max du Plessis M, Louw A (eds) The investigation and prosecution of core international crimes and the role of the international criminal court in Africa. Institute for Security Studies, Pretoria, pp 27–39

Keppler E (2011) Africa: Burkina Faso, Niger's Stand on Gaddafi and ICC Warrant. Daily Trust, 16 September 2011. Available at http://allafrica.com/stories/201109200230.html. Accessed 15 Jan 2012

Keppler E (2012) Managing setbacks for the international criminal court in Africa. JAL 56(1): 1–14

Kezio-Musoke D (2008) Rwanda: Kagame tells why he is against ICC charging Bashir. Daily Nation, 3 August 2008. Available at http://allafrica.com/stories/200808120157.html. Accessed 6 June 2013

Kioko B (2003) The right of intervention under the African Union's constitutive act: from non-interference to non-intervention. IRRC 85:807–820

Kirsch P, Holmes JT (1999) The Rome conference on an international criminal court: the negotiating process. AJIL 93:2–10

Lamamra R (2013) African Union accuses ICC of 'Hunting' Africans. BBC News Africa, 27 May 2013. Available at http://www.bbc.co.uk/news/world-africa-22681894. Accessed 10 Aug 2013

McCormack TLH (1996–1997) Selective reaction to atrocity. ALR 60:681, 683

Miglin J (2007) From immunity to impunity: Charles Taylor and the special court for Sierra Leone. Dalhous J Legal Stud 16:22

Mills K (2012) Bashir is dividing US: Africa and the international criminal court. HRQ 34(2): 404–447

Nouwen S (2005) The special court for Sierra Leone and the immunity of Taylor: the arrest warrant case continued. LJIL 18:645

Nouwen S, Werner W (2010) Doing justice to the political: the international criminal court in Ugandan and Sudan. EJIL 21:941–965

Papillon S (2010) Has the United Nations security council implicitly removed Al-Bashir's immunity? ICLR 10:275–288

Paust J (2000) The reach of ICC jurisdiction over non-signatory nationals. Vanderbilt J Transnl Law 33(1):1–16

Rabkin F (2010) Africa: world court faces charge of judicial imperialism. AllAfrica.com, 23 July 2010. Available at http://allafrica.com/stories/201007230728.html. Accessed 20 July 2012

Report of the Secretary General to the United Nations Security Council: 'The Causes of Conflict and the Promotion of Durable Peace and Sustainable Development in Africa' 16 April 1998 para 4. UN doc.A/52/871-S/1998/318

Rubin A (1993) International crimes and punishment. NI 34(fall):73

Saland P (1999) International criminal law principles. In: Roy L (ed) The international criminal court: the making of the Rome Statute. Kluwer Law International, p 202

Schabas WA (2004) United States hostility to the international criminal court: it's all about the security council. EJIL 701–720

Scharf M (1995) The politics of establishing an international criminal court. Duke J Comp Int Law 6:167–174

Scheffer D (1999) The United States and the international criminal court. AJIL 93:12–20

Simmons B, Danner A (2010) Credible commitments and the international criminal court. Int'l Org 64:225

Simpson G (1997) War crimes: a critical introduction. In: McCormack T, Simpson G (eds) The law of war crimes: national and international approaches. Martinus Nijhoff, The Hague

Simpson G (2007) Law, war and crime: war crimes trials and the reinvention of international law. Polity Press, UK, p 116

Smith P (2009) Interview: Luis Moreno-Ocampo, ICC Prosecutor. The African Report, 21 September 2009. Available at http://www.theafricareport.com/News-Analysis/interview-luis-moreno-ocampo-icc-prosecutor.html. Accessed 17 June 2013

Soares PP (2013) Positive complementarity and the law enforcement network: drawing lessons from the ad hoc tribunals' completion strategy. Israel Law Rev 46(3):319–338

Stigen J (2011) The admissibility procedures. In: Stahn C, ElZeidy M (eds) The international criminal court and complementarity: from theory to practice, vol 1. CUP, p 503

Stockholm International Peace Research Institute (SIPRI) (2000) Yearbook of world armaments and disarmaments. OUP, Oxford

Swarns R (2002) African leaders drop old guard for one that has power. N. Y Times, 9 July 2002. Available at http://www.nytimes.com/2002/07/09/world/african-leaders-drop-old-guard-fro-one-that-has-power.html. Accessed 20 Dec 2013

Tallgren I (2002) The sensibility and sense of international criminal law. EJIL 13(3):561

Themnér L, Wallensteen P (2013) Armed conflicts, 1946–2012. J Peace Res 50(4):509–521. Available at http://jpr.sagepub.com/content/50/4/509.full.pdf+html. 10 Jan 2014

Udombana N (2012) Africa and the International Criminal Court. Paper presented at the Thirteenth Justice Chukwunweike Idigbe Memorial Lecture University of Benin, Benin City Nigeria, 5 December 2012 (Copy on file with Author)

Wardle P (2011) The survival of head of state immunity at the international criminal court. Aust Int Law J 18:181–206, 183

Williams S, Sherif L (2009) The arrest warrant for president Ai-Bashir: immunities of incumbent heads of state and the international criminal court. J Confl Secur Law 14:71–92

Zeleza P (2008) Introduction: the causes & costs of war in Africa from liberation struggles to the 'War on Terror'. In: Nhema A, Zeleza P (eds) The roots of African conflicts: the causes and costs. Ohio University Press

# Chapter 6
# Institutional Preparedness for the Complementarity Regime: Nigeria as a Case Study

**Abstract** African states constitute the highest supporters of the ICC as measured by the number of ratification of the Rome Statute, as well as number of self-referrals of situations to the ICC. This support appears questionable because the same African states have begun to accuse the ICC of being fixated only on the continent. In addition to the analysis in the previous chapter of why the argument that the ICC is anti-African cannot be sustained, this chapter argues that African states lack institutional capacity to investigate and prosecute international crimes. The institutions where inadequacies are identified and discussed include the police, judiciary, prisons, as well as arguably, the lack of expertise such as judges and prosecutors that are trained specifically in the field of international criminal law. Furthermore the challenges of lack of political will, poverty as well as corruption are identified, but the analysis is focused on corruption. The chapter used Nigeria as a case study for other African states, as the challenges identified in Nigeria are replicated in other African states albeit to different degrees and with slight variations. It is hoped that African states can implement the complementarity regime domestically if they set 'their homes' in order by taking steps to address the issues identified in this chapter.

Nigeria is one of the 34 African states that have ratified the Rome Statute, thereby becoming bound to implement complementarity. In addition, the preliminary examination of the situation in Nigeria by the office of the Prosecutor (OTP) determined that there is a reasonable basis to believe that crimes against humanity, namely, acts of murder and persecution have been committed by members of the Boko Haram sect in Nigeria.[1] Consequently, the preliminary examination has progressed to phase 3 'admissibility',[2] and the OTP is currently assessing whether

[1]See OTP Article 5 Report on Nigeria 5 August 2013 (Text to note 173 in Ch 4) para 17.

[2]Report on Preliminary Examination Activities 2012 (OTP Report November 2012) para 96. Available at http://www.icc-cpi.int/NR/rdonlyres/C433C462-7C4E-4358-8A72-8D99FD00E8CD/285209/OTP2012ReportonPreliminaryExaminations22Nov2012.pdf (Accessed 20 November 2013). (The OTP retains four main phases in its preliminary examination process. Phase 1 includes an initial assessment of all information on alleged crimes; Phase 2 involves a determination whether the preconditions to the exercise of jurisdiction under Article 12 of the Rome Statute are satisfied and whether the alleged crimes fall under the subject matter jurisdiction of the ICC. Phase 3 involves



O.C. Imoedemhe, *The Complementarity Regime of the International Criminal Court*, DOI 10.1007/978-3-319-46780-1_6

the Nigerian authorities are conducting genuine proceedings in relation to the situation in order to resolve jurisdictional and admissibility issues.

Under Article 17, the test of a state's willingness and ability to investigate and prosecute international crimes is hinged upon the genuineness of the process, and which is further determined by the independence and impartiality of the domestic proceedings.[3] Therefore, this chapter demonstrates, through a case study of Nigeria, that beyond ratifying the Rome Statute, and in addition to having implementing legislation in place, African countries need credible institutions to carry out genuine proceedings domestically. This is because having a functional criminal justice system, including the police, the prison system, and the judiciary, is fundamental to the fulfilment of the responsibility implied by the primacy of domestic jurisdiction over international crimes.

Carrying out genuine proceedings is premised upon the institutional preparedness of states to implement complementarity, and an integral part is the adoption of implementing legislation, as discussed in chapter three.[4] However, even after the Rome Statute's crimes have been incorporated into domestic criminal law, adjudicating on the basis of it may still prove to be a challenge, depending on its status *vis-à-vis* other laws. Nigeria is a dualist state, as most other African states, therefore, international instruments or treaties do not have the force of law except after they have been given such force by the Nigerian legislature.[5]

As a result, when the Nigerian National Assembly simply adopts a treaty wholesale, as it did with the African Charter Act in 1983[6] and is preparing to do with the Rome Statute bill,[7] without carrying out an extensive review of existing legislation to resolve any inconsistencies, it is left to the courts to determine where a treaty ranks in relation to conflicting domestic laws. For example, in the *Abacha*[8] case, the inconsistency in the domestic Decrees[9] and the provisions of the African Charter Act was resolved in favour of the Decrees by the trial court. It was only at

analysis of admissibility in terms of complementarity and gravity. Having concluded its preliminary examination, the office takes into account the gravity of the crimes, the interests of victims and examines whether there is a reasonable basis to proceed in phase 4).

[3]Rome Statute, article 17(1)(a), (b) and 17(2)(c).

[4]Kleffner (2003).

[5]See section 12 of the Constitution of Nigeria of the Federal Republic of Nigeria. (the 1999 Constitution). Available at http://www.nigeria-law.org/ConstitutionOfTheFederalRepublicOfNigeria.htm.

[6]The African Charter on Human and Peoples' Rights (Ratification and Enforcement) Act Cap 10 Laws of the Federation of Nigeria (LFN) 1990 (now Cap A11 LFN 2011).

[7]A Bill for An Act to Enable Effect to be given in the Federal Republic of Nigeria to the Rome Statute of the International Criminal Court and for Purposes Connected Therewith—The Rome Statute of the International Criminal Court (Ratification and Jurisdiction) Bill 2004. (Copy on file with the author).

[8]*Abacha v. Gani Fawehinmi* [2000] 6 NWLR (Pt. 660) 228 (*Abacha* case).

[9]See, for example, State Security (Detention of Persons) Decree No 2 of 1984 as amended by Decree 11 of 1994; The Federal Military Government (Supremacy and Enforcement of Powers) Decree No 12 of 1994 and the Constitution (Suspension and Modification) Decree No 107 of 1993.

the Court of Appeal[10] and the Supreme Court[11] that the supremacy of the African Charter Act over the Decrees was upheld. Nevertheless, the supremacy of the Nigerian Constitution over any other law including international instruments is entrenched.[12]

Contrary to the Rome Statute, Nigerian laws allow the death penalty,[13] as well as immunity of the President and certain other persons in official government positions.[14] Legal ambiguities such as this affect states' institutional readiness to implement complementarity. When Nigeria adopts its implementing legislation, the question of whether it, and by analogy, other African nations, will then also have the institutions to prosecute international crimes is the focus of this chapter.

Institutional capacity to implement complementarity will vary from state to state depending on the local context and realities. Nevertheless, the similarities across the continent are sufficient to validate the approach of selecting one country for a case study and devising a minimum complementarity threshold that could then be applied elsewhere with slight adjustments to account for local peculiarities. Consequently, this chapter includes a discussion of whether the Nigerian police, prison system, and judiciary are equipped to carry out criminal proceedings based on complementarity.

This chapter is divided into three sections. The first section provides an overview of the current state of the Nigerian criminal justice system, in particular, the laws, the police and the prison system and identifies the reforms that would be necessary to prepare these institutions for the implementation of complementarity. It is found that international crimes have not yet been incorporated into Nigerian law. Also, it is shown that the police suffer from a lack of training and accountability, and that abuse and torture at their hands are endemic. Furthermore, the prisons are found to be insufficient and overcrowded, mainly due to the large numbers of detainees awaiting trial. It is argued that since complementarity entails criminal proceedings at the national level, the police, the courts and the prisons are institutions that should be well equipped to ensure genuine domestic proceedings.

The second section includes a discussion of the procedure for appointing judges and the professional legal skills and qualities required of a judge. It is argued that in addition to the professional legal skills required of a judge, an ICC judge, and by extension, national judges who will adjudicate international crimes should possess additional essential quality of prior training and experience in international criminal law. This is important because not only for Nigerian courts, but also for other

[10]*Fawehinmi v Abacha* [1996] 9 NWLR (Part 475) 710, 747.

[11]*Abacha v. Gani Fawehinmi* [2000] 4 FWLR 533 SC.

[12]Ibid, Per Ogundare JSC 289; Mohammed JSC 301–302; Achike JSC 317–318 and Uwaifo JSC 343.

[13]Amnesty International, 'Nigeria: Man Dragged to the Gallows will now be Executed by Firing Squad' 25 June 2013 Amnesty Annual Report 2013 https://www.amnesty.org/en/news/nigeria-man-dragged-gallows-will-now-be-executed-firing-squad-2013-06-25 (Accessed 10 March 2014).

[14]See 1999 Constitution, section 308.

African states national courts to acquire requisite judges and prosecutors who are experts in international criminal law to carry out domestic trials when the need arise and so as to avoid self-referrals to the ICC. Thus, it is argued that the unavailability of judges and prosecutors trained in the field of international criminal law may constitute a major drawback to the implementation of complementarity.

The third section discusses corruption as a bane to the implementation of complementarity in Nigeria and in Africa as a whole. Corruption in the Nigerian judiciary is analysed and the prevalence of intimidation and manipulation of judges is demonstrated. This state of affairs, coupled with security concerns and the incidence of kidnapping of judges and their family members, militate against the independence and impartiality of the judiciary, which is necessary for the implementation of complementarity. It is therefore proposed that tackling the problems of corruption and insecurity is one strategic means by which Nigeria and other African states can achieve institutional preparedness. Doing so will also restore public confidence in the justice system, which is essential to its effective function. Therefore, public impressions concerning the workings of the courts in Nigeria and a minimum complementarity threshold are expounded at the end of the section.

## 6.1 The Nigerian Criminal Justice System

According to Joseph Daudu, criminal justice is the system of practices and institutions of governments directed at upholding social control, deterring crimes or sanctioning those who violate laws with criminal penalties and rehabilitation efforts.[15] This definition identifies practices on the one hand and institutions of government on the other, as the fulcrum upon which the superstructure of crime control and justice delivery turns.[16] Therefore, in addition to criminal legislation, of importance to a criminal justice system are the institutions, infrastructure, expertise and agencies involved in the process of implementation. Thus, a criminal justice system is the collective institutions through which an alleged criminal passes until the accusations against him have been disposed of or the assessed punishment concluded.[17] Every stage of the process is dependent on a previous one; this interdependence exemplifies the nature of criminal justice as a system.[18]

The institutions are linked through a process. Michael Moore, describing the inter-connectivity in a criminal justice system, postulates that it is not a 'system' in the sense that all its agencies are directed towards a particular objective with the help of a centralised authority.[19] Rather, it is a limited system to the extent that the

[15]Daudu (2012), pp. 89–105.

[16]Ibid.

[17]Clare and Kramer (1977).

[18]Ibid. See also Schoderbek (1968).

[19]Moore (1997).

different agencies are linked through a process in which one agency's outputs become the next agency's inputs.[20]

Moore further espoused that the output of the police, for example, is the arrest of offenders, which in turn, and based on the outcome of an investigation, becomes the input into the courts. The cases, when developed as the output of the prosecution and defense, become the output of the courts after conviction and sentencing, which become input for the prisons, and so on.[21] Through a criminal justice system, due process is achieved, with offenders processed from the time of arrest until they are finally acquitted or released from prison after serving a prescribed sentence.

Thus, the objective of a criminal justice system is to deliver justice to the victims, the accused, the immediate community affected by the crime committed and to the society as a whole. To achieve this objective, there must be sufficient and available resources, there must be some coordination and collaboration among the agencies, and most importantly, there must be an existing legal framework for the coordination and collaboration of available resources.[22] A further objective of a criminal justice system is social equity, fairness and balance in the deterrence of crime. In this regard, certain institutions are indispensable to the criminal justice system; these include the police, the courts and the prisons.

### *6.1.1 The Criminal Code, the Police and Criminal Investigation in Nigeria*

As discussed in chapter four, a few African states, namely, the Democratic Republic of Congo, Kenya, Uganda and Sudan failed to meet the complementarity threshold in their domestic prosecution of international crimes in part because they attempted to prosecute these crimes as ordinary domestic crimes. Therefore, in this section, it is shown that Nigeria similarly will need to specifically proscribe international crimes, defined as such, in order to carry out genuine domestic prosecutions of international crimes. The reason for the analysis is to argue that no crime in Nigeria approximates the crimes against humanity of murder and persecution, which have been allegedly committed by members of Boko Haram, and also that existing legislation is insufficient.

The crime of murder is known to virtually all domestic criminal legislation and thus, in Nigeria, it is proscribed under section 316 of the Criminal Code.[23] This

[20]Ibid.

[21]See Sakihu Isiaka Onimajesin, 'Criminal Justice System in Nigeria: An Appraisal' 195–205. Available at http://www.unilorin.edu.ng/publications/onimajesinsi/Criminal%20Justice%20System%20In%20Nigera-%20An%20Appraisal.pdf (Assessed 2 May 2013).

[22]Idigbe (2012), pp. 111, 115–116.

[23]Criminal Code Act: An Act to Establish a Code of Criminal Law in Nigeria 1 June 1916 http://ofilispeaks.com/wp-content/uploads/criminal-act.pdf now The Nigerian Criminal Code Act Cap 77 Laws of the Federation of Nigeria (LFN) 1990; Cap C38 LFN 2004; Cap C3 LFN 2011. (Criminal Code Act), s 316.

section lists six intents, any one of which satisfies the means for murder. The section requires that the accused should have intended to kill the victim or another person. The question is; does the definition of murder in the Nigerian Criminal Code correspond to any of the crimes in the Rome Statute for which Nigeria as a state party may be able to assume jurisdiction to investigate and prosecute? It is important to note that criminal legislation in Nigeria does not include any of the international crimes categorised as such. The crime against humanity of murder is not the same as the ordinary domestic crime of murder under Nigerian criminal legislation, either in their definition or elements. Also, the crime of persecution is not recognised in Nigeria. Consequently, there are no such crimes as 'crimes against humanity' in Nigeria.

With respect to state or federal offenses, the Attorneys-General of the respective states and of the Federation have the responsibility to institute, take over and discontinue any criminal prosecution.[24] The Constitution and the Police Act are the regulatory statutes for the Nigerian Police Force (NPF). Section 4 of the Police Act defines the functions of the NPF to include the prevention and detection of crime, apprehension of offenders and preservation of law and order.[25] In addition, the NPF is vested with constitutional powers to investigate crimes.[26] Consequently, the NPF handles about 90 % of criminal investigation while the remaining 10 % is shared amongst other agencies like the Economic and Financial Crimes Commission (EFCC), the Independent Corrupt Practices and Other Related Offences (ICPC), Customs and Excise and Immigrations Service.

The management structure of the NPF is centralised and monolithic, as local or state police forces are not permitted under the Constitution.[27] Its organisation and administration are the responsibility of the Federal government.[28] With estimated staff strength of 377,000 personnel, the NPF is the largest institution in Nigeria and also Nigeria's largest employer.[29] The structure is headed by an Inspector-General of Police (IGP). Each of Nigeria's 36 states and the Federal Capital Territory (FCT) constitute a Police Command headed by a police commissioner.

Ultimately, the Nigerian government is responsible for criminal prosecution, since the NPF is a part of the executive arm and is accountable to the President of the Federal Republic of Nigeria. Since the duties of the NPF include the arrest of

[24]See sections 174 (1) & 211 (1) of the 1999 Constitution.

[25]An Act to make Provision for the Organisation, Discipline, Powers and Duties of the Police, the Special Constabulary and the Traffic Wardens Chapter P19 No 41 1967, 1 April 1943, section 24. http://www.placng.org/new/laws/P19.pdf (The Police Act).

[26]See section 214(1) of the 1999 Constitution.

[27]Section 214(1) 1999 Constitution.

[28]Open Society Justice Initiative (OSJI) and Network on Police Reform in Nigeria (NOPRIN), 'Criminal Force, Torture, Abuse and Extrajudicial Killings by the Nigerian Police Force' 2010 (OSJI & NOPRIN Report). Available at http://www.opensocietyfoundations.org/reports/criminal-force-torture-abuse-and-extrajudicial-killings-nigeria-police-force (Accessed 3 December 2013).

[29]ibid, 39.

suspected criminals and investigation of crimes,[30] their role is therefore very crucial in the criminal justice system, because for any prosecution to take place, an arrest must be made and the alleged criminal must be arraigned before a court.

The report of the Open Justice Society Initiative and the Network on Police Reforms in Nigeria documents patterns of abuse and torture committed by the NPF against the civilian population.[31] According to the report, atrocities reported are not the actions of a few rogue police officers but rather, they are examples of a culture of violence and lawlessness that pervades the police force.[32] Thus, the NPF lacks the capacity to conduct proper criminal investigations because it relies on torture to elicit confessions, being known to use different forms of brutality, including sexual violence, against detainees and suspects.[33] The failure of the Nigerian government to stop police abuse corrodes police-community relations, reinforces impunity and makes the NPF even more likely to prey on the people it is meant to protect. In fact, it is largely conventional that some members of the NPF are more willing and likely to commit crimes than to prevent their commission.[34]

The atrocities are widespread and are acknowledged by the political leadership of Nigeria. In its universal periodic review (UPR), submitted to the United Nations Human Rights Council in 2009, Nigeria acknowledged 'allegations of extrajudicial killings' but claimed that it 'neither sanctions nor will it allow such atrocities to be carried out with impunity in Nigeria'.[35] Arguably, the inaction on the part of the government to stop these atrocities makes it complicit in the atrocities.

In June 2005, the Nigerian NGO 'Access to Justice' issued a report in which it presented graphic accounts of how 'the use of torture is extremely widespread within the Nigerian Police Force and is an institutionalised and routine practice'.[36] In its July 2005 report, Human Rights Watch similarly found 'the use of torture and other cruel, inhuman and degrading treatment by the Nigerian Police Force to be widespread and routine'.[37]

In November 2006, Amnesty International in its report on investigation of sexual violence on the part of internal security agencies in Nigeria, stipulated that the 'rape of women and girls by the police and security forces... is acknowledged to be endemic in Nigeria'.[38] In the report, Amnesty International alleged that the NPF and security forces commit rape at different times and that rape is used strategically to coerce and intimidate entire communities.[39]

---

[30] See sections 24–30 of the Police Act.

[31] See OSJI & NOPRIN Report.

[32] OSJI & NOPRIN Report, 23.

[33] Ibid.

[34] Ibid, 21.

[35] United Nations Human Rights (2009), paras 72–73.

[36] Access to Justice (2005).

[37] Human Rights Watch (2007).

[38] Amnesty International (2006).

[39] Ibid, 5–11.

In April 2008, the report of the Second Presidential Committee on Police Reform admitted the existence of institutionalised police abuse.[40] Public confidence is essential to effective policing and when the police commit atrocities, they undermine the public confidence which is central to guaranteeing public safety and security. The report of the Committee determined that, arising from the pattern of violations associated with policing in Nigeria, there was profound 'loss of public confidence in the integrity of police personnel.[41] Consequently, the police is generally regarded by the public as corrupt, inept and inefficient'.[42]

It is also well-known that members of the NPF enjoy a high degree of impunity. The Police Service Commission (PSC) has the oversight function for the NPF and is responsible for preventing and investigating police abuses, but there seems to be an unwillingness to challenge the *status quo*.[43] Judicial oversight is also not effective because judges must rely on investigations conducted by the same NPF whose personnel are alleged perpetrators. With such weak oversight, few cases of police abuses are reported and fewer still are successfully prosecuted.

The foregoing analysis reveals that the current state of the NPF cannot be relied on to investigate ordinary domestic crimes let alone international crimes. Part of the problem is undoubtedly a lack of training, deprived working conditions and inadequate remuneration, and the second is non-existent facilities for communication and investigation. Detailed analyses of these factors is beyond the scope of this book, but suffice it to mention that these problems have led to corruption, extortion, a tradition of police brutality and a high propensity for violence by some members of the NPF.[44]

### *6.1.2 The Role of the Nigerian Prison Service in the Criminal Justice System*

Analysis of the Nigerian prison service is made in this section because complementarity and cooperation are two pillars upon which the Rome Statute is founded.[45] Consequently, part of the institutional preparedness to implement complementarity, is the fact that the ICC depends on states, not only to arrest and surrender suspects that it seeks to prosecute, but also for states to take up convicted persons to serve prison sentences in their domestic prisons. This is important because there are no international prisons to which individuals convicted of international crimes by the ICC could be sent to serve their prison terms. Thus, Part 10 of

[40]Federal Republic of Nigeria (2008), p. 196.

[41]Ibid.

[42]See OSJI & NOPRIN Report (2010), 31.

[43]ibid, 23.

[44]OSJI & NOPRIN Report (2010), 37, 81–90.

[45]See Silvana Arbia (2012).

the Rome Statute contains provisions on the responsibility of states in the enforcement of sentences of imprisonment by which states parties are required to ensure that their prison systems meet international standards.[46]

The importance of the foregoing is underscored by the fact that under the regime of the ICTR, Rwanda only qualified to receive convicted persons to serve sentences after it had undertaken extensive reform of its prisons to bring it in conformity with international standards.[47] The question is whether Nigerian prisons and by extension the prison systems of African states are adequate to receive convicted persons from the ICC to serve their term of imprisonment.

The objectives of the Nigerian Prisons Service (NPS) are tripartite. First, it is responsible for the legal custody of prisoners. Prisoners are deemed to be in the legal custody of the superintendent in charge of the prison and are subject to discipline and regulations.[48] Second, the NPS is required to provide adequate, humane treatment for all categories of prisoners. The third objective is that the NPS is meant to rehabilitate and reform prisoners. Rehabilitation involves encouraging the prisoners to abstain from criminal behaviour by providing them with social, educational or vocational activities which they can integrate into their social lives upon completion of their sentences.[49]

Like the criminal justice system, all three objectives of the NPS are interwoven and not mutually exclusive. Thus, it is important to determine whether the NPS is able to achieve these objectives or not. It is worthy of note that the Nigerian prisons do not only suffer from poor infrastructure, they are also overcrowded. As a result, prison congestion and the need for their decongestion presents a major challenge in relation to proposals for prison reforms in Nigeria.[50] The choice to focus the discussion on decongestion does not make other problems of less importance. Rather, it is argued that the other issues of poor facilities, neglect and lack of effective rehabilitation and reintegration programmes are entwined in the problem of overcrowding.

According to the Former Controller-General of the Nigerian Prisons Service, Olusola Ogundipe,[51] as of April 2011, the design capacity of the NPS was 46,698, while the total inmate population was 48,632.[52] This means that the capacity was exceeded by 2000 inmates. However, out of the total number of 48,632 prisoners, 34,819, representing 72 %, were awaiting trials. It was reported that in December 2007, out of a total of 42,030 inmates in custody, 28,500 were awaiting trial.[53]

---

[46]Rome Statute, Part 10 (articles 103–111).

[47]Civil Society Prison Reform Initiative (CSPRI) (2013).

[48]See Prisons Act Cap 366 LFN 1990, section 3(1).

[49]Ibid.

[50]Ogundipe (2012), pp. 175–190.

[51]Olusola Adigun Ogundipe was Controller-General of Prisons from July 2006 to December 2011. He was succeeded by Mr Zakari Ibrahim in February 2012. See 'Ogundipe Bows Out in Style' Available at http://www.prisons.gov.ng/news/news_detail.php?id=16 (Accessed March 10 2014).

[52]Ogundipe (2012), p. 177. See also US Department of State (2012), pp. 11–13.

[53]Sarkin (2008), pp. 23–49.

It is further reported that some of the 'awaiting trial inmates' have been waiting for up to 16 years or more.[54] In most cases, they have already spent well over the number of years in prison, if they were found guilty and convicted of the alleged crime.[55] However, the situation becomes irreversible where such persons are ultimately not found guilty and are acquitted. This means that one way to guarantee decongestion in the Nigerian prisons is to ensure that those awaiting trials are brought to trial as quickly as possible.

Thus, decongestion of the prisons could only be effective and work towards a comprehensive justice reform if the police and the courts were effective in justice delivery. Ultimately, admission into the prison must be based on orders of conviction from a competent court, which means that until a person is convicted, he cannot be subject to the process of rehabilitation, reform and reintegration into the society. Therefore the prison is not meant for suspects awaiting trials. The only way to ensure decongestion is to reduce the number of awaiting trial inmates and this can only be done when the investigation and prosecution of criminals are carried out promptly by the other agencies—the police and the courts.

## 6.2 The Nigerian Judiciary and Complementarity

Analysis of law enforcement and prisons in the previous section reveals that the key improvements required by Nigeria to realise its cooperation and complementarity obligations must occur in the police and the prisons. Since the inadequacies of the Nigerian police and the prison system have already been discussed, this section encompasses a discussion of the judiciary in Nigeria and whether they are able to carry out complementarity-based prosecution.

Arguably, there are no specialised courts to carry out effective investigation and prosecution of international crimes in Nigeria presently. This is not only because of the lack of a physical structure suitable for the purpose, but more importantly, it is due to the dearth of judges and prosecutors trained in the field of international criminal law. Thus, it is argued that Nigerian courts lack the capacity to investigate and prosecute members of the Boko Haram when or if they are ever apprehended.

The situation in Uganda demonstrates that a consideration of institutional preparedness at the state level must go beyond mere physical infrastructure. Arrest warrants have been issued against members of the Lord's Resistance Army (LRA) of Uganda since 2005,[56] yet till date, the ICC has not been able to commence proceedings with respect to the suspects because they have not been arrested and

[54]Ogundipe, Ibid. See also Ojo (2011).

[55]Ibid.

[56]Press Release, 'Warrant of Arrest Unsealed against Five LRA Commanders' ICC-CPI-20051014-110. *The Prosecutor v. Joseph Kony, Vincent Otti, Raska Lukwiya, Okot Odhiambo & Dominic Ongwen.*

surrendered to the ICC for that purpose. Clearly, the LRA leaders should be prosecuted but the question remains of 'how' or by 'whom'.[57] It has been argued that Uganda has one of the most effective legal systems in Africa.[58] Although this assertion needs substantiating, the fact that in the aftermath of the atrocities allegedly committed by members of the LRA, the Ugandan government established the Special War Crimes Division of the High Court may have given credence to the assertion. In addition, the Ugandan parliament has passed the ICC Bill,[59] which empowers Ugandan courts to prosecute international crimes.

Regardless of these apparent preparedness, the Ugandan judiciary seems unable to handle the investigation and prosecution of international crimes, and particularly, of members of the LRA.[60] According to Elizabeth Nahamya-Ibanda, 'despite the War Crimes Division being a significant development, the country is in great need of support . . .especially with regard to the national lack of capacity to investigate and prosecute international crimes and lack of resources'.[61]

Thus, institutional preparedness includes other factors, such as the availability of judges and prosecutors who are competent in international criminal law. This point was underscored in the *Saif Al-Islam*[62] case when the Pre-Trial Chamber I (PTCI) observed the steps undertaken by the Libyan government which involved inviting judges and lawyers versed in international criminal law from other jurisdictions.[63] In contrast, the Kenyan government merely relied on general submission in its efforts to reform its judicial system.[64]

Also, 'unwillingness' under Article 17(2)(c) may be determined with respect to situations where the proceedings are not being conducted independently or impartially.[65] Therefore, the complementarity thresholds of 'unwillingness' and 'inability', already discussed in chapter two,[66] have direct links, not only to situation of non-existent laws criminalising international crimes, but also to the unavailability of national judicial systems,[67] which includes lack of independence and impartiality of the courts at the domestic level to prosecute them. In this regard, the next

[57]Soares (2013), p. 325.

[58]Schabas (2008), pp. 9, 18.

[59]International Criminal Court Bill 2006 http://www.coalitionfortheicc.org/documents/Uganda-ICC_Bill_2006.pdf (Accessed 10 January 2014).

[60]See, for example, the use of amnesty and *mato oput* in Uganda (Text to notes 111–129 in Ch 3).

[61]Justice Elizabeth Nahamya-Ibanda, 'The Mandate and Activities of the Special War Crimes Division of the High Court Uganda' Being paper delivered on 'Challenges of Complementarity under the Rome Statute System and the Role of Lawyers: Lessons and Prospects' organised by *Advocats Sans Frontieres* in collaboration with Ugandan Law Society 1 January 2010 Kampala, Uganda. (Nahamya-Ibanda is a judge in the Special War Crimes Division).

[62]See Admissibility decision of the PTCI in the *Saif Al Islam Gaddafi* case (Text to note 96 in Ch 1).

[63]Ibid, para 213.

[64]Ibid, para 85.

[65]See Rome Statute, Article 17(2)(c).

[66](Text to notes 100–131 in Ch 2).

[67]Rome Statute, Article 17(3).

sub-section examines the question of whether the Nigerian judiciary has the quality of independence and impartiality to prosecute international crimes.

### 6.2.1 *Appointment of Judges in the Nigerian Judiciary: The Need for Focused Expertise in the Field of International Criminal Law*

In this section, it is argued that the Nigerian judiciary lacks experts in the field of international criminal law and that part of Nigeria's preparedness to implement complementarity, which means to prosecute international crimes, is having judges who are competent in the field. It is further argued that the criteria and method of appointing judges in Nigeria may account for the inadequacy. Although there appears to be no debate on the method of appointing judges, the discussion in this section includes an assessment of the extent to which the procedure can secure the requirements of independence and impartiality, essential to the judicial branch of government and specifically to the implementation of complementarity in Nigeria.

The Federal Judicial Service Commission (the FJSC) is responsible for advising the National Judicial Council (NJC) regarding the nomination of persons for appointment as judicial officers to the Supreme Court of Nigeria, the Court of Appeal, the Federal High Court and other courts in Nigeria.[68] The FJSC equally recommends the removal from office of such officers, and dismisses and exercises disciplinary control over judges.[69] The FJSC is one of the 14 Federal Executive Bodies created under section 153(1) of the 1999 Constitution.[70] It is composed of the Chief Justice of Nigeria (CJN), the President of the Court of Appeal, the Attorney-General, the Chief Judge of the Federal High Court and four other persons, two of whom must be legal practitioners and must be recommended by the Nigerian Bar Association, while the other two are not legal practitioners but persons who, in the opinion of the President, are of unquestionable integrity.[71]

According to the former CJN, Justice Dahiru Musdapher,[72] a review of the procedure for appointment to the Bench is imperative to ensure that 'knowledgeable persons of unquestionable integrity are appointed'.[73] This statement reflects

[68]See section 13(a)–(c) of Part I to the Third Schedule of the 1999 Constitution. The equivalent of the FJSC in the 36 states is the State Judicial Service Commission (SJSC). See the 1999 Constitution, section 197(1)(c).

[69]Ibid.

[70]See the 1999 Constitution, section 153(1)(e).

[71]See section 12(a)–(f) of Part I to the Third Schedule of the 1999 Constitution.

[72]Justice Dahiru Musdapher was appointed Chief Justice of Nigeria on 29 August 2011 and he retired on 14 July 2012 on attainment of 70 years in accordance with section 291(1) of the 1999 Constitution. See Agency Reporter (2012).

[73]Nnochiri (2012).

the provisions of the United Nations Basic Principles on the Independence of the Judiciary which declares that persons selected for judicial office shall be individuals of integrity and ability with appropriate training or qualifications in law.[74] In addition, the UN Basic Principles prohibits discrimination in the selection process and provides that any method of judicial selection shall safeguard against judicial appointments for improper motives.[75]

The above qualification for appointment implies that 'many qualities are required of a judge... he or she must of course know the law, and know how to apply it'.[76] It also connotes that any discussion of the appointment of judges must be based on an understanding of the nature of the judicial function and the conditions necessary for its effective performance.[77] Accordingly, Anthony Mason postulates that 'without a clear understanding of that function, it is futile to list all the desirable qualities that one might hope to find in a perfect human being and then assert that they are qualities that are expected of a judge'.[78]

The judicial function requires professional legal skills of a high order and it takes a variety of forms, each of which may call for particular qualities.[79] Common to all the forms of judicial function are the qualities of independence, impartial and neutral adjudication. Independent and impartial adjudication abnegates the notion that a judge will bring to bear a view which favours that of a particular section of the society, the president or the body that appointed him. Independence and impartiality are critical to the judicial function and these will be analysed subsequently, but first, an analysis of the professional legal skills and qualities required in the judicial function is in order.

### *6.2.2 Professional Legal Skills and Personal Qualities Required in Judicial Function*

Taiwo Osipitan once observed that 'the quality of justice depends more on the quality of men who administer the law than on the content of the law they

[74]United Nations Basic Principles on the Independence of the Judiciary 1985, Art 10. Available http://www.hjpc.ba/dc/pdf/Basic%20Principles%20on%20the%20Independence%20of%20the%20Judiciary.pdf (UN Basic Principles).

[75]Ibid.

[76]See Speech by Lord Judge Lord Chief Justice of England and Wales at 'Equality in Justice Day' at the Royal Court of Justice London 24 October 2008. (Hereinafter 'Speech by Chief Justice of England and Wales). Available at http://www.judiciary.gov.uk/Resources/JCO/Documents/Speeches/speech-lcj-equality-justice-day.pdf (Accessed 7 November 2013).

[77]Mason (2013), (Accessed 7 October 2013).

[78]Mason.

[79]Ibid.

administer'.[80] Similarly, Marai Dakolias noted that 'the quality and integrity of a judicial system can be measured by the quality and integrity of its judges'.[81] These imply that though the place of the law is important, certain legal skills and personal qualities are necessary for the judge who interprets and implement the law.

According to Anthony Mason, the requisite professional legal skills include knowledge of evidence, procedure and practice, knowledge of the law, analytical ability, the capacity to dispose of a case smoothly and efficiently, and the capacity to give a well-reasoned judgement with reasonable promptness.[82] Arguably, most of these skills will be more readily apparent in barristers than in other lawyers. Therefore, in the case of non-barristers, it may be a matter of identifying the possession of the capacity to develop these skills.[83] That means identifying lawyers with a sound general knowledge of law or relevant specialist knowledge, as the case may be, and the intellectual capacity to acquire, in a relatively short time, the requisite professional legal skills appropriate for judicial work.[84]

In addition, there are some essential personal qualities that are indispensable, namely, integrity, impartiality, industry, a strong sense of fairness and a willingness to listen to and understand the viewpoints of others.[85] No doubt, other qualities are desirable. Thus, according to Mason, the ability to communicate to the legal community and the public about the law and the workings of the court is also of high value, but not an essential quality.[86]

The specific reference to 'knowledgeable' in the statement of the former CJN,[87] suggests that some judges lack the requisite competence for the discharge of the judicial function. This deficiency can be traced to a number of reasons, including the qualifications and procedures for appointing judges.

### 6.2.3 *Appointments of Judges in Nigeria: Towards a More Representative Judiciary?*

In order of hierarchy, the Chief Justice of Nigeria and other justices of the Supreme Court are appointed by the President on the recommendation of the National

---

[80]Osipitan (2002), http://nigerianewsnow.com/News/December02/530103_lawlecture.htm. (Accessed 8 January 2006).

[81]Dakolias (1995), pp. 167, 172.

[82]Mason (2013).

[83]Ibid.

[84]Ibid.

[85]Ibid.

[86]Ibid.

[87]Nnochiri (2012).

Judicial Council (NJC), subject to a confirmation by the Senate.[88] The minimum qualification of a justice of the Supreme Court is 15 years' experience post call as a legal practitioner.[89] The appointments of the President and other justices of the Court of Appeal follow the same pattern; the President's decision is preceded by the advice and recommendation of the Federal Judicial Service Commission and the NJC, and subject to confirmation by the Senate.[90] Furthermore, whereas the Chief Judge of the Federal High Court is appointed by the President subject to confirmation of the Senate,[91] the appointments of the Chief Judge of States High Courts and other judges are carried out by the Governor of the state, subject to confirmation by the respective states' Houses of Assembly.[92]

The appointment procedure, especially the nomination of candidates by the FJSC or SJSC, as the case may be, and the subsequent screening by the NJC was designed to ensure the appointment of judges who possess the requisite competence and integrity.[93] However, the appointing authorities seem to allow personal prejudice, ethnic and political considerations to preponderate over competence.[94] Although the procedure and criteria for the appointment of judges have been expressly stipulated in the Constitution, the FJSC, in its decision to nominate a particular person for appointment, considers other factors, such as the ethnic group the proposed nominee belongs and who recommended him or her.[95] Consequently, intensive politicisation by those who aspire to become judges ultimately causes the appointment to be based not on merit but on the connections of the appointee.[96] A judge whose appointment is the product of lobbying is unlikely to be independent and impartial, in cases involving his benefactors.[97]

Appointments of judges are made subject to the principles of 'federal character of Nigeria' enshrined in section 14(3) and (4) of the Constitution that appointments should promote national unity, should not be dominated by few ethnic or sectional groups and shall reflect the diversity of the people of Nigeria.[98] Making reference to certain appointment of judges in Lagos State, which did not reflect any known criteria, Augustine Alegeh (SAN) said that the idea of appointing a person as a judge because his father was a judge, for example, should no longer be

---

[88]See Chapter VII of the Nigerian 1999 Constitution, sections 230–236 (section 230(2) provides that the number of Justices of the Supreme Court must not exceed 21); Section 231. See also 'The Judiciary in Nigeria' Available at http://fhc-ng.com/judnig.htm (Accessed 16 September 2013).

[89]The 1999 Constitution, s. 231(3).

[90]Ibid, see s 238.

[91]Ibid, see ss 250(1) &(2) for the Federal High Court's Chief Judge and Judges' appointments.

[92]Ibid, see ss 271(1)7(2) for the appointments of the Chief Judge and other Judges of a state.

[93]Nnaemeka-Agu (2002), pp. 230–236, 210.

[94]Oko (2006), pp. 9–82, 49–50.

[95]Osipitan (2002).

[96]Aniagolu (2000), p. 86.

[97]Osipitan.

[98]See the 1999 Constitution, s 14(3) & (4).

encouraged.[99] Also, former President of the Nigerian Bar Association Joseph Daudu,[100] noted that the process of appointing judges 'is fraught with all manners of irregularities', 'siblings and favoured ones have been known to be appointed as judges when more qualified persons are available...'[101]

According to Richard Akinjide, the process of appointing judges into the judiciary based on ethnicity is inappropriate: 'why should you base appointment into the judiciary on the area where somebody comes from? Supposing that area does not have the right quality, you turn appointment into the judiciary as if it is political or board appointment?'[102] Indeed, considerations of ethnic origin, social background and connections as part of the criteria for appointing judges may have compromised competence and integrity and, ultimately, the independence and impartiality of the judiciary.[103]

While these concerns seem well-founded, it is argued that this procedure is not peculiar to Nigeria, as countries in other jurisdictions are involved in the same politicised process of appointing judges. For example, Louise Arbour observed, with respect to the procedure in Canada, that 'at the highest level...the appointment of judges at the Supreme Court level is essentially the decision of the Prime Minister, after a consultation process that is neither transparent nor extensive'.[104]

Furthermore, it has been argued that the criterion for appointment of judges by reference to ethnic consideration is to allow for a more representative composition which is fairly balanced.[105] Consequently, 'an important duty lies upon the appointing authorities to ensure a balanced composition of the judiciary, ideologically, socially, culturally and the like...the judiciary is a branch of the government, not merely a dispute resolution institution. *As such it cannot be composed in total disregard of the society*'.[106]

Nevertheless, it is argued that although the ideal of appointing a judiciary whose composition is reasonably balanced may be important, it is not practicable to appoint a judiciary that approximates the composition of society as a whole for a number of reasons. The first is that the possession of professional legal skills, like the possession of professional medical skills, is not evenly distributed throughout

---

99 Benson (2013).

100 Joseph Bodurin Daudu was President of NBA from 2010 to 2012.

101 Osinuga (2011).

102 'Nigeria: Law and Human Rights: We're in Elected Dictatorship - Akinjide' 24 October 2003. Available at http://allafrica.com/stories/200310240380 (Accessed 20 August 2008).

103 Otteh (2004), cited in Oko (2006).

104 Louise Arbour, 'Building an Independent Judiciary: Process and Perceptions' address by Louise Arbour, CEO International Crisis Group, on the Occasion of the UNHCHR Conference on *Building the Future: The Challenges in Application Processes, Strengthen Justice, End Impunity* Guatemala 2 September 2013.

105 Shetreet (1987), p. 776.

106 Shetreet, (emphasis added by Mason 2013). Professor Shetreet is not alone in subscribing to the principle of fair reflection; see 'The Judiciary in England and Wales, 1992', *Justice* London 23–24; Report of the New Zealand Royal Commission on the Courts, New Zealand, 1978, para 665.

the society.[107] The second is that seeking a more representative appointment by reference to ethnic consideration ultimately leads to the appointment of persons who are less knowledgeable and who do not possess the requisite professional skills and personal qualities.

In the context of the ICC, as in the domestic, judicial independence has numerous dimensions.[108] Some of these dimensions include the procedures for nomination, selection and re-election of the judges. For the purposes of judicial independence, the procedure for selection of ICC judges is subject to varying methods and to differing terms and conditions of service, for example, regarding tenure and the permissible scope of outside activities.[109] Yet they share common characteristics with judges in the domestic setting insofar as they all play a central role in the interpretation and application of international law.

The Assembly of States Parties (ASP) consist of representatives of states parties to the Rome Statute and is responsible for the election of judges to the ICC.[110] By implication, judges of the ICC are appointed by politicians and diplomats, which brings a political element into the appointment structure.[111] For this reason, an independent appointments body, the Advisory Committee, has been established to review nominations and ensure a non-political component in the process.[112] Selection is based on the competence of the nominee in international criminal law, experience and the essential qualities articulated earlier.[113] Arguably, this mechanism for an independent review and assessment of nominations guarantees independence and impartiality.[114]

The question of judicial independence is explicitly dealt with in Articles 40 and 41 of the Rome Statute,[115] where it is stated that every judge shall be independent,[116] and shall not participate in any case in which his impartiality might reasonably be doubted on any grounds.[117] In practice, however, the nomination and election of judges to the ICC generally involve politicised processes with little transparency and which are subject to widely varying nomination mechanisms at

[107]Mason (2013).

[108]Mackenzie and Sands (2003), pp. 271–286, 276.

[109]The ICC has 18 judges with nine serving as full-time and the other nine as *ad-litem* judges. See arts 35 & 36(1).

[110]Rome Statute, Article 36.

[111]De Bertodano (2002), pp. 409–430, 421.

[112]Art 36(4)(c). The first meeting of the Advisory Committee on Nominations of judges was held on 19 April 2013. The report of the Committee is available at http://www.icc-cpi.int/iccdocs/asp_docs/ASP12/ICC-ASP-12-23-ENG.pdf (Accessed 21 October 2013).

[113]See notes 81–85.

[114]Ingadottir (2002).

[115]Rome Statute, Articles 40 & 41 on independence of the judges and excusing and disqualification of judges respectively.

[116]Rome Statute, art 40(1).

[117]Rome Statute, art 41(2)(a).

the national level.[118] This is because candidates for international judicial appointment are put forward by states, and therefore, a state might be suspected of only nominating an individual with the intention that he or she may be involved in deciding a contentious case that implicates its national interests.[119] It would be unreasonable to expect that a nominating state would put forward a candidate who does not share its values and interests.[120]

As a consequence, it has been argued that questions surround whether the ICC judges can be seen as independent and impartial dispensers of justice, handing down rule-based decisions; or whether they are merely another manifestation of state power and influence in international relations.[121] Admittedly, the procedure for the nomination, selection and appointment of ICC judges lends itself to the same politics that accompany the procedure in any domestic sphere, as in Nigeria and Africa. This is arguably so notwithstanding the work of the advisory committee, like the FJSC/SJSC and the NJC of Nigeria, which review such nominations and make recommendations for appointment.

The foregoing discussion demonstrates that to concentrate on the goal of fair representations in the appointment of judges is detrimental to the fundamental goal of an independent and impartial judiciary and could compromise both the pursuit of efficiency and public confidence. Thus, the process of ensuring a more representative judiciary and appointing persons based on ethnic considerations rather than competence has only increased the problem of corruption in the Nigerian judiciary.

## 6.3 Tackling Corruption: A Necessary Strategy for Implementing Complementarity in Nigeria

Corruption is a complex phenomenon. It is an issue that has attracted no small amount of consternation both in Nigeria and internationally. The purpose of discussing corruption in this section is to argue that part of the institutional preparedness required to implement complementarity is confronting corruption with the aim of minimising or completely eradicating it from the judicial system. A judiciary that is found to be corrupt will ultimately lead to the conclusion that a state is unable to act and therefore the ICC will intervene.

Corruption has been defined and discussed extensively by various scholars.[122] Therefore, this section does not examine the different definitions that have been

[118]Bertodano (2002), p. 420.

[119]Ibid.

[120]Mackenzie and Sands (2003), p. 278.

[121]Ibid 275.

[122]Akindele (1990); Babalobi (2005) 11–12; Victor Dike, 'Corruption Control: A New Paradigm for Effective Control in Nigeria' world.com/feature/article/corruption.html; Babalola (1995).

proffered. Rather, it adopts that by the World Bank, which states that corruption is 'the abuse of public office for private gain'.[123] This is deemed to be the case when an official accepts, solicits or extorts a bribe,[124] as well as when private agents proactively offer bribes to circumvent public policies and processes for competitive advantage and profit.[125] Highlighting this definition, Patrick Igbinovia postulates that corruption encompasses all forms of bribery, abuse of office and nepotism, any favour done in expectation of material or non-material gain or even as a reward for an earlier deed.[126]

According to Afe Babalola, corruption occurs at two levels.[127] The first level is corruption associated with politics at the law-making level, and the second is that which is perpetrated at the law-implementation level. At the first level, people try to influence law-making and policy decisions while at the second, efforts are made to pervert the course of justice.[128] This inevitably leads to the perception that corruption is linked to bad governance and leadership in Nigeria, as it is only those in government positions that get involved in the process of law-making and implementation.

The first level of corruption can be seen at both the National Assembly and the States Houses of Assembly, where certain Nigerian law-makers are motivated mostly by personal interests and selfish gains. For example, sometime ago, the National Assembly proposed a bill to legalise child Marriage,[129] because a few law-makers themselves have child brides.[130] Although a fruitful line of investigation, this level of corruption will not be explored here. Rather, the focus is on corruption at the level of law implementation, which invariably leads to the perversion of justice. The reason for this concentration is that the substratum for complementarity rests on the effectiveness of the judiciary. Thus, the National Assembly in Nigeria may adopt implementing legislation for the Rome Statute;

[123] See The World Bank Group (2013), Available at http://www1.worldbank.org/publicsector/anticorrupt/corruptn/cor02.htm> (Accessed 22 October 2013).

[124] 'The Fight Against Corruption: A world Bank Perspective' Central America Country Management Unit, Latin American and the Caribbean Region Stockholm, Sweden 25–28 May 1999. Available at http://www.iadb.org/regions/re2/consultative_group/groups/transparency_workshop6.htm (Accessed 22 October 2013).

[125] Ibid.

[126] Igbinovia (2003), pp. 1–106, 22. Available at http://www.nuc.edu.ng/nucsite/File/ILS%202003/ILS-106.pdf (Accessed 30 November 2013).

[127] Babalola, ibid.

[128] Aluko (2002), pp. 393–402, 399.

[129] On 16 July 2013, the Nigeria's senate committee voted to remove the subsection of the constitution that puts marriageable age at 18 years. See Haughton (2013). http://www.voice-online.co.uk/article/nigeria-legalises-child-marriage-girls; 'Child Marriage not in Conformity with Nigerian Law' *Vanguard* Nigeria 27 July 2013. http://www.vanguardngr.com/2013/07/child-marriage-not-in-conformity-with-nigerian-law/.

[130] Uwais (2013) (Senator Ahmad Sani Yerima at 49 years justified his marriage to a 13-year-old Egyptian girl).

thereafter, it becomes the duty of the courts to implement and to ensure that justice is delivered on the basis of the law.

### *6.3.1 Corruption in Nigeria*

Although corruption is mainly attributed to those in official government positions, it is nonetheless commonplace in Nigeria, which Transparency International rated the 35th most corrupt country in the world.[131] Corruption has permeated all aspects of the Nigerian society; private businesses can hardly make progress without engaging in corrupt practices to some degree.[132] In the public sector, corruption permeates the judiciary, police, army, universities and other institutions.[133] According to Chinua Achebe,[134] 'Corruption in Nigeria has *passed* the alarming and [has] *entered* the fatal stage and Nigeria will die if we keep pretending that she is only slightly indisposed'.[135]

According to Michael Maduagwu, the prevalence of corruption in Nigeria is attributable to the prevailing culture that condones and sometimes even encourages it.[136]

> Corruption thrives in Nigeria because the society sanctions it. No Nigerian official would be ashamed, let alone condemned by his people because he or she is accused of being corrupt... On the contrary, the official will be hailed as being smart. He would be adored as having 'made it'; he is 'a successful man'. Any government official or politician who is in a position to enrich himself [by stealing government funds] but failed to do so will in fact be ostracised by his people upon leaving the office. He would be regarded as a fool or selfish or both.[137]

The culture of patronage that exist along lines of ethnicity, family, religion or local community, facilitates the public acceptance of corrupt practices.[138] Consequently, corruption has been described as 'the mother of all crimes', 'a hydra-headed monster'[139] that appears to defy solution because of being firmly entrenched.

---

[131] Abdulmalik (2012).

[132] See Igbinovia (2003), pp. 22–26; Aluko (2002) 393 (noting that most Nigerians are corrupt in one way or the other). See also Oko (2002), pp. 397–474; Ihonvbere and Shaw (1998), p. 151.

[133] Ihonvbere (1994), pp. 17–18.

[134] Achebe (1984).

[135] Achebe, 38 (emphasis in original).

[136] Maduagwu (1996), p. 13.

[137] Maduagwu, 18–19.

[138] Aluko (2002), p. 398.

[139] See John Olusola Baiyeshea, 'Corruption: The Mother of all Crimes is Antithetical to any Notion of Justice, Equity and Fairness in Judicial Administration' Paper presented at Symposium of Mustapha Akanbi Foundation (MAF) Abuja Nigeria 21 July 2010 http://www.mafng.org/about.htm (Accessed 30 November 2013).

In 2010, a report[140] by the Intergovernmental Action Group against Money Laundering in West Africa (GIABA),[141] an agency of the Economic Community of West African States (ECOWAS), stated that Nigeria scored 87.3 %, the highest in Africa, on the scale of bribery to government officials.[142] It also noted that 10 former Governors in Nigeria embezzled a total of $250 Billion over 3 years.[143]

Furthermore, in a report by Transparency International,[144] Nigeria scored 27 out of a maximum 100 marks, where a lower score indicates more corruption and higher mark corresponded to the least corrupt country, to take the 139th position out of the 176 countries surveyed.[145] Nigeria shares this ranking with Azerbaijan, Kenya, Nepal and Pakistan.[146] Countries such as Togo, Mali, Niger and Benin to which Nigeria played and continues to play the role of a 'big brother',[147] rated better.[148]

Be that as it may, corruption is not exclusive to Nigeria, as every society is involved at various levels and to varying degrees in the fight against corruption. Thus, calling on all governments to prioritise the fight against corruption, Transparency International notes that corruption is a major threat facing humanity.[149]

> It destroys lives and communities and undermines countries and institutions. It generates popular anger that threatens to further destabilise societies and exacerbates violent conflicts. Corruption translates into human suffering, with poor families being extorted for bribes to see doctors or to get access to clean drinking water. It leads to failure in the

140 Inter-Governmental Action Group Against Money Laundering in West Africa (2010) (Accessed 2 October 2013). The report was on the assessment of seven countries, namely; Benin, Cape Verde, Cote d'Ivoire, the Gambia, Ghana, Nigeria and Senegal.

141 The GIABA is a specialised institution of the ECOWAS responsible for the implementation and coordination of anti-money laundering/counter financing of terrorism (AML/CFT) efforts in the West African region.

142 This is followed by Ghana (56.7 %) Cote d'Ivoire (55 %), Liberia (44 %) and Benin Republic (40 %).

143 Ajibade (2010), http://www.nigeriavillagesquare.com/forum/main-square/54755-10-former-governors-stole-250billion-three-years.html (Accessed 2 October 2013).

144 See Transparency International, Corruption Perception Index 2012 (CPI 2012). Available at http://cpi.transparency.org/cpi2012/results/ (Accessed 20 October 1013).

145 Comparatively, in 2011, Nigeria was placed 143rd position and came 37th most corrupt country. However, this does not mean there has been an improvement in the ranking because more countries (182) were ranked in 2011.

146 See CPI 2012.

147 Abdulwaheed (2012), p. 6. Available at http://www.onlineresearchjournals.com/ijopagg/art/91.pdf; Emmanuel Adeniyi, 'Peacekeeping: When Nigerians Pay for Others' sins' *Nigerian Tribune* 27 January 2013 (Questioning the gain of 'this Big Brother role Nigeria has been playing' particularly in the deployment of Nigerian troops to Mali in January 2013).

148 Togo with 128 position scored 30, Niger 113th position had 33, Mali at 105th position scored 34 while Benin got 94th position with 36 marks. See CPI 2012 Report.

149 See CPI 2012 Report. The CPI 2012 scored countries on a scale from 0 = Highly corrupt to 100 = very clean).

delivery of basic services like education or healthcare. It derails the building of essential infrastructure, as corrupt leaders skim funds.[150]

Admittedly, democracies all over the world face corruption.[151] However, it has been asserted that corruption in the Nigerian judiciary has become a full-blown national plague,[152] and it is a dominant, recurrent feature of the Nigerian judicial system.[153]

### 6.3.2 *Corruption in the Nigerian Judiciary*

A United Nations study found that 'corruption is an extremely serious problem for the country's justice system, second only to the lack of sufficient funding'.[154] Corruption in the judiciary includes any inappropriate financial or material and non-material gain aimed at influencing the impartiality of the judicial process by any actor within or outside the court system.[155] It generally takes the form of a bribe, which might consist of cash, a gift or, less commonly, 'status' or 'career capital', and the outcome provided in return can range from dropping an investigation, ensuring a certain verdict in a trial, or forcing the prosecution and possibly the conviction of another person.[156] Although independence and impartiality have been discussed, the analysis in this section focuses on incidents of intimidation and manipulation, which also negatively impact the independence and impartiality of the Nigerian judiciary.

The importance of this analysis is to argue that Nigeria, like the other African states examined in this book, will not be able to pass the threshold of 'genuineness' of its criminal proceedings in light of complementarity if these inhibitions are not dealt with. Besides, there are further obstacles of the death penalty, amnesties and state pardon, the lack of effective mechanisms to protect witnesses while at the same time safeguarding the rights of the accused and the efficiency of the proceedings.[157]

[150]Huguette Labelle, CPI 2012 Report (note 144).

[151]Boot (1998) (1996) (Detailing instances of corruption and abuse of judicial powers in the United States).

[152]US Dept of State, 'Country Reports on Human Rights Practices for 2012 – Nigeria' http://www.state.gov/documents/organization/204365.pdf (Accessed 23 October 2013).

[153]Bassey (2000), p. 38.

[154]United Nations Office on Drugs and Crimes (UNODC) (2006), pp. 1–174, 133 http://www.unodc.org/documents/corruption/publications_nigeria_assessment.pdf Accessed 7 November 2013.

[155]Aremu (2010).

[156]Oko, Seeking Justice (n 94), p. 39.

[157]Soares (2013).

Regrettably, corrupt practices are not restricted to politicians and the government but are extended to the judiciary as well,[158] as a few Nigerian judges have not been able to rise above the corrupt environment in which they live and operate.[159] Aluko postulates that the sociological perspective does not regard a particular form of behaviour as the problem of the individual; rather, it regards the individual behaviour as emanating from the social order in which the person lives.[160] Thus, a few judges are trapped in a culture that values wealth over honour and integrity, it is therefore not surprising that they seem unable to resist the urge to amass wealth even by engaging in corrupt and unethical practices.[161]

It was reported in 2013 that at least seven judges, namely, Abdul Kafarati, Gladys Olotu, Aliyu Liman, Ibironke Harrison, Rita Ofili-Ajumogobia, Chioma Nwosu-Iheme and Inumidun Akande were the target of corruption investigation by the EFCC.[162] Also, in 2014, two Justices; Gladys Olotu and Ufot Inyang of the Federal High Court and High Court of Justice Abuja respectively, were recommended for compulsory retirement by the Nigerian Judicial Council for charges of misconduct and corruption.[163] According to Itse Sagay, the action 'is a very healthy revival for the judiciary'.[164] It was alleged that Justice Gladys Olotu owned several accounts in local banks and in the United Kingdom, as well as owned significant stock in various companies.[165]

A judge who has accepted a bribe is under undue influence and he or she is not likely to issue decisions grounded in law. The consequence of such rulings is that those with lawful rights and interests, rather than finding protection in the courts, see their rights being violated and their interests given to other people in an officially sanctioned proceeding.[166] Far too often, the outcome of a case in Nigeria depends not on the merits and strength of the case but on extraneous factors,[167] which can be partly attributed to the intimidation and manipulation of judges from within and outside the court system.

---

[158]See Maduagwu (1996), pp. 18–19.

[159]Maduagwu (1996), p. 19.

[160]Aluko (2002), p. 398. See also Davies (1990), pp. 125–136, 127 (Noting that the judiciary as an institution is a product of its environment).

[161]Aluko, 398.

[162]See 'Seven Nigerian Judges Targets of EFCC Corruption Probe' Sahara Reporters 11 November 2013 http://saharareporters.com/news-page/seven-nigerian-judges-targets-efcc-corruption-probe (Assessed 10 March 2014). See also, Daniel (2014).

[163]See 'Nigeria's National Judicial Council Forces 2 Judges into Compulsory Retirement, Reprimands 3 Others' *Sahara Reporters* 27 February 2014 http://saharareporters.com/news-page/nigerias-national-judicial-council-forces-2-judges-compulsory-retirement-reprimands-3-othe (Accessed 10 March 2014).

[164]Madukwe (2014).

[165]Ibid, See also Ibileke (2014).

[166]Davis (2002), pp. 255, 268.

[167]Uzend (2004), cited in Oko (2006).

### 6.3.3 *Intimidation and Manipulation of Judges*

The complementarity threshold of unwillingness, set out in Article 17(2)(c), concerns the independence and impartiality of national proceedings. This Article envisaged a situation in which a state is ostensibly endeavouring to prosecute an alleged perpetrator but the proceedings are being manipulated to ensure that the accused is not found guilty.[168] This implies that even where a state is able and willing to prosecute and has actually commenced trial, machinations in the process could lead to a finding of unwillingness for which the ICC will intervene.

Instances of manipulation in court proceedings compromise the independence and impartiality of the judiciary, which is theoretically guaranteed by provisions in the 1999 Constitution of Nigeria. The Nigerian constitution proclaims that the independence, impartiality and integrity of the courts of law in Nigeria, and easy accessibility thereto, shall be secured and maintained.[169] In order to safeguard these attributes, the Nigerian constitution specifies that judges are to hold their office while they are of good behaviour until they attain the retirement age of 65 years and until they are relieved of office at the age of 70 years.[170] The constitution also entitles them to generous pension and gratuity, depending on the number of years they have held judicial office and at what age they retire.[171]

Furthermore, there are restrictions on the mode of removal of judges from office. Section 292, for example, declares that a judicial officer shall not be removed from his office or appointment before he reaches the age of retirement except in exceptional circumstances.[172] Indeed, the tenure of office of judges in Nigeria is further guaranteed by the fact that they cannot be removed by any single person. The procedure for removal involves the legislative arm of government agreeing with the FJSC or the SJSC, as the case may be, which must have recommended the removal.[173]

Other ways by which the independence of the judiciary is safeguarded in principle include charging the salaries and allowances of the judges to the Federation Account,[174] giving judges immunity in their role and separating them from politics. The first provision implies that the funds accruing to judges are paid directly to the NJC for disbursement to the heads of courts, thus shielding their emoluments from the 'whims' and 'caprices' of politicians.[175] This also implies

[168] *Saif Al-Islam* case, para 108.

[169] 1999 Constitution, section 17(2)(e).

[170] Sections 291(1) relates to justices of the Supreme Court and the Court of Appeal only. With respect to other justices or judicial officers, retirement age is 60 and the judge ceases to hold office when he attains the age of 65 years. See section 291(2).

[171] See section 291(3).

[172] The 1999 Constitution, section 292(1)(a)&(b).

[173] Ibid.

[174] Ibid, section 162(9).

[175] Davies (1990), p. 129.

that their salaries cannot be reduced while they are in office. They are thus protected from financial embarrassment which may prevent them from discharging their duties without fear or favour.[176]

Second, they enjoy absolute immunities from prosecution for anything done or said in the course of their judicial function. If anyone or a government official, for example, is dissatisfied with the ruling of a particular judge, such a person or official can only appeal to a higher court; he or she cannot commence civil or criminal proceedings against the judge for his decision.[177] Third, they are insulated from politics. Judges can exercise their constitutional rights to vote in general elections, but they are exempted from contesting an elective office, or holding a political office.[178]

However, these guarantees seem inadequate. As noted by Ikhariale,[179] 'with the constitutional guarantees given the judiciary, the political arm of the government still occasionally manages to exercise influence, and at times openly harass it, thereby making it doubtful if indeed Nigeria really possesses a constitutional system that ensures the insulation and independence of the judiciary from negative manipulations by politicians'.[180] Similarly, Ben Nwabueze observed that 'politicians are strongly inclined and prepared to use pressure of various kinds to influence in their favour the judge's decision—from lobbying to intimidation to outright bribery'.[181]

Consequently, intimidation is depicted in several ways; for instance, trials may be delayed where powerful litigants aided by some unethical lawyers and a few faithless judges, manipulate the judicial process to achieve preordained outcomes.[182] For example one of the allegations against Justice Gladys Olotu, one of the Judges recommended for compulsory retirement by the NJC, was that she delayed the delivery of judgement for 18 months after the final address by all the counsel in the case contrary to laid down judicial procedures.[183] Accordingly it was alleged that 'it was clear that there was something under-hand going on...'[184] Thus, the prevailing mind set is to bribe those who can be bribed and intimidate those who refused to be bribed.[185]

---

176 Ibid.

177 Davies (1990).

178 Ibid.

179 Ikhariale (1990), pp. 145–158.

180 Ikhariale, 147.

181 Nwabueze (1984), p. 443. Cited in Oko (2006), p. 36.

182 Oko, 'Seeking Justice', 33.

183 Madukwe (2014).

184 Itse Sagay in Madukwe.

185 Oko, Seeking Justice, 34. See also UNODC Report (note 154) 135; Aloku, 398 (Noting the Nigerian philosophy of 'if you can't beat them, then join them').

#### 6.3.3.1 Kidnapping: A Form of Intimidation of Judges

Nigerian Newspapers are replete with reports of harassment and intimidation of citizens including judicial officers.[186] Occurrences of intimidation are exemplified by the frequent kidnapping of judges or their family members for ransom.[187] This despicable act has undermined the performance of judges as they seem to now carry out their functions with fear. For example it was reported that a judge in the Delta State of Nigeria, Justice Flora Azinge, was unable to take the bench for 2 months because kidnappers had threatened to abduct her unless she paid a ransom of N20 million.[188] The kidnappers were reported to have told the judge that 'many of her colleagues had paid similar monies and that if she failed to comply, her life would be in danger'.[189]

The Governor of Delta State was accused of being complicit in the kidnappings of judges in an attempt by the Governor to intimidate judges who were presiding over certain cases,[190] which involved the state government's interests.[191] For example, On 7 August 2012, Justice Marcel Okoh of the high court of Delta State was abducted on his way to court to deliver a judgement.[192] Similarly, Justice Marshal Mukoro was attacked by gunmen.[193] Both judges were reportedly handling a case in which the Delta State government was said to have a stake. Consequently, the two judges dropped the case.[194] Furthermore, on 27 September 2013, a high court judge in Edo State, Justice Daniel Okungbowa was kidnapped.[195] This incident occurred less than 3 weeks after the release of human rights activist and

---

[186]Kidnapping occurs on a minute-by-minute basis in Nigeria even though only a few gets reported. Also abduction of judges and their family members has become prevalent in all 36 states of Nigeria.

[187]See, for example, Nnochiri (2013); Ibileke (2013).

[188]See 'Kidnappers Prevent Judge from Sitting for Two Months, Demand N20m Ransom'; Ugah (2012).

[189]Ibid.

[190]The first case involved the demand by the Okere people of the Itsekiri extraction that the court should stop the Delta State Government from using their land without following due process. The second was also instituted by the Itsekiri Host Communities and the Delta State Oil Producing Areas Development Commission (DESOPADEC), also seeking explanation from the State Government over an alleged diversion of N1 billion meant for the development of host communities.

[191]See 'Dust Over Delta Judge's Kidnap' 25 January 2013 *ThisDay* Nigeria http://www.thisdaylive.com/articles/dust-over-delta-judge-s-kidnap/137436/.

[192]Amaize (2013).

[193]'Delta High Court Judge Escapes Assassination Attempt' 12 December 2012 *TheWill* Nigeria http://thewillnigeria.com/general/17547.html.

[194]Akinrefon (2013).

[195]Adoyi (2013); Emenyonu (2013); See also Patrick Ochoga, 'Judge's Kidnap Grounds Judicial Activities in Edo' 3 October 2013 *Leadership* Nigeria http://leadership.ng/news/031013/judge-s-kidnap-grounds-judicial-activities-edo (Noting that family sources of the kidnapped judge said the abductors had demanded N200 million ransom for his release).

Senior Advocate of Nigeria (SAN) Mike Ozekhomhe, who was also abducted for several days before his release following the payment of a ransom.[196]

Indeed, 'abduction of judicial officers represents a real and mortal danger to the independence of judges and can constitute a major obstacle to the administration of justice anywhere'.[197] Regrettably, Nigeria has acquired the dubious distinction of being the 'global capital of kidnapping',[198] according to a 2011 report by the African Insurance Organisation.[199] The report noted that 'the number of kidnaps for ransom in Africa continued to increase. In the first half of 2011, Africa's proportion of the global total increased from 23 % in 2010 to 34 %. Nigeria is now the 'kidnap-for-ransom capital' of the world accounting for a quarter of globally reported cases'.[200]

Some years ago, the murder trial of those accused of killing late Attorney General, Bola Ige was delayed because three judges separately and consecutively refused to hear the case due to pressure from unnamed, highly placed individuals.[201] Justice Moshod Abaas recused himself citing instances of pressures from 'unusual quarters'.[202] Thus, judges are concerned for their lives and personal safety and they will inevitably 'tamper justice with self-preservation' as a result.[203] Consequently, more needs to be done to shield and protect judges and to ensure the safety of their family members if they are to dispense justice.

#### 6.3.3.2 Insecurity in Nigeria

Implicit in the Pre-Trial Chamber I decision in the admissibility challenge in the case regarding *Saif Al-Islam*, is the consideration of security in Libya. The PTCI determined, Libya's inability to assume full control of the detention facilities,[204] and clear inability of judicial and governmental authorities to ascertain control, ensure security throughout the country and provide adequate protection for witnesses.[205] Consequently, Libya was deemed 'unavailable' within the terms of Article 17(3) to prosecute Saif Al-Islam due to lack of security.[206] Similarly,

---

[196] See Esene (2013).

[197] Oteh (2012).

[198] See generally 'Kidnapping of Judges' 20 January 2013 *Punch* Nigeria http://www.punchng.com/editorial/kidnapping-of-judges/.

[199] Popoola (2012).

[200] Newsletter of the 18th African Reinsurance Forum and 40th Anniversary of the AIO 30 September – 3 October 2012 Balaclava, Mauritius.

[201] Ojo (2003). Cited in Oko (2006), p. 34.

[202] Ibid.

[203] Karlan (1999), pp. 535, 540 in Oko.

[204] Saif Al-Islam case, para 209.

[205] Ibid, para 211.

[206] Ibid, paras 204, 205.

Nigeria's preparedness to prosecute international crimes will be determined by Nigeria's ability to ensure security.

The Nigerian Constitution declares that the security and welfare of the people shall be the primary purpose of government,[207] and that the sanctity of the human person shall be recognised and that human dignity shall be maintained and enhanced.[208] Regrettably, these and other lofty provisions[209] are contained in chapter II of the constitution, which relates to the Fundamental Objectives and Directive Principles of State Policy,[210] and which the courts cannot enforce.[211]

Thus, Okechukwu Oko observed that Nigeria is in 'perpetual turmoil, incessantly roiled by violence, social disequilibrium, and conflicts'.[212] This assertion appears valid given that the freedoms and liberties offered by democracy have produced new anxieties and tensions which have resulted in insecurity in Nigeria. Individuals and ethnic groups have exploited these liberties to pursue destructive and violent agendas against the government, which they disparage as unjust and unable to cater to their needs.[213]

The preliminary investigation of the OTP in Nigeria reveals that members of Boko Haram are responsible for several deaths and this has resulted in a state of insecurity, particularly in the northern part.[214] Insecurity in Nigeria stems from a regime of state repression and corporate violence, which has generated lawlessness, illegal appropriations and further insecurity.[215]

Whatever the cause, security in Nigeria has collapsed under the weight of intense and implacable ethnic fervour that often erupts into violence.[216] As a result of ineffective leadership that is unable to ensure the safety and security of citizens, restive and disaffected members of the society have resorted to violence to address their economic deprivations and grudges against the government.[217]

Arguably, the failure of the Nigerian government to guarantee security opens the door to dysfunctional, extra-legal and criminal conduct that distorts the lives of citizens and undermines democratic consolidation.[218] Discussing the impact of insecurity on democratic consolidation, Jeffrey Herbst stated that 'African

---

[207] See the 1999 Constitution, section 14(2)(b).

[208] Ibid, section 17(2)(b).

[209] Includes, right to health, safety and welfare, right to medical and health facilities, right to free education, right to equal pay for equal work without discrimination.

[210] The provisions of sections 13–24 of the 1999 constitution cannot be enforced.

[211] Ibid, section (6)(6)(c).

[212] Oko (2009), pp. 1295–1332, 1300.

[213] For example the Niger-Delta crisis was precipitated by the dissatisfaction by the people in the region who constantly accused the government of neglect.

[214] OTP Report November 2012 (text to note 43 in Intro) paras 81, 84 & 85.

[215] Ikelegbe (2005), p. 208. Cited in Oko, 'Lawyers in Fragile Democracies'.

[216] Oko, 'Lawyers in Fragile Democracies' (note 210) 1301.

[217] Ibid.

[218] Ibid.

democracies are threatened by lawlessness, crime, the spill over of rebel activity from neighbouring countries and terrorist. It is imperative that the security services work better so that the security situation of individual countries can be improved'.[219] Nigeria is susceptible to being a failed state due to the inability of the government to ensure security of persons and property. This security failure has led to a general distrust of the judiciary, as it is the third arm of an ineffective government.

#### 6.3.3.3 The Attitude of the Public Towards the Judiciary

The preservation of public confidence in the impartial and independent administration of justice is a vital element in the judicial function.[220] This is because loss of confidence in the system, whether due to its inefficiency or, more particularly, due to perceptions of a want of independence or impartiality on the part of the judiciary is extremely damaging to the effective working of the justice system.

In Nigeria, there exists an appreciable popular distrust of the judiciary's integrity and its ability to protect civil rights and constrain the excesses of elected officials.[221] The late Alfred Rewane, citing the Chinese proverb, once noted, 'it is safer to put your head in a lion's mouth than it is to go to court'.[222] He maintained that the hallmarks of the Nigerian legal system are corruption, injustice, general instability, unreliability, politicisation, unpredictability and mediocrity.[223] According to Igbinovia, 'this fairly accurately characterises the general mistrust among the Nigerian people towards the judiciary'.[224]

In addition, former President Olusegun Obansanjo once observed with regard to the judiciary that 'the persisting perception of the public is that it is still battling with the widespread corruption that made prosecution and the judicial process less than effective...'[225] For a number of Nigerians, the judicial process is nothing more than an auction in which justice goes to the 'highest bidder'.[226] Such perception fosters the belief that the judiciary is corrupt and that corruption is part of the pricing component of the justice system.

> Convinced that judges issue verdicts on the basis of connections and recompense without regard to the merits of the case, many Nigerians seek to influence the outcome of cases by 'settling the judge'- [a local colloquialism for bribery]. In some parts of Nigeria, a majority

---

[219] Herbst (2004).

[220] Mason (2013).

[221] Oko, Seeking Justice (n 94), p. 18.

[222] Alfred Rewane (1995) cited in Igbinovia (2003), p. 56.

[223] Ibid.

[224] Ibid.

[225] Obasanjo (2013).

[226] Owonikoko (2003). See also UNODC Report 2006 (above note 154), 119 (Noting the perception that justice works only for the rich and the powerful).

> of citizens lack faith in the justice system to the extent that they prefer not to resolve conflicts through the courts. Arguably, those who do go to court feel the need to engage in corrupt practices like bribery or intimidation to level the playing field.[227]

The consequence of the public distrust for the judiciary is that citizens view the role of the courts as objective dispensers of justice with some scepticism. Most Nigerians seem to have discarded the notion of the court as an impartial and independent institution, resigning themselves instead to the model of 'cash and carry' where they perceive some of the judges as disregarding precedents and the law to subvert justice.[228] Motivations for deviating from judicial standards include prospect of quick though unmerited career advancement, political appointment of a judge's nominee, immediate financial gains, or even membership in a secret society with one of the parties to the dispute.[229]

In fact, the extraneous activities of certain judges in such secret societies have not portrayed them to the people as fair and non-partisan custodians of justice. The secret society which a few Nigerian judges are known to belong to are powerful and feared by their own members because they can intimidate and easily subdue people by imposing serious sanctions on them.[230] Judges who belong to such secret societies are assumed to have double loyalty; loyalty to the state and its laws as well as the secret society to which they belong.[231]

In light of the general distrust and lack of confidence in the Nigerian judiciary, former Supreme Court Justice Chukwudifu Oputa succinctly stated what the judiciary must do to regain public confidence:

> To inspire public confidence in the judicial process, judges should not only be transparently impartial but also should be seen to be accentuated only by the principles of justice and fair play. The judge should therefore scrupulously eschew bias in any shape or form. It is not merely of some importance, but is of fundamental importance, that justice should not only be done but should manifestly and undoubtedly be seen to be done. Justice must be rooted in confidence and confidence is destroyed when right minded people go away thinking – 'the judge was biased'.[232]

Confidence in the judiciary, as articulated by Justice Murray Gleeson of Australia, does not require a belief that all judicial decisions are wise, or that all judicial behaviour are impeccable, any more than confidence in representative democracy requires a belief that all politicians are enlightened and concern for the public welfare.[233] What it requires, however, is a satisfaction that the justice

[227]Okongwu (2004). See also UNODC Report 2006 (note 154) 114 (Noting that in Delta State, citizens appeared more likely to seek unofficial solutions to their complaints).

[228]Okongwu, ibid. (Describing justice in Nigeria as a 'cash and carry' affair).

[229]Abali (2003).

[230]Davies (1990), p. 133.

[231]Ibid.

[232]Oputa (2002), p. 201.

[233]Gleeson (2002).

system is based upon values of independence, impartiality, integrity and professionalism and that, within the limits of ordinary human frailty, the system pursues those values faithfully.[234] The effectiveness of the judiciary, in turn, depends largely on the public's confidence in the ability of judges to fairly and impartially administer justice.[235]

#### 6.3.3.4 Minimum Complementarity Threshold

In light of the foregoing discourse, the Nigerian judiciary and by extension most African judiciaries seem unprepared to implement the complementarity regime at the domestic level. This is because the complementarity regime of the Rome Statute is over-inclusive. According to Marti Koskenniemi, a rule is over-inclusive when it assumes to do much more than it can in practical terms.[236] One of the assumptions associated with complementarity is that there will be credible institutions at the domestic criminal justice systems to carry out genuine investigation and prosecution of international crimes. However, it has been shown in this chapter that the institutions that should partner with the ICC are either non-existent or grossly inadequate.

As a consequence, it is proposed that Nigeria could adopt a minimum complementarity threshold which could be adapted by other African states with slight variations to suit their peculiarities. The minimum threshold includes first, the transcription of the Rome Statute crimes into Nigerian criminal law. This is important because as established in previous chapters, prosecuting international crimes as ordinary domestic crimes of murder is not desirable. Second, Nigeria would have to undertake extensive review of its laws including the constitution and provisions relating to immunity and the death penalty to bring them in line with the provisions of the Rome Statute. This is because conflicting domestic laws can potentially inhibit national implementation of complementarity.

Third, the Nigerian Police Force, the Prison Service and the judiciary must be fundamentally reformed both to better protect citizens' rights and to be well-equipped to carry out investigations and prosecutions of international crimes. In this regard, there should be the appointment of qualified persons into the judiciary, including investigators, prosecutors and judges. The continuous training of judges and court personnel in international criminal law will also be of benefit. In addition, the government must provide security for all, and most especially judges, to enable them discharge the responsibilities of their office.

---

[234] Ibid.

[235] Long (2003), pp. 1, 8–9.

[236] Koskenniemi (2005). (Notes on file with Author). See also Parisi (2003), pp. 510–511.

## 6.4 Conclusion

Like every criminal justice system, the Nigerian criminal justice system is not a perfect one. Although it is evolving, there is urgent need for reforms in the criminal laws and the institutions which include the police, the prisons and the courts, to enable it carry out its complementarity role. The process of domesticating treaties, by wholesale adoption of the treaty, which the National Assembly has adopted again with regards to the Rome Statute, without first reviewing existing laws to bring them into conformity, leaves doubts as to what purpose such domestication serves.

Admittedly, the FJSC has its imperfections. Nevertheless, its advisory role in the process of appointing judges is comparable to what obtains in other jurisdictions,[237] and even at the ICC. Also, its function in the process of removing judges is considered especially reassuring to the Nigerian judiciary,[238] as it is less biased than the legislative arm, where political considerations, rather than legal competence and uprightness of a judge may be given more weight.[239]

The examination of corruption, insecurity, bias and subordination on the part of the judiciary reveals that they constitute significant obstacles not only to the goal of ensuring the rule of law but also, specifically, to the implementation of complementarity. Thus, despite constitutional safeguards for an independent and impartial judiciary, Nigerian judges and their family members suffer constant intimidation. The instances of abductions and attempted assassinations of judges, along with other attendant security problems, make Nigeria prone to becoming a failed state. While Nigeria has been singled out as being especially encumbered by kidnappings, the problem of judges being bullied, coerced, bribed, and of justice being otherwise subverted, is widespread.

In light of the complementarity of the Rome Statute, the primacy of jurisdiction comes with responsibilities, which, though are not expressly stipulated in the Statute, are nevertheless imperative for states in order to fulfil their complementarity role. Consequently, the minimum complementarity threshold proposed in this chapter is that Nigeria, can improve its justice system both in the laws and institutions by embarking on reforms to increase its capacity to investigate and prosecute international crimes.

The challenges of corruption, insecurity and lack of independence of the judiciary analysed, which are entwined and endemic to many African nations, are exemplified by Nigeria. It is proposed that in addition to adopting implementing legislation and sourcing international criminal law experts into its judiciary, a critical implementation strategy includes tackling these problems. Therefore a holistic solution is imperative. Such solution would be relevant not only to Nigeria,

---

[237]Examples are Canada and the United States. In the United States for example, judges at the state level contest election on party basis.

[238]Davies (1990), p. 130.

[239]Ibid, 131.

but could be moulded to fit the particular needs of other African states facing similar challenges in meeting their obligations as states parties to the Rome Statute.

## References


Abali D (2003) Nigeria: corruption in the judiciary. THISDAY Nigeria, 23 June 2003. http://www.support.casals.com/aaaflash1/new_busca.asp?ID_AAAControl=9579. Accessed 16 Aug 2006

Abdulmalik A (2012) Nigeria is 35th most corrupt in the world, says Transparency International 2012 Report. Premium Times, 5 December 2012. http://www.premiumtimesng.com/news/109853-nigeria-is-35th-most-corrupt-in-the-world-says-transparency-international-2012-report.html. Accessed 6 Dec 2013

Abdulwaheed I (2012) Nigeria and peacekeeping process in Africa: the Darfur peace process in Sudan. Int J Polit Good Gov 3(1):6. Available at http://www.onlineresearchjournals.com/ijopagg/art/91.pdf. 10 Dec 2013

Access to Justice (2005) Breaking Point: How Torture and the Police Cell System Violate Justice in the Criminal Investigation Process in Nigeria, 5 June 2005

Achebe C (1984) The trouble with Nigeria. Heinemann Educational Publishers

Adoyi A (2013) Edo High Court Judge Kidnapped. Daily Post Nigeria, 27 September 2013. http://dailypost.com.ng/2013/09/27/edo-high-court-judge-kidnapped/. Accessed 15 Dec 2013

AI (2006) Nigeria: rape, the silent weapon. AI Index: AFR 44/020/2006, 28 November 2006. Available at http://www.amnesty.org/en/library/asset/AFR44/020/2006/en/d6ffed15-d3e9-11dd-8743-d305bea2b2c7/afr440202006en.pdf. Accessed 20 Dec 2013

Ajibade A (2010) 10 former governors Stole $250 billion in three years. Nigerian Village Square-Marketplace of Ideas, 29 May 2010. http://www.nigeriavillagesquare.com/forum/main-square/54755-10-former-governors-stole-250billion-three-years.html. Accessed 10 May 2013

Akindele ST (1990) Corruption and economic retardation: a retrospective analysis of Nigeria's experience since independence. In: Bamisaye OA (ed) Readings in the political economy of Nigeria since independence. Ventures Limited, Lagos

Akinrefon D (2013) Lori-Ogbebor warns against kidnap of judges in delta. Vanguard Nigeria, 8 January 2013. http://www.vanguardngr.com/2013/01/lori-ogbebor-warns-against-kidnap-of-judges-in-delta/. Accessed 5 May 2013

Aluko MAO (2002) The institutionalisation of corruption and its impact on political culture and behaviour in Nigeria. Nordic J Afr Stud 11(3):393–402

Amaize E (2013) Again, kidnappers strike in delta, abduct justice Okoh. Vanguard Nigeria. http://www.vanguardngr.com/2012/08/again-kidnappers-strike-in-delta-abduct-justice-okoh/. Accessed 5 May 2013

Aniagolu A (2000) Constraint in the Administration of Justice, being paper delivered at the All Nigeria Judges Conference, 1 November 1999 Conference xxv, 86

Arbia S at the conference 'Justice for all? The International Criminal Court - 10 Year Review of the ICC' at the University of New South Wales (UNSW), Sydney, Australia, 14 February 2012. Available at http://www.icc-cpi.int/NR/rdonlyres/8C6B4B5B-D854-4F18-BA76-E0F687F2D60C/284274/Speech_10anniversary_Australia.pdf. Accessed 2 Mar 2013

Aremu I (2010) Notes on corruption and judicial administration in Nigeria. Paper presented at the Symposium organised by the Mustapha Akanbi Foundation (MAF), Abuja, Nigeria, 21 July 2010. http://www.mafng.org/about.htm

Babalobi B (2005) Causes of corruption in Nigeria, report of a workshop for civil society organisations involved in the fight against corruption. Organised by Zero Tolerance Coalition (ZCC) Lagos, Nigeria, 11–12 December 2005

Babalola A (1995) Corruption and political crisis in Nigeria: a sociological viewpoint. Paper presented at the Conference of the Nigerian Anthropological and Sociological Association

Bassey POE (2000) The Nigerian judiciary: the departing glory. Malthouse Press, Nigeria
Benson D (2013) We need to revamp Processes of Judges Appointments – Augustine Alegeh (SAN). Vanguard, 4 July 2013. http://www.vanguardngr.com/2013/07/we-need-to-revamp-processes-of-judges-appointments-augustine-alegeh-san/
Boot M (1998) Out of order: arrogance, corruption and incompetence on the bench. Basic Books
Civil Society Prison Reform Initiative (CSPRI) (2013) Rwandan Mpanga international prison commended. Available at http://ppja.org/countries/rwanda/rwandan-mpanga-international-prison-commended-2. Accessed 12 Dec 2013
Clare P, Kramer J (1977) Introduction to American corrections. Mass Holbrook Press, Boston
Dakolias M (1995) A strategy for judicial reform: the experience in Latin America. Va J Int'l L 36:167
Daniel S (2014) EFCC moves to prosecute seven corrupt judges. Vanguard, 4 January 2014. http://www.vanguardngr.com/2014/01/efcc-moves-prosecute-seven-corrupt-judges/. Accessed 10 Mar 2014
Daudu JB (2012) Criminal investigations, procedure and evidence – reform imperatives. In: Daudu J, Adekunle D (eds) Reforming criminal law in Nigeria. Nigerian Bar Association, p 89
Davies A (1990) The independence of the judiciary in Nigeria: problems and prospects. Afr Study Monogr 10(3):125–136
Davis K (2002) Purging the system: recent judicial reforms in Kazakhstan. UC Davis J Int'l L & Policy 8:255
De Bertodano S (2002) Judicial independence in the international criminal court. LJIL 15 (2):409–430
Delta High Court Judge Escapes Assassination Attempt' 12 December 2012. TheWill Nigeria. http://www.thenigerianvoice.com/nvnews/103324/1/delta-high-court-judge-escapes-assassination-attem.html. Accessed 1 June 2013
Dust Over Delta Judge's Kidnap' 25 January 2013. ThisDay Nigeria. http://www.thisdaylive.com/articles/dust-over-delta-judge-s-kidnap/137436/. 1 June 2013
Emenyonu A (2013) Courts suspend sitting in Edo over Judge's abduction, 1 October 2013. ThisDay Nigeria. Available at http://www.thisdaylive.com/articles/courts-suspend-sitting-in-edo-over-judges-abduction/160366/. Accessed 10 Nov 2013
Esene I (2013) My Experience in the Kidnappers' Den – Mike Ozekhomhe, 13 September 2013. http://www.ynaija.com/my-experience-in-the-kidnappers-den-mike-ozekhome/. 10 Nov 2013
Federal Republic of Nigeria, Presidential Committee on the Reform of the Nigerian Police Force Main Report Volume 1 April 2008, 196
Gleeson M (2002) Public confidence in the judiciary at the Judicial Conference of Australia, Launceston 27 April 2002. http://www.hcourt.gov.au/assets/publications/speeches/former-justices/gleesoncj/cj_jca.htm. Accessed 8 Nov 2013
Haughton J (2013) Nigeria legalises child marriage for girls: senate passes amendments allowing underage females to be married. The Voice, 23 July 2013. http://www.voice-online.co.uk/article/nigeria-legalises-child-marriage-girls. Accessed 10 Nov 2013
Herbst J (2004) The incomplete triumph of democracy in Africa. The American Enterprise Institute Bradley Lecture, 1 November 2004
HRW (2007) Rest in pieces: police torture and deaths in custody in Nigeria, vol 17 No II(A) 3
Ibileke J (2013) Kidnappers of wife and daughter of Supreme Court Justice Rhodes-Vivours Arrested/Paraded. Pm News, Lagos, 2 July 2013. Sahara Reporters. http://saharareporters.com/news-page/kidnappers-wife-and-daughter-supreme-court-justice-rhodes-vivours-arrested-paraded-pm-news. Accessed 13 Aug 2013
Ibileke J (2014) Sacked Nigerian Judge Sues Thisday for Libel. PM News, 27 February 2014. http://www.pmnewsnigeria.com/2014/02/27/sacked-nigerian-judge-sues-thisday-for-libel/. Accessed 10 Mar 2014
Idigbe A (2012) The role of legal practitioners in an efficient criminal justice system. In: Daudu J, Adekunle D (eds) Reforming criminal law in Nigeria. Nigerian Bar Association, p 111

Igbinovia P (2003) The criminal in all of us: whose Ox have we not taken? University of Benin, Benin City, Nigeria Inaugural Lecture 27 November 2003, pp 1–106, 22. Available at http://www.nuc.edu.ng/nucsite/File/ILS%202003/ILS-106.pdf. Accessed 20 Dec 2012

Ihonvbere J (1994) Nigeria: the politics of adjustment and democracy. Transaction Publishers, New Brunswick

Ihonvbere J, Shaw T (1998) Illusions of power: Nigeria in transition. African World Press

Ikelegbe A (2005) The economy of conflict in the oil rich Niger Delta region of Nigeria. Nordic J Afr Stud 14:208.

Ikhariale MA (1990) The independence of the judiciary under the third republican constitution of Nigeria. JAL 34(2):145–158

Ingadottir T (2002) The international criminal court nomination and election of judges, 4 June 2002. http://www.pict-pcti.org/publications/publications.html. Accessed 6 Aug 2013

Inter-Governmental Action Group Against Money Laundering in West Africa (2010) Threat assessment of money laundering and terrorist financing in West Africa, May 2010. Available at http://www.giaba.org/media/f/116_threat-assessment-on-money-laundering-and-terrorist-financing-in-west-africa---english-rev051410

Karlan P (1999) Two concepts of judicial independence. S Cal Law Rev 72:535

Kidnapping of Judges' 20 January 2013 Punch Nigeria. http://www.punchng.com/editorial/kidnapping-of-judges/. 20 May 2013

Kleffner JK (2003) The impact of complementarity on national implementation of the substantive international criminal law. JICJ 1:86–113

Koskenniemi M (2005) 'Under-inclusiveness and Over-inclusiveness of Rules' being lecture delivered at the Euromeditarranean (Bancaja) Course of International Law held at the Centre for International Peace and Development (CIPD) Castellon Spain, September 2005 (Notes on file with Author)

Long AB (2003) Stop me before I vote for this judge again: judicial conduct organisations judicial accountability and the disciplining of elected judges. W. VA. Law Review 106:1, 8–9

Mackenzie R, Sands P (2003) International courts and tribunals and the independence of the international judge. Harv Int'l L J 44(1):271–286, 276

Maduagwu M (1996) Nigeria in search of political culture: the political class, corruption and democratization. In: Gboyega A (ed) Corruption and democratization in Nigeria. Agbo Areo Publishers, Ibadan, p 13

Madukwe B (2014) Nigeria: Sack of Justice Olotu, and Justice Inyang a Healthy Revival for the Judiciary-Prof Sagay SAN. The Vanguard (AllAfrica), 6 March 2014. http://allafrica.com/stories/201403060444.html. Accessed 10 Mar 2014

Mason A (2013) The appointment and removal of judges. Judicial Commission of New South Wales. http://www.judcom.nsw.gov.au/publications/education-monographs-1/monograph1/fbmason.htm

Moore M (1997) The legitimation of criminal justice policies and practices. In: Wilson JQ et al (eds) Perspectives on crime and justice, national institute of justice research report (1996–97), Lecture Series November

Nnaemeka-Agu (2002) The position and role of a judge in a democratic state. In: Nweze CC (ed) Justice in the judicial process: essays in honour of justice Eugene Ubaezonu. p 230

Nnochiri I (2012) Review of Judges' appointment procedure imperative – CJN, 16 February 2012, Vanguard Nigeria. http://www.vanguardngr.com/2012/02/review-of-judges-appointment-procedure-imperative-cjn/. Accessed 30 Nov 2012

Nnochiri I (2013) Justice Rhode-Vivour's Wife, Daughter, Driver Regain Freedom, 28 May 2013 Vanguard Nigeria. http://www.vanguardngr.com/2013/05/justice-rhode-vivours-wife-daughter-driver-regain-freedom/. Accessed 7 Aug 2013

Nwabueze B (1984) Nigeria's presidential constitution: 1979–83 the second experiment in constitutional democracy. Longman, p 443

Obasanjo O (2013) From pond of corruption to Island of integrity. Paper presented at the 10 anniversary celebration of transparency international at Berlin, 7 November 2003. Available at http://www.dawodu.com/obas35.htm. Accessed 20 May 2013
Ogundipe O (2012) The implication of prison decongestion within the context of the proposed criminal justice. In: Daudu J, Adekunle D (eds) Reforming criminal law in Nigeria. Nigerian Bar Association, p 175
Ojo S (2003) Third Judge Abandons Omisore's Case. Daily Trust Nigeria, 31 July 2003
Ojo J (2011) The move to collapse Nigerian Prison System. ThisDay Live, 8 November 2011. Available at http://www.thisdaylive.com/articles/the-move-to-collapsenigerian-prison-system/102284/. Accessed 10 Mar 2014
Oko O (2002) Subverting the scourge of corruption in Nigeria: a reform prospectus. NYUJIL&P 34:397–474
Oko O (2006) Seeking justice in transitional societies: an analysis of the problems and failures of the judiciary in Nigeria. Brklyn J. Int'l L 31(1):9–82
Oko O (2009) Lawyers in fragile democracies and the challenges of democratic consolidation: the Nigerian experience. Fordham Law Review 77:1295–1332
Okongwu F (2004) Nigeria's judiciary requires sanitation. Daily Champion Nigeria, 13 July 2004. Westlaw: African News Database
Oputa C (2002) Judicial ethics and canons of judicial conduct. In: Nweze CC (ed) Justice in the judicial process essays in honour of justice Eugene Ubaezonu. p 201
Osinuga OO (2011) Nigeria and the ICC: the dawn of a New Era? 26 December 2011. Available at http://www.modernghana.com/news/368942/1/nigeria-and-the-icc-the-dawn-of-a-new-era.html. Accessed 20 Mar 2014
Osipitan T (2002) Thoughts on the independence and integrity of the judiciary in Nigeria. Being paper delivered at the Judicial Independence Workshop (December 2002). http://nigerianewsnow.com/News/December02/530103_lawlecture.htm
OSJI (2010) Promoting complementarity in practice-lessons from three ICC situation countries, 2. http://www.issafrica.org/anicj/uploads/OSJIComplementaritycasestudies.pdf. Accessed 10 March 2013
Oteh J (2012) Human rights group wants UN to intervene in Delta Judge Kidnap. Premium Times Nigeria, 10 August 2012. http://premiumtimesng.com/news/95143-human-rights-group-wants-un-to-intervene-in-delta-judge-kidnap.html. Accessed 20 May 2013
Otteh J (2004) Restoring the Nigerian judiciary to its pride of place. THISDAY Nigeria, 13 April 2004
Owonikoko AJ (2003) Law and human rights: tackling corruption in the administration of justice. Vanguard Nigeria, 3 April 2003; African News database
Parisi F (2003) Rules versus standard. In: The encyclopaedia of public choice. p 510
Popoola M (2012) Nigeria accounts for 25% of global kidnappings – African insurance organisation, 4 October 2012. http://www.punchng.com/business/business-economy/nigeria-accounts-for-25-of-global-kidnappings-aio/. Accessed 20 Dec 2013
Sarkin J (2008) Prisons in Africa: an evaluation from a human rights perspective. Int J Hum Rights 9:23–49. http://www.surjournal.org/eng/conteudos/pdf/9/miolo.pdf. Accessed 12 Dec 2013
Schabas WA (2008) Complementarity in practice some uncomplementary thoughts. CLF 19:5
Schoderbek P (1968) Management systems. Wiley, New York
Shetreet S (1987) Who will judge: reflections on the judicial process and standards of judicial selection. ALJ 61:776
Soares PP (2013) Positive complementarity and the law enforcement network: drawing lessons from the ad hoc tribunals' completion strategy. Israel Law Rev 46(3):319–338
The Judiciary in England and Wales, 1992. Justice London, 23–24; Report of the New Zealand Royal Commission on the Courts, New Zealand, 1978, para 665
The World Bank Group (2013) Helping countries combat corruption: the role of the World Bank. Available at http://www1.worldbank.org/publicsector/anticorrupt/corruptn/cor02.htm. Accessed 20 Dec 2013

Ugah N (2012) Judges Kidnap: I've been Vindicated, says Ogbebor. ThisDay Nigeria, 4 December 2012. http://www.thisdaylive.com/articles/judges-kidnap-i-ve-been-vindicated-says-ogbebor/132457/. Accessed 20 Dec 2013

United Nations Basic Principles on the Independence of the Judiciary 1985, Art 10. Available http://www.hjpc.ba/dc/pdf/Basic%20Principles%20on%20the%20Independence%20of%20the%20Judiciary.pdf. Accessed 10 Jan 2014

United Nations Human Rights (2009) 'Universal Periodic Review- Nigeria' National Report Submitted in Accordance with paragraph 15 (A) of the Annex to Human Rights Council Resolution 5/1 A/HRC/WG.6/4/NGA/1, 5 January 2009 paras 72–73. Available at http://lib.ohchr.org/HRBodies/UPR/Documents/Session4/NG/A_HRC_WG6_4_NGA_1_E.pdf. Accessed 16 Dec 2013

United Nations Office on Drugs and Crimes (UNODC) (2006) Assessment of the integrity and capacity of the justice system in three Nigerian States (Borno, Delta and Lagos) Technical Assessment Report January 2006, 1–174. http://www.unodc.org/documents/corruption/publications_nigeria_assessment.pdf. Accessed 20 Dec 2013

US Department of State (2012) 2011 Human Rights Reports: Nigeria, May 24, 2012, 11–13. Available at http://www.state.gov/j/drl/rls/hrrpt/2011/af/186229.htm. Accessed 12 Dec 2013

Uwais M (2013) Senator Yerima and constitutional review by Maryam Uwais. Sahara Reporters, 22 July 2013. http://mobile.saharareporters.com/article/senator-yerima-and-constitutional-review-maryam-uwais. Accessed 20 Jan 2013

Uzend M (2004) Casualties of election tribunals. Daily Champion Nigeria, 5 March 2004, WLNR 6915262

# Chapter 7
# Mutual Inclusivity: A *Sine qua non* to National Implementation of Complementarity

**Abstract** A mutually inclusive interpretation and application of complementarity is the way forward for state parties particularly African states to implement complementarity at the national level. Admittedly, no two criminal justice systems can be the same and no African states' criminal justice system can effectively mirror the ICC. However, as noted previously, complementarity was adopted in the Rome Statute without any specific direction on how it can work in practice. However, since it was imperative to preserve sovereignty, complementarity was adopted by states, to be implemented by states, for the benefit of states, the ICC as well as for the benefit of the international community as whole. This implies that the future of the ICC and international criminal justice is necessarily domestic. This chapter sums up the analysis in this book that rather than wait till situations arise in their territories, African states should take steps to adopt implementing legislation, ensure capacity building and take advantage of Article 93(10) to request legislative, technical as well as physical assistance from the ICC well in advance. The policy oriented method (New Haven School), is suggested for African states to implement complementarity as a mutually inclusive concept. The ICC's Legal Tools Project is recommended for African States to enhance their willingness and ability to implement complementarity.

The centrality of the principle of complementarity to the regime of the ICC and the importance of African states fulfilling their role under the Rome Statute by investigating and prosecuting international crimes domestically is the focus of this book. Although the components of complementarity are yet ill-defined in view of the fact that it is still evolving, the complementarity regime is vital in establishing and increasing the legitimacy of the ICC and the international criminal justice system. Thus, the future of international criminal justice is necessarily domestic.[1]

However, many challenges to implementing complementarity remain. For instance, one of the assumptions associated with complementarity is that domestic

[1]Stahn (2009) (Noting that if international criminal courts wish to leave a 'lasting footprint' on domestic societies, they must develop strategies to empower domestic institutions); Slaughter and Burke-White (2006), pp. 327, 346–350.



O.C. Imoedemhe, *The Complementarity Regime of the International Criminal Court*, DOI 10.1007/978-3-319-46780-1_7

criminal laws reflect international crimes. In practice, state authorities hardly ever consider international crimes in domestic legislation. The argument then is whether states should prosecute international crimes on the basis of ordinary domestic crimes? It is submitted that both crimes are not the same; both in their definitions, elements, nature, scale and gravity and it will be incongruous for states to fulfil their obligation under the Rome Statute without proscribing the Statute's crimes in their domestic laws.

It is further argued that since international crimes are generally not known in national legal systems, where conducts constituting these crimes have occurred, a few African states have referred the situations to the ICC. Thus, complementarity is being applied to situations that were not specifically envisioned during the drafting of the Rome Statute. For example, it was not anticipated that states will refer situations in their territories to the ICC.[2] However, the ICC is currently faced with self-referrals, and has had to come up with another complementarity threshold of 'inactivity',[3] to justify such referrals and its intervention.[4]

Thus far, the application of complementarity is based on cases where the ICC had to determine admissibility as required by Article 19 of the Rome Statute and in cases in which states claimed to be carrying out investigations domestically.[5] In the admissibility challenges by the Kenyan and Libyan governments, the ICC only had the opportunity to determine whether the investigations being carried out by both states encompassed the 'same person and substantially the same conduct'.[6] Although this is permissible under the Statute, it appears that complementarity is working in reverse. This is because the clear wording of Article 17 suggests that it is for states to be actively engaged in investigation and prosecution and it is for the ICC to allege and prove that the complementarity thresholds of 'unwillingness', 'genuine inability', or 'sufficient gravity' exist on the part of the state or the situation for which reason it would intervene. Thus, what we have seen so far is that the ICC is asserting jurisdiction, especially in the Kenyan and Libyan cases, and it is the states that then have to prove their willingness and ability in order to claim jurisdiction, as reflected in the admissibility challenges by both governments. Moreover, none of the cases that emanated from these situations have been prosecuted to conclusion; the original 'Ocampo Six' from the Kenyan situation were ultimately

[2]Nouwen and Werner (2010), pp. 948–949. See also Williams and Schabas (2008), pp. 560 and 716 respectively.

[3]'Inactivity' was developed by the OTP based on the theory of 'uncontested admissibility' (Text to notes 133–140 in Ch 2).

[4]Politi (2011), pp. 142–149.

[5]See *Muthaura et al*; *Saif Al-Islam* and the *Germain Katanga* cases (Text to notes 86, 94 & 98,102 respectively in Ch 2).

[6]See *Thomas Lubanga, Muthaura et al* and *Saif Al-Islam Gaddafi* cases (Text to notes 88, 86 & 94 in Ch 2).

dropped for lack of cooperation from the Kenyan authorities to obtain evidence to prosecute the cases.

Furthermore, of the ten situations currently before the ICC, five were referred by the respective states' governments themselves.[7] It is argued that these referrals were based on the absence of institutional and legal frameworks to carry out investigations and prosecutions domestically. This raises the fundamental question of whether the complementarity regime was intended to encourage self-referrals. Admittedly, two out of the three trigger mechanisms involve referrals, either by states or the United Nations Security Council[8]; however, it is submitted that self-referrals reveal a lack of understanding of the complementarity regime, and can also undermine the object and purpose of the Rome Statute. For this reason, a mutually inclusive interpretation and application of complementarity is proposed.

## 7.1 Conclusions

### *7.1.1 The Relevance of a Mutually Inclusive Interpretation of Complementarity*

While it may be difficult to determine the precise interpretation and application of complementarity even in the next decade, it is suggested that a mutually inclusive interpretation may be beneficial. Mutual inclusivity implies that both the ICC and national systems share the responsibility of ensuring that perpetrators of international crimes are prosecuted. This implies that the duty of states under the complementarity regime goes beyond mere ratification of the Rome Statute. For effective burden-sharing, there are certain requirements, which both the ICC and states should be engaged in to ensure that states have the same legal framework and that they attain a certain level of institutional preparedness to investigate and prosecute international crimes.

Certainly, ratification of the Rome Statute clearly demonstrates a state's abhorrence of the crimes contained therein and its commitment to joining the international community's efforts to combat them.[9] African states' efforts in this regard are indisputable. This is reflected by the continent's number of ratifications and self-referrals to the ICC. It is submitted however, that mere ratification cannot drive the complementarity regime of the Rome Statute, neither is it the objective of the Statute that all cases and situations be referred to the ICC. In fact, it is submitted

[7] See ICC, 'Situation and Cases' Available at http://www.icc-cpi.int/en_menus/icc/situations%20and%20cases/Pages/situations%20and%20cases.aspx (Accessed 3 February 2014).

[8] See 'Admissibility and Trigger Mechanisms for ICC investigation' (Text to notes 76–86 in Ch 2).

[9] Robinson (2002), p. 1867.

that self-referrals, if not curtailed, could potentially lead to a case overload for the ICC and may also defeat the objective of the Statute, which focuses on state authorities as the primary mechanism to ensure accountability.[10]

The ICC is only to fill in the gaps where and when necessary, such as where states fail and particularly where the alleged perpetrators are the state authorities themselves. It is worth noting that the primacy of jurisdiction granted to states does not mean exclusivity. Thus, in cases where the presidents are alleged perpetrators or co-perpetrators, the ICC is certainly the most appropriate forum to ensure their accountability. In line with this argument, the cases that resulted from the Kenya and Sudan situations are rightly before the ICC, since the Presidents, Vice President and other top government officials are those indicted. Admittedly, there are challenges, especially with obtaining witnesses because even though the President and Vice President of Kenya voluntarily appeared before the ICC the inability of the Prosecutor to obtain evidence led to the withdrawal of the charges against them, and the cases have all been terminated. Similarly, since March 2009, the date of the first warrant of arrest issued against President Al-Bashir of Sudan, he has not been arrested and surrendered to the ICC. Therefore, while the jurisprudence of the ICC is to prosecute those who bear the highest responsibility for the gravest crimes, the Court still needs the cooperation of states and the international community as a whole to be able to function effectively.

Consequently, in order for the ICC to truly function as a 'complement', it is submitted that African states should adopt the two prong components of the complementarity regime, namely; cooperation and complementarity legislation.[11] Based on the premise that complementarity commits states to investigate and prosecute international crimes domestically, it is argued that, although not expressly stated in the Statute, adopting implementing legislation, incorporating the crimes in the Rome Statute into their domestic criminal law, is a necessary step for states to fulfil their obligations. This would further entail that states ensure institutional capacity and confidently investigate and prosecute the crimes rather than refer to the ICC situations for which they are meant to be primarily responsible.

Two arguments are advanced in favour of implementing legislation. The first is that, embedded in complementarity is the notion that measures must be taken by individual states to prosecute international crimes domestically. The second is that, since the Rome Statute requires states to cooperate fully with the ICC, it is argued that there must be mechanisms in place at the national level to arrest and surrender to the ICC suspects that it seeks to prosecute and who happen to be within a particular state's jurisdiction.

---

[10]See generally CICC, 'Questions and Answers: ICC Implementing Legislation' Available at http://www.iccnow.org/documents/FS_CICC_Implementation_Legislation_en.pdf (Accessed 3 February 2014).

[11]AI (2012).

A critical analysis of the Pre-Trial Chamber I decision of 31 May 2013 regarding the Libyan admissibility challenge in the *Saif Al-Islam Gaddafi*[12] case reveals that implementing legislation is imperative for states to assert their criminal jurisdiction. Although the PTCI admitted that Libya could investigate and prosecute *Saif Al-Islam* based on its domestic criminal law,[13] the conclusion reached by the Chamber was different.[14] Thus, implicit in the Chamber's decision was the underlying inability based on the failure of Libya to pass the 'same conduct' limb of the 'same person same conduct' test, which arguably, Libya could have passed had it applied the international categorisation of the crimes. However, Libya, not being party to the Rome Statute, did not have any implementing legislation and the crimes against humanity of murder and persecution were not known to its domestic criminal law.

Critically, African states' rapid ratification of the Rome Statute has not been matched with corresponding legislative action.[15] Whilst the absence of implementing legislation may not be the only reasons for the inability of African states to investigate and prosecute international crimes, it is argued nevertheless that adopting implementing legislation is an appropriate starting point which would demonstrate both willingness and the ability to act. As a mechanism designed by states and to be operated by states, complementarity can benefit African states when they integrate the Rome Statute crimes into their domestic criminal law.

Admittedly, African states face significant challenges in adopting implementing legislation. These include; the time involved in the process of integrating the crimes, the difficulty in accessing experts in the field, not taking the issue as a priority and the lack of political will.[16] Other challenges are corruption and the desire of a few African leaders to preserve perpetuity in power. In view of these challenges, the express criminalisation approach is advocated.

It is submitted that mutual inclusivity can further promote the proactive complementarity model, which requires assistance from the ICC to states upon request. The distinctive provision of Article 93(10) which provides for a reverse assistance and cooperation from the ICC to states is the architecture of this model. An understanding of complementarity from this perspective would foster collaboration between national jurisdictions and the ICC for the purpose of closing impunity gaps, as envisioned in the Rome Statute.

---

[12]*The Prosecutor v. Saif Al-Islam Gaddafi and Abdullah Al-Hussein* ICC-01/11-01/11-344-Red Decision of the Pre-Trial Chamber I on the Admissibility of the case against Saif Al-Islam Gaddafi 31 May 2013. http://www.icc-cpi.int/iccdocs/doc/doc1599307.pdf (Accessed 5 February 2014).

[13]Ibid; paras 88, 108, 133, 200, 201.

[14]Ibid; paras 134, 135, 219.

[15]See Stone and du Plessis (2014). Out of the 34 African states parties to the Rome Statute, only four, namely; South Africa (2002), Senegal (2007), Kenya (2009) and Uganda (2010) are known to have implementing legislation to date.

[16]Bekou and Shah (2006).

### 7.1.2 Complementarity-Based Prosecution at the Domestic Level: The New Frontline of International Criminal Justice

The purpose of a mutually inclusive application of the complementarity regime is that states would ensure transcription of the Statute's crimes into domestic criminal law to allow for domestic prosecutions of those crimes. This argument is premised on the fact that complementarity cannot be based on two distinct bodies of laws. If existing domestic criminal laws were sufficient to deal with international crimes then the Rome Statute would not have been necessary. Therefore, a complementarity-based prosecution at the domestic level necessitates implementing legislation.

Complementarity-based prosecution refers to prosecution of international crimes conducted by states domestically, with the provisions of the Rome Statute underpinning the process. Such domestic prosecution aims at ensuring conformity with the Rome Statute both in the legal framework and in the institutional preparedness of states to prosecute international crimes. The prosecution carried out by the United Kingdom was used to illustrate this model because it carried out a domestic prosecution on the basis of its implementing legislation with the proper classification of international crimes as defined in the Rome Statute.[17]

Analysis of the crimes of genocide and crimes against humanity highlights the fact that international crimes and ordinary domestic crimes are not the same and thus domestic prosecution based on ordinary crimes cannot meet the requirements of complementarity. Significantly, international crimes are different from ordinary crimes because the context in which they are committed, the nature, scale, gravity and the overall impact are usually greater than for ordinary crimes. Crimes against humanity, for example, must be committed within the context of an attack that is characterised as 'widespread or systematic', directed against a civilian population, and the accused must have had knowledge of the attack.[18] Therefore, murder as crime against humanity, for example, cannot be the same as the ordinary crime of murder under domestic criminal law.[19]

The domestic prosecutions in African states discussed were based on ordinary crimes as defined by their respective domestic statutes, which makes them fall short of the requirements of complementarity. In addition, the states' domestic prosecutions were a reaction to the cases that were already before the ICC.[20] Admittedly, there is nothing wrong with such prosecution, taking into consideration that the ICC prosecutes only those who bear the greatest responsibility, while states must be involved in bringing the intermediate and lower-level perpetrators to justice.

---

[17] Text to notes 133–144 in Ch 4.

[18] Rome Statute, art 7.

[19] Greppi (2008).

[20] As for example the trials taking place in the SCCED in Sudan and in Kenya.

However, prosecutions in African states have thus far relied on domestic crimes.[21] Also, they appear to conflict with, rather than complement, the efforts of the ICC, particularly in Uganda where amnesty and other alternative justice mechanisms are being used as demonstrated in the *Thomas Kwoyelo*[22] case. Arguably, proceedings in the DRC may constitute complementarity-based prosecutions but the use of military courts is problematic because mobile courts were not contemplated under the Rome Statute and military jurisdictions do not guarantee due process safeguards.[23]

As there is on-going debate on domestic prosecution, whether based on ordinary crimes or on their international classification, the proposal of a complementarity-based prosecution was not without a careful examination of the different theories of domestic prosecution. These included the 'soft mirror thesis',[24] which maintains that as long as the offenders are tried for correspondingly grave domestic crimes, it does not matter whether the trial was based on the international categorisation.[25] However, this theory implies that states do not have to ratify the Rome Statute. States may also not be required to enact legislation incorporating the Rome Statute crimes into their domestic criminal law. Ultimately, the justification for the soft mirror thesis implies that the Rome Statute has little relevance.

Nevertheless, it is proposed that states should incorporate the substantive provisions of the Rome Statute, because to satisfy the complementarity criteria, it is better for states to prosecute international crimes as such rather than as ordinary crimes.[26] In line with this argument, the second approach, the 'hard mirror thesis',[27] proposes that domestic prosecution must be based on international crimes, categorised and defined as such, rather than on ordinary crimes. This is because, by such prosecution, states can avoid the possibility of being considered 'unwilling' or 'unable', which precipitates intervention by the ICC.[28]

Discounting both of these theories, Jon Heller instead advanced 'a sentence-based theory of complementarity', in which he postulates that when a domestic prosecution ends with a sentence that is the same or higher than what is prescribed by the Rome Statute or what the ICC would have given in the same case, then

[21]See, for example, the domestic prosecution in the DRC which uses military tribunal and relies on the Military Penal Code of 2002. Although the Code criminalises international crimes, yet there are gaps in the provisions which made the military court to apply the Rome Statute definitions in some cases. See the *Songo Mboyo* case (Text to notes 48–71 in Ch 4).

[22]Text to notes 114–121 in Ch 4.

[23]For example, Colonel Kibibi Mutware was sentenced to 20 years' imprisonment for crimes against humanity by the DRC military tribunal in a trial that lasted for only 10 days (Text to note 65 in Ch 4).

[24]Jon Heller (2012), pp. 86–134, 87.

[25]*Ibid*.

[26]Kleffner (2003), p. 98. See also Seman (2010), pp. 259, 266.

[27]Jon Heller (2012), pp. 87–89.

[28]See Ellis (2003); Ambos and Stegmiller (2008).

domestic prosecution can be accepted regardless of the categorisation of the crime.[29]

The sentence-based approach to complementarity that focuses exclusively on the severity of the sentence is contrary to the provisions of the Rome Statute, because it may allow the death penalty,[30] which some states apply as the maximum sentence in consideration of the gravity of particular crimes. On the contrary, the maximum penalty under the Statute is life imprisonment. Also, the sentence-based theory presents certain difficulties. The first is that a sentence-based approach does not reflect the differences in the scope, scale and gravity of the crimes.[31] Moreover, the sentence-based approach does not take into consideration that a domestic prosecution could end in acquittal.[32] Acquittal may well be the appropriate outcome of a domestic prosecution and yet, where an accused is acquitted, there is of course no sentence, and there will be nothing to compare with the Rome Statute. The sentence-based approach also implies that one must wait until the end of the prosecution to determine the acceptability of the prosecution, in which case the ICC would be barred by the *ne bis in idem* rule.[33]

In response to Jon Heller's sentence-based theory, Darryl Robinson proposed a 'process-based' approach, stating that the genuineness of the process rather than its outcome should be the focus.[34] For Robinson, once it is shown that a state is carrying out or has carried out prosecutions in relation to a case,[35] the question should be whether the state is carrying out those prosecutions 'genuinely'.[36] Accordingly, he postulates that in the context of Article 17(2) and (3), 'process' is the master theory and that charges and sentences could be looked into insofar as they reveal something about the genuineness of the process.[37]

Again, the process-based theory does not consider the difference between international crimes and ordinary domestic crimes. Consequently, the complementarity-based prosecution, which is proposed in this book, is a holistic and proactive approach which requires that states incorporate international crimes that conform to Rome Statute definitions into their domestic criminal law. It is also a practical way of avoiding a scenario in which a crime occurs that is not covered under domestic law. A typical example is the rejection of the Pre-Trial Chamber I (PTCI) of the admissibility challenge by Libya in the *Saif Al-Islam Gaddafi*[38] case, because the crime against humanity of persecution was absent from the Libyan

---

29 Jon Heller, 87–89.

30 See Schabas (2002), p. 1505.

31 Bergsmo et al. (2010), p. 801.

32 Robinson (2012).

33 See Rome Statute, articles 17(1)(c) & 20.

34 Robinson.

35 Rome Statute, art 17(1)(a)–(c).

36 Rome Statute, arts 17(1) (a) & (b), 20.

37 Robinson.

38 *Saif Al-Islam* case (n 12).

Criminal Code and a proposed higher sentence by Libya was not accepted by the PTCI.[39]

Other difficulties relating to complementarity identified include the tension between the African Union and the ICC arising from the fact that the ICC is being perceived as a form of neo-colonialism targeted against African states. However, analysis demonstrates that the conflict is not between the AU and the ICC *per se* but rather, it is between the AU and the United Nations Security Council.[40]

Therefore, a discussion of the politics of international criminal law reveals that politics cannot be entirely divorced from law and particularly international criminal law and the ICC. This is more apparent with the involvement of the United Nations Security Council, which is a political body, and yet it is empowered under the Statute to refer and defer cases to the ICC. Therefore the tension is traced to the Security Council's referral of the situation in Darfur, Sudan to the ICC and the fact that it ignored the AU's ensuing request that the case be deferred.[41] Furthermore, an examination of the 'scapegoat thesis' and 'selectivity' appeared at first to buttress the assertion that African states are inappropriately targeted by the ICC. However, proof of selectivity does not negate the carriage of justice against the individual who was selected for prosecution.[42]

Undoubtedly, other areas of misunderstandings do exist between the AU and the ICC, which arise from both political and legal sources. These include the issue of the ICC's jurisdiction over nationals of non-party states and immunities of heads of states,[43] both of which were analysed as points of misconceptions that could exacerbate the tension between not just the AU and the ICC, but also between the ICC and other state parties and non-party states alike.[44] It is suggested that Article 98 which is identified as a contradictory provision should be removed from the Rome Statute entirely. This is because the effect of the Article does not only undermine the integrity of the ICC, but it also violates the principle of equality before the law and it contravenes the obligations undertaken by state parties to the Statute.[45] Removal of the Article, however unlikely, will reduce confusion and points of conflicts in the functioning of the ICC.

The relevance of this argument is the fact that for the ICC to successfully prosecute the African cases before it, it will need the sustained support and cooperation of African states. Also, the ICC is only able to prosecute a few cases, therefore, to

[39]Ibid, paras 111, 112, 113.

[40]Keppler (2012).

[41]Text to notes 135–136 in Ch 5.

[42]See *Celebici* case (Text to note 35 in Ch 5) paras 611 & 618.

[43]Text to notes 138–186 in Ch 5.

[44]Some of the political challenges include the hypocritical stance of some of the permanent members of the United Nations Security Council and the United States exceptionality (text to notes 195–205 in Ch 5).

[45]Nsereko (2004), p. 262.

close impunity gaps, African states need credible institutions, in addition to implementing legislation, in order to prosecute lower-level and intermediate perpetrators. Thus, the cumulative effect of enhancing the relationship between the ICC and the AU would be the overall improvement of the international criminal justice system.

### *7.1.3 Institutional Preparedness of States to Prosecute International Crimes*

Another difficulty with complementarity that is yet to be resolved is the complex tension between international standards and local specificities,[46] as well as the variations between national criminal justice systems. Again, the complementarity regime assumes that states' judicial systems will necessarily be available and will be adequately prepared to handle the investigation and prosecution of international crimes as the ICC would.

Admittedly, there are significant dangers in the domestic prosecution of international crimes. First, domestic courts are potentially more likely to be biased or politically motivated than the ICC. The very proximity of the place of prosecution to the community where the crime was committed, the local press coverage, and interactions with victims and survivors may undermine the fairness of the procedure. Second, the quality of justice in local courts differs significantly. While some states have extremely well-developed legal systems, most African states lack even the most rudimentary legal tools.[47] Third, in the prosecution of international crimes, there is often a need to convince both a local and an international polity of the fairness of the proceedings and the legitimacy of the justice rendered.

Consequently, it appears that complementarity assumes homogeneity between national courts and the ICC,[48] however, in practical terms the institutions which should partner with the ICC at the domestic level simply do not exist.[49] From the point of view of the disparity exemplified by physical structures, Antoine Garapon observes that the contrast between the luxurious glass construction of The Hague and the often precarious conditions of local courts puts complementarity in danger of becoming indefensible.[50]

Certainly, the presence or absence of a credible judiciary to carry out domestic prosecutions in line with complementarity will determine the success or lack thereof of the emerging system of international criminal justice. Therefore, using

[46]Hazan (2012), p. 9.

[47]Kaplan (2014).

[48]Garapon (2012), p. 20.

[49]Ibid.

[50]Ibid.

Nigeria as a case study, it is argued that the institutional capacities of African States to investigate and prosecute international crimes are either non-existent or grossly inadequate.

The situation in Uganda also demonstrates that a consideration of institutional preparedness at the state level must go beyond mere physical infrastructure; Uganda has established a Special War Crimes Division of the High Court and has passed legislation empowering domestic courts to prosecute international crimes but still seems unable to handle the investigation of such crimes, particularly concerning members of the Lord's Resistance Army (LRA).[51] According to Elizabeth Nahamya-Ibanda, 'despite the War Crimes Division being a significant development, the country is in great need of support ... especially with regard to the national lack of capacity to investigate and prosecute international crimes and lack of resources'.[52]

Also, institutional preparedness includes the capacity of judges and prosecutors who are experts in international criminal law. This point was underscored in the *Saif Al-Islam* case when the Pre-Trial Chamber I (PTCI) observed the steps undertaken by the Libyan government which involved inviting judges and lawyers versed in international criminal law from other jurisdictions.[53] In contrast, the Kenyan government merely relied on general submission in its efforts to reform its judicial system.[54] This implies that general reform of a state's judiciary is insufficient; there should be focused appointments of experts in international criminal law.

It is further argued that 'unwillingness' under Article 17(2)(c) may be determined with respect to situations where the proceedings are not being conducted independently or impartially.[55] Therefore, the complementarity thresholds of 'unwillingness' and 'inability', have direct links not only to the nonexistence of laws criminalising international crimes, but also to the unavailability of national judicial systems,[56] which encompasses a lack of independence and impartiality of the courts at the domestic level.

Thus, in light of the complementarity regime, the primacy of jurisdiction comes with responsibilities, which, though are not expressly stipulated in the Statute, are nevertheless imperative for states in order to fulfil their complementarity role. The finding in this book is that thus far, Nigeria, like other African states, lacks the institutional preparedness to prosecute international crimes. This is because the substratum for the complementarity regime, which includes a strong judiciary, is lacking.

The examination of corruption, insecurity, bias and subordination on the part of the judiciary reveals that they constitute significant obstacles not only to the goal of

[51] See Nahamya-Ibanda (2010).

[52] Ibid.

[53] *Saif Al-Islam* case of 31 May 2013 (n 12) para 213.

[54] Ibid, para 85.

[55] See Rome Statute, Article 17(2)(c).

[56] Rome Statute, Article 17(3).

ensuring the rule of law but also, specifically, to the implementation of complementarity.[57] For instance, despite constitutional safeguards for an independent and impartial judiciary,[58] a few Nigerian judges and their family members suffer constant intimidation.[59] While Nigeria has been singled out as being especially encumbered by kidnappings, the problem of judges being bullied, coerced, bribed, and of justice being otherwise subverted, is widespread.

The challenges of corruption, insecurity and lack of independence of the judiciary analysed, are entwined and endemic to many African nations, but are exemplified by the specific analysis of Nigeria. It is proposed that in addition to adopting implementing legislation and sourcing international criminal law experts into its judiciary, a critical implementation strategy includes tackling these problems. Therefore a holistic solution is imperative. Such solution would be relevant not only to Nigeria, but could be moulded to fit the particular needs of other African states facing similar challenges in meeting their obligations as state parties to the Rome Statute.

### *7.1.4 Corruption, Unemployment, Poverty and Bad Leadership*

Aluko proposed that a major impetus for the growing corrupt practices in Nigeria is associated with poverty, unemployment and bad leadership.[60] The people are 'hurt, damaged and discounted by the very government that should protect them, their past is blighted, their present compromised and their future endangered, mortgaged and at risk'.[61] Therefore corruption can only be minimised where the material foundations for it exist, the material foundation being bread—a fair standard of living.[62]

The problem of lack of visionary leaders culminates in corrupt leadership. The struggle for political power is regarded as a chance to reap the fortunes of office by the ruling elite and an opportunity to partake of the 'national cake', which results in tension and corrupt practices.[63] In addition, in Nigeria, the government is the primary source of private wealth accumulation and this makes the struggle for

[57]See, for example, the analysis of Corruption in the Nigerian Judiciary (Text to notes 152–168 in Ch 6).

[58]See the Nigerian 1999 Constitution, s 17(2)(e).

[59]Intimidation takes varying forms; from kidnappings, to threats to life, to assassinations (Text to notes 187–204 in Ch 6).

[60]Aluko (2002), p. 398.

[61]Ibid, 399.

[62]Ake (1991) cited in Aluko.

[63]Burleigh (2013) (Noting that 'public office is so lucrative that people will kill to get it').

control of power even more intense.[64] Added to this is the 'winner takes all syndrome'[65] which makes elections a contest to win at all cost.[66] To this end, people explore every means, legal or illegal, including intimidation, kidnapping and even the murder of their opponents in order to hold on to power.[67]

In view of the pervasive nature of corruption, several anti-corruption agendas have been endorsed by the Nigerian government at different times; these include initiatives to investigate financial crimes, corruption and fraud—the Economic and Financial Crime Commission (EFCC) and the Independent Corrupt Practices and Other Related Offences Commission (ICPC). While the setting up of these bodies may have been with laudable objectives, the focus on the fight against corruption has itself breed more corruption in Nigeria.[68] Therefore, a re-focusing is advocated, that of replacing the anti-corruption fight with a fight for development and a fight for values.

In fact, it is the absence of values and development strategies that have nurtured corruption, and corruption in turn has continued to perpetuate vicious circles of underdevelopment.[69] Therefore, in terms of priority, what Nigeria and other African countries need is not anti-corruption mechanisms *per se*. Rather what is necessary is development and a reordering of values. This is because if or when the fight against corruption is won, assuming that is possible, it may only lead to the beginning of the real war; that for development, reorientation and restructuring of values. Arguably, focusing on the fight against corruption has only exacerbated the already lost values like respect, hard work, honesty and integrity. In this regard, the policy-oriented perspective is recommended for Nigeria and other African states to identify with members of the international community in the pursuit of a common interest.

---

[64] A Nigerian Legislator earns a basic wage of approximately £122,000 which nearly doubles what the British MPs earn and more than what the President of America earns. Yet 70 per cent of Nigerians live below the poverty line of £1.29 a day. See Burleigh Ibid.

[65] Aluko, 399.

[66] Former President Olusegun Obasanjo during his campaign for the PDP Governorship election in Delta and Rivers States noted that the party must win at all cost. See also Segun Olatunji, 'I'm Ready to Spend N1bn to win Ekiti Election-Kashamu' 31 August 2013 *Punch* Nigeria http://www.punchng.com/politics/hotseat/im-ready-to-spend-n1bn-for-pdp-to-win-ekiti-election-kashamu/ Marietu (2009), pp. 47–54.

[67] See Burleigh citing an instance of a text message sent to Ayo Fayose former Governor of Ekiti State by the 'Fayose M Squad'. 'M' stands for 'murder'; the text message stated that they had stabbed and bludgeoned a third candidate to death on his own bed.

[68] Akhaine (2013).

[69] UNODC (2006).

## 7.2 Recommendations

### *7.2.1 The Policy-Oriented Perspective and Complementarity*

There are different methods of international law, but due to space constraint, the methods are not analysed here. However, the policy-oriented approach is selected for African states to implement complementarity as a mutually inclusive concept. This is because the policy-oriented method does not see international law norms, procedures and institutions as immutable and autonomous, capable of self-application. Rather, it recognises that norms and institutions are the outcome of a continuous process of authoritative decision making, as actors in the international community attempt to achieve public-order goals.[70] The method highlights the complex, interdependent and decentralised system of international decision making. A derivation of this is that international law is necessarily dualistic in nature, since it will usually take authoritative decision making at the domestic level to implement its norms.

In addition, international law lacks a legislature or an institutionalised law-giver of a general competence whose legal prescriptions are binding. In a sense, legislation does exist with international organisations like the United Nations.[71] However, the dominant consent principle gives states the option to apply or not to apply rules of international law. International law also lacks police force and enforcement mechanisms.

The policy-oriented approach recognises that, although there are a variety of actors in the international community, the international legal system depends primarily on states and state institutions for enforcement. Therefore, the ability of states to implement international law norms at the domestic level is critical to the enforcement of international law. Beyond identifying the decision makers at the state level, which is the core of policy-oriented jurisprudence, the complementarity regime entails that there must be willingness and capacity to investigate and prosecute international crimes domestically. Therefore, the method suggests that the relationship between international and domestic legal systems is one of interdependence.

The policy-oriented jurisprudence is useful for the mutually inclusive implementation of complementarity because the approach reflects the need to have a continuing process of authoritative decision-making at the different levels of the world community with the objective of identifying, clarifying and securing common interests. This implies that any study of the complementarity of the Rome Statute must necessarily be addressed to persons in official government positions who are responsible for decision making and implementation. It is proposed that

[70] Chen (2000), p. 409.

[71] Barry (2000), p. 9.

authorities in Nigeria and other African states need to identify with the international community, in deed and not only in words, to secure the common interests.

These common interests consist of the maintenance of international peace and security and, ideally, the shaping and sharing of values such as respect, power, enlightenment, well-being, wealth, skill, affection and rectitude.[72] The ultimate goal of securing the common interest is the establishment of a world community of human dignity. Towards this goal, education in the broadest sense is crucial. As argued by Chen, 'we cannot be content with the status quo, we must think about new ways to build a better world'.[73] Thus the policy-oriented perspective brings a distinct dimension to citizenship education as citizens of the world must be taught to think globally, to think contextually, and to think creatively for the common interest.[74] This is because closing impunity gap requires inclusive orientation of values and education of citizens in the widest sense.

As an on-going process of authoritative decision-making, international law is dynamic. Even more dynamic is the complementarity regime of the Rome Statute, as it deepens the interdependence and interrelations amongst states and non-state participants, including international organisations, nongovernmental organisations and associations, individual and the world community as a whole. In this process, states continue to play a predominant role, with their control of unique territorial bases.[75] However, as interdependencies deepen, what happens in one state increasingly affects others and communities must take one another into account and act with mutual respect when making choices and decisions. It is only when a basic order is achieved through the curtailment of unauthorised coercion and violence that the greatest production and widest sharing of all values can be seriously pursued and attained.[76]

### 7.2.2 Minimum Complementarity Threshold: National Implementation Strategies

The benefit of national criminal jurisdiction has been highlighted. Like other international tribunals, the ICC is dependent on the cooperation of states to collect and transfer evidence as well as witnesses, suspects and accused persons to the

[72]See Article 55 of the UN Charter which emphasises universal respect for, and observance of, human rights and fundamental freedoms as indispensable to the creation of conditions of stability and well-being which are necessary for peaceful and friendly relations among states. See also the UDHR 1948.

[73]Lung-Chu Chen (2000), p. 86.

[74]Lung-Chu Chen.

[75]Ibid.

[76]Ibid, 85.

Court.[77] Even where states are cooperative, the location of the Court far away from the territories in which crimes were committed results in delays or obstacles to the pursuit of justice. Thus, it is better for states to engage their criminal justice systems in the prosecution of international crimes.

As demonstrated in the analysis of the case law of the ICC, not all the elements of complementarity have been interpreted and applied. In the *Saif Al-Islam*[78] admissibility decision, for example, the PTCI noted that consideration of 'unwillingness' was not necessary at the admissibility challenge stage since the Chamber found that Libya was genuinely unable to investigate and prosecute the suspect.[79] Thus, as with previous admissibility challenges before the ICC, only the consideration of whether or not an investigation is being carried out at the domestic level to determine the 'same person same conduct' test was evaluated.

In considering whether a case is inadmissible under Article 17(1)(a) and (b), the Appeals Chamber of the ICC noted that there are two questions that must be asked.[80] The first is whether there are on-going investigations or prosecutions at the domestic level. The second is whether there have been investigations in the past and the state having jurisdiction has decided not to prosecute the person concerned.[81] According to the Appeals Chamber, it is only when these questions are answered in the affirmative that an examination of unwillingness and inability becomes necessary.[82] As both elements, along with genuineness and sufficient gravity, are separate from the consideration of whether or not an investigation is being carried out, it is apparent that the ICC is yet to evaluate all the components of complementarity.

In order to demonstrate willingness, a minimum complementarity threshold, which includes first, the transcription of the Rome Statute crimes into domestic criminal law, is proposed. African states should undertake extensive review of their laws including the constitution and specific provisions relating to immunity and the death penalty to bring them in line with the Rome Statute. This is important because as discussed, prosecuting international crimes as ordinary domestic crimes is not desirable and conflicting domestic laws can potentially inhibit national implementation of the Rome Statute.

Second, to ensure institutional preparedness, the police forces, prison services and the judiciaries of African states must be fundamentally reformed both to better protect citizens' rights and to be well-equipped to carry out investigations and prosecutions of international crimes. In this regard, there should be the appointment of international criminal law experts into the judiciary including judges. The

[77]See Part 9 Rome Statute relating to International Cooperation and Judicial Assistance, particularly Articles 86–89.

[78]*Saif Al-Islam* case.

[79]ibid paras 204, 205, 206, 215 & 216.

[80]*Germain Katanga*, case (Text to note 98 in Ch 2).

[81]Ibid, para 20.

[82]Ibid, para 78.

continuous training of judges and other court personnel in international criminal law will also be of benefit. In addition, the government must provide security for all, and most especially judges, to enable them discharge the responsibilities of their office.

The minimum complementarity threshold is suggested so that African states can be ready, both in their laws and institutions, to implement complementarity. This is important because the problems faced by domestic institutions functioning in the context of a weak economy, lack of confidence in the judicial structure, lack of expertise in international criminal law and the questionable independence and impartiality of national judiciaries have been highlighted. Of critical importance is the fact that such operational capacity challenges are likely to be exacerbated particularly where there may be a large accumulation of cases, which usually happens in the aftermath of a mass atrocity.[83]

Since the first Review Conference of the Rome Statute held in Kampala Uganda in 2010, the role of the ICC has been streamlined to the construction of national capacity insofar as it does not interfere with the judicial function or divert funds from on-going investigations and prosecutions by the ICC. Therefore, states, international organisations and civil society are to play a leading role in encouraging and assisting national jurisdictions to ensure their legal framework and institutional capacity to investigate and prosecute international crimes.

However, outlining that states, international organisation and civil society should construct national capacity building to implement complementarity only leaves the issue of capacity building to the vagaries of international politics. For this reason, it is proposed that Article 93(10)[84] could be expounded and used by states to pursue mutually inclusive and proactive complementarity by which states could request legislative and technical assistance as well as capacity building from the ICC.

Against this background this book proffers some recommendations for African states on how to ensure their legal framework and enhance institutional capacity to carry out complementarity-based prosecution. The recommendation is structured on the three prong requirement for complementarity articulated at the Review Conference, which include legislative assistance, technical assistance and capacity building and physical infrastructures.

[83]Bergsmo et al. (2010), pp. 791–811.

[84]Article 93(10)(a) says that the Court may, upon request, cooperate with and provide assistance to a state party conducting an investigation into a trial in respect of conduct which constitutes a crime within the jurisdiction of the Court or which constitutes a serious crime under the national law of the requesting state.

#### 7.2.2.1 Legislative Assistance

In constructing the possibility of developing capacity at the domestic level to ensure implementation of complementarity, the Review Conference noted that there is need for legislative assistance. This includes the drafting of the appropriate legislative framework and assistance in overcoming domestic hurdles for passing such legislation.[85] This is apt for African states to overcome obstacles in passing implementing legislation.

In this regard, African states could draw some lessons from South Africa and states' implementing legislation, available through the ICC Legal Tools Project.[86] Areas of concern include provisions regarding amnesties and immunities, the need for the definitions and penalty of international crimes to meet the threshold of the Rome Statute and the need to adopt procedural fair trial standards.

In principle, the ICC has provided, through its Legal Tools Project,[87] ways by which states may construct functional capacity necessary for complementarity. This project was developed by the ICC and has been made available to governments, judges, prosecutors, defence counsel, NGOs and others around the world in the spirit of the complementarity of the Court. Initially developed as part of ICC's Legal Tools Project of the office of the Prosecutor, the realisation of their value as a means of increasing states' capacity led to their availability and access to use by external actors.[88] The Tools serve as an electronic library developed by lawyers with expertise in the field of international criminal justice. Notably, the legal tools database contains a specific search engine, which allows users to search for specific aspects of national legislation implementing the Rome Statute. The text in these tools reflects the need to disseminate legal information relating to the functioning of the Court.[89]

In addition, the National Implementing Legislation Database (NILD) developed by the Human Rights Centre of the University of Nottingham in conjunction with the OTP forms part of the ICC's Legal Tools.[90] It is an online knowledge transfer platform aimed to provide the general public with free access to the most comprehensive electronic library on international criminal law and justice.[91] The NILD

---

[85]Review Conference Resolution para 17(1)(a).

[86]The Project comprises of four main components which provide distinct services; Case Matrix, the Elements Digest, the Proceedings Digest and the Means of Proof Digest.

[87]The ICC's Legal Tools are available on www.icc-cpi.int/Menus/ICC/Legal+Texts+and+Tools/ Accessed 10 May 2012.

[88]Bergsmo et al. (2010).

[89]Ibid.

[90]Human Rights Law Centre (HRLC), 'National Implementation Database of the International Criminal Court'(hereinafter 'NILD') http://www.nottingham.ac.uk/hrlc/newsholding/news2009/nationalimplementinglegislationdatabaselaunchedoniccwebsite.aspx (Accessed 15 November 2013).

[91]NILD.

provides a comprehensive and up-to-date collection of national legislation that has been adopted by states in relation to the Rome Statute.[92]

Thus, it is a tool for national legislators who have not yet adopted, but are considering or drafting implementing legislation, enhancing their capability to draft effective legislation by drawing upon the previous experience of other state parties. It is recommended that African states could, in addition to the South African and Kenyan models of International Crimes Act,[93] take advantage of the NILD to facilitate their implementing legislation. The importance of the NILD goes beyond implementing legislation; even where states have already adopted such legislation, they could monitor the impact of their legislation and undertake necessary amendments whenever the content of the Rome Statute changes.

Furthermore, the NILD is relevant to judges, police forces and prison authorities, who are expected to implement such legislation but may have limited access to information, with the result that the rights of individuals and the admissibility of a trial might be jeopardised. Both of these tools represent a practical and cost-effective transfer platform for states through which legal information pertaining to core international crimes is made available.

#### 7.2.2.2 Technical Assistance and Capacity Building

Technical assistance includes, but is not limited to, the training of the police, investigators and prosecutors, capacity building with regard to the protection of witnesses and victims, forensic expertise, the training of judges and of defence counsel, security for officials and for their independence. Such assistance could take the form of supplying judges and prosecutors to assist national courts or other forms of support to special war crimes divisions at the domestic levels, as appropriate. Furthermore, assistance could be rendered for capacity building with regard to mutual legal assistance in criminal matters, to underpin cooperation in actual prosecutions.[94]

In addition, physical assistance includes support with construction of courthouses and prison facilities, and the sustainable operation of such institutions. Capacity building would, however, be needed to ensure that the functioning of such institutions comply with internationally accepted standards, and adding an element of continuous training to the operation of the institutions may be beneficial.[95]

---

[92]Ibid.

[93]The South African and Kenya implementing legislation are the only African models that have adopted the Rome Statute crimes and also adjusted other local laws, including provisions on immunities, that conflict with the provisions of the Statute.

[94]Review Conference Resolution para 17(1)(b).

[95]Ibid para 17(1)(c).

Admittedly, this will involve finances and other resources, which the ICC is not expected to handle. Currently, the ICC is funded by contributions made by Assembly of States Parties (ASP) and the United Nations,[96] and although the ICC may receive and utilise funds from voluntary contributions from governments, international organisations, individuals, corporations and other entities,[97] there is a dearth of donors to the ICC. Consequently, it is suggested that each state desiring to benefit from the technical assistance and capacity building could contribute by funding the particular project.

In this regard, Article 93(10) of the Rome Statute could be employed by states to request assistance from the ICC to ensure capacity in all institutions in line with complementarity. Since the future of international criminal justice rests on credible institutions at the domestic level, it is hoped that states and the ICC will collaborate to ensure success and effectiveness.

Credible as these recommendations are, a major challenge in actualising them is the bane of corruption, which is endemic in Nigeria and in most African states. The substratum for the complementarity regime is functional criminal justice systems at the domestic level, and, as has been noted in *Mcfoy v UAC,*[98] 'you cannot put something on nothing and expect it to stand'.[99] Unless institutions at the domestic levels are functional and effective, the culture of self-referrals will continue and this will exacerbate the already almost overburdened ICC and ultimately undermine the complementarity regime.

The complementarity regime is hinged on efforts at national levels. As already argued, although African states' support for the ICC is evident in both ratifications and referral of situations, for national implementation of the complementarity regime, African states need both appropriate legal frameworks and institutional capacity that meet a certain threshold. This is important not only for establishing the success and legitimacy of the ICC, but also for the future of international criminal justice as a whole.

The dominant theme of this book has been that national implementation of complementarity is imperative for the success and sustainability of the ICC and the international criminal justice as a whole. In order to achieve this success, a mutually inclusive interpretation of complementarity is recommended. This means that there needs to be active investigation and prosecution of international crimes at the domestic level. Thus, the minimum complementarity threshold, which includes proscribing the Rome Statute crimes in domestic criminal law and ensuring institutional preparedness of states' judiciaries, is necessary.

Whilst this may not be the complete solution to the challenges faced by African states and the ICC currently in implementing the complementarity regime, it is hoped that it will provide the needed cooperation that the ICC needs in the cases it is

[96]Rome Statute, Article 115.

[97]Ibid, Article 116.

[98]*Per* Lord Denning in *Macfoy v UAC Ltd* (1961) 3 WLR (PC) 1405.

[99]Ibid, 1409.

# Cases, Legal Documents and Other Sources

## International Instruments and Commentaries

- Agreement between the United Nations and the Government of Sierra Leone on the Establishment of the Special Court for Sierra Leone signed 16 January 2002 (The agreement was pursuant to Security Council resolution 1315 of 14 August 2000 wherein it expressed deep concern at the very serious crimes committed within the territory of Sierra Leone against the people of Sierra Leone).
- Agreement for the Prosecution and Punishment of the Major War Criminals of the European Axis, and Charter of the International Military Tribunal London 8 August 1945 http://www.icrc.org/applic/ihl/ihl.nsf/Treaty.xsp?documentId=87B0BB4A50A64DEAC12563CD002D6AAE&action=openDocument
- Charter of the United Nations 1945 https://www.un.org/en/documents/charter/
- Charter of the United Nations and the Statute of the International Court of Justice San Francisco 1945 https://treaties.un.org/doc/publication/ctc/uncharter.pdf
- Convention Against Torture and Other Cruel, Inhuman or Degrading Treatment or Punishment 1465 UNTS 85 10 December 1984.
- Draft Statute of the International Law Commission (ILC) 1994 on the Work of its Forty-Sixth Session 2 May to 22 July 1994 UN Doc A/49/10 43-44.
- Elements of Crimes, adopted by the Assembly of States Parties in New York, on 9 September 2002 and entered into force on the same date (ICC-ASP/1/3) Available at http://www.icc-cpi.int/NR/rdonlyres/9CAEE830-38CF-41D6-AB0B-68E5F9082543/0/Element_of_Crimes_English.pdf
- International Covenant on Civil and Political Rights (ICCPR) adopted by the General Assembly of the United Nations New York 16 December 1966 UNTS Vol 999 1-14668 http://www.refworld.org/pdfid/3ae6b3aa0.pdf
- International Criminal Court, Rules of Procedure and Evidence, U.N. Doc. PCNICC/2000/1/Add.1 (2000).
- Optional Protocol to the ICCPR adopted by the General Assembly of the United Nations New York 16 December 1966 UNTS Vol 999, 171 entered into force



O.C. Imoedemhe, *The Complementarity Regime of the International Criminal Court*, DOI 10.1007/978-3-319-46780-1

23 March 1976 https://treaties.un.org/pages/ViewDetails.aspx?src=TREATY&mtdsg_no=IV-5&chapter=4&lang=en

- OTP, 'Prosecutorial Strategy 2009-2012' (1 February 2010) 5. Available at <www.icc-cpi.int/NR/rdonlyres/66A8DCDC-3650-4514-AA62-D229D1128F65/281506/OTPProsecutorialStrategy20092013.pdf> (Accessed 11 January 2013).
- Protocol Additional to the Geneva Conventions of 12 August 1949 and relating to the Protection of Victims of International Armed Conflicts (Protocol 1) 8 June 1977. <http://www.icrc.org/ihl.nsf/7c4d08d9b287a42141256739003e636b/f6c8b9fee14a77fdc125641e0052b079
- Protocol Additional to the Geneva Conventions of 12 August 1949 and relating to the Protection of Victims of Non-International Armed Conflicts (Protocol II) 8 June 1977. http://www.icrc.org/ihl/INTRO/475?OpenDocument
- Special Proclamation of General MacArthur for the International Military Tribunal for the Far East (IMTFE) Tokyo 19 January 1946.
- Statute of the International Criminal Tribunal for the Prosecution of Persons Responsible for serious Violations of International Humanitarian Law Committed in the Territory of the Former Yugoslavia since 1991 SC Res 827 UN Doc S/Res/827 (25 May 1993) ('ICTY Statute').
- Statute of the International Criminal Tribunal for the Prosecution of Persons Responsible for Genocide and Other Serious Violations of Humanitarian Law Committed in the Territory of Rwanda and Rwandan Citizens Responsible for genocide and Other Such Violations Committed in the Territory of Neighbouring States Between 1 January and 31 December 1994 SC Res 1315 UN Doc 5/RES/955 (6 November 1994) ('ICTR Statute').
- The Convention for the Prevention and Punishment of Genocide adopted by Resolution 260(III) of the United Nations General Assembly on 9 December 1948.
- The Geneva Conventions of 12 August 1949 http://www.icrc.org/eng/assets/files/publications/icrc-002-0173.pdf
- The Rome Statute of the International Criminal Court, July 17, 1998, 2187 UNTS 90 (entered into force on 1 July 2002) http://legal.un.org/icc/statute/romefra.htm (Accessed 16 March 2014).
- The Universal Declaration on Human Rights (UDHR) Paris 10 December 1948 http://www.un.org/en/documents/udhr/
- United Nations Basic Principles on the Independence of the Judiciary 1985, Art 10. Available http://www.hjpc.ba/dc/pdf/Basic%20Principles%20on%20the%20Independence%20of%20the%20Judiciary.pdf
- Vienna Convention on Diplomatic Relations, done at Vienna 18 April 1961, 500 UNTS 95 entered into force 24 April 1964.
- Vienna Convention on the Law of Treaties 23 May 1969 UNTS Vol 1155, p 331 entered into force 27 January 1980. Available at http://untreaty.un.org/ilc/texts/instruments/english/conventions/1_1_1969.pdf

## States' Laws


- Argentina, Law No. 26/200 on the Implementation of the ICC Statute (2007).
- Australia, the International Criminal Court Act (Consequential Amendment) 202, No 42 (2002) section 268.4 broadens the definition of genocide to include sexual violence. See http://www.iccwomen.org/whatwedo/projects/docs/Overview_Implementing_Legislation.pdf
- C.53(1957) Law Reports: Statutes 543 as amended by the Geneva Conventions (Amendment) Act 1995, C. 27.
- CAR, Press Release, 'ICC – Prosecutor Receives Referral Concerning Central African Republic' ICC-OTP-20050107-86. 7 January 2005. Available at http://www.icc-cpi.int/en_menus/icc/press%20and%20media/press%20releases/2005/Pages/otp%20prosecutor%20receives%20referral%20concerning%20central%20african%20republic.aspx
- CICC, Press Release, 'US Congress Passes Anti-ICC Hague Invasion Act' 26 July 2002 at <http://www.iccnow.org/documents/07.26.02ASPAthruCongress.pdf
- Criminal Code Act: An Act to Establish a Code of Criminal Law in Nigeria 1 June 1916 http://ofilispeaks.com/wp-content/uploads/criminal-act.pdf now The Nigerian Criminal Code Act Cap 77 Laws of the Federation of Nigeria (LFN) 1990; Cap C38 LFN 2004; Cap C3 LFN 2011.
- DRC, Article 112 of the Constitutional Act of Transition (1994), Article 193 of the Transitional Constitution of the Democratic Republic of Congo of 4 April 2003, *Journal Officiel,* special edition of 5 April 2003 (Constitution of 2003), Article 216 of the Constitution of the Democratic Republic of Congo of 2006.
- DRC, Loi 023/2002 of 18 November 2002 Portant Code judiciaire militaire (Military Code) http://www.leganet.cd/Legislation/Droit%20Judiciaire/Loi.023.2002.18.11.2002.pdf and Loi 024/2002 of November 2002 Portant Code Penal Militaire (Military Penal Code) http://www.leganet.cd/Legislation/Droit%20Judiciaire/Loi.024.2002.18.11.2002.pdf (Assessed 2 November 2012).
- DRC, Press Release, 'ICC – Prosecutor Receives Referral of the Situation in the Democratic Republic of Congo' ICC-OTP-20040419-50 19 April 2004. Available at http://www.icc-cpi.int/en_menus/icc/press%20and%20media/press%20releases/2004/Pages/prosecutor%20receives%20referral%20of%20the%20situation%20in%20the%20democratic%20republic%20of%20congo.aspx
- DRC, The Constitution of the Democratic Republic of Congo of 2006.
- DRC, The DRC Constitution of 18 February 2006, *Journal Officiel,* special edition of 18 February 2006 (DRC Constitution of 2006) states that civilian and military courts may apply ratified treaties provided they are consistent with the laws. See articles 153 & 215. The Constitution is available (in French) at: http://democratie.francophonie.org/IMG/pdf/Constitution_de_la_RDC.pdf (Accessed 28 June 2012).
- DRC, The DRC Legislative Decree no. 003/2002 of 30 March 2002 *Journal Officiel* of 5 December 2002 (special edition).

- DRC, The Legislative Decree no. 003/2002 of 30 March 2002 authorised the ratification of the Rome Statute, *Journal Officiel* of 5 December 2002 (special edition 'International and Regional Instruments Relating to Human Rights Ratified by the Democratic Republic of Congo'). Ratification instrument was deposited on 11 April 2002 http://www.icc-cpi.int/asp/statesparties/country&id=5.html (Accessed 28 June 2012).
- DRC, The Transitional Constitution of the Democratic Republic of Congo of 4 April 2003, *Journal Officiel,* special edition of 5 April 2003 (Constitution of 2003).
- England, The International Criminal Court (England) Act 2001c.17, (2001) 1 Law Reports: Statutes 1367 (ICC Act).
- Federal Republic of Nigeria Official Gazette 19 January 2007 B50. Available at www.population.gov.ng/pop_figure.pdf
- Geneva Conventions Act Uganda (Ch 363) 16 October 1964 <http://www.ulii.org/ug/legis/consol_act/gca1964208/ Article 2 (Accessed 14 June 2012).
- Helsinki, An Act on the Implementation of the Provisions of a Legislative Nature of the Rome Statute of the International Criminal Court and on the Application of the Statute. No 1284/2000 Issued in Helsinki 28 December 2000. Available at http://www.finlex.fi/en/laki/kaannokset/2000/en20001284.pdf. (Accessed 12 December 2012).
- Kenya, Armed Forces Act (Chapter 199) Laws of Kenya, available online at http://www.kenyalaw.org/kenyalaw/klr_app/frames.php (Accessed 13 December 2011).
- Kenya, Chapter 63 Laws of Kenya, available at <http://www.kenyalaw.org/kenyalaw/klr_app/frames.php (Accessed 13 December 2011).
- Kenya, Findings of the Commission of Inquiry into the Post-Election Violence in Kenya. Available at <http://www.kenyalaw.org/Downloads/Reports/Commission_ofInquiry_into_Post_Election_Violence.pdf (Accessed 13 December 2011) 345–346.
- Kenya, The Constitution of the Federal Republic of Kenya 2010 Available at <http://kenyahighcommission.ca/wp-content/uploads/2013/04/constitution-of-kenya-2010.pdf
- Kenya, The International Crimes Act 2008 (Kenya International Crimes Act), gazetted and entered into force January 2009. Available at<http://www.kenyalaw.org/Downloads/Acts/The_International_Crimes_Act_2008.pdf (Accessed 30 June 2013).
- Mali, 'Referral Letter by the Government of Mali' ICC-01/12 13 July 2012. Available at http://www.icc-cpi.int/NR/rdonlyres/A245A47F-BFD1-45B6-891C-3BCB5B173F57/0/ReferralLetterMali130712.pdf
- Nigeria, A Bill for An Act to Enable Effect to be given in the Federal Republic of Nigeria to the Rome Statute of the International Criminal Court and for Purposes Connected Therewith- The Rome Statute of the International Criminal Court (Ratification and Jurisdiction) Bill 2004. (Copy on file with the author).
- Nigeria, An Act to make Provision for the Organisation, Discipline, Powers and Duties of the Police, the Special Constabulary and the Traffic Wardens Chapter P19 No 41 1967, 1 April 1943. http://www.placng.org/new/laws/P19.pdf

- Nigeria, State Security (Detention of Persons) Decree No 2 of 1984 as amended by Decree 11 of 1994; The Federal Military Government (Supremacy and Enforcement of Powers) Decree No 12 of 1994 and the Constitution (Suspension and Modification) Decree No 107 of 1993.
- Nigeria, The African Charter on Human and Peoples' Rights (Ratification and Enforcement) Act Cap 10 Laws of the Federation of Nigeria (LFN) 1990 (now Cap A11 LFN 2011) African Charter Act.
- Nigeria, The Constitution of the Federal Republic of Nigeria 1999. Available at http://www.nigeria-law.org/ConstitutionOfTheFederalRepublicOfNigeria.htm (Accessed 2 May 2013).
- Organic Law No 11/2007 of 16 March 2007 Concerning Transfer of Cases to the Republic of Rwanda from the International Criminal Tribunal for Rwanda (ICTR) and from Other States. Available at http://www.refworld.org/docid/476644652.html (accessed 26 August 2013).
- Rwanda, 'Mpanga, A Stronghold for the UN in Rwanda' *International Justice Tribune* 5 May 2008. Available at http://www.rnw.nl/international-justice/article/mpanga-stronghold-un-rwanda
- Rwanda, Gazette of the Republic of Rwanda. Year 46, no. special, 25 July 2007).
- Rwanda's Organic Law No. 66/2008 of 21 November 2008 which modified Organic Law No. 31/2007 of 25 July 2007 relating to the Abolition of the Death Penalty.
- Samoa, International Criminal Court Act 2007; Burundi Law No. 1/004, 08 May 2003.
- Scotland, The International Criminal Court (Scotland) Act 2001, 2001 ASP 13 House of Lords Hansard, Vol. 623, cols 418–419.
- South Africa, Implementation of the Rome Statute of the International Criminal Court Act No 27 of 2002 Government Gazette No 23642 of 18 July 2002. Available at http://www.info.gov.za/gazette/acts/2002/a27-02.pdf and http://www.iccnow.org/documents/SouthAfricaLegEng2002.pdf (Assessed 11 April 2013).
- Sudan: Special Criminal Court on the Events in Darfur (SCCED). Available at http://www.justiceinperspective.org.za/africa/sudan/special-criminal-court-on-the-events-in-darfur.html (Accessed 13 February 2012).
- The American Service-Members Protection Act 2002, 26 July 2002. Available at http://www.house.gov/legcoun/Comps/aspa02.pdf
- The Code of Crimes against International Law (CCAIL) entered into force on 30 June 2002: *Bundesgestzblatt* (*BGBI*) 2002, 1, 2254).
- The Constitution Amendment Act Kenya http://www.kenyalaw.org/Downloads/Bills/2008/The_Constitution_of_Kenya(Amendment)_Bill_2008.pdf (Accessed 13 December 2011).
- The Constitution of the Republic of South Africa 1996 (Act No 108 1996) adopted 8 May 1996 as amended by Notice No 78 in Government Gazette No 33899 of 24 December 2010. Available at http://www.info.gov.za/documents/constitution/1996/a108-96.pdf (Accessed 30 November 2013).
- The Criminal Code Act: An Act to Establish a Code of Criminal Law in Nigeria 1 June 1916 http://ofilispeaks.com/wp-content/uploads/criminal-act.pdf now

The Nigerian Criminal Code Act Cap 77 Laws of the Federation of Nigeria (LFN) 1990; Cap C38 LFN 2004; Cap C3 LFN 2011.

- The Geneva Conventions Act, 1968 (Chapter 198 Laws of Kenya). Available at http://www.kenyalaw.org/kenyalaw/klr_app/frames.php (Accessed 13 December 2011).
- The UK International Criminal Court Act 2001, 2001 Ch 17 was passed on 24 September 2001. Available at http://www.legislation.gov.uk/ukpga/2001/17/pdfs/ukpga_20010017_en.pdf (Accessed 13 May 2013).
- Trinidad and Tobago, International criminal Court Act 2006.
- Uganda Constitution Amendment Act 2005 and Constitution Amendment (No 2) Act 2005.
- Uganda International Criminal Court Bill 2006 http://www.coalitionfortheicc.org/documents/Uganda-ICC_Bill_2006.pdf
- Uganda, Agreement on Accountability and Reconciliation between the Government of Uganda and the Lord's Resistance Army/Movement, Juba, Sudan, June 29, 2007, paras 4 & 6; Annex to the Agreement on Accountability and Reconciliation between the Government of Uganda and the Lord's Resistance Army/Movement, Juba, Sudan 19 February 2008. Available at http://www.iccnow.org/documents/Annexure_to_agreement_on_Accountability_signed_today.pdf
- Uganda, Press Release, 'ICC – President of Uganda refers situation concerning the Lord's Resistance Army (LRA) to the ICC' ICC-20040129-44 29 January 2004. Available at http://www.icc-cpi.int/en_menus/icc/press%20and%20media/press%20releases/2004/Pages/president%20of%20uganda%20refers%20situation%20concerning%20the%20lord_s%20resistance%20army%20_lra_%20to%20the%20icc.aspx
- Uganda, The Constitution of the Republic of Uganda 1995. Available at http://www.ugandalawlibrary.com/ull/files/constitution/constitution_1995.pdf (Accessed 30 June 2013).
- Uganda, The International Criminal Court Act 2010 Act 11 (Act Supplement No 6 Act to the Uganda Gazette No 39 Vol CIII) 25 June 2010. Available at http://www.issafrica.org/anicj/uploads/Uganda_ICC_Act_2010.pdf (Accessed 30 June 2013).
- Uganda: Laws of Uganda Amnesty Act 2000 (Cap 294); Article 3. Available at http://www.ulii.org/ug/legis/consol_act/aa2000111/ (Accessed 24 March 2012).
- Uganda's Chief Justice, 'ICD Practice Directions' Legal Notice No 10 of 2011. Legal Notice Supplement, Uganda Gazette No 38 vol CIV 31 May 2011.

## Cases

- Abacha v. Gani Fawehinmi [2000] 4 FWLR 533 SC
- Abacha v. Gani Fawehinmi [2000] 6 NWLR (Pt. 660) 228
- Andrei Sawoniuk. R. v. Sawoniuk [2000] 2 Criminal Appeal Reports 220.

- Appeals Chamber, The Prosecutor v Francis Kirimi Muthaura, Uhuru Muigai Kenyatta and Mohammed Hussein Ali Judgment on the Appeal of the Republic of Kenya against the decision of Pre-Trial Chamber II of 30 May 2011 entitled 'Decision on the Application by the Government of Kenya challenging the Admissibility of the case Pursuant to Article 19(2)(b) of the Statute' 30 August 2011 ICC-01/09-02/11-274 para 39. http://icc-cpi.int/iccdocs/doc/doc1223134.pdf
- Appeals Chamber, The Prosecutor v William Samoei Ruto, Henry Kiprono Kosgey and Joshua Arap Sang Judgement on the Appeal of the Republic of Kenya against the decision of Pre-Trial Chamber II of 30 May 2011 entitled 'Decision on the Application by the Government of Kenya Challenging the Admissibility of the case Pursuant to Article 19(2)(b) of the Statute' 20 August 2011 ICC-01/09-01/11-307 para 40.
- Arrest Warrant of 11 April 2000 (Democratic Republic of Congo v. Belgium), ICJ decision 14 February 2002.
- Attorney General of Anambra State & Others v Attorney General of the Federation [1993] NWLR (Part 302) 692.
- Baha Mousa case. BBC News 19 September 2006 http://news.bbc.co.uk/1/hi/5360432.stm
- Darfur, Sudan, The Prosecutor v. Omar Hassan Ahmad Al Bashir, Case No ICC-02/05-01/09, ICC-CPI-20130716-PR932 Decision of the Pre-Trial Chamber II Regarding Omar Al Bashir's Visit to Nigeria) 15 July 2013.
- Decision on Immunity in Prosecutor v. Taylor SCSL-2003-01-1 Appeals Chamber 31 May 2004, para 51.
- Decision on the Admissibility of the Case Under 19(1) of the Statute ICC-02/04-01/05-377, Pre-Trial Chamber II 10 March 2009, para 37.
- Decision on the Prosecution's Application for Al Bashir's Arrest Warrant 4 March 2009, paras 41–45.
- Fawehinmi v Abacha [1996] 9 NWLR (Part 475) 710, 747.
- ICC Office of the Prosecutor, 'ICC issues a warrant of arrest for Omar Al-Bashir, President of Sudan' 4 March 2009; Situation in Darfur, Sudan (ICC-02/05-157) 'Public Redacted Version of Prosecutor's Application under Article 58 filed on 28 July 2008'; The Prosecutor v. Omar Al-Bashir (ICC-01/05-157), 'Decision on the Prosecution's Application for a Warrant of Arrest against Omar Hassan Ahmad Al-Bashir' Pre-Trial Chamber I, 4 March 2009.
- ICC Trial Chamber 1, Situation in the DRC Case No ICC-01/04-01/06 Tuesday 27 January 2009 ICC-01/04-01/06-T-109-ENG WT 27-01-2009 1/59 NB t 31 http://www.icc-cpi.int/iccdocs/doc/doc623848.pdf
- ICTY, Prosecutor v Tadic, Appeals Chamber, 2 October 1995, para 141. Available at http://www.icty.org/case/tadic/4 (Accessed 28 August 2013).
- Justice Jackson in Trial 1, Trial of Major War Criminals Nuremberg 51. Available at http://law2.umkc.edu/faculty/projects/ftrials/nuremberg/jackson.html
- Kenya, 'Situation in the Republic of Kenya and Authorisation to Open an Investigation' ICC-01/09 31 March 2010. Available at http://www.icc-cpi.int/en_menus/icc/situations%20and%20cases/situations/situation%20icc%200109/Pages/situation%20index.aspx

- Military Prosecutor v Lieutenant Colonel Kibibi Mutware et al. in ASF, 'Case Study of the Application of the Rome Statute of the ICC in the DRC' available at http://www.asf.be/wp-content/publications/ASF_CaseStudy_RomeStatute_Light_PagePerPage.pdf
- Per Lord Denning in Macfoy v UAC Ltd (1961) 3 WLR (PC) 1405, 1409.
- Press Release, ICC Statement of the Prosecutor on the Opening of the Investigation into the Situation in Libya 3 March 2011 http://www.icc-cpi.int/NR/rdonlyres/035C3801-5C8D-4ABC-876B-C7D946B51F22/283045/StatementLibya_03032011.pdf
- Pre-Trial Chamber II decision in Prosecutor v Joseph Kony, Vincent Otti, Okot Odhiambo and Dominic Ongwen ICC-02/04-01/05-377 10 March 2009 para 34. (Decision on the Admissibility of the case under Article 19(1) of the Statute).
- Pre-Trial Chamber II in The Prosecutor v. Kony et al., Decision on the Admissibility of the Case under Article 19(1) of the Statute, 10 March 2009, ICC-02/04-01/05-377, paras 17–18.
- Pre-Trial Chamber III in The Prosecutor v. Jean-Pierre Bemba Gombo, Decision on the Prosecutor's Application for a Warrant of Arrest against Jean-Pierre Bemba Gombo, 10 June 2008, ICC-01/05-01/08-14-tENG (Translation notified 17 July 2006), para. 16.
- Prosecutor v Delalić, Mucić, Delić and Landžo Judgement, IT-96-21-A 20 February 2001 (Čelebići case).
- Prosecutor v Germain Katanga and Mathieu Ngudjolo Chui Case No ICC-01/04-01/07-123tENG (Reasons for the Oral Decision on the Motion Challenging the Admissibility of the Case under Art 19) 16 June 2009.
- Prosecutor v Tihomir Blaskic ICTY Case No. IT-95-14-AR108bis Appeals Chamber decision of 29 October 1997
- Prosecutor v. Anto Furundzija Case No: IT-95-17/1-T Judgment of 10 December 1998 paras 153–157
- Prosecutor v. Charles Ghankay Taylor Case No SCSL-03-1-T (Judgment of 26 April 2012).
- Prosecutor v. Francis Kirimi Muthaura and Uhuru Muigai Kenyatta Case No ICC-01/09-02/11 (Prosecution notification of withdrawal of Charges against Francis Kirimi Muthaura). Available at http://www.icc-cpi.int/iccdocs/doc/ICC-01-09-02-11-687.pdf (Assessed 11 April 2013).
- Prosecutor v. Slobodan Milosevic IT-99-37, Decision on Preliminary Motions 8 November 2001, paras 8–10
- PTCI decision of 10 February 2006 in the Lubanga and Ntaganda cases ICC-01/04-01/07; The ICC, 'Understanding the International Criminal Court' Available at http://www.icc-cpi.int/iccdocs/PIDS/publications/UICCEng.pdf paras 37 & 38.
- PTCII: The Prosecutor v William Samoei Ruto, Henry Kiprono Kosgey and Joshua Arap Sang Case No ICC-01/09-01/11.
- Questions Relating to the Obligation to Prosecute or Extradite (Belgium v. Senegal) ICJ decision of 20 July 2012 para 72-76. Available at http://www.icj-cij.org/docket/files/144/17064.pdf (Accessed 3 October 2012).

- R v Payne, General Court Martial Charge Sheet (2006), available at http://www.army.mod.uk/apa/courtsmartial-trials (Accessed 18 October 2007).
- Situation and cases before the ICC available at http://www.icc-cpi.int/en_menus/icc/situations%20and%20cases/Pages/situations%20and%20cases.aspx (Accessed 5 June 2013).
- Situation in Cote d'Ivoire No ICC-02/02/11, Decision on the Authorisation of an Investigation into the Situation in the Republic of Cote d'Ivoire 3 October 2011 http://www.icc-cpi.int/iccdocs/doc/doc1240553.pdf>
- Situation in Kenya No ICC-01/09 Decision on the Authorisation of an Investigation 31 March 2010 http://www.icc-cpi.int/iccdocs/doc/doc854287.pdf
- Situation in the Republic of Kenya, The Prosecutor v. Francis Kirimi Muthaura, Uhuru Muigai Kenyatta and Mohammed Hussein Ali ICC-01/09-02/11-274 30-08-2011 1/43 NM PT OA Available at http://icc-cpi.int/iccdocs/doc/doc1223134.pdf (Judgment on the Appeal of the Republic of Kenya against the decision of Pre-Trial Chamber II of 30 May 2011 entitled 'Decision on the Application by the Government of Kenya Challenging the Admissibility of the Case Pursuant to Article 19(2)(b) of the Statute).
- SS Lotus, PCIJ Series A No 10 (1927).
- Statement by ICC Prosecutor on the Notice to Withdraw Charges against Mr Muthaura' 11 March 2013. Available at http://www.icc-cpi.int/en_menus/icc/press%20and%20media/press%20releases/Pages/OTP-statement-11-03-2013.aspx (Accessed 11 April 2013).
- Summary of decision in the two Kenya Cases, 23 January 2012. Available at http://www.icc-cpi.int/en_menus/icc/press%20and%20media/press%20releases/news%20and%20highlights/Pages/summary%20of%20decision%20in%20the%20two%20kenya%20cases.aspx (Assessed 11 April 2013).
- The Prosecutor v Francis Kirimi Muthaura et al Case No: ICC-01/09-02/11 (The Decision on the Confirmation of Charges Pursuant to Article 61(7)(a)&(b) of the Rome Statute) 156-193 23 January 2012. Available at http://www.icc-cpi.int/iccdocs/doc/doc1314543.pdf (Accessed 30 June 2013).
- The Prosecutor v Jean-Baptiste Gatete ICTR-2000-61-1 TCI (Decision on the Prosecutor's Request for transfer to the Republic of Rwanda 17 November 2008.
- The Prosecutor v Jean-Bosco Uwinkindi ICTR-2001-75-R11bis T Ch (Decision on the Prosecutor's Request for Referral to the Republic of Rwanda) 28 June 2011 http://www.unhcr.org/refworld/pdfid/4e5602ca2.pdf (Accessed 20 June 2012).
- The Prosecutor v Jean-Bosco Uwinkindi ICTR-2001-75-R11bis T Ch (Decision on the Prosecutor's Request for Referral to the Republic of Rwanda) 28 June 2011 http://www.unhcr.org/refworld/pdfid/4e5602ca2.pdf (Accessed 28 June 2012).
- The Prosecutor v Mr Germain Katanga ICC-01/04-01/07-1497 OA 8 (Oral Decision of the Trial Chamber II of 12 June 2009 on the Admissibility of the Case) para 81–82.
- The Prosecutor v Omar Hassan Ahmad Al-Bashir ICC case No ICC-02/05-01/09, 'Decision informing the United Nations Security Council and the Assembly

of States Parties to the Rome Statute about Omar Al-Bashir's visit to Chad' 27 August 2010 http://www.icc-cpi.int/iccdocs/doc/doc931075.pdf (Accessed 15 July 2011).

- The Prosecutor v Saif Al Islam Gaddafi and Abdullah Al-Senussi ICC-01/11-01/11 Application on Behalf of the Government of Libya relating to Abdullah Al-Senussi Pursuant to Article 19 of the ICC Statute 2 April 2013 http://www.icc-cpi.int/iccdocs/doc/doc1575650.pdf (Accessed 30 November 2013)
- The Prosecutor v Saif Al Islam Gaddafi and Abdullah Al-Senussi ICC-01/11-01/11 Decision on the admissibility of the case against Saif Al-Islam Gaddafi 31 May 2013 http://www.icc-cpi.int/iccdocs/doc/doc1599307.pdf (Accessed 10 January 2014).
- The Prosecutor v Thomas Lubanga Dyilo, Decision on the Prosecutor's Application for a Warrant of Arrest, ICC-01/04-01/06 10 February 2006, para 29.
- The Prosecutor v Yusuf Munyakazi ICTR-97-36-R11bisAC (Decision on the Prosecutor's Appeal against Decision on Transfer under Rule 11bis) 8 October 2008.
- The Prosecutor v. Ahmad Muhammad Harun and Ali Muhammad Ali Abd-Al-Rahman Decision on the Prosecution Application under Article 58(7) of the Statute, 27 April 2007, ICC-02/05-01/07-1-Corr, para. 24.
- The Prosecutor v. Bahr Idriss Abu Garda, Decision on the Prosecutor's Application under Article 58, 7 May 2009, ICC-02/05-02/09-l-Conf, para. 4 (public redacted version in ICC-02/05-02/09-12-Anxl).
- The Prosecutor v. Francis Kirimi Muthaura, Uhuru Muigai Kenyatta and Mohammed Hussein Ali ICC-01/09-02/11 (The decision of Pre-Trial Chamber II of 30 May 2011 on the Application by the Government of Kenya Challenging the Admissibility of the Case Pursuant to Article 19(2)(b) of the Statute). Available at http://icc-cpi.int/iccdocs/doc/doc1078823.pdf
- The Prosecutor v. Francis Kirimi Muthaura, Uhuru Muigai Kenyatta and Mohammed Hussein Ali Case No: ICC-01/09-02/11 http://www.icc-cpi.int/iccdocs/doc/doc1314543.pdf (Decision on the Confirmation of Charges Pursuant to Article 61(7) (a) and (b) of the Rome Statute).
- The Prosecutor v. Francis Kirimi Muthaura, Uhuru Muigai Kenyatta and Mohammed Hussein Ali ICC-01/09-02/11 (The decision of Pre-Trial Chamber II of 30 May 2011 on the Application by the Government of Kenya Challenging the Admissibility of the Case Pursuant to Article 19(2)(b) of the Statute). Available at http://icc-cpi.int/iccdocs/doc/doc1078823.pdf (Accessed 20 July 2013).
- The Prosecutor v. Francis Kirimi Muthaura, Uhuru Muigai Kenyatta and Mohammed Hussein Ali, Decision on the Application by the Government of Kenya Challenging the Admissibility of the Case Pursuant to Article 19(2)(b) of the Statute, 30 May 2011, ICC-01/09-02/11-96, para. 48.
- The Prosecutor v. Gasper Kanyarukiga Case No. ICTR-2002-78-R11bis (Decision on the Prosecutor's Appeal Against Decision on Referral Under Rule 11bis) 30 October 2008.

- The Prosecutor v. Germain Katanga, Decision on the evidence and information provided by the Prosecution for the issuance of a warrant of arrest for Germain Katanga, 6 July 2007, ICC-01/04-01/07-4.
- The Prosecutor v. Ildephonse Hategekimana ICTR-00-55-R11bis AC (Decision on the Prosecutor's Appeal against the Decision on the Transfer under Rule 11bis) 4 December 2008.
- The Prosecutor v. Joseph Kony, Vincent Otti, Raska Lukwiya, Okot Odhiambo & Dominic Ongwen.
- The Prosecutor v. Mathieu Ngudjolo Chui, Decision on the evidence and information provided by the Prosecution for the issuance of a warrant of arrest for Mathieu Ngudjolo Chui, 6 July 2007, ICC-01/04-01/07-262, para 2.
- The Prosecutor v. Omar Hassan Ahmad Al Bashir, Decision on the Prosecution's Application for a Warrant of Arrest against Omar Hassan Ahmad Al Bashir, 4 March 2009, ICC-02/05-01/09-2-Conf, para. 50 (public redacted version in ICC-02/05-01/09-3).
- The Prosecutor v. Omar Hassan Ahmad Al-Bashir ICC-02/05-01/09.
- The Prosecutor v. Saif Al-Islam Gaddafi and Abdullah Al-Hussein ICC-01/11-01/11-344-Red Decision of the Pre-Trial Chamber I on the Admissibility of the case against Saif Al-Islam Gaddafi 31 May 2013. http://www.icc-cpi.int/iccdocs/doc/doc1599307.pdf (Accessed 20 June 2013).
- The Prosecutor v. Thomas Lubanga Dyilo Case No ICC-01/04-01/06.
- The Prosecutor v. Thomas Lubanga Dyilo, Decision concerning Pre-Trial Chamber I Decision of 10 February 2006 and the Incorporation of Documents into the Record of the Case against Mr Thomas Lubanga Dyilo, 24 February 2006, ICC-01/04-01/06-8-Corr.
- The Prosecutor v. William Samoei Ruto, Henry Kiprono Kosgey and Joshua Arap Sang, Decision on the Application by the Government of Kenya Challenging the Admissibility of the Case Pursuant to Article 19(2)(b) of the Statute, 30 May 2011, ICC-01/09-01/11-101, para 54.
- The Prosecutor v. Yusuf Munyakazi (Judgement and Sentence) ICTR-97-36A-T ICTR 5 July 2010. Available at http://www.unhcr.org/refworld/docid/4c722d350.html
- The Prosecutor v. Yusuf Munyakazi (Judgement and Sentence) ICTR-97-36A-T ICTR 5 July 2010. Available at http://www.unhcr.org/refworld/docid/4c722d350.html (Accessed 22 October 2012).
- TMG de l'Ituri, Affaire Bongi, 24 March 200610-11 (Military Prosecutor v Blaise Bongi) in ASF, 'Case Study: The Application of the Rome Statute of the International Criminal Court by the Courts of the Democratic Republic of Congo' March 2009, 8 http://www.asf.be/wp-content/publications/ASF_CaseStudy_RomeStatute_Light_PagePerPage.pdf
- TMG de l'Ituri, Affaire Bongi, 24 March 200610-11 (Military Prosecutor v Blaise Bongi)
- TMG de Mbandaka, Affaire Songo Mboyo, 12 April 2006, RP 084/05; CM de l'Equateur, Affaire Songo Mboyo 7 June 2006, RPA 014/06.

- Trial Chamber I in Prosecutor v Lubanga, Decision on the Practice of Witness Familiarisation and Witness Proofing icc-01/04-01/06 8 November 2006 paras 34 & 38.
- Warrant of Arrest Unsealed against Five LRA Commanders' ICC-CPI-20051014-110. The Prosecutor v. Joseph Kony, Vincent Otti, Raska Lukwiya, Okot Odhiambo & Dominic Ongwen (The warrants of arrest were issued under seal by the Pre-Trial Chamber II on 8 July 2005 and unsealed on 13 October of the same year).


## AU/UN Documents


- AU Assembly Decision on the Application by the International Criminal Court Prosecutor for the Indictment of the President of the Republic of Sudan (Doc. 221 (XII) 3 February 2009.
- AU Peace and Security Council Decision (PSC/MIN/Comm CXLII) 21 July 2008 paras 3, 5, 9 and 11(i).
- AU Press Statement, 'The Chairperson of the Commission Expresses Deep Concern at the Decision of the Pre-Trial Chamber of the International Criminal Court on Darfur' 4 March 2009.
- AU Summit, 'Decision on the progress report of the Commission on the implementation of decision Assembly/AU/Dec.270 (XIV) on the second ministerial meeting on the Rome Statute of the International Court: Doc.Assembly/AU/10 (XV) in Decisions, Declarations, Resolution of the 15th ordinary session of the AU Assembly: Assembly /AU/Dec.296 (XV) (Kampala 27 July 2010). Available at http://www.au.int/en/sites/default/files/ASSEMBLY_EN_25_27_July_2010_BCP_ASSEMBLY_OF_THE_AFRICAN_UNION_Fifteenth_Ordinary_Session.pdf
- AU Summit, 'Towards Greater Unity and Integration Through Shared Values' 31 January 2011 AU Assembly 16th Ord. Sess. AU Doc Assembly/AU/Decl. 1 (XVI).
- Charter of the Organisation of African Unity (OUA) 25 May 1963 in Addis-Ababa Ethiopia. Available at http://www.au.int/en/sites/default/files/OAU_Charter_1963_0.pdf
- Charter of the United Nations. available at https://www.un.org/en/documents/charter/chapter7.shtml
- Completion Strategy for the ICTR, United Nations Security Council Resolution 1503 of 2003; Judge Vagn Joensen, 'Report on the Completion Strategy of the International Criminal Tribunal for Rwanda (as at 10 May 2013)' S/2013/310 http://www.unictr.org/Portals/0/English/FactSheets/Completion_St/S-2013-310e.pdf
- Declaration on the Inter-Sudanese Peace Talks in Darfur 5 July 2005 AU Assembly 5th Ord. Sess AU Doc Assembly/AU/Decl.3(V).
- Peace and Security Council Decision (PSC/PR/Comm CLXXV) 5 March 2009.

- RPE Rule 11*bis* (A), Rule 11*bis*: Suspension of Indictment in case of Proceedings before National Courts Available at http://ictr-archive09.library.cornell.edu/ENGLISH/rules/050702/amend12.html (Accessed 9 June 2012).
- The Constitutive Act of the African Union. Available at http://www.au.int/en/sites/default/files/ConstitutiveAct_EN.pdf
- The Protocol for the Establishment of the Peace and Security Council (The Protocol) of the African Union adopted by the 1st Ordinary Session of the Assembly of the African Union in Durban, 9 July 2002. Available at http://www.africa-union.org/root/au/organs/psc/Protocol_peace%20and%20security.pdf
- United Nations Security Council Resolution 1593 S/RES/1593 (2005) Adopted by the Security Council at its 5158th Meeting on 31 March 2005 http://www.icc-cpi.int/NR/rdonlyres/85FEBD1A-29F8-4EC4-9566-48EDF55CC587/283244/N0529273.pdf (Accessed 30 January 2014).
- United Nations Security Council Resolution 1970 S/RES/1970 (2011) Adopted by the Security Council at its 6491st Meeting on 26 February 2011 http://www.icc-cpi.int/NR/rdonlyres/081A9013-B03D-4859-9D61-5D0B0F2F5EFA/0/1970Eng.pdf (Accessed 30 January 2014).

Printed by Printforce, the Netherlands